# STANDARD ENCYCLOPEDIA OF

# CARNIVAL GLASS

## 5TH EDITION

BILL
EDWARDS

**COLLECTOR BOOKS**
*A Division of Schroeder Publishing Co., Inc.*

## Searching For A Publisher?

We are always looking for knowledgeable people considered to be experts within their fields. If you feel that there is a real need for a book on your collectible subject and have a large comprehensive collection, contact Collector Books.

## On the Cover:

Hearts and Flowers Plate, vaseline (rare), $17,000.00;
Good Luck Bowl, marigold, $425.00+;
Ripple Vase, amber, $130.00.

Cover design by Beth Summers
Book design by Terri Stalions

Additional copies of this book may be ordered from:

Collector Books
P.O. Box 3009
Paducah, Kentucky 42002-3009

@$24.95. Add $2.00 for postage and handling.

Copyright: Bill Edwards, 1996

This book or any part thereof may not be reproduced without the written consent of the Author and Publisher.

Printed by IMAGE GRAPHICS, INC., Paducah, Kentucky

# Contents

# Dedication

For my family — Milford, Lorraine, Kim, Pam, Mike, Nick, Mark, Lauren, Alex, Abby, and Hayley.

# Acknowledg-ments

A very special thanks to John and Lucille Britt for years of friendship and help, and my thanks to the following people for once again coming to my aid to improve this book over its forerunner: Dean Hanson, Russ Bibbee, Bob and Pat Davis, Bill Stoetzel, Thelma Harmon, Norman Archer, Eileen Moake, John Woody, Joe Cobb, Jim Halacz, Kathi Johnson, Mr. and Mrs. John Rogers, Lewis Price, Bob Gallo, Richard Conley, Carl and Eunice Booker, Arlene and Joe Johannets, the Ernie L. Pyles, Linda Blanton, Raymond Johns, Mercedes Titus, Don Doyle, Frank Bounds, Gloria and Vicky Balander, R.G. Klein, William Banks, Mark Sadowski, Mike and Janet Carwile, J.L. Salmon, Dennis Pinkham, Katherine Thomson, the Jerry Parrs, Joe and Dorothy Baur, Eugene and Ellen Reno, Rick and Bonnie Boldt, the Preston VerMeers, Sharon Klek, Richard Lanz, Dennis Addy, Donald L. Clark, Elaine Benedict, as well as anyone else I may have overlooked.

# Author's Note

I have spent a major portion of my life learning about, living with, and writing about carnival glass. Let me say that aside from the pure pleasure of handling so much of this beautiful glass, I've met so many very wonderful people, I feel my life has been enriched beyond measure by the experience.

# Introduction

For the benefit of the novice, carnival glass is that pressed and iridized glass manufactured between 1905 and 1930. It was made by various companies in the United States, England, France, Germany, Australia, Czechoslovakia, Sweden, and Finland.

The iridization, unlike the costly art glass produced by Tiffany and his competitors, was achieved by a spray process on the surface of the glass before firing, thus, producing a very beautiful product at a greatly reduced cost, giving the housewife a quality product well within her budget.

In addition, carnival glass was the last hand-shaped glass mass produced in America and remains as a beautiful reminder of the glassmaker's skills.

In this volume, we will show the variety of shapes and colors of carnival glass and will also attempt to define the patterns by manufacturer and for the first time, put the entire field of carnival glass into one reference book for the collector.

It is my hope that this effort will bring new interest to this truly beautiful glass and stimulate its growth as a collectible; and my only regret is a lack of space to show every known pattern.

Having researched carnival glass for nearly 25 years, I sometimes forget there are collectors just beginning, who haven't learned the fine points of this remarkable glass; so for them, here are some basic thoughts.

First comes color. To tell the true color of a piece of carnival glass, hold the piece to a strong light; the base color you see is the color of the piece. The colors given off by the iridescence have little or nothing to do with the true color of the glass. Many have asked me to provide a color chart to aid beginners, but capturing glass colors on paper is nearly impossible. The best advice I can offer on color is to handle as much of this glass as you can, holding it to the light and observing; soon, colors will come naturally, at least the basic colors.

Next, perhaps we should discuss shapes. Bowls and plates are easy to understand as are pitchers, tumblers, and vases; but even those have variations: bowls can be ruffled, unruffled (shallow unruffled bowls are called ice cream shape), deep, or shallow. Pitchers can be standard, smaller (milk pitcher), taller (tankard), or squat. Tumblers can be standard size, tall (lemonade), or small (juice), even as small as shot glasses. Vases can range from tiny 4" bud vases to monster 22" sizes called funeral vases (any vase over 16" tall is considered a funeral vase). Vases may be straight topped, flared, or JIP (jack-in-the-pulpit) shaped with one side down and one side up. In addition there are table sets, consisting of a creamer, a sugar, a covered butter dish, and a spooner (this piece has no lid). There are decanters and stemmed goblets of several sizes; there are rose bowls, evident by the lips being pulled in equally around the top of the piece; candy dishes that have the rims flared out; and nut bowls that have the rim standing straight up. There are banana bowls that are pulled up on two sides, baskets that have handles, bon-bons that have handles on opposite sides, and nappies with only one handle. In addition we have berry sets (small and large bowls that are deep and usually come with one large bowl and six small ones), orange bowls (large footed bowls that held fruit), handled mugs, and plates (these are shallow without any bowl effect, coming straight out from the base and no higher from base to rim than 2"). Specialized shapes include candlesticks, hatpins, hatpin holders (footed pieces with the rim turned in to hold hatpins), epergnes (pieces that hold flower lilies), card trays (flattened bon-bons or nappies), toothpick holders, cracker and cookie jars with lids, stemmed compotes (or comports as they were originally called), hair receivers, powder jars with lids, as well as many, many novelties that include paperweights, animal novelties, and wall pocket vases. Finally we have punch sets which consist of a punch bowl, standard or base, and matching cups. These are all the general shapes of carnival glass. In addition we have many, many specialty shapes that include light shades, beads, beaded purses, odd whimsey shapes of all sorts that have been fashioned from standard pieces, pintrays, dresser trays, pickle casters in metal frames, and bride's baskets likewise. The list of shapes is almost endless and the beginner should study these and ask other collectors about odd pieces they can't identify.

Now, let's talk briefly about the iridescence itself. By far the major portion of carnival glass items will be found with a satiny finish that has many colored highlights across the surface, like oil on water; but another very popular finish was developed by the Millersburg Company and used by all other makers in limited amounts. This is called "radium" finish and can be recognized by its shiny, mirror-like luster on the surface. Often, with radium finish, the exterior of the pieces has no iridization and the piece has a light, watery shine. Beyond that, some items, especially pastels such as white, ice blue, and ice green, have a frosty look. This treatment is always satin, never radium. Finally, there is the addition of the milky edge on treatments that are called opalescent. Added to the marigold finish, this is called "peach opalescent" and with the ice blue, it becomes "aqua opalescent." Other opalescent treatments with carnival glass are: blue opalescent, amethyst opalescent, lime green opalescent, ice green opalescent, vaseline opalescent, and red opalescent.

Finally, let me say there are many new color labels that have come about over the last few years. These are mostly shadings of primary or secondary colors; they are often hard to understand and harder to describe. Here are a few: moonstone (opaque glass, not as dense as milkglass); clambroth (pale ginger ale color); black amethyst (nearly black glass iridized); horehound (a shade darker than amber); Persian blue (opaque, like moonstone but blue); smoke (grayish, with blue and gold highlights); teal (a mixture of blue and green); vaseline (a mixture of green and yellow); lavender (a pale amethyst); and lime (green with a yellow mix). Lastly, there are a handful of colors, now in vogue, that nobody seems to agree on a definition: things like Renniger blue, a tealish, sapphirey blue, according to some! Have we carried all this too far? Of course, but it isn't in my hands to stop this proliferation of colors. I can only hope the above information proves helpful in some way. Remember, we are all learning and knowledge comes in time and with patience. The trip is worth the effort.

# The Dugan Story

The Dugan Glass Company of Indiana, Pennsylvania, began production on April 14, 1892, calling itself the Indiana Glass Company with Harry White as its president and operating for less than a year before closing. The vacant plant was first leased, then purchased by Harry Northwood in 1895. For the next two years it poured out a stream of Northwood glass until Northwood decided to join the National Glass Combine and moved his main operation to the old Hobbs, Brockunier plant, leasing the Indiana plant to its managers, Thomas E. Dugan and W.G. Minnemeyer, who changed the name to the Dugan Glass Company (also called the American Glass Company).

They produced basically the same sorts of glass as Northwood until 1913 when the name was changed again to the Diamond Glass Company with John P. Elkin as president; H. Wallace Thomas, secretary; D.B. Taylor, treasurer; and Ed Rowland, plant manager. During this time, many Northwood molds were reworked, a trademark with a "D" within a diamond registered and most of the carnival glass from the company was produced under the supervision of Thomas Dugan.

The plant operated until 1931 when it was destroyed by fire and never rebuilt because of the Depression that gripped the country and the industry.

# The Fenton Story

First organized in April 1905, the Fenton Art Glass company didn't really materialize until the following July. At that time the glass decorating shop was opened in Martins Ferry, Ohio, in an abandoned factory rented by Frank L. Fenton and his brother, John (who was later to found the famous Millersburg Glass Company).

The next few months were occupied in obtaining financial backers, glass workers, buying land to be plotted into lots as a money-raising venture, and construction of their own plant in Williamstown, West Virginia. At times, everything seemed to go wrong, and it wasn't until 1907 that the company was "on its way."

From the first, the design abilities of Frank Fenton were obvious, and each pattern seemed to bear his own special flair. He (along with Jacob Rosenthal who had come to the Fenton factory after fire had destroyed the renowned Indiana Tumbler and Goblet Company in Greentown, Indiana) was greatly responsible for sensing what the public admired in glass ornamentation.

In 1908 friction arose between the two brothers, and John exited to pursue his dreams in Millersburg, Ohio. By this time, the Fenton process of iridization has taken the mass-scale art glass field by storm and carnival glass was on its way.

For the next 15 years, the Fenton company would produce the largest number of patterns ever in this beautiful product, and huge amounts of iridized glass would be sent to the four corners of the world to brighten homes. While the company made other decorative wears in custard, chocolate glass, mosaic inlaid glass, opalescent glass, and stretch glass, nothing surpassed the quality and quantity of their iridized glass. Almost 150 patterns are credited to the company in carnival glass alone, and many more probably credited to others may be of Fenton origin.

All this is truly a remarkable feat, and certainly Frank L. Fenton's genius must stand along side Harry Northwood's as inspiring.

While the Imperial Glass Company of Bellaire, Ohio, was first organized in 1901 by a group of area investors, it wasn't until January 13, 1904, that the first glass was made; and not until nearly five years later the beautiful iridized glass we've come to call carnival glass was produced.

In the years between these dates, the mass market was sought with a steady production of pressed glass water sets, single tumblers, jelly jars, lamp shades, chimneys, and a full assortment of table items such as salt dips, pickle trays, condiment bottles, and oil cruets.

All of this was a prelude, of course, to the art glass field which swept the country, and in 1909, Imperial introduced their iridescent line of blown lead luster articles as well as the Nuruby, Sapphire, and Peacock colors of carnival glass.

Quite evident then, as now, this proved to be the hallmark of their production. Huge quantities of the iridized glass were designed, manufactured, and sold to the mass marketplace across America and the European Continent for the next decade in strong competition with the other art glass factories. Especially sought was the market in England early in 1911.

In quality Imperial must be ranked second only to the fine glass produced by the Millersburg Company and certainly in design, is on an equal with the great Northwood Company. Only the Fenton Company produced more recognized patterns and has outlasted them in longevity (the Imperial Glass Company became a subsidiary of the Lenox Company in 1973).

Along the way came the fabulous art glass line called "Imperial Jewels" in 1916. This was an iridescent product often in freehand worked with a stretch effect. This is so popular today, many glass collectors have large collections of this alone.

In 1929 Imperial entered the machine glass era and produced its share of what has come to be called Depression glass and in the early 1960s, the company revived their old molds and reproduced many of the old iridized patterns as well as creating a few new ones for the market that was once again invaded by "carnival glass fever." While many collectors purchased these items, purists in carnival glass collecting have remained loyal to the original and without question, the early years of carnival glass production at the Imperial Company will always be their golden years.

Interestingly enough, if John and Frank Fenton hadn't had such adverse personalities, there would have been no Millersburg Glass Company. Both brothers had come to the Martins Ferry, Ohio, area in 1903 to begin a glass business in partnership, but Frank was conservative and level-headed while John was brash and eager – a constant dreamer and the pitchman of the family. Each wanted to make a name in the business, and each wanted to do it his way.

By 1908 with the Fenton Art Glass Factory going strong, the clashes multiplied, and John went in search of a location for a plant of his own. He was 38, a huge strapping man with a shock of heavy brown hair and a pair of steely eyes that could almost hypnotize. He would sire five children.

After weeks of travel and inquiry, he came to Holmes County, Ohio, and was immediately impressed with the land and the people. Here were the heartland Americans whose families had come from Germany and Switzerland. They were hard workers like the Amish that lived among them, good businessmen who led a simple life.

Word soon spread that John Fenton wanted to build a glass plant, and the people welcomed him. By selling his interest in the Fenton plant and borrowing, John secured option on a 54.7 acre site on the north edge of Millersburg. Lots were plotted and sold, and ground was broken on September 14, 1908. And like John Fenton's dreams, the plant was to be the grandest ever. The main building was 300' x 100', spanned by steel framing with no center supporting. A second building, 50' x 300', was built as a packing and shipping area as well as a tool shop. The main building housed a 14-pot furnace, a mix room, an office area, a lehr area, and a display area for samples of their production.

During construction gas wells were drilled to supply a source of power, and stocks were sold in the company, totaling $125,000.00

On May 20, 1909, the first glass was poured. The initial molds were designed by John Fenton and were Ohio Star and Hobstar and Feather. While at the Fenton factory, he had designed others, including the famous "Goddess of Harvest" bowl as a tribute to his wife. The glass that now came from the Millersburg factory was the highest quality of crystal and sample toothpick holders in the Ohio Star pattern were given to all visitors that first week.

In addition to the crystal, iridized glass in the Fenton process was put into production the first month in amethyst, green, and soft marigold. A third pattern — a design of cherry clusters and leaves — was added and soon sold well enough to warrant new molds, bringing the Multi-Fruit and Flowers design into being as a follow-up pattern.

Early in January 1910 the celebrated "radium" process was born. It featured a softer shade of color and a watery, mirror-like finish on the front side of the glass only; it soon took the glass world by storm and became a brisk seller. Noted glassworker, Oliver Phillips, was the father of the process, and it was soon copied by the Imperial Company and others in the area.

In June of that same year, the famous Courthouse bowl was produced as a tribute to the town and to the workers who had laid the gas lines to the factory. These bowls were made in lettered, unlettered, radium, and satin finish and were given away by the hundreds at the factory, just as the crystal Ohio Star punch sets had been given to all the town's churches and social organizations, and the famous People's Vase was to be made as a tribute to the area's Amish.

During the next years the Millersburg plant was at its zenith, and dozens of new patterns were added to the line from molds produced by the Hipkins Mold Company. They included the noted Peacock patterns as well as the Berry Wreath, Country Kitchen, Poppy, Diamond, Pipe Humidor, and Rosalind patterns. By late March 1911 Hipkins wanted pay for their work, as did other creditors, and John Fenton found his finances a disaster. The plant was kept producing, but bankruptcy was filed, and Samuel Fair finally bought the works in October, renaming it the Radium Glass Company. In the next few months, only iridized glass in the radium process was produced while John Fenton tried to find a way to begin again.

But time soon proved Fair couldn't bring the factory back to its former glory, and he closed the doors, selling the factory and its contents to Frank Sinclair and the Jefferson Glass Company in 1913. Sinclair shipped many of the crystal and carnival molds to the Jefferson plant in Canada for a run of production there which included Ohio Star, Hobstar and Feather, and Millersburg Flute. The rest of the molds were sold for scrap despite the success of the patterns with the Canadians who bought the graceful crystal designs for several years. Jefferson's production at the Millersburg plant itself was brief. The known pieces include a 6" Flute compote just like the famous Millersburg Wildflower, marked "Crys-tal" with no interior pattern.

In 1919 the empty plant was again sold to the Forrester Tire and Rubber Company; the great stack was leveled and the furnace gutted. The Millersburg Glass factory was no more. But as long as one single piece of its beautiful glass is collected, its purpose will stand, and the lovers of this beautiful creation will forgive John Fenton his faults in business and praise his creative genius.

An entire book could be written about Harry Northwood, using every superlative the mind could summon and still fail to do justice to the man, a genius in his field. Of course, Harry had an advantage in the glass industry since his father, John Northwood, was a renowned English glassmaker.

Harry Northwood came to America in 1880 and first worked for Hobbs, Brockunier and Company of Wheeling, West Virginia, an old and established glass-producing firm. For five years, Harry remained in Wheeling, learning his craft and dreaming his dreams.

In 1886 he left Hobbs, Brockunier and was employed by the La Belle Glass Company of Bridgeport, Ohio, where he advanced to the position of manager in 1887. A few months later, a devastating fire destroyed much of the La Belle factory, and it was sold in 1888.

Harry next went to work for the Buckeye Glass Company of Martin's Ferry, Ohio. Here he remained until 1896 when he formed the Northwood Company at Indiana, Pennsylvania. Much of the genius was now being evidenced, and such products as the famous Northwood custard glass date from this period.

In 1899 Northwood entered the National Glass Combine only to become unhappy with its financial problems, and in 1901 he broke away to become an independent manufacturer once again. A year later, he bought the long-idle Hobbs, Brockunier plant, and for the next couple of years, there were two Northwood plants.

Finally in 1904, Northwood leased the Indiana, Pennsylvania, plant to its managers, Thomas E. Dugan and W.G. Minnemeyer, who changed the name of the plant to the Dugan Glass Company. In 1913 the plant officially became known as the Diamond Glass Company and existed as such until it burned to the ground in 1931.

In 1908 Harry Northwood, following the success of his student, Frank L. Fenton, in the iridized glass field, marketed his first Northwood iridescent glass, and Northwood carnival glass was born. For a 10-year period carnival glass was the great American craze, and even at the time of Harry Northwood's death in 1919, small quantities were still being manufactured. It had proved to be Northwood's most popular glass, the jewel in the crown of a genius, much of it marked with the well-known trademark.

Besides the five major producers of carnival glass in America, several additional companies produced amounts of iridized glass.

These companies include: Cambridge Glass Company of Cambridge, Ohio; Jenkins Glass Company of Kokomo, Indiana; Westmoreland Glass Company of Grapeville, Pennsylvania; Fostoria Glass Company of Moundsville, West Virginia; Heisey Glass Company of Newark, Ohio; McKee-Jeanette Glass Company of Jeanette, Pennsylvania; and U.S. Glass Company of Pittsburgh, Pennsylvania.

The Cambridge Company was the "leader" of the lesser companies, and the quality of their iridized glass was of a standard equal to that of the Millersburg Glass Company. Actually, there appears to have been a close working relationship between the two concerns, and some evidence exists to lead us to believe some Cambridge patterns were iridized at the Millersburg factory. The Venetian vase is such an item. Known Cambridge patterns are:

| | | |
|---|---|---|
| Horn of Plenty | Inverted Thistle | Sweetheart |
| Double Star (Buzz Saw) | Buzz Saw Cruet | Near Cut Souvenir |
| Cologne Bottle | Proud Puss | Forks Cracker Jar |
| Tomahawk | Inverted Feather | Toy Punch Set |
| Inverted Strawberry | Venetian | Near-Cut Decanter |

Many of the Cambridge patterns are beautiful near-cut designs or patterns intaglio; and while amethyst and blue are colors rarely found, most Cambridge carnival glass was made in green and marigold.

The Jenkins Glass Company made only a handful of carnival glass patterns, mostly in marigold color, and nearly all patterns in intaglio with a combination of flower and near-cut design. Their known patterns are:

| | | |
|---|---|---|
| Cane and Daisy Cut | Stork Vase | Cut Flowers |
| Diamond and Daisy Cut | Oval Star and Fan | Stippled Strawberry |

The Westmoreland Company also made quality carnival glass in limited amounts. Known patterns are:

| | | |
|---|---|---|
| Checkerboard | Strutting Peacock | Footed Drape |
| Pillow and Sunburst | Footed Shell | Shell and Jewel |
| Basketweave and Cable | Wild Rose Wreath #270 | Prisms |
| Corinth Vt. | Orange Peel | Carolina Dogwood |
| Fruit Salad | Little Beads | |

The Fostoria Company had two types of iridized glass. The first was their Taffeta Luster line which included console sets, bowls, and candlesticks; the second was their Brocaded patterns which consisted of an acid cutback design, iridized and decorated with gold. These patterns include:

| | | |
|---|---|---|
| Brocaded Acorns | Brocaded Palms | Brocaded Daffodils |
| Brocaded Rose | Brocaded Summer Garden | |

Heisey made very few iridized items and those found have a light, airy luster. Patterns known are:

| | | |
|---|---|---|
| Heisey #357 | Heisey Flute | Heisey Colonial |
| Heisey Tray Set | Paneled Heisey | |

The McKee-Jeanette Company had a few carnival glass patterns as follows:

| | | |
|---|---|---|
| Aztec | Rock Crystal | Heart Band Souvenir |
| Hobnail Panels | Lutz | Snow Fancy |

The U.S. Glass Company was a combine of 17 companies, headquartered in Pittsburgh, Pennsylvania. Their plants were usually designated by letters, and it is nearly impossible to say what item came from which factory. However, some of the patterns we have classified as U.S. Glass are:

| | | |
|---|---|---|
| Beads and Bars | Louisville Shrine | Daisy in Oval Panels |
| Rochester Shrine | Field Thistle | Champagne |
| Golden Harvest | New Orleans Shrine Champagne | Shrine Toothpick |
| Palm Beach | Feather Swirl | Vintage Wine |
| Cosmos and Cane | Butterfly Tumbler | |

In addition to all the glass produced by these minor concerns, specialty glass houses contributed their share of iridized glass in the large "Gone With The Wind" lamps, shades, chimneys, etc.; as well as minute amounts of iridized glass from Libby, Anchor-Hocking, Tiffin, DeVilbiss, Hig-Bee, and Jeanette are known.

It is not possible in our limited space to show all these patterns from the smaller makers, but we'll try to give a sampling from many of them.

In addition, many patterns in carnival glass have not been attributed to definite producers at this time, and so you will find a few items shown where we must say "maker unknown." While we wish this didn't have to be, sooner or later, these too will find their proper place in the history of carnival glass.

Besides the British and Australians, factories in Sweden, Finland, Denmark, Czechoslovakia, Holland, Mexico, France, and Argentina are now known to have produced some amount of iridized glass. While it would be impossible for us to catalog all these companies, I will list a few of the more prolific and their currently known patterns.

### Finland
Finnish carnival glass wasn't made until the early 1930s and was made primarily at four factories, including one at Riihimaki which seemed to specialize in copying some best-selling American patterns like Lustre Rose, Four Flowers, and Tiger Lily.

### Czechoslovakia
Several researchers trace such patterns as Zipper Stitch, The Fish Vase, and the Hand Vase to this country's production. If so, they also made some red for I have seen one red Hand Vase! Everything else named is in marigold including the Star and Fan Cordial set.

### Sweden
Swedish carnival glass was made in the Varmland region at a factory called the Eda Glassworks with such patterns as Rose Garden, Curved Star, Sunk Daisy, and Sunflower and Diamonds. Colors are primarily marigold and blue, and I suspect the Sungold epergne may have come from this factory.

### Argentina
The Regollcau Cristalerias Company is in Buenos Aires, and here a handful of little-known patterns were made including the Beetle ashtray and an ashtray I call CR since that is just how it is shaped. I've seen it in both marigold and blue.

### Mexico
Recent information into the mysterious patterns of Votive Light, Ranger, and Oklahoma all point to a Mexican production by Cristales de Mexico in Nuevo Leon, Mexico. Each of these patterns is marked with the "M" inside a "C."

In addition, small amounts of iridized glass, often decorated with hand painting, was made in France, Germany, Holland, and Belgium. Some of these pieces are very intricate and the design top-notch. I have seen a very beautiful custard glass bowl in a bride's basket that has a candy-ribbon edge; it is iridized and has an enamel design. It was pretty enough to be in a museum, and I've envied the owner ever since I saw it.

When iridized glass caught the buyer's fancy in this country, the major companies (especially Imperial and Fenton) began to ship carnival glass to England, Europe, and Australia, and it wasn't long until the glasshouses there began to enter the iridized field. In England the chief producer of this glass was the Sowerby Company of Gateshead-on-Tyne. However, other concerns made some iridized glass, including Gueggenheim, Ltd., of London; and Davisons of Gateshead.

The movement of carnival glass in England began later than in America and lasted about five years after sales had diminished in this country. Many shapes were made, including bowls, vases, compotes, and table pieces. However, water sets and punch sets were pretty much overlooked, and only a few examples of these have come to light. Colors in English glass were mainly confined to marigold, blue, and amethyst, but an occasional item in green does appear. The pastels apparently were not popular for few examples exist.

Here then is a list of known English patterns and its volume may surprise many collectors:

| | | |
|---|---|---|
| African Shield | Cathedral Arches | Diamond Ovals |
| Apple Panels | (Hobstar and Cathedral) | Diving Dolphins |
| Art Deco | Chariot | Fans |
| Banded Grape and Leaf | Covered Hen | Feathered Arrow |
| Beaded Hearts | Covered Swan | Fine Cut Rings |
| Buddha | Daisy Block | Flute Sherbet |
| Cane and Scroll | Daisy and Cane | Footed Prism Panels |

| English Carnival Glass (Cont.) | | |
|---|---|---|
| Grape and Cherry | Moonprint | Spiralex |
| Heavy Prisms | My Lady's Powderbox | Split Diamond |
| Hobstar Cut Triangles | Pineapple | Star |
| Hobstar Reversed | Pinwheel | Stippled Diamond Swag |
| Intaglio Daisy | Pinwheel Vase | Thistle and Thorn |
| Kokomo | Sacic Ashtray | Tiny Berry Tumbler |
| Lattice Heart | Saint Candlestick | Triads |
| Lea (and variants) | Scroll Embossed Vt. | Vining Leaf |
| May Basket | Signet | |

# Australian Carnival Glass

Just as England caught the "fever," so did the populace of Australia, and in 1918 the Crystal Glass Works, Ltd. of Sydney began to produce a beautiful line of iridized glass, whose finish ranks with the very best (mostly in bowls and compotes but with occasional table items and two water sets known).

Australian carnival glass is confined to purple, marigold, and an unusual amber over aqua finish, and patterns known are:

| | | |
|---|---|---|
| Australian Swan | Emu (Ostrich) | Magpie |
| Australian Grape | Feathered Flowers | Pin-ups |
| Banded Diamonds | Flannel Berry | Rose Panels |
| Beaded Spears | Flannel Flower | S-Band |
| Blocks and Arches | Interior Rays | Sun Gold Epergne |
| Butterflies and Bells | Kangaroo (and variants) | Thunderbird (Shrike) |
| Butterflies and Waratah | Kingfisher (and variants) | Waterlily and Dragonfly |
| Butterfly Bower | Kiwi | Wild Fern |
| Butterfly Bush | Kookaburra (and variants) | |
| Crystal Cut | | |

# Patterns

**Absentee Dragon**

## Absentee Dragon

If you take a close look at this very rare 9" plate, you will see it is very different from the Dragon and Berry pattern it resembles. It is the only one known, and while I hate the name, I consider it a top rarity in Fenton glass. It has a Bearded Berry reverse pattern, and the color is excellent. It was, no doubt, an experimental piece.

## Acanthus

An Imperial pattern found mostly on bowls and occasionally on plates, the Acanthus is quite graceful. Colors known are marigold, smoke, green, and blue, but certainly Imperial purple is possible. The exterior pattern is Wide Panel or Flute.

## Acorn (Fenton)

It would be hard to imagine a more naturalistic pattern than this. Realistic acorns and oak leaves arranged in three groupings fill much of the allowed space and form a pleasing design. Acorn is found on bowls and plates in a wide range of colors including marigold, amethyst, green, red, vaseline, ice blue, and iridized milk glass.

**Acanthus**

**Acorn (Fenton)**

13

*Acorn (Millersburg)*

*Acorn Burrs*

*Adam's Rib*

# *A*corn (Millersburg)

What a shame the Millersburg company didn't make this realistic design in other shapes; the compote is one of the best designed in all of carnival glass. Realistic acorns and leaves with an exterior of flute and the typical Millersburg clover base. Colors are marigold, amethyst, green, and a rare vaseline.

# *A*corn Burrs

Other than the famous Northwood Grape and their Peacock at Fountain pattern, Acorn Burrs is probably the most representative of the factory's work, and one eagerly sought by carnival glass collectors. The pattern background is that of finely done oak bark while the leaves are those of the chestnut oak. The mold work is well done, and the coloring ranks with the best. Acorn Burrs is found in a wide range of colors and shapes and always brings top dollar.

# *A*dam's Rib

This scarce Dugan-Diamond pattern dating from the 1920s can be found on tall, dome-shaped pitchers and stemmed and handled tumblers. This is actually a lemonade set. Colors are pastel in green, blue, and frosty white.

# *A*dvertising Items

These come in dozens of varieties, shapes, and colors, and it would be impossible in our limited space to show them all. Advertising items were a much-welcomed area of business by all carnival glassmakers, because they were a guaranteed source of income without the usual cost-lost factor of unsold stock. Also, they could often be made with less care, since they were to be given away; old molds could often be utilized to avoid expensive new molds. Many Northwood advertising items were small plates with simple floral designs.

*Advertising Items*

*African Shield*

## African Shield

This small vase shape originally had a wire flower holder that held the stems of freshly cut blossoms in a neat arrangement. It is 2⅞" tall and 3¼" wide at the top, and while I can't be certain who made it, I believe it is English. Marigold is the only color reported so far.

## Age Herald

Another famous advertising pattern, known to have come from the Fenton factory, is found only in amethyst. Both bowls and plates are known, and the pattern was designed as a give-away item from the well-known Birmingham, Alabama, newspaper. The exterior pattern is a wide panel.

## Amaryllis

This unusual compote is a treasure for several reasons. First is the size (2¼" high, 5¼" wide). The shape is roughly triangular, rising from a slightly domed base. The underside carries the Poppy Wreath pattern, and the only colors reported are a deep purple, cobalt blue, and marigold. Amaryllis is a rather scarce Northwood pattern and isn't often mentioned in carnival glass discussions. It is, however, a unique and interesting addition to any collection.

*Age Herald*

*Amaryllis*

*American*

*Apple and Pear Intaglio*

*Apple Blossom
(Northwood)*

*Apple Blossoms*

# A merican

From the Fostoria glasshouse the American pattern was one of their most important patterns in crystal, and it is no surprise to find it among their iridized items. The footed tumbler shown is slightly taller than most tumblers.

# A pple and Pear Intaglio

Like its cousin the Strawberry Intaglio, this rather rare bowl is a product of the Northwood Company and is seen mostly in crystal or goofus glass. The example shown measures 9¾" in diameter and is 2¾" high. The glass is ½" thick!

# A pple Blossom (Northwood)

The tumbler shown is only part of a grouping painted by the same artist that consists of a water set, berry set, and table set. Usually found in blue, both amethyst and marigold are known in smaller quantities.

# A pple Blossoms

Found only in small bowls or plates, Apple Blossoms seems to be an average carnival glass pattern, produced for a mass market in large quantities. Most often seen in marigold, it is occasionally found in vivid colors as well as pastels, especially white. A quarter-size chunk of this pattern in white was found at the Dugan dump site in 1975.

*Apple Blossom Twigs*

# *A* pple Blossom Twigs

This is a very popular pattern, especially in plates where the design is shown to full advantage. The detail is quite nice with fine mold work, much like that of Acorn Burrs. Found mostly in marigold, peach, and purple, Apple Blossom Twigs has as its exterior pattern, the Big Basketweave pattern. Shards in this pattern at the Dugan site have been identified.

# *A* pple Panels

Found only in the breakfast set shown so far, Apple Panels is an intaglio pattern. The design consists of two panels with an apple, stem, and leaves; these are separated by panels of hobstars and fans. Colors are marigold and green but others may someday surface.

*Apple Panels*

# *A* pple Tree

It certainly is a pity Fenton chose to use this realistic pattern on water sets only. It would have made a beautiful table set or punch set. Apple Tree is available in marigold, cobalt blue, and white, and I've seen a rare vase whimsey formed from the pitcher with the handle omitted. The coloring is nearly always strong and bright.

*Apple Tree*

17

*April Showers*

*Arcs*

*Art Deco*

*Asters*

18

# April Showers
Like the bubbles in a carbonated soft drink, the tiny beads seem to float over this very interesting vase pattern. Found in all sizes from 5" to 16", April Showers is sometimes found with Peacock Tail pattern on the interior. The colors are marigold, blue, purple, green, and white. The top edge is usually quite ruffled in the Fenton manner.

# Arcs
This pattern is often confused by beginning collectors with the Scroll Embossed pattern, and it's easy to see why. Perhaps they were designed by the same person since they are both Imperial patterns. Arcs is found on bowls of average size, often with an exterior of File pattern and on compotes with a geometric exterior. The usual colors are marigold or a brilliant amethyst, but green and smoke do exist.

# Art Deco
We don't often see such a plain carnival pattern, but this one has a good deal of interest, despite its lack of design. The very modern look was all the rage in the Art Deco age, so I've named this cute little bowl in that manner. I don't know who the English manufacturer was.

# Asters
Recently, I've seen this very pretty intaglio exterior pattern on a 6" compote as well as a 10" bowl, both in a very strong marigold, and Mrs. Hartung lists it in a 6" bowl. I suspect this pattern is English, probably from Sowerby.

*Aurora Pearls*

# Aurora Pearls

Since I first showed this beautiful iridized custard piece, I've seen a larger version that was 12½" wide as well as a version in red and one in cobalt, both iridized and decorated. All were beautiful! I'm sure this is European and bridges the space between art glass and carnival glass.

# Australian Flower Set

Used like the Water Lily and Dragonfly flower set, this Australian beauty has no design except the slender thread border on the bowl's exterior. The iridescence is fantastic, as you can see.

# Australian Sugars

These two beauties are kissing cousins and both Australian. The marigold one is called Australian Panels and the purple one Australian Diamonds (not Concave Diamonds as previously listed). Other shapes may exist, but I haven't seen them.

*Australian Flower Set*

*Australian Sugars*

*Australian Swan*

*Autumn Acorns*

*Aztec*

### Australian Swan

Pictured is the Australian Black Swan on a beautiful bowl design. The floral sprays remind us of lily of the valley but are probably some Australian plant. Colors are purple and marigold in both large and small bowls.

### Autumn Acorns

Apparently a spin-off pattern from the Fenton Acorn, Autumn Acorns has replaced the realistic oak leaf with the grape leaf used on the Vintage pattern bowls. Found mostly in bowls, an occasional plate is seen in green. The bowls are found in marigold, blue, green, amethyst, vaseline, and red.

### Aztec

While McKee didn't make much carnival glass, the few existing pieces are treasures and certainly the Aztec pattern is one. Known only in a creamer, sugar, rose bowl, tumblers, and pitcher, the coloring ranges from a good strong marigold to a clambroth with a fiery pink and blue highlights. Each shape in Aztec is rare and important.

## Balloons

Balloons is one of those border-line items that could be called either carnival glass or stretch glass since it has characteristics of both. Found in various shapes, including vases of different sizes and shapes, plates with a center handle, compotes, and perfume atomizers. The colors are marigold or smoke. The design is ground through the luster and appears clear, and, of course, there is the stretch effect on many of the pieces.

## Band

Like most of the violet basket inserts, this one relies on a metal handle and holder for any decoration it might have. It was made by Dugan and probably came in marigold as well as the amethyst shown.

## Banded Diamond

Now known to be an Australian pattern, Banded Diamond is found in water sets and berry sets that are scarce. The colors are a very rich amethyst and a strong marigold.

## Banded Diamonds and Bars

Three sizes of this Finnish tumbler are known thus far, and all have a deep, rich marigold color and strong iridization. The smallest one (shown) is only 2¼" high; the second one shown is the largest, and it is just slightly over 3½" high.

*Balloons*

*Band*

*Banded Diamond*

*Banded Diamonds and Bars*

21

*Banded Drape*

*Banded Grape and Leaf*

*Banded Rib*

*Band of Roses*

## Banded Drape

Banded Drape is another of Fenton's decorated water sets, but the shape is quite distinctive, being almost urn-shaped. The colors are very beautiful with much luster and are found in marigold, amethyst, cobalt blue, white, and ice green. The enameled flower seems to be a lovely calla lily.

## Banded Grape and Leaf

Here is the only water set I've heard about in English glass. As you can see, the design is quite good, and the color is better than average. The only color I've seen is marigold, and at least two sets of this pattern are in American collections.

## Banded Rib

Another rather late pattern, this is one of the taller water sets, probably intended for iced tea or lemonade. The only color reported is the marigold, and the only shapes are tumblers and pitchers.

## Band of Roses

Besides this tumble-up and matching tray, a pitcher and tumbler are known in this pattern. It came from Argentina I understand, but is probably a product of a glass firm in Europe. At any rate, it is pretty and quite rare in any shape.

22

*Barbella*                    *Barber Bottle*

## Barbella

Made by Northwood, this scarce tumbler is 3½" high. It has a collar base and has for a design, 14 panels on the interior. The Northwood "N" is on the inside of the base. The coloring is a strong, pure vaseline, but other colors may exist.

## Barber Bottle

This pattern is certainly misnamed since it is actually a cordial bottle and has a matching tray and stemmed cordials! The bottle stands over 11" tall in good marigold trimmed in black, as are the cordials. These are from Czechoslovakia.

## Basket

Novelty items are a very important area of glass production, and this little item is one of the best known. Standing on four sturdy feet, the Northwood Basket is about 5¾" high and 5" wide. Often the basket is simply round, but sometimes one finds an example that has been pulled into an eight-sided shape. Made in a wide range of colors including marigold, purple, vaseline, cobalt, ice green, ice blue, aqua, and white. This is a popular pattern.

*Basket*

## Basketweave (Northwood)

Here's a secondary Northwood pattern found often on bowls and now and then on compotes and bonbons. It's a pretty, all-over filler that does the job.

*Basketweave (Northwood)*

*Basketweave and Cable*

*Beaded Acanthus*

*Beaded Band and
Octagon Lamp*

*Beaded Basket*

## Basketweave and Cable

Much like the Shell and Jewel breakfast set from the same company, the Westmoreland Basketweave and Cable is a seldom-found pattern and surely must have been made in limited amounts. The mold work is excellent, and the luster is satisfactory. Colors are marigold (often pale), amethyst, green, and rarely white.

## Beaded Acanthus

It's hard to believe this outstanding pattern was made in this one shape only, but to date I've heard of no other. This milk pitcher, like the Poinsettia, measures 7" high and has a base diameter of 3¾". It is found mostly on marigold glass or smoke, but a very outstanding green exists, and I suspect amethyst is also a possibility. The coloring is usually quite good, and the iridescence is what one might expect from the Imperial Company.

## Beaded Band and Octagon Lamp

Here is a seldom-seen oil lamp that is really very attractive. The coloring is adequate but watery, indicating 1920s production. It was reportedly made in two sizes, 7½" and 9¾", but I can't confirm this. The maker is unknown.

## Beaded Basket

While the beaded basket is, in many respects, just as attractive as the footed Northwood version and less expensive, it can be found with the upper edge flared or flattened down. It has been seen in several colors including marigold, blue, amethyst, lavender, smoke, vaseline, and white. Green has now been reported, but not confirmed at this time.

## Beaded Bull's Eye

There are several variations of this vase pattern often caused by the "pulling" or "slinging" to obtain height. Nevertheless, the obvious rows of bull's eyes on the upper edge serve to establish identity. Found mostly in marigold, these Imperial vases are not easily found.

## Beaded Cable

The Beaded Cable rose bowl has long been a favorite with collectors for it is a simple yet strong design made with all the famous Northwood quality. Usually about 4" high, these rose bowls stand on three sturdy legs. The prominent cable intertwines around the middle and is, of course, edged by beads. Nearly all pieces are marked and are made in a wide variety of colors. Of course, these pieces are sometimes opened out to become a candy dish, like many Northwood footed items.

## Beaded Panels and Grapes

Reportedly made in Czechoslovakia, this 4½" tumbler has beaded panels that remind one of the old Holly Amber design. Three panels feature grapes and leaves that drop from a band of vines, leaves, and grape clusters. Marigold is the only color I'm aware of, but others may exist.

## Beaded Panels Compote

This little beauty was made by the Dugan-Diamond company and can be found in marigold, amethyst, a rare milk glass with a vaseline finish, and the peach opal finish shown. It isn't rare but certainly is a pretty addition to any collection.

*Beaded Bull's Eye*

*Beaded Panels and Grapes*

*Beaded Cable*

*Beaded Panels Compote*

*Beaded Shell*

*Beaded Spears*

*Beaded Star*

### Beaded Shell
Known also in custard glass, Beaded Shell is one of the older Dugan patterns and is found in a variety of shapes, including berry sets, table sets, water sets, and mugs. Colors are purple, blue, green, marigold, and white with blue and purple somewhat more easily found.

### Beaded Spears
Beaded spears is a scarce water set, made in Czechoslovakia for export and shipped to many areas of the world. The set shown lives in Australia. Marigold is the only reported color, but tumblers are known in two sizes (shown is the flared lemonade version). The design of peaks, prisms and plain circles is unique and very pretty.

### Beaded Star
Besides the variation of this pattern that is shown (sometimes called Moon and Beaded Stars) there is a variant that is known in opalescent glass as Beaded Stars and Swag. Both were made by the Fenton Company and in carnival glass are found a small bowl, rose bowl, plate, and a banana bowl.

## Beaded Star Medallion

Here is a Northwood shade, shown with the complete wall fixture, holding both gas and electric shades. These are marked Northwood and the coloring is just superb. Notice there is stippling on the exterior.

## Beaded Swirl

Now known to be a Sowerby pattern and found in covered butterdish, sugar, compote, and milk pitcher, this pattern is also known as Beads and Panels and can be found in blue as well as marigold. The compote shape has been seen with the top flattened also to make a shallow, stemmed bowl.

## Beads

It's really a shame this pattern isn't found more often and is restricted to the exterior of average-size bowls, because it is a well-balanced, attractive item, especially on vivid colors. Combining three motifs — daisy-like flowers, petalish blooms, and beads — this pattern, while not rare, is certainly not plentiful and is a desirable Northwood item.

## Bearded Berry

One of Fenton's primary exterior patterns the Bearded Berry pattern has six branches of berries and leaves. The berries themselves have small whisker-like lines from their ends. Tying all the bunches together is a thin cable-like line above them, circling the bowl.

*Beaded Star Medallion*

*Beaded Swirl*

*Beads*

*Bearded Berry*

Bee Ornament

Beauty
Bud Vase

Beetle Ashtray

Bellaire Souvenir

## Beauty Bud Vase

This Dugan pattern was a popular one, which was made in large runs and is easily found today, mostly in marigold. You will notice that except for the missing limbs around the base, it is exactly like the Twigs vase from the same maker.

## Bee Ornament

This tiny solid glass ornament is only about 1½" long and reminds me of the famous Butterfly ornaments that were made to attach to flower arrangements. The Bee Ornament has been found in marigold, and I finally got to hold one of the scarce white ones at an ACGA Convention this year. I've been told Westmoreland is the maker.

## Beetle Ashtray

Unusual is the word for this rare ashtray. It was made by the Regolleau Christalerias Company of Buenos Aires, Argentina, around 1925. As you can see, the mold work is outstanding, and the cobalt blue coloring is excellent. To date only two of these have been reported.

## Bellaire Souvenir

This curious bowl measures 7" in diameter and is roughly 2½" deep. The lettering and little bell are all interior work while the fine ribbing is on the outside. Just when this bowl was given, or why it remains is a mystery to me, but I'm quite sure it would have great appeal to the collector of lettered glass. This was made by Imperial.

*Bell Flower (Fuchsia)*

## Bell Flower (Fuchsia)

This very rare stemmed compote with handles has been mistaken with a similar pattern called Bells and Beads but is really quite different on close examination. It is made by the Fenton Company and to date only blue is known but certainly marigold is a possibility. The current owners prefer the name Fuchsia although Bell Flower was the first name used so I'm listing both here.

## Bells and Beads

Shards of this pattern turned up in the Helman digs, so we know this is another Dugan pattern. Found in small bowls, plates, hat shapes, nappies, compotes, and a handled gravy boat, Bells and Beads' colors are marigold, blue, amethyst, green, and peach opalescent.

## Bernheimer Bowl

The only difference between this much sought bowl and the famous Millersburg Many Stars pattern is, of course, the advertising center, consisting of a small star and the words: Bernheimer Brothers. This replaces the usual large star and demonstrates how a clever mold designer can capitalize on a good design. While not nearly as plentiful as the Many Stars bowls, the Bernheimer bowls are found in blue only.

*Bells and Beads*

*Bernheimer Bowl*

*Big Basketweave*

*Big Fish*

*Big Thistle Punch Bowl*

## Big Basketweave

This Dugan pattern is found on the exterior of Fanciful and Round-Up bowls, the base pattern for the Persian Garden two-piece fruit bowls and for vases, as well as a handled basket in two sizes. Colors are marigold, amethyst, blue, peach opalescent, and white.

## Big Fish

Rarer than the Trout and Fly pieces that were also made by the Millersburg company, the Big Fish has more realistic mold work. It can be found in a host of shapes; round, tri-cornered, square, and tightly ruffled. Colors are the usual Millersburg ones; marigold, amethyst, green, vaseline, and rarely clambroth.

## Big Thistle Punch Bowl

I could spend pages raving about this very superb Millersburg rarity, but let me simply say I consider it the most beautiful of all the carnival glass punch bowls. Two are known, and both are amethyst. One has a flared top while the other is straight up. Needless to say, the glass is clear, the mold work superior, and the iridescence beyond belief.

*Birds and Cherries*

## Birds and Cherries

Found quite often on bonbons and compotes, this realistic Fenton pattern is sometimes found on rare berry sets and very rare plates. The birds, five in number, remind me of grackles. I've heard of this pattern in marigold, blue, green, amethyst, white, pastel-marigold, and vaseline.

## Bird with Grapes

Larger than the Woodpecker wall vase, the Bird with Grapes vase is also called Cockatoo. The coloring tends to be somewhat amberish, and the flat back has a hole to attach it to a wall hook. The maker is unknown, at least to me.

## Blackberry (Fenton)

Found often as an interior pattern on the open-edge, basketweave, hat-shape Fenton produced in great numbers, Blackberry is a very realistic pattern, gracefully molded around the walls of the hat. It is known in many colors including marigold, cobalt blue, green, amethyst, ice blue, ice green, vaseline, and red. The example shown is blue with marigold open-edge.

*Bird with Grapes*

*Blackberry (Fenton)*

31

*Blackberry (Northwood)*

# Blackberry (Northwood)

While several companies had a try at a Blackberry pattern, Northwood's is one of the better ones and quite distinctive. The pattern covers most of the allowed space, be it the interior of a 6" compote or an 8½" footed bowl. Combined with the latter is often a pattern called Daisy and Plume. The colors are marigold, purple, green, and white.

# Blackberry Banded

Like many Fenton patterns, Blackberry Banded is limited to the hat shape and without an exterior pattern. These ruffled hats are usually between 3¼" and 3¾" high with a base diameter of 2½". Found mostly in marigold or cobalt blue, they are rarely found in green and milk glass with marigold iridization.

# Blackberry Block

This is one of the better Fenton water set patterns and can be found in marigold, blue, amethyst, green, and rarely white. The all-over pattern of wire-like squares with berries and leaves vining over them is very pleasing.

**Blackberry Banded**

**Blackberry Block**

*Blackberry Bramble*

# Blackberry Bramble

A very available pattern on bowls and compotes. Blackberry Bramble is a very close cousin to the Fenton Blackberry pattern but has more leaves, berries, and thorny branches. The bowls are rather small with diameters of 6" to 8¼", and the compotes are of average size. Colors are marigold, green, and cobalt blue, but others may certainly exist.

# Blackberry Spray

I've always felt this a poorly designed pattern, but others may disagree. There isn't too much graceful about the four separate branches, and the fruit isn't spectacular. Nevertheless, it can be found on hat shapes, bonbons, and compotes in marigold, cobalt blue, green, amethyst, aqua, and red. The examples of aqua I have seen do not have opalescence.

*Blackberry Spray*

# Blackberry Whimsey (Fenton)

This rare Fenton whimsey is shaped from the two-row open edge basket with Blackberry pattern interior. The vase has been shaped into an 8¼" high beauty. The only color reported is a beautiful cobalt blue, but others may certainly exist.

*Blackberry Whimsey (Fenton)*

*Blackberry Wreath*

*Black Bottom (Fenton)*

*Blaze*

## Blackberry Wreath

In all the years I've been writing about glass, this pattern along with its sister pattern of Grape Wreath and Strawberry Wreath have provoked the most inquiry. Just remember Blackberry Wreath always has a berry and four leaves in the center of the design. Colors are typical Millersburg ones: marigold, green, amethyst, vaseline, and clambroth, the large bowl in a rare blue.

## Black Bottom (Fenton)

This very Art Deco little candy jar once had a lid but it has long since been separated. These are shown in the old Fenton ads in a host of colors in stretch glass, but this is the first one I've seen in marigold. The base has a spray-painted finish that has been then fired to keep its black color.

## Blaze

This strange name was given to this pattern by Rose Presznick and I have no idea why. The pattern is on a large bowl shape on the exterior only with a standard eight-sided crimp. As far as I know, the maker hasn't been determined but it looks very English in design.

*Blocks and Arches*

## Blocks and Arches

Often confused with the very similar Ranger pattern, Blocks and Arches is really an Australian design found only on tumblers and pitchers like the one shown. Colors are marigold and amethyst.

## Blossom and Shell

While most opalescent glass collectors call this pattern Blossom & Shell, carnival glass collectors have long lumped it with the Northwood Wild Rose pattern (which it isn't). As you can see there are important differences, including more petals to the flowers, more leaves, and a scrolling below the flowers that doesn't appear on Wild Rose. The coloring shown is called Alaskan and is an amber finish over green glass.

## Blossoms and Band

Blossoms and Band is not a very distinguished pattern, and its origin is questionable. Found primarily on berry sets in marigold, a car vase is also known, as shown. The design is quite simple with a row of blossoms, stems, and leaves above a band of thumbprints and prisms. The color has a good deal of pink in the marigold, much like English glass. The mold work is adequate but far from outstanding. Needless to say, this is not the same pattern as that found on the Millersburg Wild Rose lamps that are often called by the same name. This is possibly an Imperial pattern.

*Blossom and Shell*

*Blossoms and Band*

*Blossomtime*

*Blown Candlestick*

*Blueberry*

*Booker Cider Set*

## Blossomtime

Even if this outstanding compote was not marked, we'd surely assign it to the Northwood company because it is so typical of their work. The flowers, the thorny branches (twisted into a geometrical overlapping star), and the curling little branchlets are all nicely done and are stippled, except for the branchlets. The background is plain and contrasts nicely. Blossomtime is combined with an exterior pattern called Wild Flower and is found in marigold, purple, green, and pastels. The stem is quite unusual, being twisted with a screw-like pattern. Blossomtime is a scarce pattern and always brings top dollar.

## Blown Candlestick

Very thin and hollow from the base to the bottom of the candleholder, this European candlestick is quite tall (12¼") and has the even light lustre associated with items from the continent. Other colors may exist, but I haven't heard of them.

## Blueberry

May I say in the beginning, I'm quite prejudiced about this Fenton water set for I think it is outstanding in both design and execution. What a shame it wasn't made in other shapes such as a table set. I've heard of Blueberry in marigold, cobalt blue, and white only, but that doesn't mean it wasn't made in other colors.

## Booker Cider Set

This cutie is in the collection of Carl and Eunice Booker, so I've named it after them. It is smaller than most, has a beautiful spray of enameled flowers and an amethyst handle! It is probably European. A matching pitcher exists.

*Bo Peep Mug and Plate*

## Bo Peep Mug and Plate

While the Bo Peep mug is simply scarce, the plate is a quite rare item, seldom sold or traded from one collection to another. The color is good marigold and reminds us of that found on most of the Fenton Kitten items. Of course, all children's items in glass were subjected to great loss through breakage, but I doubt if large amounts of the Bo Peep pattern were made in the beginning. So, of course, small quantities have survived.

## Border Plants

Typical of many Dugan-Diamond designs this dome-based bowl (also found in a collar base) has a large central flower design bordered by stippling and a series of stemmed flowers that alternate with a series of three-leafed designs. Colors are amethyst, lavender, and the usual peach opalescent.

*Border Plants*

## Bouquet

If you look quite closely at this bulbous water set, you'll notice several common devices used by the Fenton company, such as fillers of scales surrounding an embroidery ring. No other shapes exist, and the water set is found in marigold, blue, and white. The mold work is quite good, and the colors are typically Fenton.

*Bouquet*

*Boutonniere*

*Breakfast Set (Heisey)*

*Brocaded Acorns*

### Boutonniere

This little beauty is a Millersburg product. It usually has a fine radium finish and is most often seen in amethyst. And although I haven't seen one, I've been told there is a variation sometimes found with a different stem and base. Boutonniere is also found in marigold and green.

### Breakfast Set (Heisey)

While it isn't so marked, I'd guess this very attractive marigold breakfast set was a Heisey product. The coloring is very dark and rich, and the handles are like those on known Heisey products.

### Brocaded Acorns

The lacy effects of all these brocaded patterns by the Fostoria company are a joy to behold. This was achieved by an acid cutback process, and after the iridescence was fired a gold edging was applied. Found in several shapes, Brocaded Acorns was made in pink, white, ice green, ice blue, and vaseline.

*Brocaded Daffodils*

## Brocaded Daffodils

Like the other brocaded patterns, this was made by Fostoria. The shape is a 7½" x 6½" handled bowl in pink. The lovely pattern consists of beautifully realistic daffodils, leaf swirls, and small star fillers.

## Brocaded Palms

Shown is one example of Fostoria's Brocaded series, a large, handled cake plate in Brocaded Palms pattern. As you can see, the design is created with an acid cutback effect on the glass before iridization, and the edges are gold trimmed. All the patterns are generally handled in this manner, and colors found include ice green, ice blue, pink, white, and a lovely and rare rose shade, as well as a rare vaseline color.

*Brocaded Palms*

## Broken Arches

Broken Arches is a beautiful geometric Imperial pattern found only in punch sets of rather stately size. Not only is the coloring good, but the mold work is outstanding. The colors are marigold and amethyst. Often there is a silver sheen to the latter which detracts from its beauty, but when a set is found without this gunmetal look, the result is breathtaking. The marigold set is more common and sells for much less than amethyst. A green Broken Arches would be a great rarity.

*Broken Arches*

*Brooklyn Bottle*

*Bull's Eye and Leaves*

*Brooklyn Bridge*

*Bull's Eye and Loop*

### Brooklyn Bottle

I suspect this beautiful 9⅝" cruet may be of European origin. The glass is very thin, and the non-iridized handle and stopper are very attractive amethyst glass.

### Brooklyn Bridge

Like the Pony bowl pattern, this beautiful advertising bowl apparently came from the Dugan factory. The only color reported is marigold, and the mold work is outstanding. Brooklyn Bridge is a scarce and desirable pattern. A rare unlettered example is also known.

### Bull's Eye and Leaves

Confined to the exterior of bowls and found mostly in green or marigold, this pattern is a trifle too busy to be very effective and is certainly not one of Northwood's better efforts. All in all, there are five motifs, including leaves, beads, circles, fishnet, and a petal grouping. Although each appears on other Northwood products, not in this combination.

### Bull's Eye and Loop

This is one of the nicer small Millersburg vases. It has four rows of loops with bull's eyes appearing on alternating loops in a staggered pattern. It is quite rare and usually brings a premium price. All examples I've seen had a radium finish, and colors known are marigold, amethyst, and green.

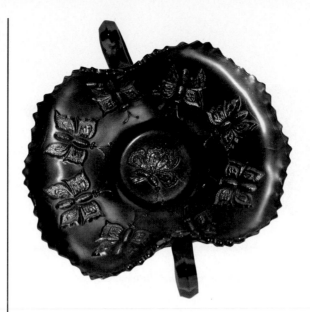

*Butterflies*

# Butterflies

This outstanding Fenton pattern is found only on bonbons often flattened into a card tray shape. The colors are very good with eight butterflies around the edges and one in the center. The exterior carries a typical wide panel pattern and often is found with advertising on the base. Colors are marigold, cobalt blue, green, amethyst, and white. At least these are the ones about which I've heard.

# Butterflies and Waratah

Normally seen in the compote shape, this one has been flattened into a very stylish footed cake stand. The beautiful purple is typical of Australian carnival glass and can stand with the best. It is also found in marigold.

# Butterfly (Northwood)

This popular Northwood bonbon pattern shows a well-designed butterfly with rays emanating from the center. The usual exterior is plain but a rare "threaded" exterior can sometimes be found. Colors are marigold, amethyst, blue, purple, green, electric blue, ice blue, lavender, and smoke.

*Butterflies and Waratah*

*Butterfly (Northwood)*

*Butterfly and Berry*

*Butterfly and Corn Vase*

*Butterfly and Fern*

### Butterfly and Berry

One of Fenton's prime patterns, found on a large array of shapes including footed berry sets, table sets, water sets, a hatpin holder, vase whimseys, spittoon whimsey, nut bowl whimsey, and a centerpiece whimsey. Colors are marigold, cobalt blue, green, amethyst, red, white, and a very rare Nile green opalescent shown.

### Butterfly and Corn Vase

This interesting vase is rare for several reasons, and it is a pleasure to show it here. First is the pattern which has been reported only twice in the past few years. Both examples are identical in size (5⅞" tall and 2¾" base diameter). Secondly, the base color of the glass is vaseline with a marigold finish. While this coloring is found rarely on both Millersburg and Northwood items, I believe the Butterfly and Corn vase to be a product of the latter.

### Butterfly and Fern

Made by the Fenton Art Glass Company, this is a very pretty water set. Colors are marigold, amethyst, green, and blue and all are Fenton at its best with outstanding moldwork and rich coloring.

*Butterfly and Tulip*

*Butterfly Lamp*

### *B*utterfly and Tulip

Make no mistake about it, this is a very impressive Dugan pattern. The bowl is large, the glass heavy, and the mold work exceptional. Found in either marigold or purple, this footed jewel has the famous Feather Scroll for an exterior pattern. Typically, the shallower the bowl, the more money it brings with the purple bringing many times the price of the underrated marigold.

### *B*utterfly Bower

The interior design of a stippled central butterfly flanked by trellis work and flora is hard to see. However, the exterior's S-Band pattern shows quite well. This deep bowl is 6½" across and stands 3" tall. It can be found in marigold and purple. The rim has a bullet edge. Manufactured in Australia.

### *B*utterfly Lamp

Named for the wing-like projections of the metal base, this very unusual lamp stands approximately 13" tall to the burner. The very rich marigold font has a series of stylized designs around the curving that resemble the Art Deco bowl shown elsewhere in this book, and I suspect the lamp may well be from England also.

*Butterfly Bower*

*Butterfly Bower (S-Band Exterior)*

43

*Butterfly Ornament*

*Butterfly Pintray*

*Butterfly Tumbler*

*Buttermilk Goblet*

### Butterfly Ornament

I'm told this interesting bit of glass was made as a giveaway item and attached to bonbons, baskets, and compotes by a bit of putty when purchasers visited the Fenton factory. This would certainly explain the scarcity of the Butterfly ornament for few are around today. Colors I've heard about are marigold, amethyst, cobalt blue, ice blue, white, and green.

### Butterfly Pintray

While most of these are seen in marigold, often pale and washed out, this example is the pastel version with pink wings and blue body and is a richly iridized beauty. It measure 8" across and is 7" tall. These were made by the same company that made the Tall Hats.

### Butterfly Tumbler

The tumbler shown is one of the top prizes in tumbler collecting. The color is an unusual amber-marigold and the design, four butterflies, a stippled background, and bands of circles at top and bottom is very pretty. It was made by U.S. Glass. In addition to the one marigold example, four smoky-olive ones have been found.

### Buttermilk Goblet

Exactly like the Iris goblet also made by Fenton, the plainer Buttermilk Goblet is a real beauty and rather hard to find, especially in green or amethyst. As you can see, the iridescence is on the interior of the goblet only, and the stem is the same as the Fenton Vintage compotes.

**Button and Daisy Hat**

## Button and Daisy Hat

Again, here is an item that has been reproduced in every type of glass known, but the example shown is old and original and has resided in one of the major carnival glass collections in the country for many years. Like so many of the miniature novelty items, the coloring is a beautiful clambroth with lots of highlights. Manufacturer unknown.

## Buzz Saw Cruet

This eagerly hunted Cambridge novelty always brings top dollar when it comes up for sale. Found in two sizes, the colors seen are green and marigold. The mold work is fantastic as is the iridescence. Oddly, the base shows a pontil mark indicating the cruet was blown into a mold. Again, these were probably designed as container for some liquid, but just what, we can't say

## Cactus (Millersburg)

This Rays and Ribbons exterior reminds me of the famous Hobstar and Feather pattern with its incised fans, edged with needles and the hobstars above. In addition, there is a small file filler near the base, merging into a diamond where the feathers meet.

## Cambridge #2351

This Cambridge near-cut pattern was made in a host of shapes in crystal, but in iridized glass only the punch set pieces and a bowl have been reported so far. The punch set was advertised in marigold, amethyst, and green, and the one reported bowl is also green.

**Buzz Saw Cruet**

**Cactus (Millersburg)**

**Cambridge #2351**

*Candle Vase*

*Canada Dry Bottle*

*Cane and Scroll (Sea Thistle)*

*Cane*

46

## *Canada Dry Bottle*
Used in the mid-20s, the bottle shown says "Canada Dry Incorporated – Gingerale #13" on the base. It was used for a product from that company called "Sparkling Orangeade" and has remarkably good iridization for a throw-away bottle.

## *Candle Vase*
While I know nothing about this unusually-shaped vase except that it is 9½" tall, I can say with some certainty it was probably shaped in several other ways in many instances. I haven't had any other colors reported, but they may exist.

## *Cane*
One of the older Imperial patterns, Cane is found on wine goblets, bowls of various sizes, and pickle dishes. The coloring is nearly always a strong marigold, but the bowl has been seen on smoke, and I'm sure amethyst is a possibility. Cane is not one of the more desirable Imperial patterns and is readily available, especially on bowls; however, a rare color would improve the desirability of this pattern.

## *Cane and Scroll (Sea Thistle)*
I'd guess there are other shapes around in this pattern, but the small creamer shown is the only one I've seen so far. As you can see, there are four busy patterns competing with one another but their combination isn't unattractive. The marigold has a reddish hue.

*Cannon Ball Variant*

## Cannon Ball Variant

While the shape of this Fenton water set is the same as the Cherry and Blossom usually found in cobalt, this marigold version has a much different enameled design. The tumblers have an interior wide panel design, and I'm sure this is quite a scarce item.

## Captive Rose

Captive Rose is a very familiar decorative pattern found in bowls, bonbons, compotes, and occasional plates in colors of marigold, cobalt blue, green, amethyst, amber, and smoke. The design is a combination of embroidery circles, scales, and diamond stitches, and is a tribute to the mold maker's art. The roses are like finely stitched quilt work. Manufactured by Fenton.

## Carnival Beads

I have always resisted showing strands of beads before, even though they are very collectible and quite attractive, but when Lee Briix sent this very interesting photo using a Diamond Point Columns vase as a prop, I changed my mind. Most of these beads were made in smaller glass factories or in Europe.

*Captive Rose*

*Carnival Beads*

*Carolina Dogwood*

*Caroline*

*Cartwheel*

### Carolina Dogwood
Westmoreland made this rather hard-to-find pattern in both marigold and aqua finish on milk glass and a very rare marigold bowl that is on clear glass. The design of dogwood sprays with a single center blossom is a good one.

### Caroline
Made by Dugan-Diamond, this hard-to-distinguish pattern offers little in design and only the shapes and coloring make it a good item. It is mostly found on peach opalescent, but marigold is sometimes found on the bowl and plate shapes. The design is all exterior.

### Cartwheel
Marked twice, this Heisey piece had a matching lid and is a pale, flashed iridization like the few other Heisey pieces we've seen in a carnival treatment. These were not iridized by Heisey, of course, but for them. At any rate, this is a candy dish.

*Cathedral (Curved Star)*

# Cathedral (Curved Star)

After years of uncertainty and guessing, we've traced this pattern to Sweden and the Eda Glassworks. Several shapes exist including a chalice, pitcher, bowl, flower holder, epergne, compote, butter dish, creamer, open sugar, two-piece fruit bowl, and a rare rose bowl. Colors are marigold and blue.

# Central Show Store

Perhaps this is one of the more scarce Northwood advertising pieces and like most it is a shallow bowl, nearly 6" in diameter. Its lettering reads "Compliments of the Central Shoe Store – Corner of Collinsville and St. Louis Avenues – East St. Louis, Illinois." The floral sprays are much like others used on similar pieces from the Northwood Company.

# Chariot

Possibly English, the Chariot compote is about 4½" tall and has a bowl diameter of 6½". It isn't often found and the only ones I've seen are marigold with good color. The pattern is exterior only and the base has a 20-rayed star.

*Central Shoe Store*

*Chariot*

*Chatelaine*

## Chatelaine

Most of the authorities in the field agree this very rare, beautiful water set pattern is an Imperial item. However, I'm listing it as a questionable one because I've seen no proof of its origin. Of course, I can't emphasize too strongly its quality or scarcity, and the selling price on the few examples to be sold publicly verify this. The only color I've heard of is a deep rich purple.

## Checkerboard

It has been pretty well established that Checkerboard was a Westmoreland product, which partially explains its rarity today. I've seen about half a dozen tumblers over the years, but the pitcher shown is one of only three known to exist. The color, iridescence, and mold work are outstanding. A rare goblet is occasionally found iridized.

*Checkerboard*

*Checkerboard Panels*

## Checkerboard Panels

This shallow flat bowl is also known as Zipper Round in England and is English. It has an interesting exterior pattern of rows of file, raised bands, and borders at top and bottom of file edging. The base has a very pretty star design. The interior is plain and heavily iridized.

## Cherry (Dugan)

The Dugan-Diamond version of the Cherry pattern can be found in berry set pieces, footed bowls that are often quite deep, a 6" plate, and a very rare cruet in white carnival. Other colors are marigold, amethyst, and peach opalescent. Sometimes the exterior has the Jeweled Heart pattern but not always.

## Cherry (Millersburg)

Sometimes called Hanging Cherries this very realistic pattern is simply the best of the cherry patterns in all of carnival glass. It can be found in many bowl sizes, a water set, a table set, rare plates, a rare compote, a milk pitcher, and several whimsey shapes. Colors are marigold, amethyst, green, blue, clambroth, and vaseline.

*Cherry (Dugan)*

*Cherry (Millersburg)*

51

*Cherry and Cable*

*Cherry Chain*

*Cherry Circles*

## Cherry and Cable

Sometimes called Cherry and Thumbprint, this is a very difficult Northwood product to locate, and to date I've seen one tumbler, one pitcher, a table set, and a small berry bowl. The pattern is very much a typical Northwood design and reminds one of the famous Northwood Peach, especially in the shape of the butter dish bottom which carries the same exterior base pattern as the Prisms compote. I know of no colors except a good rich marigold, but others may certainly exist.

## Cherry Chain

Cherry Chain is a close relative of the Leaf Chain pattern shown elsewhere in this book. Found on bowls, plates, and bonbons, this all-over pattern is well done and effective. The colors are marigold, blue, green, amethyst, and white. There is an extremely rare example of this pattern on a red slag base glass, and it is the only one I've heard about. There is a variant also.

## Cherry Circles

This Fenton piece employs a pattern of fruit combined with a scales pattern, the latter being a favorite filler device at the Fenton factory. Cherry Circles is best known in large bonbons, but compotes, bowls, and occasional plates do exist in marigold, cobalt blue, green, amethyst, white, and red.

*Cherry/Hobnail (Millersburg)*

## Cherry/Hobnail (Millersburg)

On comparison, the interior cherry design varies enough from the regular Millersburg Cherry to show its separate example with the hobnail exterior. These bowls are quite rare and are found in marigold, amethyst, and blue, and measure roughly 9" in diameter. A 5" bowl can also be found, both with and without the hobnail exterior.

## Cherry Variant (Millersburg)

Shown is a very rare plate, thought to be a Millersburg product by most experts. It measures some 10¾" in diameter and has three clusters of fruit and leaves that match other Millersburg Cherry designs, but the exterior is plain except for a rayed star on the marie. Color is a strong amethyst and the outer edges have fluting. So far, only this one example is reported.

## Christmas Compote

What an elegant large compote this is in either purple or marigold. The interior has a fine rib radiating from the center with holly and leaves while the exterior sports the same holly and leaves with four partial poinsettias near the rim. The Christmas Compote measures 9½" across the rim, is 5½" tall, and has a base diameter of 5½". The maker has not yet been confirmed.

*Cherry Variant (Millersburg)*

*Christmas Compote*

*Chrysanthemum*

*Chrysanthemum Drape Lamp*

*Circle Scroll*

# *C*hrysanthemum

For years I thought this might be an Imperial pattern for it so reminded me of the Windmill pattern, but it really is Fenton. Found on large bowls, either footed or flat, Chrysanthemum is known in marigold, blue, green, ice green, white, and a very beautiful red.

# *C*hrysanthemum Drape Lamp

This beauty would grace any glass collection. As you can see, the font is beautifully iridized and has been found in pink glass as well as white. Strangely, most of these lamps have been found in Australia, but the maker is, thus far, unknown.

# *C*ircle Scroll

Dugan's Circle Scroll is not an easy pattern to find, especially in the water sets, hat shape, and vase whimseys. Other shapes known are berry sets, compotes, creamers, and spooners. The colors I've seen are marigold and purple, but certainly others may exist with cobalt a strong possibility.

*Classic Arts*

# Classic Arts

What an interesting pattern this is. It is available in a covered powder jar, a rose bowl, a 7" celery vase, and a rare 10" vase. The design is very "Greek" in feeling, and the tiny figures quite clear. The green paint gives an antiquing effect which adds greatly to the beauty. It was made in Czechoslovakia.

# Cleveland Memorial Tray

Undoubtedly made to celebrate Cleveland's centennial birthday, this cigar ashtray depicts the statue of James Garfield, his tomb in Lake View cemetery, the Soldiers and Sailors Monument, the Superior Street viaduct, and the Cleveland Chamber of Commerce building. The coloring and iridescence are typically Millersburg, and the mold work compares favorably with that of the Courthouse bowl. A real treasure for any glass collector. Found also in amethyst.

# Coal Bucket (U.S. Glass)

These rather rare little match holders can be found in both marigold and green, and are a miniature collector's dream come true. Few are around, and they bring high prices when sold.

*Cleveland Memorial Tray*

*Coal Bucket (U.S. Glass)*

*Cobblestones*

*Coin Dot (Fenton)*

*Coin Dot (Westmoreland)*

### Cobblestones

This simple Imperial pattern is not often seen, but certainly is a nice item when encountered. Found on bowls of various sizes – often with Arcs as an exterior pattern. Cobblestones is also found on handled bonbons where a beautiful radium finish is often present, and the exterior is honeycombed. A curious circumstance to say the least. The colors are marigold, green, blue, amethyst, and amber. There is also a variant, as well as a rare plate.

### Coin Dot (Fenton)

This pattern is fairly common on medium size bowls but can sometimes be found on plates and a handled basket whimsey. The colors are marigold, cobalt blue, green, amethyst, and red, but not all shapes are found in all colors. The bowl and rose bowl are the only shapes reported in red.

### Coin Dot (Westmoreland)

Once these were all thought to be made only by the Fenton company. The variations and some timely research have disclosed that the rose bowl shown, as well as a compote shape and bowl from which the rose bowl was pulled, are from the Westmoreland plant. Colors are marigold, amethyst, green, milk-glass iridized, blue milk-glass iridized, teal, and aqua opalescent.

*Coin Spot*

## *Coin Spot*

This undistinguished little Dugan compote holds a dear spot in my heart for it was the first piece of carnival glass we ever owned. Made in opalescent glass also, in carnival glass it is found in marigold, green, purple, peach, white, and blue. The design is simple, consisting of alternate rows of indented stippled ovals and plain, flat panels. The stem is rather ornate with a finial placed midway down. Often in marigold, the stem remains clear glass.

*Colonial*

## *Colonial*

Imperial's Colonial pattern is simply one version of wide paneling. The shapes I've heard about are vases, toothpick holders, open sugars, candlesticks, and the handled lemonade goblet shown. Colors are marigold, green, and purple, usually of the very rich nature.

*Colonial Lady*

## *Colonial Lady*

Just look at the color on this rare vase! It certainly rivals Tiffany and only proves Imperial was topped by no one in purple glass. Colonial Lady stands 5¾" tall and has a base diameter of 2¾". I've heard of no other color except marigold, but certainly others may exist. Needless to say, these are not plentiful.

## *Colonial Variant*

Perhaps this isn't really a variant, but with the lid it looks different. It was made by Imperial and is found in marigold and sometimes clear carnival.

*Colonial Variant*

*Columbia*

*Columbia Variant*

*Compass*

## Columbia

Made first in crystal, Columbia is found in carnival glass on a rare cake plate, compotes, and vase shapes, all from the same mold. The coloring is usually marigold, but amethyst and green are known. While the simplicity of Columbia may not be appreciated by some collectors, it certainly had its place in the history of the glass field and should be awarded its just dues. Manufactured by Imperial.

## Columbia Variant

Please compare this true compote to the regular Columbia pattern and you will see the design is very similar, yet the base is a bit different. Few of these variants seem to have been made and in old Imperial ads which shown some 16 shapes from the standard Columbia design, not a single example of this variant is shown.

## Compass

A Dugan pattern of hobstars, hexagons, and other geometric designs that manages to fill nearly all the allowed space. Compass is found on exteriors of Dugan Heavy Grape bowls, and the example shown demonstrates why peach opalescent is such a collected color.

*Compote Vase*

# Compote Vase

Approximately 6" tall, this well done stemmed piece is found in all the standard colors but is mostly seen in amethyst or green. Often, the stem is not iridized, but the luster on the rest of the compote vase more than makes up for it. I believe it to be a Dugan product, since I catalog pieces of it from the Dugan digs.

# Concave Diamond

Most of us have seen the Concave Diamond water sets in ice blue and tumblers in vaseline, but I hadn't seen another shape until encountering this quite rare pickle caster in a beautiful marigold. That brought back a memory of finding a small fragment of this pattern in the Dugan shards from the 1975 Indiana, PA, diggings, so I would speculate this rare item originated at that factory. Also known are "tumble-ups" in aqua, marigold, and aqua opalescent.

*Concave Diamond*

# Concave Flute (Westmoreland)

Found mostly on somewhat plain looking rose bowls, this Westmoreland pattern really comes to life on the bowl shape or even the rare banana bowl. The only design is exterior, a series of nine flutes that bleed out from a sharp arch. Colors are marigold, amethyst, green, teal, and a very pretty amber with much gold.

*Concave Flute (Westmoreland)*

*Concord*

*Cone and Tie*

*Connie (Northwood)*

*Constellation*

## Concord

Even among all the other grape patterns in iridized glass, I'm sure you won't confuse Concord with the others, for the net-like filler that covers the entire surface of the bowls' interior is unique. Found in both bowls and plates, Concord is a very scarce Fenton pattern and is available in marigold, green, amethyst, blue, and amber. It is a collector's favorite and doesn't sell cheaply.

## Cone and Tie

The simple beauty of this very rare tumbler (no pitcher is known) is very obvious; and while most collectors credit it to Imperial, I cannot verify its maker. The coloring is a very outstanding purple on the few examples known, and the selling price only emphasizes its desirability. Rarely does one of these move from one collection to another.

## Connie (Northwood)

This beautiful Northwood water set, shaped much like the Swirl tankard from the same company, is a tribute to the decorator's skill. Floral sprays in whites, pinks, and blues nearly cover both pitcher and tumbler, and the iridization, while light and airy is obvious in the photo, giving the set a frosty whiteness.

## Constellation

One of the smaller compotes, the Constellation is 5" tall and about the same size across the rim. It has an exterior pattern called Seafoam which is much like the S-Repeat pattern. The Constellation pattern consists of a large center star with bubble-like dots over the area and a series of raised bars running out to the rim. Colors are marigold, amethyst, peach opalescent, white, and a frosty pearlized finish over vaseline glass.

*Cooleemee, N.C.*

# Cooleemee, N.C.

This 9" advertising Heart and Vine plate is a rare one. Only four or five are known, and all are marigold. The plate was sold to promote the J.N. Ledford Textile Mill Company of Cooleemee, NC, and undoubtedly was a giveaway item. Today it is a rare and valuable collector's item. Of course, it was made by Fenton.

# Coral

I'd guess the same designer who gave us the Peter Rabbit and Little Fishes pattern is also responsible for Coral; the bordering device for all three is almost identical. Coral is found in bowls mostly, but a rare plate and rarer compote are known in various colors, including marigold, blue, green, vaseline, and white. Manufactured by Fenton.

# Corinth

Made by both Dugan-Diamond and Westmoreland, Corinth can be found in vases, bowls, and a beautiful banana bowl. Colors are marigold, green, teal, amethyst, peach opalescent, amber, and an odd iridized milk glass. Vases are often JIP style.

*Coral*

*Corinth*

61

**Corn Bottle**

**Corn Cruet**

**Corning Insulator**

**Cornucopia Vase**

### Corn Bottle

Perhaps the Corn Bottle is not an Imperial product, but the beautiful helios green has always made me feel it was. So while I list it as a questionable Imperial product, I stand convinced it is. Colors found are marigold, green, amethyst, and smoke (another indication Imperial made it), all of good quality. The iridescence is usually outstanding as is the mold work. It stands 5" tall and usually has a cork stopper.

### Corn Cruet

Since I first saw this years ago, I've been able to learn little about it. The only color reported is the white. Rumor places it in the Dugan line, but I can't be sure.

### Corning Insulator

While I've never been very excited by insulators, this one has super color and is marked "Corning – Reg. USA Pat." It is only one of several sizes that can be found.

### Cornucopia Vase

Since this vase is pictured in a Jeanette catalog that dates from the 1920s, the maker of this vase is no longer in question. It is 5" tall and 4¼" across the base. It has typical light iridization like most carnival glass of this period. It is similar in design to the Cornucopia candleholder found in white made by Fenton except for the base design and size variation.

*Corn Vase*

# Corn Vase

This is one of the better-known Northwood patterns, and that's little wonder because it is such a good one. Usually about 7" tall, there are certain variants known; especially noteworthy is the rare "pulled husk" variant that was made in very limited amounts. The colors are marigold, green, purple, ice blue, ice green, and white. The mold work is outstanding, the color superior, and the glass fine quality – truly a regal vase.

# Coronation (Victorian Crown)

This bulbous vase shape stands 5" tall and measures 3" across the lip. It has four Victorian crowns around and suspended coronets between. It is, of course, English, but from what company I can't say, nor can I pin down its use except to call it a vase shape.

*Coronation (Victorian Crown)*

# Cosmos

Green seems to have been the only color in this Millersburg pattern, and small bowls abound; however, an occasional 7" plate can be found. The radium finish is spectacular, and the mold work is outstanding.

*Cosmos*

# Cosmos and Cane

Made in berry sets, table sets, water sets, a rose bowl, a tall compote, plates, a short compote, and several whimsey shapes, this U.S. Glass pattern is a scarce one. The design, an incised cosmos flower and leaves banded by rows of cane, can be found in marigold, honey-amber, white, and a rare amethyst.

*Cosmos and Cane*

*Cosmos and Hobstar*

## Cosmos and Hobstar

There is something special about these fruit bowls on a metal standard, and this is one of the pretty ones. The pattern is one I don't recall seeing before and is a series of diamond panels with hobstars and cosmos blossoms alternating. Above the diamonds are fans and below, half-diamonds filled with a file pattern. The marigold is very rich, but I can't say if other colors were made or just who the maker was.

## Cosmos Variant

Cosmos Variant is a Fenton pattern found in bowls and occasionally plates (a compote has been reported but I haven't seen it). Amethyst is probably the most available color, but Cosmos Variant can be found in marigold, purple, blue, white, iridized milk glass, and red.

## Country Kitchen

Used as both a primary and secondary pattern, this hard-to-come-by design is quite artistic. The berry sets are next to impossible to locate, and the four-piece table sets are quite scarce and expensive. These, of course, are all primary uses; however, Country Kitchen is more often seen as an exterior pattern on the lovely Fleur-de-lis bowls where it compliments the latter perfectly. Millersburg seemed to have a flair for creating outstanding near-cut patterns, and this is certainly one of them. A variant is called Potpourri.

*Cosmos Variant*

*Country Kitchen*

*Courthouse*

## Courthouse

The Millersburg Courthouse 7 – 7½" bowl is one of the best loved advertising pieces in all of carnival glass. Found only in amethyst, the bowl can be seen in both ruffled and plain shapes, in regular with the lettering: "Millersburg Souvenir – Millersburg Courthouse" or the so-called unlettered bowl with "Millersburg Courthouse," which is much rarer.

## Covered Hen (Chic)

The Covered Hen is probably the best-recognized piece of English carnival glass made at the Sowerby Works. Known in a good rich marigold as well as a weak cobalt blue, the Covered Hen is 6⅞" long. The mold work is very good but the color ranges from very good to poor. While reproductions have been reported, my British sources tell me this isn't true, and that no examples have been made since the 1940s.

## Covered Frog

Made by the Co-Operative Flint Glass Company of Beaver Falls, PA, this novel covered dish is a stand-out in design and color. It measures 5½" long and 4" tall and has been seen in pastel green, pastel blue, marigold, and rarely amethyst. The eyes are painted black and are very realistic.

## Covered Swan

This beautiful English pattern is a companion to the Covered Hen and can be found in both marigold and amethyst. It measures 7¾" long, and the neck doesn't touch the back! What a mold maker's achievement! The base is similar to that of the Covered Hen dish. Both are butter dishes.

*Covered Hen (Chic)*

*Covered Frog*

*Covered Swan*

**Crab Claw**

# Crab Claw

Crab Claw is indeed a curious near-cut pattern that very seldom enters discussion by collectors but isn't as readily found as many other geometrics from the Imperial Company. Found on bowls of various sizes, a two-piece fruit bowl and base, and scarce water sets, the pattern is most often found in marigold, but amethyst and green are known in the bowl shapes. The design features hobstars, curving file, and diamond devices, and daisy-cut half-flowers, all seemingly interlocking.

# Crackle

Crackle is a very common, very plentiful pattern available in a large variety of shapes, including bowls, covered candy jars, water sets, auto vases, punch sets, plates, spittoons, and a rare window ledge planter. Marigold is certainly the most found color, but green and amethyst do exist on some shapes. And often the color and finish are only adequate. Crackle was mass produced in great amounts, probably as a premium for promotional giveaways, so I suppose we can't expect it to equal other carnival items.

# Crucifix

Now known to be from the Imperial Glass Company, these rare candlesticks are known in marigold carnival glass and crystal. The Crucifix candlestick is 9½" tall and is very heavy glass.

**Crackle**

**Crucifix**

*Crystal Cut*

*Curtain Optic*

## Crystal Cut

This beautiful compote comes to us from Australia and as you can see, is a very nice geometric design. Other colors and shapes may exist, but if so, I haven't seen them. It measures 7" in diameter.

## Curtain Optic

Made in the 1920s by the Fenton Company, this beautiful pattern is a kissin' cousin to the stretch pieces. It can be found on ice tea sets, guest sets, and possibly other shapes as well. The pastel coloring is a pleasant relief and compliments the opal drapery effect.

## Curved Star (Cathedral)

Here is another view of this Swedish pattern. Shown is the base of the fruit set which, upended, makes a nifty compote as you can see. It is probably used more often in this capacity than its original purpose.

*Curved Star (Cathedral)*

67

*Cut Arches*

*Cut Arcs*

*Cut Cosmos*

# Cut Arches
While I'm fairly confident this is another geometric pattern of English origin, I can't remember even seeing another shape in this pattern. As you can see, it is a banana boat of quite heavy glass. The only color reported is the marigold shown, and it has the typical marigold look of English glass. The deeply cut design would certainly lend itself to a water set.

# Cut Arcs
While it is most often found on the exterior of 8"–9" bowls, Fenton's Cut Arcs is occasionally seen on compotes of standard size and a vase whimsey, pulled from the bowl shape. On the example shown the edging is a tight candy-ribbon, and the interior carries no pattern at all.

# Cut Cosmos
How I wish I knew who made this beautiful tumbler! The design is top-notch and certainly deserves full recognition, but the maker remains unknown. The only color reported is the marigold shown, and it has the typical marigold look of English glass. The deeply cut design would certainly lend itself to a water set.

**Cut Flowers**

**Cut Grecian Gold Lamp**

## Cut Flowers

Here is one of the prettiest of all the Jenkins' patterns. Standing 10½" tall, the intaglio work is deep and sharp, and the cut petals show clear glass through the luster, giving a beautiful effect. Most Cut Flowers vases are rather light in color, but the one shown has a rich deep marigold finish. Cut Flowers can also be found in a smoke color.

## Cut Grecian Gold Lamp

Fenton made several items with similar wheel-cut designs including Engraved Grape and Engraved Zinnia but this is the first lamp font I've seen. The coloring is very good and while I suspect this item came along in the late 1920s, it would add to any collection.

## Cut Ovals

This Fenton pattern falls into the stretch glass field, but because of the etching it is considered carnival glass. Known in both candlesticks and bowls, Cut Ovals can be found in marigold, smoke, ice blue, ice green, pink, white, tangerine, lavender, red, and vaseline. The candlesticks are 8½" tall, and the bowls are known in 7", 8", 9", and 10" sizes.

**Cut Ovals**

*Dahlia*

*Daisy*

*Daisy and Cane*

*Daisy and Drape*

# Dahlia

Make no mistake, Dahlia is an important, often scarce, always expensive, Dugan pattern. The glass is fine quality, the design highly raised and distinct, and the iridescence super. Found only in marigold, purple, and white, Dahlia is made only in berry sets, table sets, and water sets, all useful shapes, which probably explains the scarcity due to breakage in use. The water sets are much sought.

# Daisy

Found only in the bonbon shape, Fenton's Daisy pattern is very scarce. The pattern is a simple one of four strands of flowers and leaves around the bowl and one blossom with leaves in the center. While marigold has been reported, blue is the color most found, and although I haven't seen amethyst or green, they may exist.

# Daisy and Cane

Shown is the decanter shape in this scarce pattern. It can also be found in a stemmed wine, a vase, and a spittoon whimsey shape. Colors are mostly marigold, but the spittoon has been found in blue. The pattern of file squares holding alternating daisies and large cane circles is a good one.

# Daisy and Drape

This pattern is probably a spin-off of the old U.S. Glass pattern Vermont, the main difference being the standing row of daisies around the top edge. Made in most of the Northwood colors, the purple leads the vivid colors, while the aqua opalescent is the most sought of the pastels. White is probably the most available color, but even it brings top dollar.

# Daisy and Plume

While the Northwood Company seems to be the primary user of this pattern, the Dugan-Diamond Company also had a version. Most Northwood pieces are marked and include a stemmed rose bowl, a compote with Blackberry interior, and a three-footed novelty bowls or rose bowl (very much like the Dugan one). Dugan pieces sometimes have the Dugan Cherry interior but not always. Both companies made this pattern in opalescent glass also and carnival colors are marigold, white, purple, electric blue, green, and aqua in Northwood and peach opalescent, marigold, green, and amethyst in Dugan-Diamond.

# Daisy Basket

Like many other of the Imperial handled baskets in shape and size, the Daisy Basket is a large hat-shaped one with one center handle that is rope patterned. The basket stands 10½" tall to the handle's top and is 6" across the lip. The colors are a good rich marigold and smoke, but be advised this is one of the shapes and patterns Imperial reproduced in the 1960s.

# Daisy Block Rowboat

Originally used as a pen tray in crystal, this Sowerby product had a matching stand, but I've never seen the stand in carnival. Daisy Block was made in marigold, amethyst, and aqua in iridized glass. It measures 10½" in length.

# Daisy Cut Bell

What a joy this very scarce Fenton pattern is. It was called a Tea Bell in a 1914 catalog, and as you can see, the handle is clear and scored, and the Daisy design is all intaglio. The Daisy Cut Bell stands 6" tall and is found in marigold only. It is a four mold design and has a marking inside "PATD APPLD."

*Daisy and Plume*

*Daisy Basket*

*Daisy Cut Bell*

*Daisy Block Rowboat*

*Daisy Dear*

*Daisy Squares*

*Daisy Web*

*Daisy Wreath*

## Daisy Dear

I've always called this pattern Triplets, based on Mrs. Hartung's drawing of it in her book V, but since I am told the pattern should really be identified as Daisy Dear, I am happy to make that correction. It is a Dugan exterior pattern, found on smallish 7 – 7½" bowls in marigold, amethyst, lavender, peach opalescent, green, and white.

## Daisy Squares

Found in stemmed rose bowls, compotes, and goblets this very pretty pattern has a simple design of daisies, stems, and leaves arranged to form squares. Around the raised base is a row of raised beads and the inside has honeycombing. Colors are marigold, amethyst, amber, and a soft green, sometimes over an amberish base glass.

## Daisy Web

What a hard-to-find pattern this is. Only the hat shape is known, and the only colors I've seen are amethyst, blue, and marigold. From the exterior design of Beaded Panels we know this pattern came form the Dugan company, so peach is a definite possibility.

## Daisy Wreath

Apparently Westmoreland decided this pattern looked best on a milk glass base for I haven't heard of it any other way. The 9" bowl in marigold on milk glass is quite scarce. Equally scarce is the aqua blue on milk glass shown.

*Dance of the Veils*

# Dance of the Veils

I've heard of three of these beauties by the Fenton Company in iridized glass, and they are truly a glassmaker's dream. Marigold is the only carnival color although crystal, pink, green, custard, and opalescent ones are made.

# Dandelion

I have serious misgivings about labeling both of the pictured items as the same pattern, but since this is how they are best known, I will yield to tradition. Actually, the mug is certainly a Dandelion pattern that is quite rare and popular, especially in aqua opalescent. Occasionally a mug bears advertising on the base and is called the Knight Templar mug; it brings top dollar! The water set, while known as Dandelion, is not the same design, but nonetheless is an important Northwood pattern. It is found in marigold, purple, green, ice blue, white, and a very rare ice green. The tankard pitcher is regal.

*Dandelion*

# Dart

Dating to the 1880s, the Dart pattern has heretofore been found only on crystal items in many shapes. It is a pleasure, this very rare and attractive oil lamp. The iridescence is soft with lots of pinks and blues and the coloring is a fine pastel marigold.

# Deep Grape

Millersburg made beautiful compotes, and this is a fine example of their art. It can be found in various shapes including a rare stemmed rose bowl, a squared-top compote, and a cone-shaped one. The design of grapes, tendrils, and leaves wind around the top and hang down the sides realistically. Colors are marigold, amethyst, green, and blue with vaseline rumored. All colors and shapes are rare.

*Dart*

*Deep Grape*

73

*Delta Base Candlesticks*

*Diamond and Daisy Cut*

*Diamond and Daisy Cut Variant*

## Delta Base Candlesticks

I certainly wish I had more information about these candlesticks. They have the same base design as an old pressed glass pattern called Delta so I've appropriated the name. As you can see, the marigold iridescence is on the top half of each piece and is very strong at the top. The glass is thick, heavy, and very clear.

## Diamond and Daisy Cut

This beautiful pattern is found on 10" vases, compotes, and rare water sets (which have been mistakenly labeled Mayflower). Found primarily in a good rich marigold, the compote has been in amethyst so perhaps other colors exist.

## Diamond and Daisy Cut Variant

While not exactly like the water set with the same name, this punch bowl is near enough to be termed a variant, resembling the compote more nearly. It is the only example thus far reported and I know of no base or cups but certainly there must have been.

*Diamond and Fan (Millersburg)*

# Diamond and Fan (Millersburg)

This is a beautifully designed exterior pattern, always found with the Nesting Swan bowl in carnival glass. As you can see, the pattern literally covers all available space but doesn't seem busy.

# Diamond and File

I'm not at all sure this pattern is Imperial but list it here as a possible one. It hasn't a great deal of imagination, but may have been intended as giveaways or quick sales. The small bowl shown is quite deep, possibly intended as a jelly holder. The color is adequate, and I've heard of these in smoke as well as marigold.

*Diamond and File*

# Diamond and Rib

Diamond and Rib is a Fenton pattern that has caused great confusion on the collecting world. This is because the jardiniere shape was long suspected to be a Millersburg product. This size has been found in large vases just like the smaller ones, so that we know there were two sizes of molds used. Colors are marigold, green, amethyst, smoke, and blue.

# Diamond and Sunburst

Found in bowls, decanters, goblets, and a rare oil cruet whimsey, this Imperial pattern is a very nicely done geometric design. Colors are marigold, green, purple, amethyst, and amber.

*Diamond and Sunburst*

*Diamond and Rib*

*Diamond Flutes*

*Diamond Fountain*

*Diamond Lace*

### Diamond Flutes

Besides the 7¼" parfait glass shown, the Diamond Flutes pattern was made in a creamer and sugar. Marigold is the only reported color at this time, and sometimes it tends to be very light on this U.S. Glass pattern.

### Diamond Fountain

This beautiful cruet has now been traced to the Higbee company and appears in their 1910 ads as a pattern called Palm Leaf Fan in crystal. As you can see, the mold work is quite good and the color adequate.

### Diamond Lace

Over the years, I've seen scores of purple water sets in this pattern and not one has been anything but well-iridized and a sight to behold. The pattern is found in berry sets also in marigold and purple, and the water sets are also found rarely in marigold, lavender, and rumored in white.

*Diamond Ovals*

## Diamond Ovals

Found in a creamer on a foot, stemmed compote, stemmed plate, and stemmed sugar, Diamond Ovals is a Sowerby pattern. The creamer measures only 4½" tall and the compote is medium sized, measuring 8". Marigold is the only reported color to date.

## Diamond Pinwheel

Perhaps there are other shapes in this pattern, but if so, I haven't seen them. As you can see, it is a simple geometric design, but very pleasing. The glass and luster all have good quality and certainly add to any collection.

## Diamond Point

While this Northwood pattern is quite typical of most vase patterns, it has a certain distinction of its own. While refraining from "buoyness," it manages an interesting overall pattern. It is found in purple, blue, aqua opalescent, green, marigold, peach, and white and is normally of standard height, being 10" to 11" tall.

## Diamond Point Columns (Fenton)

While this pattern bears the same name as the simple berry sets so often seen, the patterns are really quite different, and one need only examine the ribbed column area to see why. Shown is a beautifully iridized green vase 9½" tall with very strong color. It is found in all the standard colors as well as pastels of white, ice green, and ice blue.

*Diamond Pinwheel*

*Diamond Point*

*Diamond Point
Columns (Fenton)*

*Diamond Point Columns (Imperial)*

*Diamond Points Basket*

*Diamond Prisms*

## Diamond Point Columns (Imperial)

I haven't heard of this Imperial pattern in any other color than a good rich marigold, but that certainly doesn't mean they do not exist. The shapes known are compotes, plates, vases, table sets, and powder jars (which are rare). While the design of alternating rows of plain and checkered panels is quite simple, the overall appearance is quite effective. It is also found in small bowls.

## Diamond Points Basket

Although the dimensions are nearly the same as Northwood's Basket, the Diamond Points Basket is a much rarer pattern. And while some collectors have credited the Fenton company with this much-sought novelty, I lean toward Northwood as the maker. The colors found are marigold, purple, and a radiant cobalt blue. The mold work is sharp and precise and the iridescence heavy and outstanding. I have heard of less than a dozen of these baskets, so you are lucky if you own one.

## Diamond Prisms

I've seen this same compote shaped with the sides squared, and it was also on the same shade of marigold with much amber in the tint.

*Diamond Ring*

# Diamond Ring

This typical geometric design of file fillers, diamonds, and scored rings is found on berry sets as well as a fruit bowl of larger dimensions. The usual colors of marigold and smoke are to be found, and in addition, the fruit bowl has been reported in a beautiful deep purple. While Diamond Ring is not an outstanding example of the glassmaker's art, it certainly deserves its share of glory. Manufactured by Imperial.

# Diamonds

Most collectors are familiar with this pattern in the water sets, but it does appear on rare occasion in a punch bowl and base (no cups have yet come to light). Like its cousin, Banded Diamonds, the design is simple but effective. The glass and iridescence are very good, and all have the "Millersburg look."

# Diving Dolphins (English)

For many years, this scarce item was credited to the Imperial company, but we know now it was a Sowerby product. The interior carries the Scroll Embossed pattern, and Diving Dolphins is found in marigold, blue, green, and amethyst with the latter easiest to find. It measures 7" across the bowl and may be round, ruffled, turned in like a rose bowl, or five-sided.

*Diamonds*

*Diving Dolphins (English)*

*Dogwood Sprays*

*Dolphins Compote*

*Dotted Diamonds and Daisies*

# Dogwood Sprays

This is a pattern so very familiar to all carnival collectors, for there are probably more bowls with various floral sprays than any other design. Dogwood Sprays, while well done, is not extraordinary in any sense of the word. Found on both bowls and compotes, the color most seen is peach, but purple and a rare blue does turn up from time to time. Manufactured by Dugan.

# Dolphins Compote

Millersburg created many fine glass items but nothing better in design or execution than the Dolphins Compote. From the Rosalind interior to the three detailed dolphins that support the bowl from the plate base, it is a thing of beauty. Colors are amethyst, green, and a rare blue.

# Dotted Diamonds and Daisies

Here's another of those very plain tumblers whose only mold design is the series of narrow interior ribs. Its main appeal lies in the very nice enamel work of stylized leaves, daisies, and a diamond grid of dots. It is reported in marigold only.

*Double Dolphin*

# Double Dolphin

Some people will probably question this pattern appearing here for it is rightly considered stretch glass, but the mold work of the dolphins tends to bridge the gap between the stretch and carnival glass so I've shown it here. This Fenton pattern was made in many shapes, including bowls, compotes, vases, covered candy dishes, candlesticks, and cake plates. Colors are ice blue, ice green, white, pink, red, topaz, tangerine, and amethyst.

# Double Dutch

While it's difficult to say whether this pattern came before or after Windmill and the NuArt plate, it is quite obvious they were all the work of the same artist. All depict various rural scenes with trees, a pond, and bridge. This Imperial pattern is featured on a 9½" footed bowl, usually in marigold but occasionally found in smoke, green, and amethyst. The coloring is superior and the mold work very fine. The exterior bowl shape and pattern is much like the Floral and Optic pattern.

*Double Dutch*

# Double Loop

This Northwood pattern is found on creamers, as shown, and an open sugar with a stem. Often these are trademarked, but not all are. The colors known are marigold, green, purple, aqua opalescent, and cobalt with the latter most difficult to find.

*Double Loop*

*Double Scroll*

*Double Star*

*Double Stem Rose*

# Double Scroll

The Double Scroll pattern was Imperial's try at an Art Deco pattern in iridized glass and can be found on candlesticks, a dome-based console bowl, and a punch cup in marigold, green, amethyst, smoke, and red (not all colors in all shapes). The candlesticks measure 8½" tall, and the oval-shaped console bowl that went with them is 10½" x 8½" in diameter and stands 5" tall. The scrolls are of solid glass. The glass is thick and fine and the coloring is excellent.

# Double Star

In reality, this is the same pattern as the Buzz Saw cruet, but for some reason it has been called by this different name. Found in water sets and a rare spittoon whimsey formed from a tumbler, this Cambridge pattern is seen mostly in green, but marigold and amethyst can be found. I consider Double Star one of the best designed water sets in all of carnival glass.

# Double Stem Rose

Like other patterns made at the Dugan plant, this pattern has mistakenly been attributed to the Fenton company. Double Stem Rose is found on dome-footed bowls of average size in marigold, blue, green, lavender, amethyst, and white. The design is interesting and well executed.

*Dragon and Berry (Strawberry)*

# Dragon and Berry (Strawberry)

Obviously a companion piece to well-known Dragon and Lotus pattern, Dragon and Berry apparently didn't have the popularity of its cousin for few examples are to be found. Known in both footed and flat-based bowls and in colors of marigold, green, and blue, this Fenton pattern is a much-sought item.

# Dragon and Lotus

Probably one of the best known of all carnival glass patterns, Dragon and Lotus was a favorite of all Fenton patterns produced over several years. Shapes are flat or footed bowls and rare plates. Colors are marigold, green, blue, amethyst, peach opalescent, iridized milk glass, aqua opalescent, vaseline opalescent, red, and the pastels.

*Dragon and Lotus*

# Dragon's Tongue

Known mostly in light shades in a milk glass with marigold iridescence, Dragon's Tongue is also found on a large footed bowl that has a diameter measurement of 11". The only color reported on the bowl shape is marigold, but certainly other colors are possible, especially Fenton's famous cobalt blue.

*Dragon's Tongue*

**Dragon Vase**

**Drapery Variant (Northwood)**

**Drapery**

**Dugan's Many Ribs**

# Dragon Vase

Many years ago I saw a large iridized plate with a Dragon motif. When I returned to the shop to buy it someone else had, and until now I haven't seen another item with this pattern until I was sent this photo. As you can see, the vase is six-sided, and all sides have a dragon. The base carries a many-rayed, geometric star. The color is a rich amethyst, and I have no idea who made it.

# Drapery

Long a favorite of rose bowl and candy dish fanciers, this graceful Northwood design of three ribs and drapery looks good from any angle. Also found in the vase shape, Drapery is known in marigold, blue, purple, green, aqua opalescent, ice blue, ice green, and white.

# Drapery Variant (Northwood)

This variant is just that because the ribbing, unlike the regular Northwood Drapery, doesn't run over the base to created any footed look. It is marked "Northwood," however, and stands about 8¼" tall. Colors seen by the author are marigold, amethyst, and green but others may certainly exist.

# Dugan's Many Ribs

Shown in the hat shape in peach opalescent this seldom discussed Dugan pattern can also be found in small vases. Colors are marigold, peach opalescent, blue, and amethyst. The ribs are slightly wider than either Northwood or Fenton's Fine Rib patterns. The hat shape shown is 4½" tall and 6½" across the top and has a base diameter of 2⅝".

*Dugan's Stippled Rays*

# Dugan's Stippled Rays

As you can see this is a very undistinguished, little discussed pattern, confined to unimaginative bowls and an occasional hat shape like the one shown. The pattern is all on the inside, leaving a plain shiny exterior.

# Dugan's Vintage Variant

I certainly wish we could avoid all the variants, but for the life of me, I don't know what else to call this very rare plate. It is one of five or six known. It is much different in arrangement of grape clusters and the tendrils of the leaf center, and the edging is different. It has a 1" collar base and is found in blue and amethyst as well as the marigold shown.

# Egg and Dart

These candlesticks stand 3½" tall and have a base diameter of 4½". The color is rather pale but the iridescence is quite good. The name comes from the famous decoration often used by wood workers in furniture and architects for mouldings. I suspect this pattern is European and may be English.

*Dugan's Vintage Variant*

*Egg and Dart*

*Elegance*

*Elks (Fenton)*

*Elks (Millersburg)*

# E*legance*

What a pretty all over pattern this is! It has a bit of everything: a stippled center blossom, a row of beading, alternating triangles of stippling and flowers, more beads, and an edging of flowers. Elegance is a rare pattern, known in the marigold shallow bowl shown, an ice blue bowl, and an ice blue plate.

# E*lks (Fenton)*

Given or sold as souvenirs at their conventions, the Elk pieces are very collectible today. Fenton's pattern can be found in bowls, plates, and bells, and the design of each is outstanding. Colors are cobalt blue, green, amethyst, and marigold all with heavy luster. Not all shapes in all colors, however.

# E*lks (Millersburg)*

Larger than the Fenton Elk bowl, the Millersburg example is called Two-Eyed Elk and is more detailed. It is found only in amethyst with a radium finish. Millersburg also made a rare Elks paperweight with the same design in amethyst and green.

*Elks Nappy (Dugan)*

# E *lks Nappy (Dugan)*

For many years I thought this beautiful nappy (two known) was a Millersburg product, but recent information assures us it came from the Dugan factory. As you can see, it is a real beauty with stunning color and fine mold work. The only color is purple.

# E *lks Paperweight (Millersburg)*

Besides the rare bowls, Millersburg also made these very rare paperweights in both amethyst and green. These are 4" long and 2⅝" wide and except for a rim on the underside are solid glass. A copycat weight was made in the 1970's in other colors, but a close look will distinguish the real thing from the copy.

*Elks Paperweight*
*(Millersburg)*

# E *mbroidered Mums*

A close cousin to the Hearts and Flowers pattern, also made by the Northwood company, Embroidered Mums is a busy but attractive pattern. It can be found on bowls, plates, and stemmed bonbons in a wide range of colors including marigold, pastel marigold, ice blue, ice green, purple, teal blue, electric blue, aqua opalescent, lavender, sapphire blue, lime opalescent, and the bonbons in white.

*Embroidered Mums*

# E *mu*

The Emu bowl is one of the better Australian patterns and is available on 4½" and 10½" bowls as well as large compotes and footed cake stands. The color most found is purple, but marigold and the amber over aqua base glass are found rarely. Some call this pattern Ostrich, but the Ostrich lives in Africa, and the Emu is an Australian bird with a similar appearance.

*Emu*

*Enameled Carnival Glass*

*Enameled Panel*

*Enameled Prism Band*

*Encore*

# E nameled Carnival Glass

Toward the latter years of the carnival glass "craze," patterns become simpler, and in order to give the customer something different, items (especially water sets and bowls) were marketed with hand-painted enamel work on them. Most of these were simple floral sprays, but occasionally an interesting fruit pattern emerged like the scarce water set shown here. Today, these seem to be gaining in popularity and certainly deserve a place in carnival glass history. This is a Northwood pattern called Enameled Grape.

# E nameled Panel

While this very pretty goblet has all sorts of designs, one matched against another such as etching, gold enameling, and mold work, it is the applied enamel panel with beautifully hand-painted roses that makes it quite elegant. The base is hollow, giving another strange twist to the whole, but the marigold coloring is very rich and the look very much one of quality.

# E nameled Prism Band

This beautiful Fenton tankard water set is a standout in the series of enameled water sets. It can be found in marigold, blue, green (rarely), and a very impressive and scarce white. Also the floral work may vary slightly from one item to another.

# E ncore

I try not to show contemporary glass but this bottle, made in 1970 for the Schlitz Brewery by Owens Glass is a really interesting bit of advertising and is highly collectible. It was a limited run of production and today isn't too easy to find.

## English Hob and Button

This pattern has been reproduced in the last few years in this country, especially on tray and bowl shapes in an odd shade of amberish marigold on very poor glass. The English version shown is another thing, however. The glass is clear and sparkling. The shapes are bowls, mostly, in marigold, green, amethyst, and blue.

## English Hobstar

This oddly shaped bowl was made to fit into a fancy silvered holder. The bowl is 6" long and just under 4" wide. The pattern is two hobstars on each side and one on each end, all separated by X-cuts with diamond centers. The metal holder is very ornate with metal maple leaves branching from stems to support the bowl.

## Engraved Daisy and Spears

Made by Fenton in their Grecian Cut Gold Assortment, this very interesting small goblet (4½" tall) is very much like the Engraved Daisy tumblers except for the added "spears" to the design. All the Grecian Cut Gold items date from 1916 – 1918 and are color flashed.

## Engraved Grape

This lovely etched pattern is from the Fenton factory and has been seen on many shapes including vases, candy jars, tall and squat pitchers, tumblers, juice glasses, and a tumble-up. Colors are marigold and white.

## Engraved Zinnia

While the engraving of tall- and short-stemmed flowers is rather difficult to see, the tumbler has good luster, and the shape is quite nice. Has anyone seen the pitcher?

*English Hob and Button*

*English Hobstar*

*Engraved Daisy and Spears*

*Engraved Grape*

*Engraved Zinnia*

*Estate*

*Etched Vine*

*Etched Deco*

*Evelyn*

# *E state*

Estate is a Westmoreland pattern found in mugs, perfumes, a creamer, and a sugar. The items known are small in size (the mug is only 3" tall) and the design a maze-like wide band around the lower portion of the piece. Colors reported are marigold, aqua, aqua opalescent, and a very rare smoke.

# *E tched Deco*

This footed 8" plate is typical in many respects of English and European glass and surely came from one or the other. The only decoration are the five etched bars with crosshatching around the rim, but the color is good and the iridization adequate.

# *E tched Vine*

I know very little about this tumbler, but it has good color and finish with an interesting paneling around the base and a many rayed star on the bottom. The etching is good and much like Fenton pieces in the 1920s but I can't identify the maker at this time.

# *E velyn*

Since I showed this rare Fostoria pattern, a second one identical in size and color has been found in Washington State. So at least two of the trial run were not destroyed as thought. The design of hobstars and file windmills is a good one, and the rich emerald green top-notch.

*Fan*

# Fan

Despite the fact most collectors have credited this pattern to Northwood. I'm really convinced it was a Dugan product. In custard glass it has been found with the well-known Diamond marking. Of course, many more shapes of the Fan pattern were made in custard. In carnival glass, the availability is limited to the sauce dish and an occasional piece that is footed and has a handle. The colors seen are marigold, peach, and purple. Peach is the most available color.

*Fanciful*

# Fanciful

Probably many collectors will challenge this pattern being attributed to Dugan, but shards from the Dugan factory were identified by this author in both marigold and purple, so here it is. Actually, if a comparison is carefully made with the Embroidered Mums, Heart and Flowers, and Fancy patterns, one finds a close similarity that isn't evident on first glance. Fanciful is available on bowls and plates in colors of marigold, peach, purple, and white. The familiar Big Basketweave adorns the exterior.

*Fancy Cut*

# Fancy Cut

Much like the small creamers in design, Fancy Cut is actually the pitcher from a child's water set (tumblers to match are known in crystal). The color is a good rich marigold and the pitcher measures 4" tall and has a base diameter of 2¼". The design is a bit busy, combining several near-cut themes, but the rarity of the iridized version more than makes up for this.

# Fans

This English pattern was made by Davison Glass and can be found in the small pitcher shown (5" tall, 7" across the handle), a matching tumbler, and a cracker jar with metal lid. The pattern is very pretty with an allover design, and the color is usually quite rich. Reported in marigold only.

*Fans*

*Fan-Star (Millersburg)*

*Fan-Tail*

*Farmyard*

**F**an-Star (Millersburg)
Except for the base, this very unusual Millersburg exterior is completely plain. The base has a very odd star, bursting into a fan of root-like fingers that match the ones on the Tulip Scroll vase exactly. The interior pattern is Zig-Zag and is found in the usual Millersburg colors.

**F**an-Tail
Fan-Tail is a pattern found on occasion as the interior design of Butterfly and Berry bowls. Actually, the design is made up of a series of peacock's tails swirling out from the center of the bowl, and while it is an interesting pattern, it certainly is not a designer's success. This Fenton pattern has been reported in marigold, cobalt blue, green, and white.

**F**armyard
The only word for this Dugan-Diamond pattern is bold. The chickens scratching in a barnyard is pure whimsey but very well done, and the exterior pattern of Jeweled Heart is quite complimentary. Colors are purple, fiery amethyst, green, and peach opalescent; all are scarce and sought. Shapes are many including a square bowl and a near-plate shape.

*Fashion*

# Fashion

Fashion is probably the most familiar geometric pattern in all of carnival glass. It was manufactured in huge amounts over a long period of time and was originally called "402½" when first issued. The shapes are creamers, sugars, punch sets, water sets, a bride's basket, and a fruit bowl and stand. While marigold is the most often seen color, smoke, green, and purple are found but are scarce. This pattern was made by Imperial. A rare red punch set was made since cups exist.

# Feather and Heart

This fine Millersburg water set, found in green, marigold, and amethyst is typical in many ways of all the Millersburg water sets. The pitcher lip is long and pulled quite low, while the rim is scalloped quite like its cousin, the Marilyn set. The glass is quite clear, rather heavy, and has excellent iridescence. A little difficult to find, the pattern adds greatly to any collection.

# Feathered Flowers

This pretty exterior pattern is found on the Australian Kiwi bowls. It is an intaglio pattern of swirls and stylized blossoms and is quite attractive.

*Feather and Heart*

*Feathered Flowers*

*Feathered Serpent*

*Feathers*

*Feather Stitch*

### Feathered Serpent

Available on large and small bowls as well as a spittoon whimsey that is rare, this Fenton pattern has an exterior design called Honeycomb and Clover. Colors are marigold, green, blue, and amethyst. The luster is usually heavy and the finish a satin look.

### Feathers

Northwood certainly made its share of vases, perhaps because they were so decorative and useful. The Feathers vase is an average example usually found in marigold, purple, and green and is of average size and quality.

### Feather Stitch

This pattern is a kissing cousin of the well-known Coin Dot design and as such is found on bowl shapes only, although I suspect a plate shape does exist. The colors seen are marigold, blue, green, and amethyst, and the bowls may vary in size from 8½" to 10". Feather Stitch was produced by Fenton.

*Fentonia*

*Fenton Smooth Rays*

*Fern*

*Fern Brand Chocolates*

## Fentonia

Known in berry sets, table sets, fruit bowls, and water sets, Fentonia is an interesting allover pattern of diamonds filled with the usual Fenton fillers of scales and embroidery stitchery. Colors are marigold, blue, green, and occasionally amethyst, but the pattern is scarce in all colors and is seldom found for sale. There is a variant called Fentonia Fruit.

## Fenton Smooth Rays

If you examine the shape and edging of this bowl (Fenton's #212 mould), you might just think this was a Scale Band item with a Stippled Rays interior. It isn't. There is no pattern on the exterior and the interior design is Smooth Rays! I'm sure this came in the usual Fenton colors and maybe white as well. And while it certainly isn't a show stopper, it can't be too plentiful.

## Fern

Again we find a pattern that is sometimes combined with the well-known Northwood pattern, Daisy and Plume. Fern is usually found as an interior pattern on bowls and compotes. It is an attractive pattern but really not an outstanding one.

## Fern Brand Chocolates

Like so may of the small Northwood advertising pieces, this is a treasure for collectors, and a real beauty for advertising buffs. The only color is amethyst, and it measures 6¼" across.

*Fern Panels*

*Field Flower*

*Field Thistle*

*File*

## Fern Panels

Like so many of the Fenton novelty pieces of carnival glass, Fern Panels is found only on the hat shape. Not too exciting, but then it apparently had an appeal of its own then as now. The colors are the usual ones: marigold, blue, green, and occasionally red.

## Field Flower

Originally called 494½, this much overlooked Imperial pattern is really a little jewel. Found only on a standard size water set and a rare milk pitcher, Field Flowers is found in marigold, purple, green, and a very beautiful clambroth. The design, basically a flower framed by two strands of wheat on a stippled background, is bordered by double arches that edge the stippled area and continue down to divide the area into panels. All in all, this is a beautiful pattern that would grace any collection.

## Field Thistle

Field Thistle is a U.S. Glass Company pattern, scarce in all shapes and colors. Shapes known are berry sets, table sets, water sets, a vase, plate, and small creamer and sugar called a breakfast set. Colors most found are marigold or green, but the breakfast set is known in a beautiful ice blue, so other colors may exist. The pattern is all intaglio, and sometimes the marigold coloring is a bit weak.

## File

For many years, File was designated as a product of the Columbia Glass Company, but was actually made by the Imperial Glass Company and is shown as such in their old catalogs in many shapes, including bowls, water pitchers, compotes, and table sets. The colors are marigold, green, smoke, and amethyst, and usually the luster is quite good with much gold in evidence. The mold work is far above average.

*Filigree*

# $F$*iligree*

As part of a group of designs called the Filigree line, this very strange, single item shown may well be the first piece of carnival glass produced by the Dugan-Diamond company. The same shape and pattern can also be found in emerald glass with gold decoration as well as ruby and royal blue. Date of production is 1904 – 1909.

# $F$*ine Block Shade*

While I am not a shade fan, I find this one exceptional. The interior is lined vertically and the exterior has horizontal lines, giving a beautiful quality to the iridescence. The coloring is a very rich, amber-like marigold and the size is 4" tall with a 2" top opening and a 5½" base diameter.

*Fine Block Shade*

# $F$*ine Cut and Roses*

The real pleasure of this Northwood pattern is the successful combination of a realistic floral pattern with a pleasing geometric one. Of course, rose bowls have a charm all their own. Really well done mold work and super color both add to its attraction, and even though it is slightly smaller than many rose bowl patterns, it is a favorite of collectors.

*Fine Cut and Roses*

# $F$*ine Cut Heart (Millersburg)*

Here is the back pattern of the beautiful Primrose bowl, but the one shown is something special. An experimental piece with a goofus finish under iridization. I've seen one other Millersburg example of this on a Peacock and Urn ice cream bowl, and it was also amethyst.

*Fine Cut Heart (Millersburg)*

*Fine Cut Ovals (Millersburg)*

*Fine Prisms and Diamonds*

*Fine Cut Rings*

*Fine Rib (Northwood)*

## Fine Cut Ovals (Millersburg)

As a companion to the Whirling Leaves pattern, Fine Cut Ovals has eight ovals, each containing two sections of fine cut and two of file. At the edges, a fan flares from a diamond center, giving interesting contrast.

## Fine Cut Rings

From a set of copyright drawings we know this pattern was made by the Guggenheim, Ltd. Company of London in 1925. Shapes shown in the drawing are an oval bowl, vase, footed celery, covered butter dish, creamer, stemmed sugar, round bowl, footed cake plate, and covered jam jar. The only color I've seen is marigold, and as you can see, the coloring, mold work, and luster are outstanding.

## Fine Prisms and Diamonds

This large English vase stands some 13½" tall and has a hefty base diameter of nearly 4". Obviously it was intended to be used and not just a decorative item. And while the design qualities aren't impressive, the glass is of good color and luster.

## Fine Rib (Northwood)

Can you imagine anything simpler? Yet the Fine Rib pattern was, and is, a success to the extent it was used time and time again by the Northwood company as secondary patterns and is the primary one in attractive vases like the one shown. While common in marigold and purple, the green color is a scarce one in Fine Rib.

## *Fine Rib Vase (Fenton)*

While both Northwood and Fenton produced a Fine Rib vase pattern, there are differences in the design. On the Northwood vase, the ribbing extends all the way down on the base, while the Fenton design ends in a distinctive scalloped edge above the base. Of course, Fenton made this shape and pattern in red too.

## *Fisherman's Mug*

This very popular mug pattern has the fish and waterlily on one side only with the reverse side plain. The mug is generous in size and heavy. It was made by Dugan-Diamond and is usually seen in amethyst. Other colors known are marigold, lavender, purple, peach opalescent, horehound, and ultra-rare cobalt blue.

## *Fishnet Epergne*

Made by the Dugan Glass Company, this classy one-lily epergne can be found in amethyst or peach opalescent. The netting is all on the lily, and the bowl is perfectly plain except for the dome base where a series of scoring lines radiate from top to bottom. Note that the base is sometimes clear.

## *Fish-Scales and Beads*

Most of these bowls I've seen are small – 6" to 7" in diameter. Nevertheless, they are well done, interesting, and add much to any collection. The Fishscale pattern is on the interior while the Beads design is on the exterior. When held to the light, one pattern fits happily into position to complement the whole, giving a pleasant experience.

*Fisherman's Mug*

*Fine Rib Vase (Fenton)*

*Fishnet Epergne*

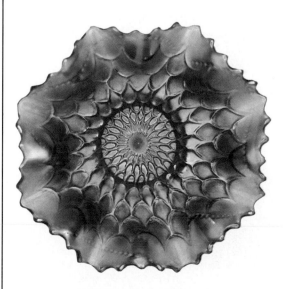

*Fish-Scales and Beads*

*Standard Encyclopedia of*
*Carnival*
*Glass*

*Fish Vase*

*Five Hearts*

*Five Panel*

*Flared Wide Panel Atomizer*

## F*ish Vase*

This handsome vase has finally been traced to the makers of the Zipper Stitch pattern as well as the Hand Vase and is believed to come from Czechoslovakia. I've seen only marigold, but have had both amethyst and green reported to me by a British collector.

## F*ive Hearts*

Like so many of the Dugan patterns in peach opalescent, Five Hearts is found only on dome-footed bowls of average size. It has been estimated that 60% to 75% of all peach carnival was made by this company. Personally, I'd say it would be closer to 90%.

## F*ive Panel*

Most companies had a try at these stemmed candy jars (the one shown is missing its lid), but the Five Panel seems to have a different dividing rib than either the Fenton or Northwood versions. The coloring is a good marigold, and most of these were made in several colors, especially pastel shades.

## F*lared Wide Panel Atomizer*

I've often wondered just how many iridized patterns in atomizers there really are. Certainly it was a popular item in the days of carnival, and each of them seem to have a charm of its own. This one, while rather plain, is a real cutie.

*Fleur de Lis (Czech)*

# *F*leur de Lis (Czech)

Until recently only a beautiful vase was known in this pattern, but recently a bowl has surfaced. The pattern is deeply intaglio and very richly iridized. The vase stands 10½" tall and the bowl measures 8½" across. Marigold is the only reported color and the pieces are known to be from Czechoslovakia.

# *F*leur de Lis (Millersburg)

Named, of course, for the stylized figures which symbolize the lily of the French royal family, this beautiful Millersburg design is found on bowls of all shapes and as an interior pattern on an occasional Hobstar and Feather punch bowl. The overall pattern is formal though well balanced, and the quality of workmanship, iridescence, and color rank with the best. Espe cially beautiful is the dome-footed three-cornered bowl in amethyst.

*Fleur de Lis (Millersburg)*

# *F*lora

Known as a float bowl and made by Sowerby, this 10" all-exterior patterned piece (the interior is plain and was advertised with a glass figural flower holder) was made in amber, blue, green, and a color called Rosalin in regular glass and the blue iridized treatment shown. Dates of production are from 1924 to 1936 with the carnival pieces coming first.

*Flora*

*Florabelle*

*Floral and Grape*

# *F*lorabelle

What a beauty this pastel water set with enameled flowers and gold foliage is. While it is shown in pastel green, I suspect it may have been made in white. The wide rolling of the lip and the reeded handle give it a look of quality.

# *F*loral and Grape

Without question, Floral and Grape is one of the most familiar Dugan patterns. The water sets are plentiful, especially in marigold. The only other shape is a hat whimsey pulled from the tumbler and other colors are cobalt blue, amethyst, green, and a scarce white. Also, there are variations due to the wear of molds and creation of new ones. A variant is credited to the Fenton company.

# *F*loral and Grape Variant

Here is the variant design, made by the Fenton company. It is, while similar to Dugan's, a crisper patterning and there is no cable above the center band as there is in the Dugan version. Just remember, the Fenton pieces are less cluttered with pattern. Colors are marigold, cobalt blue, green, and amethyst (no white like the Dugan pattern).

*Floral and Grape Variant*

*Floral and Optic*

## Floral and Optic

Most people are familiar with this pattern in rather large footed bowls in marigold or clear carnival, although it exists on rare cake plates and rose bowls and in smoke, iridized milk glass, red, a stunning aqua, white, and iridized custard glass. The pattern is quite simple, a series of wide panels edged by a border band of vining flower and leaf design. A green or amethyst bowl in Floral and Optic would be a real find in this Imperial pattern.

## Floral and Wheat

Floral and Wheat is an exterior pattern found on compotes and stemmed bonbons. Often it accompanies an interior pattern called Puzzle. Colors are marigold, amethyst, blue, and peach opalescent. It was made by the Dugan-Diamond company.

## Floral Sunburst

This very impressive vase is rather large and has an intaglio design of two panels of stylized daisies amid free-form leaves that are separated by large sunbursts that end at the top in stylized blossoms. I suspect this scarce vase is from England, and the flower reminds us of the one found on the Sunflower and Diamond vase. The color is a rich, dark marigold. It is 8½" tall and 5" across the top.

*Floral and Wheat*

*Floral Sunburst*

*Florentine*

*Florentine Hat*

*Flower Block*

# F *lorentine*

Both Fenton and Northwood made these candlesticks, and it is difficult to tell them apart. These shown are the Fenton version, however. They come in many colors including pastels and red as well as the usual carnival glass colors.

# F *lorentine Hat*

I've seen these hat-shaped pieces in several sizes and colors, and some have a stretch finish. The one shown, from Fenton, has a beautiful yellow-marigold finish and is pure carnival glass. It measures 4¼" tall, 3½" across the base, and nearly 7" across the rim. I'm sure similar shapes were made by other glass factories also.

# F *lower Block*

This pattern is a spin-off of the Curved Star pattern, and I'm showing it here in its entirety so collectors will be able to see the complete block as designed. Most of the ones around have lost their fancy wire base and wire arranger on the top.

*Flowering Dill*

# *F*lowering Dill

Once again we encounter a Fenton pattern that was chosen for the hat shape only, but Flowering Dill has a bit more to offer than some in that the design is graceful, flowing, and covers much of the allowed space. Flowering Dill can be found in marigold, cobalt blue, green, and red.

# *F*lowering Vine

The Flowering Vine compote is indeed a very scarce Millersburg item. To date, I've heard of only two examples, one in green and one in amethyst. The compote is a large one, some 9" high and 6½" across. The interior pattern is one of grape-like leaves and a dahlia-like flower. The finish is a fine radium one on heavy glass.

# *F*lower Medallion

While I can't tell you who made this tumbler, I can say I am impressed with its design. It reminds me of Curved Star in many ways. The Flower Medallion is a pale marigold, stands 4½" tall, and has a flashed look. The design, a series of arches filled with a lily-like flower, is very well balanced.

# *F*lower Pot (Blue)

While both Imperial and Fenton made these flower pot and saucer planters, the one shown is from the Fenton Art Glass Company. It is a beautiful ice blue and is 5" tall and 4¾" in diameter. The plate is 6¼" in diameter. It has been seen mostly on pastels including pink but can also be found on marigold.

*Flowering Vine*

*Flower Medallion*

*Flower Pot (Blue)*

*Flowers and Frames*

*Fluffy Peacock*

*Flute (Millersburg)*

*Flute (Northwood)*

# Flowers and Frames
Here is another of Dugan's dome-footed bowls found primarily in peach opalescent, but also available in marigold as well as purple and green. The bowls vary from 8" to 10" depending on the crimping of the rim and usually have very sharp mold detail.

# Fluffy Peacock
This is Fenton at its best, and it is a shame it is only found on water sets. The design is very flowing from the stylized peacocks to the tall strands of feathering that run from top to bottom. Colors are marigold, blue, green, and amethyst, and all are desirable.

# Flute (Millersburg)
The Millersburg Flute has one or two distinct differences from any of the other Flute patterns. One, of course, is the clarity of the base glass itself but the most pronounced is the ending of the flutes themselves plus the clover-leaf base. It is found in punch sets, berry sets, vases, and a rare compote.

# Flute (Northwood)
While it is certainly true that all of the major makers of carnival glass used the Flute pattern one way or another, apparently only Imperial and Northwood thought enough of it to make it a primary pattern. Thus, we find many useful shapes in an array of colors coming from the Northwood factories – including sherbets, water sets, table sets, berry sets, and even individual salt dips (an item seldom encountered in carnival glass). The green water set is probably the rarest color and shape in this pattern. Shown is a rare plate.

*Flute #3 (Imperial)*

# Flute #3 (Imperial)

Made in table sets, water sets, a toothpick holder (small), cruet, celery vase, a punch set, berry set, and a two-handled toothpick holder, the Imperial Flute design is quite strong with a flaring edge at the bottom. Colors of marigold, purple, green, clambroth, amber, and rarely blue are usually very rich, especially the purple which is highly prized.

# Flute and Cane (Imperial)

Found in wines, champagnes, punch cups, a milk pitcher, and the water set pieces shown, this is a very scarce pattern indeed. All shapes are found in marigold, but the water pitcher is reported in white also and is much sought in either color as are the marigold tumblers.

*Flute and Cane (Imperial)*

# Flute and Honeycomb (Millersburg)

Here's a better look at the 5" bowl I showed in *Millersburg, Queen of Carnival Glass.* You can see by the design above the base why I've renamed it rather than simply calling it a Flute variant. Super amethyst is the only color I've seen, and it matches the Big Thistle punch bowl in color and finish.

# Fluted Scrolls

Perhaps this should be called a spittoon, but regardless of the name it is a very rare, one-of-a-kind product in carnival. While often found on opalescent glass, this is the only iridized item in this pattern of which I've heard. Perhaps it was a novelty a Dugan worker produced for himself. The coloring is a good amethyst with average luster.

*Flute and Honeycomb (Millersburg)*

*Fluted Scrolls*

107

*Flute Sherbet (English)*

*Folding Fan Compote*

*Footed Prism Panels*

*Footed Shell*

### Flute Sherbet (English)

This little cutie is signed "British" in script on the underside of the base. In size they are small, measuring 3¼" tall and 3" across the top. The only color reported is a good marigold of deep hue.

### Folding Fan Compote

The only shape I've seen for this Dugan pattern is the stemmed shallow compote shown. Most have the ruffled edge, and the average size is 7½" in diameter and 4" tall. Colors are marigold, amethyst, green, and peach opalescent. The one shown has a clear base, but this isn't always the case.

### Footed Prism Panels

What a nice design this pretty 10" footed vase is! It is a Sowerby product, and the only reported colors are a good rich marigold and a scarce green. The design is a series of six panels filled with star prisms in graduating sizes. The stem base is domed and gently scalloped, giving great space to the appearance.

### Footed Shell

Made in two sizes, 5" and 3", this little novelty from the Westmoreland company is a scarce item, especially in the smaller size. The shell rests on three stubby feet, and the iridization is on the inside only. Colors I've seen are amethyst, green, marigold, and blue. Also milk glass iridized.

*Forks*

# Forks

I first showed this rare cracker jar in my *Rarities in Carnival Glass* book as an unlisted pattern but have since learned it was called Forks in old Cambridge ads. The only color I've seen is a very rich green, but I wouldn't rule out marigold or amethyst.

# Formal

Evidence points to Dugan as the maker of this interesting pattern found only on the vase shaped in a jack-in-the-pulpit manner and a quite scarce hatpin holder. The colors most seen are purple and marigold, but I'm told pastels do exist. The hatpin holder stands 7¼" tall.

*Formal*

# Fountain Epergne

From Sowerby, this very attractive epergne has a sterling frame that is hallmarked. The lilies have a twisted swirl in the design and are clear except for the marigold carnival tops. There are three smaller lilies and the massive center one and while the whole piece is similar to the Five Lily epergne, the Fountain epergne is more graceful and seems to be of better quality.

*Fountain Epergne*

# Four Flowers

For many years I've been puzzled by the origin of this beautiful design, but since peach opalescent is a prominent color, I'm satisfied it was also a Dugan product. Known in bowls and plates from 6" to 11", colors are purple, green, marigold, peach, blue, and smoke.

*Four Flowers*

*Four Flowers Variant*

*474*

*Four Pillar*

*49er*

## Four Flowers Variant

With all the recent research on this pattern, I seem to grow even more confused, but for argument's sake, I'll say the theory now seems to place this pattern's maker in the Scandinavian orbit of glassmaking. It is a beauty, whoever made it, much prettier than the regular Four Flowers and is found in bowls, plates, and a stunning salver on a metal base.

## Four Pillar

Often credited to Northwood, examples in amber, green, and amethyst have also been seen with the Diamond-D mark. Other colors known are marigold, ice blue, ice green, white, aqua opalescent, and the strange yellow-green shown called citrine. Occasionally, advertising appears on the base, and pieces with gold decoration on the lip are found.

## 474

Here is a very pretty near-cut pattern that really looks quite good on all shapes. I know of punch sets, table sets, water sets, and a milk pitcher in 474, as well as a nice fluted bowl. The color is usually marigold, but amethyst and green do exist in some shapes and are highly prized. The glass is heavy and clear, the coloring extra fine, and the mold work superior – all making Imperial's 474 a real treat to own. Rare vases are also known.

## 49er

Rarely found or discussed by collectors, the 49er pattern is found on a variety of shapes including a wine decanter, stemmed wines, a squat pitcher, tumblers, and a dresser set as shown, consisting of atomizer, perfume bottles in three sizes, a ring tray, a pin dish, a pin box, and a powder box. The maker of 49er is believed to be European. Only marigold has been reported at this time. There is also a variant tumbler.

*French Grape*

# French Grape

While the photo certainly does not do justice to the design of this 5″ bowl, the pattern is one I hadn't seen before. The design is a simple grape and leaf design and the finish is a watery flashed iridescence of vaseline color. It is marked "Made in France."

# French Knots

I suppose most people credit this pattern to Fenton because of the shape – a typical hat with ruffled top. The design is quite nice and gracefully covers most of the space except the base. The exterior is plain but nicely iridized, and the only colors I've heard about are marigold and blue. French Knots is 4″ tall and has a base diameter of 2½″.

*French Knots*

# Frolicking Bears

Rare is hardly the word for this distinguished pattern, and I certainly wish I could identify the maker positively, but I can't (although I lean toward the U.S. Glass Company). The coloring is an odd gunmetal luster over an olive green glass. The mold work is good but not exceptional. To date the Frolicking Bears tumbler has sold for more money than any other, and the pitchers rank near the top of the market.

*Frolicking Bears*

# Frosted Block

Frosted Block is a very Imperial pattern found in several shapes including bowls, creamers, sugars, compotes, plates, milk pitchers, pickle dishes, and rose bowls. The color most seen is a good even marigold, but as you can see from the photo, a beautiful fiery clambroth is known in most shapes. In addition, some pieces are marked "Made in USA." These pieces are much scarcer and are well worth looking for.

*Frosted Block*

**111**

*Frosted Oxford Bobeche*

*Fruit and Flowers*

*Fruit Basket (Millersburg)*

*Fruit Salad*

## Frosted Oxford Bobeche

Shown years ago in a drawing, Rose Presznick named this item and listed it as being made in marigold, blue, and white carnival glass. To date, I've only seen this marigold example which measures 4½" across, with a 1½" opening diameter and nearly 1" thickness. It is a bobeche, used to catch candle wax on a candlestick.

## Fruit and Flowers

Apparently a very close relative to the Three Fruits pattern, this is another of Northwood's floral groupings so well designed and produced. Also, there are several variations of this pattern, some with more flowers intermingled with the apples, pears, and cherries, often meandering almost to the very outer edge of the glass. Again the Northwood Basketweave is the exterior pattern, and Fruits and Flowers is found on compotes with handles as well as bowls and rare plates.

## Fruit Basket (Millersburg)

I couldn't quite believe my eyes when I first saw this Millersburg compote. But there it was with the exterior design and shape exactly like the Roses and Fruit compote with an interior basketweave design and a pineapple, grapes, and fruit! It was a real find, and I've been grateful ever since for the privilege of photographing it. It is my belief that this compote was the original pattern design but had to be modified because of the difficulty in producing the intricate design and remain in a competitive price area. At this time, four have been found. Of course, it must be classified as an extreme rarity.

## Fruit Salad

Westmoreland seems to be the maker of this beautiful and rare punch set after years of speculating. Found in marigold, amethyst, and peach opal, the design is outstanding and desirable.

**Garden Mums**

## Garden Mums

Here is the Northwood design used on so many of their advertising pieces. The flat plate is 6" across, and the coloring is a typical amethyst. Just why these few examples were left unlettered is a mystery, but they certainly add much to any collection.

## Garden Path

Just why there are two nearly identical patterns as this one and the variant shown elsewhere is puzzling. The major difference are the addition of minor embellishments at the outer edge of the design. Not much reason in my opinion to call for a second mold but evidently reason enough for the makers.

## Garden Path Variant

Essentially the same as the regular Garden Path pattern except for the addition of six winged hearts and an equal number of five-petaled flora, the Garden Path Variant can be found on 9" bowls, 10" fruit bowls, 6 – 7" plates, and a rare 11" plate. The exterior pattern is Soda Gold and colors found are amethyst and peach opalescent.

## Garland

Quite often you'll spot one of these nicely done footed rose bowls in cobalt blue or marigold, but the green is quite rare. I haven't heard of an amethyst one, but I suspect it was made in that color. Made around 1911, these are shown in Fenton ads well up into the later dates of iridized glass and must have been quite popular. There are three sets of wreaths and drapery around the heavily stippled bowl.

**Garden Path**

**Garden Path Variant**

**Garland**

113

*Gay 90s*

**George W. Getts Plate**

*Gibson Girl*

*German Steins*

# *Gay 90s*

Not only because of its extreme rarity but because the design is so very well suited for a water set is this pattern recognized as one of two or three top water sets in all of carnival glass. In every regard excellence of workmanship is obvious. Even the solid glass handle shows leaf veining at the top and intricate petal sliping at the base. Add to this the beautiful Millersburg finish and the clarity of superior glass, and you have a real winner – the Gay 90s water set.

# *George W. Getts Plate*

Here is still another of the Northwood advertising small plates with the Garden Mums design. As you can see, this one's claim to fame is the backward "S" in "Grand Forks." Whether intentional or not, it catches the eye. Amethyst is the only reported color.

# *German Steins*

Until I received the photos of these enameled steins (one is dated Nov. 17, 1892), I had no idea carnival glass examples even existed. The sizes are 8", 10", 11", and 12". The lettering is in German (one says "PROSIT," another "ZUR EVINNERUNG," and the dated one says "STUTTGART").

# *Gibson Girl*

What a cute little toothpick holder this is despite having no pattern whatsoever! It stands 2⅜" tall. Who made it and in what other colors I haven't a clue.

*God and Home (Dugan)*

# God and Home (Dugan)

For many years little was known about this unusual water set, except that it was found only in cobalt blue. It has a laurel wreath, a sun, and rays. On one side it reads "In God We Trust" and on the other side "God Bless Our Home." This rare set is now thought to have been made at the Dugan-Diamond factory, and it is a real pleasure to show it here, thanks to the Yohes of Stuttgart.

# Goddess of Harvest

Goddess of Harvest is the rarest of all Fenton bowl patterns and certainly deserves all the attention it gets. I've heard of six or seven of these beauties in colors of marigold, blue, and amethyst, and each is highly treasured by its owner. The bowl measures about 9" in diameter and is usually found with a candy ribbon edge.

# Golden Cupid

This very scarce beauty is something to behold. In size it is only 5¼" in diameter and quite shallow. The glass is clear with the cupid in gilt and a strong iridescence over the surface. It may be an ashtray, but I can't be sure. Large bowls are reported also.

*Goddess of Harvest*

*Golden Cupid*

*Golden Flowers*

*Golden Grape*

*Golden Harvest*

*Golden Honeycomb*

### Golden Flowers

Made by Jenkins just as the Stork vase, the Golden Flowers is much harder to find and usually has a richer finish. It is 7½" tall with a top opening of 3" and a base measuring 2⅞". The background has a heavy stippling, and the flowers are two types, large and small.

### Golden Grape

Known only in bowls or rose bowls on a collar base, this is a neatly molded item without much elaboration. The exterior is completely plain, and the only colors found are green, marigold, or pastel marigold, usually with a satin finish. Golden Grape was manufactured by Dugan.

### Golden Harvest

Here is another U.S. Glass pattern found mostly in marigold but occasionally seen in amethyst and reported in white. As you will notice, the wines are different from the decanter but are the proper ones. The stopper is solid glass.

### Golden Honeycomb

This interesting Imperial pattern provides an allover design without being busy. The small bowls have odd little solid glass handles that are like the ones on the breakfast set while the plate and compote do not. The only color I've heard of is a good deep marigold with very rich iridescence. While this certainly isn't in the same class as the Dugan Honeycomb rose bowl, it is a better than average item to own.

*Golden Thistle*

## Golden Oxen

While this mug has never been one of my favorites like the Heron, it is hard enough to find so that many people want one. Taller than most mugs, the only color I've seen is marigold.

## Golden Thistle

Much like the Golden Cupid piece shown elsewhere, this even rarer 5" tray is the first I've seen. The glass is clear with gilding in the exterior design and iridization on the surface only. A third pattern in this technique called Diana at the Hunt is known but I haven't been lucky enough to see it.

## Golden Wedding

I am very pleased to show the complete item, just as sold. Notice that the cap is still sealed, the whiskey is still inside, the labels are intact, and the beautiful box, dated December 31, 1924, gives us a time frame for the bottle. Several sizes exist from a full quart down to the tiny ¹⁄₁₀ pint size.

## Good Luck

Harry Northwood must have loved this pattern for the color range available is staggering. The design is simple – floral sprays around the inside of the bowl with a horseshoe and riding crop centered and the words, "Good Luck" above. There are minor mold variations and some pieces have stippling and others do not. Both bowls and plates with various edge treatments are known.

*Golden Oxen*

*Golden Wedding*

*Good Luck*

117

*Gothic Arches*

*Graceful Tumbler*

*Graceful*

## Gothic Arches

Unlisted up until now, this beautiful vase stands 10" tall. The flared or morning glory style top adds to the interest as does the fine smoke coloring. The maker is unknown, but I suspect Imperial. To date other colors have not been reported but probably exist.

## Graceful

Once again we find a very simple pattern, so very different from most Northwood offerings in the carnival glass field. Found mostly in marigold, occasionally a rich purple or deep emerald green vase in this pattern will surface, and when one of these is found, the simple beauty of the Graceful pattern becomes obvious.

## Graceful Tumbler

While there is a well-known Northwood vase pattern by this same name, most collectors will not confuse the two. The tumbler name honors Grace Rinehart (and it's about time) and is from Europe. It stands 4" tall and can be found in cobalt blue and amber. Its main design features are the series of scrolls and rococo fillers.

## Grand Thistle (Wide Paneled Thistle)

Regardless of which of the three names you choose to call this pattern (the third is Alexander Floral), the beautiful intaglio pattern and the rich luster are quality. Colors are marigold and cobalt blue with the marigold a bit on the amber side on at least one of the tumblers.

*Grand Thistle (Wide Paneled Thistle)*

*Grape (Imperial)*

# Grape (Imperial)

Perhaps reproductions have detracted too much from this beautiful Imperial pattern for most of us, but regardless of that, it remains a beautifully designed, nicely done pattern. In fact, for sheer realism, it doesn't take a back seat to any Grape pattern! The shapes are almost endless, and the colors range from marigold to amethyst, green, smoke, clambroth, and amber, all usually with a very fine luster.

# Grape and Cable (Fenton)

Yes, Fenton made a Grape and Cable pattern, and it is often hard to distinguish it from Northwood's. Fenton's contribution is found in bowls (both flat and footed), plates, and large orange bowls usually with the Persian Medallion interior. Colors are marigold, green, amethyst, blue, and rarely red.

*Grape and Cable (Fenton)*

# Grape and Cable (Northwood)

Without question this is the all-time favorite Northwood pattern. It led the field when made, and it is still very popular. The shapes available are staggering, and the color range is almost as large. I've heard of entire collections built around this one pattern and hardly a collection would be complete without one example.

*Grape and Cable (Northwood)*

*Grape and Cherry*

*Grape and Gothic Arches*

*Grape Arbor*

*Grape Basket*

# *G*rape and Cherry

Known only on large bowls, this Sowerby pattern is a real beauty. The design is exterior and all intaglio, and is a series of grapes and cherries separated by an unusual torch and scroll design. The base has a grape and leaf design, also intaglio. The only colors I've heard about are marigold and cobalt blue, but others may certainly exist.

# *G*rape and Gothic Arches

Made in a variety of kinds of glass including crystal, custard, gold decorated, and carnival, this pattern is certainly one of the earlier grape patterns. The arches are very effective, reminding one of a lacy arbor framing the grapes and leaves. While the berry sets often go unnoticed, the water sets are very desirable and are a must for all Northwood collectors.

# *G*rape Arbor

This is an underrated pattern, especially in the large footed bowl shape which carries the same exterior pattern as the Butterfly and Tulip. Of course, the tankard water set is popular, especially in the pastel colors of ice blue, ice green, and white. The marigold set seldom brings top dollar, and this is a shame since it is quite nice. The only other shape in Grape Arbor is a scarce hat shape.

# *G*rape Basket

Made by Imperial, this very attractive basket is rather scarce. Colors are marigold or smoke but a green or purple would be a great catch. Iridization is on both the inside and outside of the example shown, and measured to the top of the handle, this basket stands nearly 8" tall.

*Grape Delight*

# Grape Delight

Here is a pattern I'm sure will bring on a few outcries, because I've often heard it declared to be a Fenton product. I'm very sure, however, that it came from the Dugan family. On close comparison with several Dugan products, the mold work is certainly compatible. Not only does it come in the scarce nut bowl shape shown but in the more often seen rose bowl. The colors are both vivid and pastel and the most unusual feature, the six stuffy feet.

# Grape Leaves (Dugan?)

Yes, this bowl is marked "Northwood" but in over twenty years of research, I haven't seen another Northwood bowl with this edging used so often by Fenton and Dugan! Add to that the unusual coloring of this bowl, described by the owner as "sea green" (it has also been seen in cobalt blue) and one has to wonder if this mold was left at Indiana, PA, when Northwood left and was put into limited production by Dugan!

# Grape Leaves (Millersburg)

Seldom found and always costly, this rare Millersburg pattern is quite like the Blackberry, Grape, and Strawberry Wreath patterns except for its rarity. The major design difference lies in the center leaf and grapes, and it is found in marigold, amethyst, green, and vaseline.

*Grape Leaves (Dugan?)*

*Grape Leaves (Millersburg)*

*Grape Leaves (Northwood)*

*Grapevine Lattice*

# Grape Leaves (Northwood)

While it doesn't get the raves of the famous Grape and Cable pattern, this Northwood design is just as attractive. With four grape stems and leaves and four bunches of grapes, it is very balanced. Colors are marigold, amethyst, green, blue, black amethyst, ice blue, amber, and smoke. The exterior is the Blossom and Palm (sometimes called Blossom and Shell) from Northwood's opalescent glass era.

# Grapevine Lattice

I personally doubt the plate is really the same pattern as the water set known by the same name, but I will give in to tradition and list them as one and the same. The plate and bowl could be called Twigs, since they closely resemble the Apple Blossom Twigs pattern minus the flowers and leaves. The colors are both vivid and pastels, usually with very good iridescence. This pattern was manufactured by Dugan.

# Grape Wreath

This bowl might be called the "missing link" for it stands squarely between the Blackberry Wreath and the Millersburg Strawberry and seems to be a part of the series – perhaps from the same designer. Besides the various sizes of bowls, a rare spittoon whimsey, and 6" and 10" plates are known.

*Grape Wreath*

# Grape Wreath Multi-Star Variant

Here is the third example of a Millersburg variant in this pattern and as you can see, the difference lies in the center design of concentric stars. Some collectors call this the Spider Web Center, and I can certainly see why. It can be found on the same sizes the other Grape Wreath bowls were made and in the same colors.

# Grape Wreath Variant (Millersburg)

Actually, only the center design has been changed on these, and as you can see, it is a stylized sunburst. I've seen several sizes of bowls with this center, but it looks best on the large 10" ice cream bowls. Colors are marigold, green, amethyst, and a beautiful clambroth with much fire in the luster.

# Grecian Urn

Perfume bottles seem to have a charm all their own and this graceful example is a prime item. It stands 6" tall and has a gilt stopper with a dauber attached. And while it isn't marked, an atomizer that is marked DeVilbiss is known that matches in size and shape. The coloring is a good strong marigold.

# Greek Key

This simple continuous Northwood pattern, called Roman Key in pressed glass, is really very attractive when iridized. Actually, there are three motifs used: the ray center pattern, the Greek Key, and the beads (in the much sought water set a fourth motif of prisms is added). Besides the water set, there are flat and footed bowls as well as plates. The colors are both vivid and pastels.

*Grape Wreath Multi-Star Variant*

*Grape Wreath Variant (Millersburg)*

*Grecian Urn*

*Greek Key*

*Greek Key and Scales (Northwood)*

*Hamilton, Montana Souvenir Vase*

*Halloween*

*Hammered Bell*

# Greek Key and Scales (Northwood)

Here's a rather nice Northwood secondary pattern usually found on dome-based bowls with the Stippled Rays variant interior. The design is crisp and does a nice job.

# Halloween

This is a very appropriately named pattern since the bright rich marigold is contrasted nicely with narrow black banding at top and bottom. There are two sizes in both tumblers, and the matching pitchers and the pitchers have black handles.

# Hamilton, Montana Souvenir Vase

I'm not sure this advertising vase dates back to the original carnival glass era, but it has fair iridescence and I hadn't heard of one before. The lettering is applied, then fired, and the stem and base is clear. The vase stands 6½" tall and has a flared top.

# Hammered Bell

This well-known light shade is a very imaginative work of art and was used in a variety of ways: as a hanging shade, suspended over lights on a chandelier, or even in pairs or alone as a shade for a sconce. The metal fittings vary from one shade to the next with the example shown a very pretty Art Deco hanger that matches a neat wall sconce dated 1913.

# Handled Vase (Imperial)

Mrs. Hartung shows this neat vase with the lip turned down, and Rose Presznick drew it cupped in like a rose bowl. But here it is in the original shape, and it is very pretty indeed. It stands about 9" tall, and the coloring is a deep rich marigold well down before paling to a lighter shade.

# Harvest Flower

Here is a seldom-seen pattern, found only on a pitcher and tumbler in marigold, amethyst, and green on the latter and only in marigold in the pitcher. The tumblers have been reproduced in a dingy purple as well as white, so beware.

# Harvest Poppy

Seldom found or discussed this very well designed compote has been seen in marigold, amethyst, peach opalescent, and white, and I strongly suspect it may have been made in other colors as well. The design is very strong with poppies, stems of wheat, leaves, and stippling between the flowers.

# Hattie

While there is little to be called outstanding about Hattie, it nonetheless has its own charm and has the distinction of having the same pattern on both the exterior and interior. Most often found on 8" bowls with a collar base, it is also found in a scarce rose bowl and two sizes of plates, both of which are rare. The color most seen on this Imperial product is marigold, but green and amethyst do exist, and I've heard of both amber and smoke bowls.

*Handled Vase*
*(Imperial)*

*Harvest Flower*

*Harvest Poppy*

*Hattie*

Hawaiian Moon

Headdress

Heart and Horseshoe

Heart and Trees

## Hawaiian Moon

Like the Late Waterlily tumbler shown elsewhere, this is a machine-enameled item with a flashed finish. It has been seen in marigold and a scarce cranberry and came along in the Depression era.

## Headdress

Here is a pattern found in two varieties because it was made both in America and in Sweden. It is found in 9" bowls and on compotes in marigold, green, and blue.

## Heart and Horseshoe

Yes, Fenton had a version of the Good Luck pattern, and it is much harder to find than the one Northwood produced. Note that it is simply the familiar Heart and Vine pattern with the horseshoe and lettering added. Colors are marigold and green with the marigold most prevalent and the green very hard to find.

## Heart and Trees

Found as an interior pattern on some of the footed Butterfly and Berry bowls, Heart and Trees is a combination of three well-known Fenton standards. Colors known are marigold, green, and blue, but certainly others may exist.

# Heart and Vine

Apparently this was one of Mr. Fenton's favorite designs for he used several variations of it combined with the Butterfly and Berry pattern as Stream of Hearts or on the Heart and Horseshoe pattern. The Heart and Vine pattern can be found on both bowls and plates and occasionally with advertising on the latter (the Spector plate). Colors are marigold, green, amethyst, blue, and white.

# Hearts and Flowers

Intricate though it is, the Hearts and Flowers pattern is one of Northwood's best and much resembles the Embroidered Mums design in that respect. It can be found in bowls (mostly with Fine Rib exterior but rarely with a basketweave), plates, and stemmed compotes. The color range is very broad including marigold, amethyst, blue, green, ice blue, purple, white, ice green, aqua opalescent, clambroth, blue opalescent, and a rare marigold on custard (ivory).

# Heavy Banded Diamonds

Perhaps designed as a companion to the Banded Diamonds water set, this beautiful Australian berry set, available in both marigold and purple, is a joy to behold. The diamonds are heavily molded and stand out below the narrow thread lines, and the iridescence is very rich.

# Heavy Diamond

I'd always thought this pattern to be a Dugan product until this vase shape in smoke appeared, so apparently it is an Imperial product. Previously reported only in marigold, shapes known besides the vases are large bowls, creamers, and sugars, but others probably are around.

*Heart and Vine*

*Heavy Diamond*

*Hearts and Flowers*

*Heavy Banded Diamonds*

*Heavy Grape (Dugan)*

*Heavy Grape (Imperial)*

### Heavy Grape (Dugan)

So similar in many ways to the Millersburg Vintage bowls, this Dugan pattern does have several distinctive qualities of its own. The most obvious one is, of course, the grape leaf center with grapes around its edge. Also missing are the usual tendrils and the small leaflets, and the exterior doesn't carry a hobnail pattern but a typical near-cut design.

### Heavy Grape (Imperial)

Once called a Fenton product, this beautiful Grape design is now known to be an Imperial pattern and is available on berry sets, nappies, custard sets, and plates in three sizes. The colors on most pieces are simply spectacular and include marigold, green, purple, smoke, amber, pastel green, smoky blue, and clambroth. The 11" chop plate is highly sought and always brings top dollar when sold.

### Heavy Hobnail

I first showed this unusual item in *Rarities in Carnival Glass.* At that time, only the white version was known, but since then a spectacular purple example has been seen. These were the Fenton Rustic vases that weren't pulled or slung into the vase shape and very few are known.

*Heavy Hobnail*

*Heavy Iris*

*Heavy Prisms*

# Heavy Iris

Just why Dugan-Diamond didn't use this very spectacular pattern on shapes other than the water set has always puzzled me for it is a first-class design. It is bold and heavy and certainly uses its space to the best advantage. Colors are marigold, amethyst, purple, white, pastel marigold, peach opalescent, amber, and ice blue, but beware, this pattern was reproduced by Wright in 1978.

# Heavy Pineapple

Made by the Fenton company, Heavy Pineapple is a very scarce pattern, found on large footed bowls in marigold, cobalt blue, and white. The pattern is all exterior and highly raised.

# Heavy Prisms

This beautiful celery vase stands 6" tall and shows the quality English carnival glassmakers attained. The maker is Davisons, and the colors reported are marigold, amethyst, and blue. The glass is very thick and heavy, and the luster top-notch.

# Heavy Shell

Found only on white carnival, this Dugan pattern is rather scarce. The shapes are oval bowls and matching candlesticks. The glass is quite heavy, and the luster very rich.

*Heavy Pineapple*

*Heavy Shell*

129

*Heavy Web*

## Heavy Web

Found primarily on large, thick bowls in peach opalescent, Heavy Web is a very interesting Dugan pattern. It has been found with two distinct exterior patterns – a beautifully realistic grape and leaf design covering most of the surface and an equally attractive morning glory pattern. I've seen various shapes including round, ruffled, square, and elongated ones. A vivid purple or green bowl in this pattern would certainly be a treasure.

## Heisey Colonial

Shown is a very pretty dresser set, each piece marked "Heisey – patent 1910." The Heisey company did not iridize glass I have been assured, so just who added the light, watery iridization on some of their glass is a mystery (at least to me), but it isn't often found and each piece is a treasure. To find this complete set is a real accomplishment.

## Heron Mug

Like the Fisherman's mug this pattern came from Dugan-Diamond also but is harder to find and in my opinion, better designed. The Heron is on one side of the mug only, but does fill more space in a graceful rendering of the bird, and its marshy domain. The Heron mug has been reported in marigold, purple, and amethyst only.

*Heisey Colonial*

*Heron Mug*

# Herringbone and Beaded Oval

This very hard to find compote was listed in Imperial advertising as #B-54½, and the pattern was shown on a light shade. The compote has superb marigold color on the bowl, and the stem and base is clear. No other color has been reported and only three or four are known.

# Herringbone and Mums

Made by the Jeanette Glass Company in the late 1920s, this rare Depression era tumbler is a close relative to the Iris and Herringbone pattern by the same company. Both are found only in marigold, but the Herringbone and Mums is shorter and has the novel six-sided block base.

# Hex Base Candlestick

Nearly every glassmaker had a try at candlesticks shaped like this one, especially in stretch glass. The one shown is reported to be from the Imperial Company and has a very rich dark marigold coloring. Most of these candlesticks were sold in pairs with a console bowl and in a wide range of colors including green, purple, and even red.

# Hex Optic

Produced in the late days of carnival glass, the Hex Optic pattern like the Treebark Variant came from the Jeanette Company. The line consisted of water sets, various table pieces including large and small bowls, saucers, and jelly and relish dishes. Sometimes light in iridization, the mold work is less complicated than early glass, even from the same company.

*Herringbone and Beaded Oval*

*Hex Base Candlestick*

*Herringbone and Mums*

*Hex Optic*

*Hobnail*

*Hobnail Soda Gold*

*Hobnail Variant*

*Hobstar*

### Hobnail

While plentiful in many other types of glass, Hobnail is quite a rare item in carnival and one of real beauty. The very pattern seems perfectly suited for iridescence. The base carries a many-rayed design, and all the pieces I've seen are top-notch. The pitchers and tumblers are very rare and extremely hard to locate, but even the rose bowl is a prize, and the lady's spittoon is a little darling. Hobnail was made by Millersburg.

### Hobnail Soda Gold

While most spittoons found in carnival glass are of a daintier size, Imperial's Hobnail Soda Gold spittoon is a larger, more practical size. It measures 7" across the top and stands 5" high. I've seen examples in marigold and green as well a peculiar dark shade of amber. Many of these have a great deal of wear on the bottom indicating they were actually used!

### Hobnail Variant

This rare and exciting Millersburg pattern is quite different from the regular Hobnail made by the same company, because it has 11 rows of dots with 18 in each row around. The top row has only nine hobs, however. I suspect this was a copycat item from Fenton's Heavy Hobnail, but it is definitely Millersburg since mold drawings from there exist. Shapes known are vases, rose bowls, and a jardiniere. Colors reported are marigold, amethyst, and green.

### Hobstar

Apparently this was one of the early near-cut patterns from Imperial. I'd guess it experienced great popularity from the first for it was carried over from crystal to carnival glass in many shapes, including berry sets, cookie jars, table sets, bride's baskets, and a very rare pickle caster in an ornate holder. Marigold is the common color with purple and green quite scarce.

132

*Hobstar and Arches*

# Hobstar and Arches

Found mostly in bowls, this well-done Imperial geometric pattern was also sold with the same base as the Long Hobstar fruit set (most companies got double mileage whenever possible with patterns) giving them a footed fruit bowl in this pattern also. Colors are marigold, green, amethyst, and smoke.

# Hobstar and Cut Triangles

This very unusual pattern is typically English in design, with strong contrast between geometrically patterned areas against very plain areas. Rose Presznick lists bowls, plate, and a rose bowl in this pattern in both green and amethyst, but the only shapes I've seen are bowls, rose bowls, and compotes in marigold or amethyst.

# Hobstar and Feather

This Millersburg pattern is simply the best geometric pattern in carnival glass. Bold, deeply cut, and impressive, it is massive in concept. Found in punch sets, table set pieces, a giant footed rose bowl, small bowls of various shapes, a compote, a dessert, and several whimseys. Colors are marigold, amethyst, purple, green, and rare examples of blue and vaseline.

*Hobstar and Cut Triangles*

*Hobstar and Feather*

133

*Hobstar and Fruit*

*Hobstar Band*

*Hobstar Diamonds*

*Hobstar Flower*

# Hobstar and Fruit

Made by Westmoreland, this seldom found, seldom discussed pattern is found mostly on small bowls but is known on a larger 10" bowl and a 10½" plate. Colors are mostly peach opalescent, but we are happy to show a banana bowl whimsey in marigold and a 6½" shallow bowl in blue opalescent.

# Hobstar Band

This scarce Imperial pattern is found only on handled celery vases and water sets of two varieties. The usual pitcher is flat based, but as you can see a quite rare pedestal variant is known. The only color reported is a good rich marigold.

# Hobstar Diamonds

Another rare tumbler, this very pretty geometric pattern has eight small hobstars around the base, eight larger ones at the top of the design, and long panels of plain diamonds between. The coloring is a pretty honey-marigold.

# Hobstar Flower

This beautiful little Northwood compote is seldom seen and usually comes as a surprise to most collectors. I've heard it called Octagon or Fashion at one time or another, and most people say they've never seen it before. It is a rather hard-to-find item. It is known in marigold, but is mostly found in amethyst.

*Hobstar Panels*

# Hobstar Panels

Apparently the English glassmakers like the creamer shape, for they certainly made their share of them. Here is a well-conceived geometric design with hobstars, sunbursts, and panels integrated into a very nice whole. The only color I've seen is the deep marigold shown, but certainly there may be others.

# Hobstar Reversed

Shown is what was called a "sideboard set" in the advertising by Davisons of Gateshead. It consists of a flower frog and holder that is footed and two-sided vases which were also used as spooners. Also known is a covered butter dish. The colors listed are marigold, amethyst, and blue, but not all colors are found in all shapes.

# Hobstar Whirl (Whirligig)

While I can't be certain who made this very nice compote, I wouldn't rule out Dugan or Northwood. The design is simple but effective, and the luster very good. The coloring is cobalt blue.

# Hocking Mixing Bowl

While most of these mixing bowls date to Depression glass times, this is the first iridized one I've heard about. It has very strong color and iridescence, indicating it came along at the end of one period of glass production of carnival, but certainly not in the time of the Sungold items that are truly Depression glass. It is marked "Hocking" and has a top diameter of 7", I believe. Ads show this same bowl mold used in 1929.

*Hobstar Whirl (Whirligig)*

*Hobstar Reversed*

*Hocking Mixing Bowl*

*Holiday*

*Holly*

*Holly and Berry*

# Holiday

Holiday is a Northwood pattern that so far has turned up only on this 11" tray. It is shown here in marigold and has the Northwood mark. It is also known in crystal but seems to have no accompanying pieces.

# Holly

Most collectors are familiar with this Fenton pattern, found on bowls, plates, compotes, goblets, and hat shapes. The design is simple: tendrils of holly and leaf vining from the center out to the rim of the piece. Colors are marigold, green, amethyst, fiery amethyst, lavender, blue, aqua opalescent, white, vaseline, red, celeste blue, lime green opalescent, and cobalt opalescent.

# Holly and Berry

This Dugan pattern, found mostly in rather deep bowls and nappies (one-handled bonbons) as well as an occasional sauce boat, is so similar to the Millersburg Holly pattern that most people simply accept it as a product of that company. The one distinguishing difference is the leaf and berry medallion in the center of the Holly and Berry pattern while the Millersburg design has no such center motif. Holly and Berry is found in purple, green, marigold, blue, and most often peach opalescent. A large piece of this pattern was discovered in the Dugan diggings.

*Holly Sprig (or Whirl)*

## Holly Sprig (or Whirl)

I have combined these two Millersburg patterns under one title, because, frankly, I can distinguish no discernible difference in them. Either can be found with or without a wide panel or the near-cut wreath pattern. The holly leaves and berries do vary somewhat from shape to shape, but certainly not enough to warrant separate titles. At any rate, it is a simple, well-executed pattern, especially nice on a one-handled nappy. The colors are usually green, marigold, and a fine amethyst.

## Holly Wreath Variant (Millersburg)

Besides the Grape Wreath variants, Millersburg's Holly patterns were often given the three same center patterns of feathers, stylized clovers, and multi-ringed stars. Here is a very pretty example of the feather center on a bowl with a candy-ribbon edge. All of these are found on 7" – 8" bowls in the usual Millersburg colors.

*Holly Wreath Variant*
*(Millersburg)*

## Holly Wreath Variant with Multi Stars

A close comparison with the two other Millersburg variants in this pattern shown elsewhere will exhibit the only differences are in the center design. Just like the Grape Wreath pattern, three different center designs are found.

## Homestead Shade

There seems to be several painted scenes on these shades; some with castles, mountains, or winter landscapes. The example shown has a cabin on one side and trees and pasture on the rest. It was named by Marian Hartung. It is 5" tall and has a bell diameter of 4¼". The finish is dull but does show iridescence.

*Holly Wreath Variant*
*with Multi Stars*

*Homestead Shade*

137

*Honeybee Pot*

*Honeycomb and Clover*

*Honeycomb and Hobstar*

*Honeycomb Panels*

## Honeybee Pot

Shown in a Jeanette catalog as late as 1959, this cute honey container stands 4¼" tall. Besides the lightly iridized one that has a yellowish color, it was made in shell pink milk glass as well as clear and amber glass that was not iridized.

## Honeycomb and Clover

While this Fenton pattern is best known as the exterior design of Feathered Serpent pieces, it is also used as the primary pattern for bonbons and the scarce compote. Colors I've heard about include marigold, green, blue, amethyst, amber, and white, but others may exist!

## Honeycomb and Hobstar

This very rare vase is from the Millersburg Company and has never been out of the Ohio area. As you can see, it is a very rich blue with heavy even luster. The base design is the same as the Hobstar and Feather rose bowl. The vase stands 8¼" tall. This example was found years ago on a shelf in a defunct Millersburg business and has remained in its present home for many years. Another blue and one amethyst are reported.

## Honeycomb Panels

I have been assured this tall tumbler is old, and I must admit it appears so to me. It is rather tall with excellent color and iridization in a rich purple. Three rows of honeycombing above a series of eight panels make the design simple yet effective. I suspect it came from one of the European glass companies but can't be sure at this time.

*Honeycomb Rose Bowl*

## Honeycomb Rose Bowl

Found only in marigold or peach opalescent glass, this well-designed novelty rose bowl from the Dugan-Diamond Glass Company is a very popular item with collectors, especially of rose bowls. They stand 4½" tall.

## Horn of Plenty

What can I say about this bottle that isn't obvious from the photo? It isn't rare or even good carnival, but it certainly has a place in the history of our glass.

## Horses' Heads

Sometimes called Horse Medallion, this well-known Fenton pattern can be found in flat or footed bowls, a scarce plate shape, and the rare rose bowl. The edges often are varied in ruffling and can resemble a jack-in-the-pulpit shape. Colors are marigold, blue, green, white, vaseline, aqua, and red.

## Horseshoe Shot Glass

If it weren't for the pretty horseshoe design in the bottom of this shot glass, it would be just another piece of glass. But with the design, it is very collectible, highly sought, and not cheap. Marigold is the only color so far reported.

*Horn of Plenty*

*Horses' Heads*

*Horseshoe Shot Glass*

*Hot Springs Vase*

*Howard Advertising Vase*

*Idyll (Fenton)*

*Illinois Daisy*

# Hot Springs Vase

This very interesting vase is a beauty. It measures 9⅞" tall and 4½" wide across the top. The coloring is a pale amber and the iridescence is quite good. It is lettered: "To Lena from Uncle, Hot Spring, Arkansas, Superior Bath House, May 20, 1903." Who says carnival glass was first made in 1907?

# Howard Advertising Vase

A well-known vase pattern that is called Four Pillars, the vase shown has advertising on the base which says "Howard Furniture Co., 109 & 11 Nth Howard St." The vase shown is 12" tall and has a 4" base diameter. The coloring is a strong emerald green with good iridescence.

# Idyll (Fenton)

While I apologize for the poor quality of the picture, I have only praise for this very rare vase. It is one of only two ever reported and is a design jewel. The coloring is amethyst, and it stands 7" tall. The pattern of water lilies and butterflies is just right.

# Illinois Daisy

How strange the name of this pattern sounds on a British pattern, but Illinois Daisy was a product of Davisons of Gateshead. Shapes known are the familiar covered jar and an 8" bowl. The only color I've heard about is marigold, often very weak, but perhaps time will turn up another color.

*Illusion*

# Illusion

It is rather difficult to describe this seldom-discussed Fenton pattern. It is found on bowls occasionally, but mainly on bonbons and is a combination of flowers, leaves, and odd geometric shadow-like blotches. Colors seen are marigold and blue, but I certainly wouldn't rule out green amethyst. A red Illusion bonbon would be a real treasure, but so far I haven't heard of one.

# Imperial #284

If you compare this Imperial vase, shaped much like the Jester's Cap vase by Westmoreland shown elsewhere, you will see it has fewer ribs (eight as opposed to Westmoreland's twelve). In point of fact, these vases should not really be called anything but Corinth vases by different makers, regardless of shaping, but I will bow to earlier naming. This vase was designated as #284 in Imperial ads, and so I've named it.

*Imperial #284*

# Imperial Basket

This Imperial handled basket is identical in size and shape to the Daisy basket and, as you can see, the handle patterns are the same. The coloring is unusual in that it is mostly smoke carnival with just a touch of marigold around the top.

*Imperial Basket*

# Imperial Grape Shade

Apparently these shades are not in great supply for I've seen very few of them over the years. They are a standard 5½" tall and 5" across, are marked "Nuart" and are very attractive with good color. The pattern is well raised, and the scalloped edging very nice.

*Imperial Grape Shade*

*Imperial Jewels Candleholders*

*Imperial Paperweight*

*Inca Bottle*

*Inca Vase*

# *I*mperial Jewels Candleholders

These beautiful Imperial Jewels candleholders are 7¼" tall. As you can see, they have a bold red iridized finish, and there is no stretch effect. Some are marked with the "Iron Cross" mark, but these are not.

# *I*mperial Paperweight

This very rare advertising paperweight was shown in my book on carnival glass rarities for very few of these are known. The paperweight is roughly rectangular, 5½" long, 3⅛" wide, and 1" thick. A depressed oval is in the center of the weight, and it is inscribed: "Imperial Glass Company, Bellaire, Ohio, USA," "Imperial Art Glass," "Nucut," "NuArt," and "$^{IM|PE}_{RI|AL}$ ." These are all trademarks of the company, of course. The glass is a fine amethyst with good, rich luster.

# *I*nca Bottle

I can't recall ever hearing about the unusual 9½" bottle shown here. A paper label on the back says: "Huaco de oro Peruano." And while the color isn't all that dark the iridization is quite good and the charm of the design is outstanding.

# *I*nca Vase

Like its sister design, the Sea Gulls vase, this is a foreign pattern also. It's probably Scandinavian. The feeling is Art Deco and very well done. The only color reported is a rich marigold.

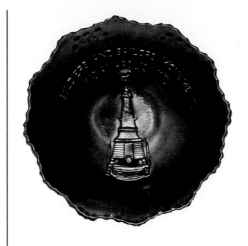

*Indiana Soldiers and
Sailors Plate*

*Indian Canoe*

## Indiana Soldiers and Sailors Plate

For more years than I care to remember, I've wanted to show this very rare Fenton plate, but was never able to photograph one of the three known. All are cobalt blue with a design of the monument that dominates the Circle in downtown Indianapolis. The exterior pattern is a typical Fenton one, Berry and Leaf Circle (Horse Chestnut). The iridization is superb!

## Indiana Statehouse

Besides the two versions of the Soldiers and Sailors plates, Fenton also made this very rare plate shown in blue. The size is identical to the other two, and the exterior carries the same Berry and Leaf Circle design. This was made in marigold also.

## Indian Canoe

This small novelty is really very heavy glass for its 6½" length. The coloring is touched with a bit of amber, but the iridization is quite good. Other measurements are 1½" tall and 2¼" wide. The maker is a mystery to me.

## Intaglio Daisy

Again, the English have designed a neat, useful near-cut pattern. The bowl stands 4" tall and has a 7½" width. The design is all intaglio, and the only color I've seen is marigold. Sowerby is the maker.

*Indiana Statehouse*

*Intaglio Daisy*

143

*Intaglio Stars*

*Interior Flute*

*Interior Panels*

*Interior Rays*

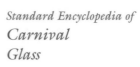
### Intaglio Stars

What a pretty tumbler this is! It stands 4" tall, has 12 panels that are ¾" wide around the upper portion and a band of three stars and three sunbursts, all intaglio. The marigold coloring is very rich and has a radium-like finish. The maker is unknown at this time.

### Interior Flute

Here's another one of the many Flute patterns so popular in their day. There was probably a matching sugar. I haven't seen any other colors, but they probably exist.

### Interior Panels

Here is a familiar treatment, plain on the outside with ribbing, optic, or paneling on the interior. It has very good color and iridescence and the matching stopper adds a lot to the look. The color is a very rich marigold with purple highlights.

### Interior Rays

Since I first showed this table set pattern, we've learned that it may be a U.S. Glass product closely resembling a Depression glass pattern called Aunt Polly. Here are the covered sugar and the creamer which show the design to the best advantage. There is also a covered butter dish as well as a covered jam jar which casts a shadow on an American origin in my mind.

*Interior Swirl and Wide Panel*

# *Interior Rib*

This very classy 7½" vase is tissue-paper thin, and the only design is the inside ribbing that runs the length of the glass. The color is a strong smoke with high luster, and I've seen only two of these over the years.

# *Interior Swirl and Wide Panel*

Despite its long name, this squat pitcher is a really cute one with good coloring and lots of character. Other colors and shapes may exist, but I haven't seen them and don't know who the maker is.

*Interior Rib*

# *Inverted Coin Dot*

The tumbler shown is part of a scarce water set made by the Fenton Company, and to the best of my knowledge is not found in other shapes. As you can see, the pattern is all interior. Colors known are marigold, amethyst, and green, but blue may exist.

*Inverted Coin Dot*

# *Inverted Feather*

This is probably the best known of all Cambridge carnival glass patterns and is found in a variety of shapes including a cracker jar, table set, water set, compote, sherbet, wine, milk pitcher, and punch set. All shapes are rare except the cracker jar, and colors known are marigold, green, and amethyst.

*Inverted Feather*

145

*Inverted Prisms*

*Inverted Strawberry*

*Inverted Thistle*

*Iris*

## *Inverted Prisms*

This very impressive creamer has the look of British design and I suspect it is indeed from that country. I haven't seen any companion pieces but surely an open sugar exists. The coloring is a strong marigold with good luster.

## *Inverted Strawberry*

Like its cousin, Inverted Thistle, this beautiful Cambridge pattern is all intaglio and can be found on several shapes including berry sets, water sets, candlesticks, large compotes, sherbets, milk pitchers, creamers, spooners, a stemmed celery, powder jars, and a lady's spittoon. All shapes are rare, and colors known are marigold, green, amethyst, and blue.

## *Inverted Thistle*

Cambridge was responsible for very original patterns and superior workmanship and here is a prime example. Known in water sets, a spittoon, a covered box, a pickle dish, and a breakfast set, this is an intaglio pattern. Colors are marigold, amethyst, green, and a rare blue.

## *Iris*

Along with the plain Buttermilk Goblet, this pattern found in both compotes and goblets, is Fenton. Colors seen are marigold, green, amethyst, and a very rare white.

***Iris and Herringbone***

# *I*ris and Herringbone

Made late in carnival history, this Jeanette pattern can be found in a host of shapes, all useful. Its coloring runs from good to awful, and many pieces are found in crystal, also.

# *I*saac Benesch Bowl

This cute 6¼" advertising bowl is quite easily identified, because of its distinct design. It bears the labeling "The Great House of Isaac Benesch and Sons, Wilksbarre, Pa., Baltimore, Md., Annapolis, MD." The center theme is bracketed by springs of daisy-like blossoms and leaves. The exterior carries the familiar wide panel design and a rayed base. The predominant color is amethyst.

# *I*vy

This cute little souvenir wine has the same stem and base design as Fenton's small Orange Tree compote so we are sure it came from that factory. It is found in both the wine and claret size with various advertisements. Marigold is the only color I've seen, but certainly others may have been made.

# *J*ack-in-the-Pulpit (Dugan)

Besides the Northwood version of this vase, Dugan had a try at it too, and here is their version. It's a bit plainer and isn't nearly as pretty without the footing, but it does come in several colors and adds a pleasant touch of color and artistry.

***Isaac Benesch Bowl***

***Ivy***

***Jack-in-the-Pulpit (Dugan)***

147

*Jack-in-the-Pulpit*
*(Northwood)*

*Jacobean Ranger*

*Jackman Whiskey*

*Jacob's Ladder Variant (U.S. Glass)*

## *Jack-in-the-Pulpit (Northwood)*

While both Dugan and Fenton made Jack-in-the-Pulpit vases, the one shown is a Northwood pattern and is so marked. It stands 8¼" tall and has an exterior ribbing. Colors known are marigold, purple, green, aqua opalescent, and white, but others may exist.

## *Jackman Whiskey*

Much like its cousin, the Golden Wedding bottle, this was designed to hold whiskey for commercial sale. It is scarcer than the former and generally has better iridescence. The maker is unknown.

## *Jacobean Ranger*

Found in several shapes including pitchers, tumblers in three sizes, bowls of various sizes, a stemmed wine, and decanter, this very attractive pattern has been reported first to have come from England and then from Czechoslovakia. The examples I've seen have all been an outstanding marigold with excellent mold work.

## *Jacob's Ladder Variant (U.S. Glass)*

Besides the Jacob's Ladder perfume, I've heard of this rose bowl shape in the variant and nothing else. Just why more shapes haven't surfaced, I don't know, for the pattern is interesting and well done. The only color is a good marigold.

# Jelly Jar

For years I found the lids to these Imperial jelly jars in shops and thought they were late carnival glass "coasters," but a few years back, I saw the two parts put together and was really quite surprised at what I saw. The jar itself is 3" wide and 2¾" tall and of deep, well iridized marigold. All the pattern is interior, so when the jar was upended onto the lid, a design was formed in the jelly. The lid itself also carries an interior design of spokes and an exterior one of a many-rayed star. Again, here is a true rarity, well within any collector's range.

# Jester's Cap

Called Northwood's Jester's Cap by Marian Hartung, this interesting pattern is actually a product of Westmoreland. The design is much like the Corinth pattern and features twelve ribs running the length of the vase. The top is flared and pulled up on one side, giving the pattern its name. Colors are amethyst, marigold, green, blue, white, peach opalescent, and a very pretty aqua blue over milk glass.

# Jeweled Heart

Carried over from the pressed glass era, Jeweled Heart is, of course, the famous exterior pattern of the Farmyard bowl. However, Dugan used it as a primary pattern on very scarce water sets when the pitcher is footed – an uncommon shape for water pitchers in carnival glass. I have seen Jeweled Heart in purple, peach, and marigold, but other colors may exist. If so, they would be considered ultra-rare. A tumbler is reported in white, but I haven't seen it.

# Jewels

Both Imperial and Dugan-Diamond made similar products in this very pretty finish of high gloss iridization with stretch finish. The colors are many as are the shapes, but the example shown is a patented shape by Dugan called a candle bowl, dating to 1924. It can be found in a color called Vesuvius blue, white, and amber, as well as the green shown.

*Jelly Jar*

*Jester's Cap*

*Jeweled Heart*

*Jewels*

*Jockey Club*

*J.R. Millner Co.,*
*Lynchburg, Va.*

*Kangaroo*

*Keyhole (Dugan)*

## Jockey Club

Although very much akin to the Good Luck pattern, Northwood's Jockey Club is certainly a separate pattern and a quick once-over will establish this fact. The floral arrangements are entirely different, even the horseshoe and riding crop are not the same. Jockey Club is found on trademarked bowls which carry the Northwood Basketweave as an exterior pattern. The ones I'm familiar with have been on a good amethyst glass, well iridized.

## J.R. Millner Co., Lynchburg, Va.

This rare tumbler has the advertising on the base and is a beautiful honey amber. The lettering says: "J.R. Millner Co., Lynchburg, Va." The tumbler pattern is, of course, Cosmos and Cane by U.S. Glass and can be found in white without the advertising as well as marigold. All are scarce but the advertising example is considered rare.

## Kangaroo

This beautiful Australian pattern typifies the quality of the Crystal Glass Factory. Known in large and small bowls, in marigold and purple, Kangaroo has the Wild Fern pattern as its exterior. There is a variant.

## Keyhole (Dugan)

Used as the exterior pattern on Raindrop bowls, this Dugan secondary pattern is much more interesting than the one it complements. Colors are marigold, amethyst, and peach opalescent.

**Keystone Colonial (Westmoreland)**

## Keystone Colonial (Westmoreland)

At least three of these have been reported, all with the Keystone trademark containing a "W." They stand 6¼" tall and are very much like the Chippendale pattern compotes credited to Jefferson Glass. The only color I've seen is a very dark purple.

## Kingfisher

Like many of the other "bird patterns" from down under, this nice Australian bowl has both the animal and flora shown. Kingfisher has a stippled aura, a registration number, and comes in large and small bowls.

## Kingfisher Variant

The primary difference between this and the regular Australian Kingfisher pattern is the addition of a wreath of wattle. Both marigold and purple are found.

## King's Crown (U.S. Glass)

In crystal and ruby flashed glass, this pattern can be found in many shapes, but this is the only piece in carnival glass I've ever heard about. It is a dainty wine goblet in good marigold and very, very rare indeed.

**King's Crown
(U.S. Glass)**

**Kingfisher Variant**

**Kingfisher**

151

*Kitten Paperweight*

*Kittens*

*Knotted Beads*

*Kiwi*

## Kitten Paperweight

This slight bit of glass is a rare miniature heretofore unreported in any of the pattern books on carnival glass. Its coloring, as you can see, is a good even marigold, and the iridization is well applied. In size, it is much like the 3" long Bulldog paperweight. The Kitten paperweight is truly a rare little item.

## Kittens

For many years this Fenton pattern has been a favorite of collectors and the Kittens pieces rise steadily in price and popularity. This is a child's pattern and is known in bowls, cup and saucer, banana bowl, spooner, plate, vase, and a very rare spittoon whimsey. Colors are marigold, vaseline, and cobalt blue.

## Kiwi

This very odd bird is a native of New Zealand. This Australian bowl shows two of them with a mountain range in the background and a border of fine fern branches. Colors are a fine purple and marigold.

## Knotted Beads

In many ways this is a combination of the April Showers and the Diamond and Rib vase pattern for the tiny grouping are gathered into pulled ovals. I know of examples of Knotted Beads in marigold, blue, green, white, and vaseline, and sizes range from 4" to 12" in height. A Fenton product.

*Kokomo*

# Kokomo
In England this pattern has come to be called Geometric but it has long been known in America with the Kokomo name. The most unusual feature of the design is the three odd feet that are angled into a blockish finish. The bowl's design seems to consist of sections of file, cut stars, and odd prisms. The only shape is the rose bowl. It was made by Sowerby.

# Kookaburra
Familiar to the Kingfisher pattern, the Australian Kookaburra has an upper edging of flannel flower, wattle, and two large groups of waratah flowers flanking a flannel flower blossom.

# Kookaburra Variant
In this Australian variant the obvious differences are the fine large waratah flowers around the stippled circle, and, of course, the edging is a bullet rim pattern.

*Kookaburra*

*Kookaburra Variant*

153

*Lacy Dewdrop*

**Late Enameled
Bleeding Hearts**

**Late Enameled
Grape**

**Late Enameled
Strawberry**

**Late Waterlily**

# *L*acy Dewdrop

There seems to be some very disturbing questions about the origins of this pattern, but currently most collectors believe the iridized pearl pieces were made by Phoenix Glass in the 1930's rather than Westmoreland. So, I'll accept that until more information is available. It was made in water sets, covered compotes, covered bowls, and a banana bowl as well as a table set.

# *L*ate Enameled Bleeding Hearts

Again we show a tall tumbler that many call a vase. It has a light airy iridization and delicate white and colored enameled flowers. Like most items with this finish, the Enameled Bleeding Hearts tumbler came along fairly late.

# *L*ate Enameled Grape

Like so many items made near the end of carnival glass popularity this cute goblet has a light airy luster, but the bold white enameling of leaves and grapes are the real attraction. The goblet stands only 4½" tall and I have seen a very similar tall tumbler called Late Strawberry in the Whitley book.

# *L*ate Enameled Strawberry

Very similar to the same pattern shown in the Whitley book, this example, a lemonade glass, has only one roll of glass above the bulging base while the Whitley example has three rolls. The coloring is light, and the enamel work is all white.

# *L*ate Waterlily

For one of the later patterns in carnival glass, this certainly is a good one. The coloring is superior, the shape symmetrical, and the design of cattails and waterlilies attractive.

# Lattice and Daisy

Most often seen on marigold water sets, Dugan's Lattice and Daisy was also made on very scarce berry sets. The other colors known are cobalt blue and white, but I certainly would not rule out green or amethyst, especially on the water sets.

# Lattice and Grape

If you examine the shape of this Fenton water set, you'll find it is almost identical to that of the Grapevine Lattice water set, but Lattice and Grape is distinctive in its own right. The mold work is very good, and the design appealing. Available in a rare spittoon whimsey pulled from a tumbler in addition to water sets, Lattice and Grape is found in marigold, cobalt blue, green, amethyst, peach opalescent, and white.

# Lattice and Leaves

Much like the Footed Prism Panels vase, the Lattice and Leaves vase stands 9½" tall from a dome foot. It has been found in both deep blue and the stunning marigold shown, both with superior iridization. I suspect it to be a Sowerby product from England.

# Lattice and Points

Distinctive for its latticework as well as the flame design above the base and the distinct cable separating the two, this Dugan pattern is one known in marigold, amethyst, and white. Pressed into the bottom is the daisy design often found on the Vining Twigs bowl and indeed the Lattice and Points vase was pulled from the same mold.

# Laurel and Grape

I know very little about this previously unreported pattern except that it is a vase shape and stands 7" tall. The design, a cluster of grapes inside a laurel wreath is a nice one and reminds me of the English Grape and Cherry pattern. Marigold is the only reported color.

*Lattice and Leaves*

*Lattice and Daisy*

*Lattice and Grape*

*Lattice and Points*

*Laurel and Grape*

*Laurel Band*

*Laurel Leaves*

*LBJ Hat*

*Lea*

## *Laurel Band*

While the dome-base tumblers are seen frequently in this late pattern, the pitcher shown is a find and seldom finds its way out of collections. The pitcher measures 8" tall and has a 4" dome base while the tumbler stands 4⅞" tall. The only color reported is a strong marigold.

## *Laurel Leaves*

While Mrs. Hartung showed this pattern in a round plate, here is an eight-sided one. The pattern is on the exterior, and while the design will never win any awards, the color is rich, and the iridization is good. It is well known in marigold, green, and amethyst.

## *LBJ Hat*

This late carnival ashtray has been called this for the last few years. It has a diameter of 6¼" and stands 3" tall. While not in the class of a Cleveland Memorial ashtray, it is an attractive specimen of iridized glass.

## *Lea*

Found in a handled pickle dish, a footed creamer, and a footed bowl that can be in various shapes, Lea and the Lea variants are patterns produced by the Sowerby company. Most examples are marigold, but I have heard of an amethyst creamer.

156

*Leaf and Beads*

## Leaf and Beads

Here is another very well-known Northwood pattern found not only in carnival glass, but clear and opalescent glass as well. Available on bowls as well as rose bowls, the twig feet are used by more than one carnival glassmaker. However, the trademark is usually present. Leaf and Beads is found in a wide range of colors including marigold, green, purple, ice green, ice blue, and white.

## Leaf and Beads Variant

Here is the variant bowl on a dome base, and as you can see, the design is not so strong as the regular Leaf and Beads. These seem to be found mostly in green, as shown, but marigold and amethyst are known. It is marked Northwood. The shape is considered a nut bowl by many collectors.

## Leaf and Little Flowers

This little Millersburg cutie is rather unique, not only in size but also in design. The four free-floating blooms arc similar to those on the Little Stars design, but the four large prickly-edged leaves with a center cross blossom is unique. It seems cactus-like. Just 3" tall, the Leaf and Little Flowers compote has an octagon-shaped base and has been seen in amethyst, green, and rarely marigold.

*Leaf and Beads Variant*

*Leaf and Little Flowers*

*Leaf Chain*

## Leaf Chain

Very close to Cherry Chain in design, Fenton's Leaf Chain is more commonly found, indicating it was made in larger amounts. Known in bowls, plates, and bonbons. Leaf Chain was made in a wide variety of colors including marigold, cobalt blue, green, amethyst, white, vaseline, lavender, smoke, aqua, and red. The mold work is quite good and the finish above average.

## Leaf Column

While not a spectacular pattern, here is a Northwood vase that takes on new importance on second glance. It is a well-balanced allover pattern that does the job nicely. The iridescence, especially on the dark colors, is quite nice. The shape is attractive, and the vase is, of course, a very useful item. Certainly any collection of carnival glass would benefit by adding one of these.

## Leaf Rays

Found mostly on a one-handled, spade-shaped nappy, this Dugan pattern was also made in the ruffled version. Colors are marigold, peach opalescent, amethyst, green, blue, white, and clear.

## Leaf Swirl

I've always liked this Westmoreland compote, because it has such a good design and is so well balanced. The lines and leaves swirl upward from the base in six strong panels. Colors are marigold, deep purple, amethyst, lavender, amber, and a pretty teal blue. The compote is 5" tall and can be either opened widely or almost goblet shaped.

*Leaf Column*

*Leaf Swirl*

*Leaf Rays*

## Leaf Swirl and Flower

What a beautifully graceful vase this is. It appears to be a Fenton product, stands 8" tall, and has a trail of etched leaves and flowers around the body. I'd guess it was made in marigold and pastels, too but can't be sure.

## Leaf Tiers

For some reason, this pattern is difficult to locate. Apparently it was not made in large quantities, although it was made in usable shapes, including berry sets, table sets, and water sets. The twig feet were used by both Fenton and Northwood to some degree, and while Leaf Tiers is mostly seen in marigold, very scarce water sets in purple, green, and blue are known. A Fenton product.

## Lightning Flower

This very rare Northwood pattern, shown on a handled nappy, was shared by Fred and Cathy Roque. The pattern is exterior with an inside design of poppies that reminds me of the Imperial Pansy bowl. There are several narrow rings around the scalloped rim, and the color is good. Rose Presznick reports the Lightning Flower pattern on compotes and plates as well, but neither have been confirmed.

## Lightolier Luster and Clear Shade

This very collectible shade is 5½" tall and measures 5" across. The panels are on the interior and the outside is smooth. It was a product of Lightolier Company and has, as you can see, very strong iridization.

*Leaf Swirl and Flower*

*Lightolier Luster and Clear Shade*

*Leaf Tiers*

*Lightning Flower*

*Lily of the Valley*

*Lined Lattice*

# Lily of the Valley

Personally, I feel this is the very best of all Fenton water sets, and the price this rare pattern commands bears me out. Aside from being beautiful, Lily of the Valley is an imaginative pattern. Found only in cobalt blue and marigold, Lily of the Valley would have made a beautiful table set pattern.

# Lined Lattice

From Dugan-Diamond, this very pretty vase shape with the odd feet-projections was originally an opalescent pattern called Palisades. carnival colors are marigold, amethyst, blue, green, peach opalescent, white, and the very odd example shown of flint opalescent with a marigold carnival interior!

# Lion

Someone at the Fenton factory had to be an animal lover for more animal patterns were born there than at any other carnival glass factory in America. The Lion pattern is a nice one, rather scarce and available in bowls and plates. The colors are marigold and blue in the bowls, but I've seen only marigold in the rare plates.

*Lion*

*Little Barrel*

## Little Barrel

Most collectors acknowledge these small containers as being Imperial Glass products. They are rumored to have held liquid samples of some sort, and some have been found with paper labels attached. Colors are marigold, amber, green, and smoke and all are desirable. They stand just under 4" tall.

## Little Beads

Made by the Westmoreland Company, this odd little pattern is seen mostly on peach opal, but the example shown has an aqua base glass. It measures 2" tall and 5½" across and has a 2½" base.

## Little Daisies

Made by Fenton, this very pretty pattern was made in small amounts, for few examples seem to be around today. Found only in bowls, colors known are marigold and blue. The daisy design covers most of the interior, the outside is plain.

*Little Beads*

*Little Daisies*

161

*Little Fishes*

*Little Flowers*

*Little Stars*

## Little Fishes

A close comparison with the Coral pattern will reveal many similarities to this pattern. Little Fishes can be found in large or small bowls, both flat based and footed, and in rare plates that measure about 9". Colors are marigold, blue, green, amethyst, aqua, vaseline, amber, ice green, and white, which is rather rare.

## Little Flowers

Here's another pattern once felt to be Millersburg but now known to be a Fenton product. Little Flowers is found in berry sets and two sizes of rare plates in marigold, green, blue amethyst, amber, aqua, vaseline, and red.

## Little Stars

I've found this Millersburg pattern a bit difficult to locate and don't believe many of these bowls are around. The amethyst ones are especially nice, but green and marigold exist. Also a larger size is known as is the plate shape in green. Shown is a rare blue bowl.

*Loganberry*

## Loganberry

Despite the reproduction of this impressive vase in the 1960s, Imperial's Loganberry has remained one of the collector's favorites. The vase is 10" tall and has a base diameter of 3¾". There are four mold marks. The colors found are green, marigold, amber, smoke, and purple with the latter the hardest to find. Of course, the quality of design and the beautiful luster make this a real treasure.

## Long Buttress

Made in many shapes in crystal and often mistaken for a similar pattern called Portland (I did), Long Buttress can be found in iridized glass in tumblers, a water pitcher, and large and small berry bowls. Iridization may range from a good marigold to a frosty clambroth. Long Buttress is a Fostoria pattern and dates to 1904.

## Long Hobstar

Imperial was famous for nearcut designs, and Long Hobstar is a prime example of their skills. Shown in a very rare punch bowl and base (no cups known), Long Hobstar can also be found in bowls and a beautiful bride's basket. The colors are marigold, smoke, green, and occasionally purple.

*Long Buttress*

*Long Hobstar*

**Long Thumbprint**

**Louisa**

**Lotus and Grape**

**Lotus Land**

## Long Thumbprint

Found in bowls, compotes, creamers, sugars, and vases, this Dugan pattern has little going for it design-wise, but sometimes it is quite nice when the coloring is as good as on the vase shown. Colors are mostly marigold, but amethyst, blue, and green are occasionally found, and I've seen the breakfast pieces in a smoky marigold and the vase in peach opalescent.

## Lotus and Grape

Please note the similarities between this pattern and Fenton's Water Lily and Two Flowers. All have a feeling of the small ponds once so much a part of backyard garden displays. Lotus and Grape is found on bonbons, flat or footed bowls, and rare plates in colors of marigold, green, blue, amethyst, white, and red.

## Lotus Land

What a privilege to show this very rare bonbon, generous in size (8¼" across) and rich in design. From its stippled center flower to the whimsical outer flowers, the pattern is one you won't soon forget. Amethyst is the only reported color on the few examples.

## Louisa

Louisa is a very pretty, well designed floral pattern that seems perfectly suited for the rose bowl shape shown. Also known on footed candy dishes and a rare footed plate (all from the same mold), Louisa is found in marigold, green, blue, amethyst, and the rare deep amber called horehound. This is by Westmoreland.

## Lovely

Lovely is a seldom-seen interior pattern found on footed bowls with Leaf and Beads as an exterior pattern. While we can't be certain, it is possible this motif was added at the Dugan factory, since shards of Leaf and Beads were found there. The colors seen, thus far, are green, marigold and purple with very good iridescence.

## Lucille

Seldom seen, I've long believed this set to be new glass, but after learning what John Britt had to say about it, I have become a believer. The water set shown is a beautiful cobalt blue and tumblers are known in marigold. Brochwitz Glass of Germany is reputed to be the maker, but I can't confirm this.

## Lustre and Clear

Shown is the handled creamer in this pattern, and I've seen the matching sugar also. Other shapes reported are a berry set, covered butter dish, a water set, and table shakers. Found mostly in marigold, the creamer and sugar are known in purple. The pattern is all interior and the outside plain.

## Lustre Flute

Again we have a very familiar pattern to most collectors, but one that is not really too distinguished. I suppose not every pattern should be expected to be spectacular. The shape I've seen most often is the hat shape in both green and marigold, but punch sets, berry sets, breakfast sets, bonbons, nappies, and compotes do exist in marigold, green, and purple. The base is many rayed and usually the Northwood trademark is present.

*Lovely*

*Lucille*

*Lustre and Clear*

*Lustre Flute*

*Lustre Rose*

*Maday and Co.*

*Magpie*

*Maize*

# Lustre Rose

Aside from Imperial's Grape or Pansy patterns, this is probably their biggest seller in the early years. It was made in berry sets, table sets, water sets, plates, fruit bowls, and a beautiful fernery in colors of marigold, green, purple, cobalt, amber, smoke, and clambroth. Reproduction has devalued this beautiful pattern, but the old pieces are still outstanding examples of glassmaking with superb craftsmanship and color.

# Maday and Co.

This quite rare advertising bowl is found as the exterior of Fenton's Wild Blackberry 8½" bowl. The only colors known to date are amethyst and green, while the normal bowls are primarily found in green and marigold. The advertising reads "H. Maday and Co. 1910."

# Magpie

The magpie is a different bird altogether, and the one shown on this Australian bowl is probably a New Zealand parson bird. The flowers are typical flannel flowers and wattle.

# Maize

Made by the Libby Glass company, this famous pattern can be found in several types of glass including custard. The example shown is clear with pastel blue staining on the husks and a soft iridescence over the rest of the piece. Shapes in the carnival treatment are rare and include the cruet or syrup shown, a celery vase, and a 9" pitcher. All have the blue husks and a very rare tumbler also turns up with this treatment.

***Mallard Duck***

# Majestic

This is a well-designed tumbler made by the McKee Glass company and is very rare. It is 3⅞" tall and has a 24-point star on the base. The design features double fans that enclose a four-section block. Majestic items can also be found in crystal and ruby stained glass.

# Malaga

Malaga is rather difficult pattern to find, indicating production must have been small on this Dugan design. What a pity for the allover grape pattern is a good one with imaginative detail throughout. Found only on large bowls and plates, I've heard of marigold, amber, and purple only, but green is a strong possibility.

# Mallard Duck

I certainly wish I knew more about this rare item, but it's the only true carnival one I've seen. I believe these were made by Tiffin (mostly in milk glass), and I once saw an example with applied ruby luster. However, I can say with assurance the one shown is old, has been in one of the country's major collections for years, and is a prized rarity of the owner. The coloring is a beautiful clambroth with fiery blue and pink highlights.

# Many Fruits

This is a truly lovely fruit pattern, something that any company would be proud to claim. The mold work is heavy and distinct, the design is interesting and quite realistic, and the coloration flawless. I personally prefer the ruffled base, but that is a small matter. This Dugan pattern would have made a beautiful water set. The colors are marigold, blue, white, purple, and green.

***Majestic***

***Malaga***

***Many Fruits***

*Many Stars*

*Maple Leaf*

*Marilyn*

*Martec*

168

# Many Stars

Which came first – the chicken or the egg? Or in this case, the Many Stars or the Bernheimer bowl? For they are exactly the same except for the center design where in the former a large star replaces the advertising. These bowls are generous in size and can be found in amethyst, green, marigold, and blue. The green is often a light, airy shade just a bit darker than an ice green and is very attractive when found with a gold iridescence. Millersburg manufactured this pattern.

# Maple Leaf

Maple Leaf is a carry-over pattern from the custard glass line, but in carnival glass is limited to stemmed berry sets, table sets, and water sets. I examined shards of this pattern from the Dugan dump site, so items in carnival glass were obviously turned out at that factory. The background is the same Soda Gold pattern as that found on the exterior of Garden Path bowls and plates. Maple Leaf was made in marigold, purple, cobalt blue, and green. The secondary pattern on the berry set pieces is Peacock Tail.

# Marilyn

This water set pattern is probably one of the most unusual and outstanding in the field of carnival glass. First look at the pitcher's shape. Notice the unusual upper edging, so different from those of other companies. Then there is the drooping pouring lip so favored by the Millersburg Company. The finish is, of course, the fine radium look, and the glass is heavy. All in all, a real prize for any collector.

# Martec

Another McKee pattern in the Tec series like Aztec, this nice pattern has only been found in the tumbler in carnival glass. It stands 4" tall and is marked "Prescut." The design is geometric with two major hobstar variations.

*Martha*

# Martha

Rose Presznick named this large compote-shaped piece because she said she saw one engraved with that name. It looks English but I have no proof of that. I do know it isn't often seen and in 20 years this is the first one I've had a chance to show. The compote has a 7½" top diameter and stands 4½" tall, and the base is slightly over 4½" also.

# Mary Ann

I don't believe I've heard of another one of these loving cups in collections I'm familiar with, and yet I've always known these existed. As you can see, they are much different from the vase shape, having three handles and no scalloping around the top edge or base. Of course, it is quite rare, and it is a real pleasure to show it here. The Mary Ann vase is Dugan.

*Massachusetts (U.S. Glass)*

*Mary Ann*

# Massachusetts (U.S. Glass)

While the vase shape shown is the only shape I've heard about in this very attractive pattern, I'd bet it was made in a creamer and sugar as well. It is found only in marigold and brings a good price when sold, for it is a scarce and desirable item.

# Mayan

Always one of my favorites this Millersburg bowl pattern is usually found in ice-cream shapes in green that tends toward olive, but a recent find has been a very rare marigold bowl that is ruffled. The design of six feather-plumes that radiate from a large beaded center is quite distinctive.

*Mayan*

*May Basket*

*Mayflower (Millersburg)*

*Mayflower Shade*

# May Basket

This beautiful basket is called Diamond and Fleur de Lis by Mrs. Presznick. It was made by Davisons of Gateshead and has a diameter of 7½" and is 6" tall. Can you imagine how difficult it was to remove this beautiful novelty from the mold? May Basket was made in marigold and has been reported in smoke.

# Mayflower (Millersburg)

Found with the rare Millersburg Grape Leaves bowl, Mayflower is a series of flower-like designs, separated by eight diamond and near-cut sections. Held to the light, the effect is a real surprise through the Grape design. Colors are marigold, green, amethyst, and vaseline, and every one is rare.

# Mayflower Shade

This very attractive shade was named many years ago by Marion Hartung, who also listed bowls, nappies, and compotes in the same pattern. In design it is much like the Four-Seventy-Four pattern by Imperial and I suspect there is some confusion about the two patterns over the years. At any rate, the coloring is quite good and a fine stippling on the surface holds the iridescence well.

*Meander (Northwood)*

# Meander (Northwood)

Here's the exterior of the gorgeous Three Fruits Medallion bowl shown elsewhere, and as you can see, the glass is truly black amethyst and has no iridizing on the exterior. The pattern of Meander, however, is a good design and very complimentary.

# Melon Rib

Another pattern credited to Imperial, Melon Rib can be found on water sets, candy jars, salt and pepper shakers, and a covered powder jar, all in marigold. As you can see, the pitcher is tall, stately, and very pretty.

# Memphis

While an interesting geometrical pattern, Northwood's Memphis has never been one of my favorites possibly because of its limited shapes. I can imagine how much my interest would increase if a water set were to appear! I have seen an enormous banquet punch set in crystal, but the size was not made in carnival glass. The shapes are a berry set, punch set, fruit bowl on separate stand, and a compote. The colors found are both vivid and pastel.

# Mexican Bell

Similar to the Swirled Threads goblet shown elsewhere, this pretty goblet has a pale green base glass with a strong marigold iridescence over the bowl. The glass is rather thin and the stem has a large globe shape separating the bowl from the base.

*Melon Rib*

*Mexican Bell*

*Memphis*

*Mikado*

*Milady*

**Miniature Blackberry Compote**

*Miniature Hobnail Cordial Set*

# Mikado

Called giant compotes, these beautiful 8½" tall fruit stands have two outstanding patterns – cherries on the exterior and the beautiful Mikado on the inside of the bowl. This design consists of a center medallion of stippled rays around which are three large chrysanthemums and three Oriental scroll devices. The colors are marigold, blue, a rare green, and a very rare red. Mikado was made by Fenton.

# Milady

Again, we show one of the better water sets by the Fenton Company. The pitcher is a tankard size, and the design is paneled with very artistic blossoms and stems with graceful leaves. Colors most seen are marigold and blue, but scarce green and a rare amethyst do exist.

# Miniature Blackberry Compote

This little Fenton cutie is most often seen on blue or marigold and is quite scarce in either color. The white one shown is very rare. Standing only 2½" high with a bowl diameter of 4⅛", this miniature or jelly compote would be a treasure in any collection and certainly would highlight a compote grouping.

# Miniature Hobnail Cordial Set

What a nice little set this is! Probably from Europe, it is the only one about which I've heard. The decanter stands 8" tall to the top of its stopper and, needless to say, the set is quite a rare item.

*Miniature Loving Cup*

# Miniature Loving Cup

Many collectors have a weakness for miniatures and the one shown here would bring joy to any of them. It stands 3½" tall and measures 3" from handle to handle. The color is strong and the iridescence good.

# Miniature Rose Bowl

Sometimes called a Bubble Bowl, this thin piece is 4" high and 4" wide. These probably came in several sizes and perhaps other colors. This one has a very rich marigold finish and would grace any collection.

# Miniature Urn

Like the other miniatures shown, this piece relies on its smallness and omits any design other than the shape. It stands 3" tall, has a width of 1½", and the glass is very thin. Color and iridescence are super.

*Miniature Urn*

*Miniature Rose Bowl*

# Mirrored Lotus

Here is a Fenton pattern that is quite scarce, especially in some colors. Found mostly on 7" ruffled bowls in blue, green, marigold, or white, it is also known on the rare ice-cream shaped 7" bowl in celeste blue, a rare plate in the same color, and a rare white rose bowl.

# Mirrored Peacocks

For some reason, I'm very excited by the design of this tall tumbler. It is reputed to have come from either Finland or Czechoslovakia and has a very whimsical touch. The design, two large, stylized peacocks stand over several ram-like figures!

*Mirrored Lotus*

*Mirrored Peacocks*

*Mitered Diamonds and Pleats*

*Mitered Ovals*

*Moderne*

*Moonprint*

# Mitered Diamonds and Pleats

This British pattern is most often seen as shown, a 4½" handled sauce dish, but I've seen 8½" bowls. Mrs. Presznick reports a tray in 10" size as well. The coloring is top notch marigold, but a smoky blue shade has been reported.

# Mitered Ovals

This beautiful vase is a Millersburg product. It is a rare item seldom found for sale. The colors seen are amethyst, green, and very rarely marigold. In size it is outstanding, being some 10½" tall. The mold work is superior.

# Moderne

I've named this cute cup and saucer the very first name that entered my head, but it seems to fit. I'd guess it is fairly late carnival, but it still has good coloring and a nice luster.

# Moonprint

Here is one of the prettiest of all English carnival patterns. The shapes are a banana bowl, covered jar, vase, covered butter, covered cheese-keeper, compote, milk pitcher, creamer, and bowls that range in size from 8" to 15". Marigold is the basic color with a super finish. I've heard of a peach opalescent covered jar but cannot confirm its existence. I'd guess Sowerby made this pattern.

# Morning Glory

If there is one water set that stands above all others in sheer beauty, this Millersburg pattern is surely it. Almost 14" tall, the pitcher is stately. It has heavily raised morning glory vines around its center and the applied handle has been shaped to resemble a leaf where it joins the pitcher. The matching tumbler is 3¾" tall and has a rayed base. The glass is sparkling clear, the radium finish is excellent, and the mold work impressive. Along with the Gay 90s, the Morning Glory water set has to be near the top of anyone's list.

# Morning Glory Vase

Several companies made similar vases with the flaring top resembling morning glories, but the one shown happens to come from Imperial and is a whopping 17" tall. The color is fabulous! I've seen these as small as 5" and every size between, in several colors including marigold, smoke, green, blue amethyst, white, ice green, teal, aqua, and even one in a strange pale blue and marigold combination.

# Mt. Gambier Mug

I can't be sure this mug is Australian, but this one comes from there. It is etched "Greetings from Mt. Gambier." The color is a good rich marigold.

# Moxie Bottle

I normally avoid the bottle cycle unless they are as attractive as this well-designed scarcity. The coloring is obviously a very frosty white with heavy luster, and the design of plain and stippled diamonds is a good one. Moxie was a soft drink that went out of favor in the mid 1920s.

*Morning Glory*

*Morning Glory Vase*

*Moxie Bottle*

*Mt. Gambier Mug*

175

*Multi-Fruits and Flowers*

*Muscadine*

*Mystic*

*My Lady's Powder Box*

# Multi-Fruits and Flowers

Grape clusters, leaves, blossoms, cherries, peaches, and pears! What an imaginative collection to grace beautiful lustered glass! This fantastic Millersburg pattern is seen mostly on punch sets of medium size, but here is a very scarce water set and a stemmed fruit goblet or compote. The base of the punch set can double as a compote when up-ended and is iridized inside and out.

# Muscadine

Almost a twin to the Beaded Panels and Grapes tumbler, the Muscadine has a band of geometric squares-within-squares and diamonds-within-diamonds instead of a band of grapes and leaves. Again we have a pattern made in Czechoslovakia for export. The color is marigold, and the tumbler stands 5⅛" tall.

# My Lady's Powder Box

Here is a favorite with collectors and a good price is always assured when one of these sell. Found only in marigold of a good rich quality, the powder jar stands 5½" tall and has a base diameter of 3¼". The figure on the lid is of solid glass. I suspect Davisons is the manufacturer but have no proof.

# Mystic

I named this 7" vase. So if anyone knows it by another name, I'd be happy to hear from them. The design of elongated shields separated by a hobstar and file filler is interesting. The very mellow coloring reminds me of other Cambridge products, and that is just who made it, according to a 1908 advertisement.

# Nautilus

It is a shame there aren't more shapes of this pattern in carnival glass, because every piece of the custard is a joy. In carnival we find only the small novelty piece described as a boat shape. (Actually one large footed berry bowl has been seen in marigold – a very, very rare piece of carnival glass!) It appears with either both ends turned up or one end turned down, and the colors are peach and purple. A Dugan product from old Northwood molds.

# Near-Cut

This attractive Northwood pattern is quite similar to the Hobstar Flower shown elsewhere in this book. In addition to the compote and goblet made from the same mold, there is a very rare water pitcher. I have heard of no tumblers, but they may exist. The colors are marigold and purple with the latter most seen. A rare green compote is known also.

# Near-Cut Decanter

What a triumph of near-cut design this rare Cambridge pattern is! Standing 11" tall, this beauty is found in a sparkling green, but I wouldn't rule out amethyst or marigold as possibilities. The mold work is some of the best, and the finish is equal to any from the Millersburg plant.

# Nesting Swan

This pattern has become one of the most sought Millersburg bowl patterns, and it is certainly easy to see why. The graceful swan, nesting on a bed of reeds, surrounded by leaves, blossoms, and cattails is a very interesting design. The detail is quite good, and the color and finish exceptional. The beautiful Diamond and Fan exterior contrasts nicely and echoes the fine workmanship throughout. In addition to the beautiful green, marigold, and amethyst, Nesting Swan can be found in a beautiful honey-amber shade and a very rare blue.

*Nautilus*

*Near-Cut*

*Near-Cut Decanter*

*Nesting Swan*

177

*New Orleans Champagne*

*Night Stars*

*Nippon*

## New Orleans Champagne

Like the other champagnes from U.S. Glass, this version is on clear iridized glass with the design areas hand painted. The alligators along the sides are quite unique in carnival glass, and the crowned and bearded man represents Rex, King of the Mardi Gras. I really can't think of anything more fitting for a piece of carnival glass.

## Night Stars

What a rare little beauty this Millersburg pattern is! Found on the bonbon shape shown in an unusual olive green, marigold, and amethyst. It has also been seen in a very rare card tray in amethyst and vaseline and an equally rare spade-shaped nappy in amethyst only. All shapes and colors are rare and desirable, so never pass one up.

## Nippon

Certainly Nippon must have been a popular pattern in its heyday, for it is readily found today. The pattern is simple but effective; it is a central stylized blossom with panels of drapery extending toward the outer edges of the bowl. Found in a wide variety of colors, including marigold, green, blue, purple, ice green, ice blue, and white. This Northwood is a nice pattern to own.

*Northern Star*

# Northern Star

I have some misgivings about this being a Fenton pattern, but since it is listed as such by a noted glass author, I will consider it one. Shown is the 6" card tray, but Northern Star can also be found on a ruffled mint dish, small bowls, and plates, all in marigold. The design is all on the exterior, and both outside and inside are iridized.

# Nu-Art (Homestead)

If you will take a few moments to compare this Imperial pattern with the Double Dutch found elsewhere in this book, you will find very similar designs, probably done by the same artist. The Nu-Art plate, however, is a rarer, more important design that sells for many times the amount of a Double Dutch bowl. Found in many colors including marigold, green, purple, smoke, amber, white, ice green, and the rare cobalt blue, the Nu-Art plate is sometimes signed. It measures 10½" across and has been reproduced.

*Nu-Art (Homestead)*

# Nu-Art Chrysanthemum

Apparently the popularity of the regular Nu-Art plate prompted this, a sister design of striking beauty. Also 10½" in diameter, the Chrysanthemum plate has the same Greek key border device. The flowers are very graceful and heavily raised, and of course, the iridescence is outstanding. I've seen this plate in marigold, smoke, amber, green, clambroth, and purple, but other colors may exist. Again, this pattern was reproduced in the 1960s. This was produced by Imperial.

*Nu-Art Chrysanthemum*

179

*Nu-Art Drape Shade*

*Nugget Beads*

#4

#5

### Nu-Art Drape Shade

Made by the Imperial Company, this very attractive shade has a design that is all interior. It is 5" tall and has a bell spread of 5½". The color and iridescence is super and the drapes all have tiny stitching lines, showing fine mold work.

### Nugget Beads

Here is another string of carnival beads, but much more impressive than the set shown elsewhere in this book. The stringing includes gold spacers, regular iridized beads, and graduated nugget-shaped chunks. The coloring is a very rich amethyst.

### #4

Made first in crystal, like so many Imperial patterns, this is a rather simple, not too impressive pattern found on compotes as well as small footed bowls. The colors are usually marigold or smoke, but I've seen it in clear carnival as well as green.

### #5

This pattern dates from the early days of the Imperial Company and was first issued in crystal. The shapes known are a celery holder, 6" tall, and the beautiful dome-footed bowl shown, where the pattern is exterior. The color most encountered is marigold, but, as you can see, the bowl is a rich amber.

#9

**#9** This little Imperial cutie is very nice, especially when found on a rich smoky color with golden highlights. Of course, it is also known on marigold, and I suspect green is a possibility. While the pattern is relatively simple – a series of arches filled with small hexagonal buttons – it is quite effective. Sometimes called Tulip and Cane, #9 is also found in wine, claret, and goblet shapes.

**#270** Made by the Westmoreland Company, this little open-stemmed bowl is found in amber, peach opalescent milk glass, as well as, the aqua color shown. It is a simple but effective pattern well worth collecting.

#270

**O***ctagon*
Next to the Fashion pattern, this is probably Imperial's most common near-cut design, especially when found in marigold. But dark colors show up now and then, and the shape shown is rare in marigold. In the beautiful purple, the toothpick is extremely rare. Octagon is found in table sets, water sets, wine sets, footed vases, milk pitchers, goblets, and rare toothpicks. It is a pleasing allover pattern.

**O***ctet*
Even if this pattern were not marked, we would attribute it to the Northwood Company, because the exterior pattern is the Northwood Vintage found on the Star of David and Bows bowl. Octet is also a dome-footed bowl, usually about 8½" in diameter. It is a simple but effective pattern – one that wouldn't be easily confused with others. The colors are marigold, purple, green, white, and ice green. The purple is the most common.

Octet

*Octagon*

**Ohio Star**

**Omnibus**

**Olympic Compote**

**Open Edge Basketweave**

### Ohio Star

This beautiful near-cut vase is almost 10" tall and certainly is a standout in the carnival vase field. While the majority of vases are of simple design, this one flaunts its multi-cut pattern even to the star in the high domed base. The coloring is excellent and not only is Ohio Star found in the usual marigold, green, and purple but is reported in a beautiful blue! Certainly Millersburg blues are not easily found, and one of these would enhance any collection. A rare compote is known, and a super-rare white vase also.

### Olympic Compote

The Millersburg Olympic miniature compote is extremely rare. Its measurements are the same as the Leaf and Little Flowers compote made by the same company, and the exterior and base are identical also. If ever the old adage "great things come in small packages" could apply, certainly it would be to the Olympic compote.

### Omnibus

This interesting tumbler has been credited to the U.S. Glass Company and is rather rare (six known) and little recognized. The primary design is a sunburst teamed with two diamonds of file and a pulled diamond of bubble-like filler along with fanning. The sunburst moves from top to bottom in a series around the tumbler. The design is quite good; the color is super. A rare find.

### Open Edge Basketweave

This well-known Fenton pattern seems to grow in popularity, especially in the large pastel pieces which are scarce to rare. Found in hat shapes, bowls, J.I.P. shapes, banana bowls, vase whimseys, and plates. Colors are marigold, blue, green, amethyst, pink, smoke, ice blue, ice green, white, aqua, celeste blue, and red. Shown is a rare plate in smoke.

*Open Rose*

# Open Rose

This pattern is very similar to the Lustre Rose pattern but is not found on as wide range of shapes as the latter. The plate shown is the most sought shape, but there arc also footed and flat bowls of many sizes available. Colors of marigold, smoke, green, purple, clambroth, and amber are known, and each is usually outstanding. The amber plate shown typifies the Imperial quality.

# Optic (Imperial)

Each panel in this pattern is curved, thus the name and an interesting design above the ordinary. Besides bowls and small compotes, a creamer and sugar are known in marigold and smoke.

*Optic (Imperial)*

# Optic and Buttons

In crystal this pattern is found in many shapes including table sets, plates, oil bottles, decanters, shakers, and sherbets, but in carnival glass Optic and Buttons is limited to berry sets, a goblet, a large handled bowl, a small pitcher, tumblers in two shapes, and a rare cup and saucer. Many of the items in carnival are marked with the Imperial Iron Cross mark including the milk pitcher and the cup. All shapes I've seen are in marigold only.

*Optic and Buttons*

# Optic Flute

This Imperial pattern is seldom mentioned but can be found on berry sets as well as compotes. Colors I've seen are marigold and smoke, but others may have been made.

*Optic Flute*

183

*Optic Variant*

*Orange Tree and Scroll*

*Orange Peel*

*Orange Tree*

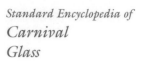
# Optic Variant

If you examine the Optic Flute, you will recognize the base of this Imperial bowl but will notice the fluting is missing. These have been found on berry sets, but I'm sure other shapes were made. The interior of the 6" bowl shown was highly iridized and had a stretch appearance, and the exterior had only slight luster.

# Orange Peel

This is a sister design to the Fruit Salad pattern and both are made by Westmoreland. Orange Peel, while not as rare, is made in a punch set, custard set, and a stemmed dessert in marigold, amethyst, and teal, all Westmoreland prime colors.

# Orange Tree

No other Fenton pattern had more popularity or was made in more shapes than the Orange Tree and all its variants. Known in berry sets, table sets, water sets, ice cream sets, breakfast sets, compotes, mugs, plates, powder jars, hatpin holders, rose bowls, a loving cup, wines, punch sets, and goblets. Orange Tree is found in marigold, blue, green, amethyst, peach opalescent, lustered milk glass, aqua opalescent, white, amber, vaseline, aqua, red, and amberina.

# Orange Tree and Scroll

What a beauty this hard-to-find tankard set is. The orange trees are like those on the regular pieces and the Orange Tree Orchard set, but below the trees are panels of scroll work much like the design on the Milady pattern. Colors are marigold, blue, and green, but I wouldn't rule out amethyst or white on this Fenton product.

*Orange Tree Orchard*

# Orange Tree Orchard

Obviously a spin-off pattern of the Orange Tree, this rather scarce Fenton water set has a nicely shaped, bulbous pitcher. The design is a series of orange trees separated by fancy scroll work and has been reported in marigold, blue, green, amethyst, and white.

# Oriental Poppy

Here is a very impressive, realistic pattern, especially effective on the chosen shape – a tankard water set. The mold work on this Northwood product is clear and clean, and the glass is quality all the way. Colors are marigold, green, purple, white, ice green, ice blue, and blue.

# Ostrich Cake Plate

This Australian pattern is actually the emu on a footed cake stand but has been misnamed. The exterior is a beautiful Rib and Cane pattern. Colors are marigold and purple, but these are rare.

*Oriental Poppy*

*Ostrich Cake Plate*

*Oval and Round*

*Pacifica*

*Pacific Coast Mail Order House*

*Painted Pansy Fan Vase*

# *O*val and Round

While Imperial's Oval and Round may certainly be thought of as a very ordinary pattern, it does have its own charm on a bowl as nicely ruffled as the one shown. Simple in execution, the pattern is found on plates of large size and bowls of various sizes only. The colors are marigold, green, smoke, or purple, and are usually very richly lustered.

# *P*acifica

Made by the U.S. Glass Company, the Pacifica tumbler is quite rare. Originally catalogued as #6425 by the maker, Pacifica has a rather complex pattern of hobstars, file sections, and small daisy-like flowers. Lustre is light, and the coloring has a bit of amber in the marigold.

# *P*acific Coast Mail Order House

Shown are two colors in a very rare advertising item. The exterior is, of course, Grape and Cable. Three examples are known in each color of marigold and blue. The bowls are footed. They were made by Fenton.

# *P*ainted Pansy Fan Vase

Shown first by Rose Presznick, this very pretty vase has a fine stippling over the entire exterior surface. She lists two sizes but I can't confirm this and as for the painted or enameled floral spray, I imagine there were several designs other than pansies that were used. The vase shown is 5½" tall and has a spread across the top of 7½". The base is 3½".

*Palm Beach*

# Palm Beach

Apparently this U.S. Glass pattern was carried over from the pressed glass days. It is scarce in all shapes but can be found in a variety of useful pieces, including berry sets, table set, a cider set, rose bowls, vase whimseys, a plate, and a miniature banana bowl whimsey. The color is often rather weak and marigold, purple, and white are known. The example shown is a bowl whimsey with an iridized goofus finish.

# Paneled Dandelion

Fenton's Paneled Dandelion is another of those spectacular tankard water sets that are so eye-catching. The panels of serrated leaves and cottony blossoms are very realistic and fill the space allowed nicely. Colors are marigold, blue, green, and amethyst.

# Paneled Diamond and Bows

For some reason this Fenton vase pattern isn't often found, despite not being rare. It ranges in size from the small 6½" version shown to the standard 11" vases and in colors of marigold, blue, green, amethyst, white, and an unusual peach opalescent. The design, a panel of geometric hobstars in diamonds separated by rayed bows, appears on alternating panels (three of six).

# Paneled Holly

This Northwood pattern is found in crystal, gilt glass, and carnival glass. However, the range of shapes is much less in the latter, limited to the exteriors of bowls, footed bonbons, a rare breakfast set, and an extremely rare water pitcher. While fairly attractive, Paneled Holly is really not a great pattern. It appears a trifle busy and a bit confused. The most often seen color is green, but purple and marigold do exist. I've seen a combination of green glass with marigold iridescence.

*Paneled Dandelion*

*Paneled Diamond
and Bows*

*Paneled Holly*

187

*Paneled Smocking*

*Paneled Treetrunk*

*Pansy*

*Panther*

## Paneled Smocking

I've always felt this pattern was from either England or Australia, but I may be wrong on both counts. Marigold is the only color I've seen, and there are no other shapes reported.

## Paneled Treetrunk

While similar to the Northwood Treetrunk vase, this scarce and interesting vase has an appeal all its own. The example shown is 7½" tall and has a base diameter of 4⅞". It has eight panels, and the coloring is a fine amethyst. I suspect it was made by Dugan but can't be positive.

## Pansy

The Pansy bowl shown typifies the Imperial quality so often found in iridized glass. The luster is outstanding with a gleaming finish equal to the best Millersburg we all treasure so much. The mold work is super, enhanced by the very rich gold finish. While the Pansy pattern doesn't bring top dollar, it is a pleasure to own such a beautiful item.

## Panther

Fenton made some of the best animal patterns, and this one is at the top of the heap. Found in footed berry sets with a Butterfly and Berry exterior, the Panther bowl can be found in marigold, blue, green, amethyst, red (small bowls only), white, and the very rare Nile green opalescent bowl shown.

*Parlor Panels*

## Parlor Panels

If you haven't had a chance to see one of these beautiful vases, especially the Imperial purple shown, you've certainly missed a real experience, for these are a glass collector's dream. Parlor Panels was shown in old Imperial catalogs and has not been reproduced to date. I've heard of marigold, blue, smoke, purple, and green. Some examples are swung to 12" lengths.

## Parquet

Here is the creamer in a seldom-seen pattern that may well be English for the matching sugar is a collar-based 5½" bowl. The creamer stands nearly 4" tall and measures 4½" across the spout to the handle. Color and iridescence is typically English.

*Parquet*

## Pastel Swan

Made by Northwood, Dugan, and Fenton, these master salt holders were very popular indeed. They can be found in opalescent glass as well as the iridized versions, and the colors are marigold, purple, ice blue, ice green, peach opalescent, celeste blue, amethyst opalescent, and pink. The example shown is Fenton's and is an experimental piece of amber, cobalt, and aqua glass mixed at the end of day's production.

*Pastel Swan*

## Peach

Once more we show a Northwood pattern that was also produced in other types of glass. This was more than likely one of the earlier Northwood carnival glass patterns and is found in a very fine cobalt blue as well as white, the latter often with gilding. What a shame more shapes were not made in Peach, for only berry sets, table sets, and water sets are known. The pattern is scarce and always brings top dollar.

*Peach*

189

*Peach and Pear*

*Peacock (Millersburg)*

*Peacock and Dahlia*

190

## Peach and Pear

While no shards of this pattern were catalogued from the Dugan digs, I'm convinced it was their product. It is available mostly in marigold with an occasional amethyst one turning up. The mold work is excellent, and only the one shape and size are known.

## Peacock (Millersburg)

While both Fenton and Northwood had similar patterns, the Millersburg Peacock is most noted and by far the best example of this design. The detailing is considerably greater, the bird more realistic, and the quality of glass and finish superior. There are slight differences between the large bowl and the individual berry bowls in the Peacock pattern, but most of these are in the detail permitted on the allowed space, and a complete berry set is worth searching for. The color most often seen is a fine fiery amethyst, but green, marigold, clambroth, and blue exist as well.

## Peacock and Dahlia

While this Fenton pattern is related in design to the Peacock and Grape, it is a better design and much scarcer. Known only in bowls and plates, Peacock and Dahlia carries the Berry and Leaf Circles pattern on the exterior. Colors known are marigold, blue, green, amethyst, vaseline, white, and aqua.

*Peacock and Grapes*

# Peacock and Grapes

Obviously, this Fenton design and Peacock Dahlia were from the same artist. This too, is found on bowls, flat or footed, and scarce plates. Colors are marigold, blue, green, amethyst, aqua, vaseline, white, red, and peach opalescent.

# Peacock and Urn (Fenton)

The Fenton version of this pattern (both Northwood and Millersburg had their own) is most often seen on stemmed compotes in marigold or aqua. Other shapes are bowls, plates, and a scarce goblet from the compote mold. Colors known are marigold, blue, green, amethyst, white, aqua, lavender, and red.

# Peacock and Urn (Millersburg)

Millersburg Peacock and Urn differs from the regular Peacock pattern in that it has a bee by the bird's beak. The shapes known are large bowls, small 6½" bowls, a chop plate, and a giant compote in the usual colors of marigold, green, and amethyst.

*Peacock and Urn (Fenton)*

*Peacock and Urn (Millersburg)*

191

*Peacock and Urn (Northwood)*

*Peacock and Urn "Mystery" Bowl*
*(Millersburg)*

*Peacock and Urn Variant*
*(Millersburg)*

### Peacock and Urn (Northwood)

Similar to the Millersburg version of Peacock and Urn, the Northwood design has three rows of beading on the urn and has more open area outside the design itself. It is found on ice cream sets, berry sets, a chop plate, and a very rare 6½" plate. Color range is wide, from vivid to pastel, including aqua opalescent.

### Peacock and Urn "Mystery" Bowl (Millersburg)

There is little mysterious about this bowl any longer. It is indeed from Millersburg, has a bee and two rows of beading on the urn, and is found in both the ruffled and ice cream shape in 8" and 8½" diameters. Colors are the usual marigold, amethyst, and green, and all are rare.

### Peacock and Urn Variant (Millersburg)

Over the years, so much controversy has arisen over all the Millersburg Peacock designs, I'm showing all of them including this 6⅛" very shallow bowl. Note that there is a bee, and the urn has three rows of beads! The only color reported on this piece is amethyst. So far, four are known, so it is rather rare.

*Peacock at the Fountain*

### Peacock at the Fountain

One of Northwood's best patterns, this well-done, intriguing design can be found in berry sets, table sets, punch sets, water sets, compotes, and a large footed orange bowl. Colors include all the standard ones plus ice green, white, ice blue, and aqua opalescent. Dugan made a copycat water set.

### Peacock Garden Vase

In addition to the marigold vase previously shown, I am now thrilled to add the rare white opalescent carnival example. There is also a reported white carnival without the opalescence. We believe Northwood made this vase in the 1912 – 1916 era and Fenton began their version in 1933 calling it their #791. Fenton has continued production in many types of glass over the years.

*Peacock Garden Vase*

### Peacock Lamp

Made on a crystal base, this beautiful lamp base has an enameled interior and an iridized exterior. Colors are red, marigold, amethyst, smoke, and white, and all are rare. It's 10¼" tall, and sometimes has no hole indicating these were sold as both lamps and vases.

*Peacock Lamp*

*Peacocks*

*Peacock Tail*

*Peacock Tail and Daisy*

## Peacocks

Often called Peacocks on the Fence, this Northwood pattern typifies what carnival glass is really all about. An interesting pattern, well molded, and turned out in a variety of appealing colors, Peacocks is a delight. Only average size bowls and plates are known, but the color range is wide, including vivid colors, pastels, and a really beautiful aqua opalescent. The exterior usually carries a wide rib pattern.

## Peacock Tail

Very reminiscent of the Northwood Nippon pattern, Fenton's Peacock Tail is known on bowls of all sizes, bonbons, compotes, hat shapes (some with advertising), and vase interiors. Colors I've seen are marigold, blue, green, amethyst, amber, and red.

## Peacock Tail and Daisy

I am very thrilled to finally show this very rare Westmoreland bowl pattern. Besides the marigold, there is an amethyst and a blue opal milk glass that isn't iridized, but I've heard of no other shapes or colors. As you can see, the pattern is graceful as can be, and the design is very well balanced.

*Peacock Tail Variant*

## Peacock Tail Variant

One look at the iridescence of this little compote, and it becomes quite obvious it is a Millersburg product, culled from three common motifs used by most glass companies of the day – the peacock tail rings, the stippled rays, and the feather. At any rate, it is a nice little item and quite enjoyable to own. Amethyst seems to be the most often seen color, but marigold and green are known.

## Peacock Variant (Millersburg)

This extremely rare 7½" (same size as the Courthouse bowls) variant is an outstanding example of Millersburg craftsmanship. The mold work is very sharp with great detail, and there is a bee, but no beading. Also the urn is quite different than the other peacocks. Colors are marigold, green, and amethyst, but blue may exist.

## Pebble and Fan

This very attractive vase is 11½" tall with a base diameter of 4½" and is truly a triumph. The mold work as well as the basic design is quite good. Colors I've heard about are cobalt blue, marigold, and a rather unusual amber with vaseline finish.

*Peacock Variant (Millersburg)*

*Pebble and Fan*

195

Pebbles (Dugan)

*Penny Match Holder*

*People's Vase*

*Pepper Plant*

### Pebbles (Dugan)

Here is the Dugan version of Coin Dot, and as you can see, it has no stippling. Found on open bowls and plates, colors are amethyst, marigold, and green.

### Penny Match Holder

Once again we picture a rare but useful novelty that is seldom found. The octagonal base is 3⅜" across and the entire match holder is 3½" tall. Purple is the only color about which I've heard, and the iridescence is very rich and heavy, very much like the better Northwood products in this color. However, the maker remains unknown.

### People's Vase

We are told this masterwork of art glass was produced by the Millersburg Company to show appreciation for the help of the Amish people of the area in getting the factory started. The dancing figures represent Amish children, hands clutching, prancing happily in thanks for a successful harvest – the only time their religion permitted such merriment. In the background Grandfather looks on with pleasure. But regardless of the circumstances surrounding the vase's conception, there is no doubt that this is at the very top of Millersburg's best and surely deserves a place in the history of American glass. The only pattern variation occurs in the lip which is usually straight but very occasionally appears in scallops. The vase is 11½" high, 5½" in diameter, and weighs 5 pounds. The colors are marigold, amethyst, green, and cobalt blue.

### Pepper Plant

On first glance this appears to be a Fenton Holly hat in cobalt blue, but examine it closely. You will find that while the stems and leaves are the same, the berries are really pulled into peppers, and each stem ends in a flower design at the top of the hat. The piece shown is 6½" across the top and stands 3" tall with 2" octagonal base.

*Perfection*

# Perfection

This beautiful water set is a fitting companion to its sister design, the Gay 90s. Outstanding mold work, color, and iridescence are the hallmark of Millersburg, and the Perfection pattern certainly fits this description. The pitcher is 9½" tall and quite bulbous. It has four mold marks. The tumblers are 4" tall and taper from 2⅞" diameter at the top to 2⅛" at the base which has a 24-point rayed star.

# Persian Garden

Found in berry sets, ice cream sets, and two sizes of plates, this very well designed pattern came from the Dugan factory. It is available in marigold, amethyst, green, blue, white, ice blue, and ice green.

# Persian Medallion

Very Oriental in flavor, Persian Medallion is one of those well-known Fenton patterns that was extremely popular when it was made and is available on bowls of all shapes and sizes, plates both large and small, compotes, rose bowls, and even a hair receiver (not to mention interiors on punch sets). Colors are marigold, blue, green, amethyst, white, amber, and red.

*Persian Garden*

*Persian Medallion*

*Petal and Fan*

*Petal Band*

*Petals*

*Petals and Prisms*

## Petal and Fan

Found only in bowls of various sizes, this Dugan pattern also has the Jeweled Heart as an exterior design. The motif itself is simple but attractive – a series of alternating stippled and plain petals on a plain ribbed background with a fan-like design growing from each plain petal. The feeling is almost one of ancient Egypt where such fans were made of feathers. Petals and Fans is available in many colors including peach opalescent.

## Petal Band

This very pretty compote vase is a real mystery and I finally stopped looking for the pattern in other listings and simply named it Petal Band, so if someone out there can identify it, please let me know. It stands about 6" tall and has very nice color. The stem is well proportioned and aside from inside wide ribbing, the only design is the band of stippled petal-like sections around the bottom of the compote's bowl.

## Petals

This Dugan pattern is primarily a bowl pattern but is occasionally seen in a compote as well as a super banana bowl shape. Colors are the usual Dugan ones and the exterior seems to be found with a wide panel design.

## Petals and Prisms

Here is another of those foreign patterns, probably English, that can be found on several shapes including the collar-based sugar shown. Other shapes known are a stemmed sugar, a creamer, a 9" bowl, and a large (10½") bowl. The stemmed sugar can be upended and used as a base for the larger bowls making a fruit set. The design is all exterior, consisting of incised petals and circles, edged with prism bands that are vertical.

*Peter Rabbit*

## Peter Rabbit

Peter Rabbit is one of Fenton's rare treasures, much sought by collectors and always priced for top dollar when sold. The shapes are 9" bowls and 10" plates in marigold, honey amber, green, blue, and amethyst. The design is closely related to both Little Fishes and Coral patterns.

## Pickle Paperweight

Of all the oddities I've come across in carnival glass, this is probably the oddball of all time. It measures 4½" in length and is hollow. As you can see, it has a super color and finish. I assume it to be a paperweight for I can think of little else it could be used for. The maker is unknown, and the only color reported is amethyst.

## Pillar and Flute

Shown is the compote piece of this appealing Imperial pattern. Found in many shapes including a breakfast set, wall vase, 8" celery tray, berry set, and rose bowl which often has the Imperial Iron Cross marking, the colors are nearly always marigold or clambroth. The design is a simple flute convex on both inside and out.

## Pillow and Sunburst

This pattern is credited to the Westmoreland Company, and while it has been seen on several shapes in crystal, the only reported iridized shape is the bowl shape. The pattern is exterior and can be found in marigold or purple. The example shown is an 8½" bowl.

*Pickle Paperweight*

*Pillar and Flute*

*Pillow and Sunburst*

*Pin-Ups*

*Pinched Rib*

*Pinched Swirl*

*Pineapple*

## Pin-Ups

This scarce Australian pattern, simple but distinctive, is found mostly on 8½" bowls in a rich purple, but here we show a very scarce marigold. The exterior carries a slender thread border.

## Pinched Rib

Just why the glassmakers collapsed the sides of these vases remains a mystery to me, but certainly they thought there was a reason for several sizes exist. Most are found in marigold or peach opalescent glass, and they range in size from 4" tall to over a foot. The one shown has a pretty crimped lip. Some are Dugan products, but I'm sure other makers had a try at them.

## Pinched Swirl

We seldom hear much about this attractive design, but it is known in both rose bowls and a rare spittoon, both in peach opalescent. I don't believe the maker has been confirmed, but Dugan or Westmoreland seem likely candidates.

## Pineapple

Sometimes called Pineapple and Bows, this Sowerby pattern is available in 7½" dome-footed bowls, a compote, and a creamer. The mold work is quite good with much attention paid to detail. The luster is very good on the items I've seen, and colors of marigold, purple, and blue are known.

*Pineapple Crown*

## Pineapple Crown

Named by Marian Quintin-Baxendale, the bowl shown has been found in two sizes, the one shown being 8½" x 4" and 2½" tall. It is oval with a light airy coloring, and the mold work is quite good with most of the surface covered with design. The maker is unknown to me, but I'm sure it is either English or European.

## Pine Cone

What a little beauty this design is! Known only on small bowls and scarce plates. Fenton's Pine Cone is seen mostly on marigold, blue, or green, but an occasional amber plate has been seen. The design is well molded, geometrically sound, the iridescence is usually quite good.

*Pine Cone*

## Pinwheel Vase

Now known to be of English origin, these pretty vases are found in three sizes in colors of marigold, blue, and amethyst. The mold work and coloring are very good, and so is the design. Originally, this pattern was called Derby.

## Pipe Humidor

Here is a fantastic Millersburg pattern many collectors haven't even seen, because it is just that rare. And what a pity so few of these are around since it is lovely enough to grace any collection. The coloring and iridescence are exceptional and the design flawless. Imagine how difficult to remove the lid from the mold without damage to the pipe and stem. The humidor is just over 8" tall and measures 5" across the lid. A three-pronged sponge holder is inside the lid, intended of course, to keep the tobacco moist. Around the base is a wreath of acorns and leaves above another leaf-like pattern that runs down the base.

*Pinwheel Vase*

*Pipe Humidor*

*Plaid*

## Plaid

On the few occasions this Fenton pattern is found, the coloring is usually cobalt blue with heavy luster or a rare red. As you can see, the coloring is very bright with rich iridescence. Needless to say, these 8½" bowls are a collector's dream and certainly would complement any collection of red carnival glass.

## Plain Jane (Imperial)

The only design whatsoever is the many-pointed star in the base of the bowl. It is found in berry sets in smoke, marigold, green, and purple; it is a close relative to the Plain Jane handled basket.

## Plain Jane Basket

Long credited to the Imperial Company, this large basket, while rather plain, has great appeal. It has been seen in smoke as well as marigold, and measures 9¼" to the top of the handle.

## Plain Petals

Here is a pattern seldom discussed, yet it is found as the interior design of some pieces of Leaf and Beads. It is my opinion the latter was made by both Northwood and Dugan, and these pieces with the Plain Petals interior as well as the famous rose bowl are Northwood. The example shown is on a very interesting leaf-shaped nappy.

*Plain Jane (Imperial)*

*Plain Jane Basket*

*Plain Petals*

## Plume Panels

For years I felt this rather stately vase was a Northwood product, but as you can see, it has been found in a beautiful red so I'm rather sure it came from the Fenton factory. Other colors known are marigold, blue, green, amethyst, and white.

## Plums and Cherries

Also known as Northwood's Two Fruits, this very rare pattern is known on a spooner, a lidless sugar, and tumblers. On one side we have three cherries, and the other features two plums. The table pieces have a series of small bands near the top and bubble-like lumps around the base, while the tumblers have only the bands. All are found in cobalt blue, and the tumbler in a rare marigold.

## Poinsettia (Imperial)

Found only on one shape (the beautiful milk pitcher shown), Poinsettia is an outstanding Imperial pattern. Standing 6½" tall, the Poinsettia is usually found in marigold or smoke color, but as you can see, a rare and beautiful purple does exist as does an equally rare green. What a shame more shapes do not exist in this beautiful design!

## Poinsettia (Interior)

Here is something unusual – a tumbler with all the pattern on the inside. Of course, we've all seen the Northwood Swirl pattern which is also an interior one, but that was a simple geometrical design, while the Interior Poinsettia is an offering of a large flower. Apparently these were never very popular for they are very scarce. Also, to the best of my knowledge, no pitcher has been found. The iridescence is on both the inside and outside and is a good rich marigold. Only some of these Northwood tumblers are marked.

*Plume Panels*

*Plums and Cherries*

*Poinsettia (Imperial)*

*Poinsettia (Interior)*

203

*Poinsettia (Northwood)*

*Pond Lily*

*Pony*

## Poinsettia (Northwood)

For some reason, in years past someone attributed this very stylish pattern to the Fenton Glass Company. Just why, I can't guess, for Poinsettia was made by Northwood in custard glass and was illustrated in their advertising of the day. At any rate, this mistake has been corrected, and we now recognize this well-done bowl as a Harry Northwood design. Poinsettia is found either as a flat-based or footed bowl with the Fine Rib as an exterior pattern. The finish is nearly always superior. The colors are marigold, green, purple, black amethyst, fiery amethyst, white, and ice green.

## Pond Lily

Much like other Fenton patterns such as Two Flowers and Water Lily, Pond Lily has both scale filler and the Lotus-like flower. The only shape I've seen is the bonbon, and colors reported are in marigold, blue, green, and white. Of course, other colors may exist, and certainly red is a possibility.

## Pony

For years the origin of this attractive bowl has been questioned, and only recently has it been attributed to the Dugan Company. Colors seen are marigold, amethyst, and ice green. The mold work is quite good.

*Pool of Pearls*

# Pool of Pearls

Found only on the exterior of Persian Garden plates, this very attractive pattern is not easy to find and often goes unnoticed by collectors. It is a kissin' cousin to the opalescent pattern called Jewel and Flower and also resembles the Garden Path design.

# Poppy (Millersburg)

Large open compotes seem to have a fascination all their own, and this one from Millersburg is certainly no exception. It is quality all the way, whether found in green, purple, or marigold. Standing 7" tall and being 8" across, Poppy has four mold marks. It has the Potpourri as a secondary pattern. The poppy flowers and leaves are well done and stippled.

# Poppy (Northwood)

This Northwood pattern is most often found on small oval bowls, described as trays or with the sides crimped as pickle dishes. However, it is also found as an exterior pattern on larger bowls, some with plain exteriors, others with a large Daisy in the center of the bowl. The colors are electric blue, marigold, peach, purple, aqua, opal, and white. Others may exist, but these are the ones I've seen.

*Poppy (Millersburg)*

*Poppy (Northwood)*

205

*Poppy Show (Northwood)*

## Poppy Show (Northwood)

Let me state from the beginning this is not the same pattern as the Poppy Show Vase. It is a beautiful well-made item, very much akin to the Rose Show pattern in concept and design. It is found only on large bowls and plates in a wide range of colors, including marigold, green, blue, purple, white, ice blue, and ice green. This Northwood pattern brings top dollar whenever offered for sale.

## Poppy Show Vase (Imperial)

What a shame this beauty was chosen to be reproduced by Imperial in the 1960s. The old Poppy Show Vase is a real show stopper, standing about 12" tall with a lip diameter of 6¾"! The mold work is very fine with the graceful poppy in a series of four panels around the vase. I've seen this artistic gem in marigold, clambroth, pastel marigold, amber, green, and purple. Naturally, the darker colors are quite scarce and are priced accordingly.

## Portland Elks Bell (Fenton)

Like the other Fenton Elks bells, this rare, previously unreported, Portland bell has the usual elk's head within a clock face and the ribbed handle. The coloring is a fine cobalt blue with heavy luster.

*Poppy Show Vase (Imperial)*

*Portland Elks Bell (Fenton)*

*Potpourri (Millersburg)*

# Potpourri (Millersburg)

I certainly welcome the chance to show this very rare pitcher in the Potpourri pattern, a kissin' cousin to Millersburg's Country Kitchen pattern. Only two of these pitchers have been reported and both are marigold, smaller than a water pitcher, and were used for milk.

# Prayer Rug

Known only in the finish shown, beautiful custard glass with a marigold iridescence, Fenton's Prayer Rug is a seldom-seen item. The only shape is a handled bonbon, but I suspect time will bring to light additional ones, since uniridized pieces are known in small bowls, vases, and hat shapes.

*Prayer Rug*

# Premium

Not only found in the well-known candlesticks shown, but also in 8½" bowls, 12" bowls, and 14" plates. Imperial's Premium pattern is shown in old catalogs in marigold, clambroth, purple, green, and smoke. The candlesticks are 8½" tall, heavy, and beautifully iridized! While not in the class with the Grape and Cable candlesticks, they are still quite nice. Used with the medium size bowl, they make a nice console set.

*Premium*

*Pressed Hexagon*

*Pretty Panels*

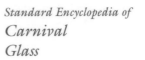

### Pressed Hexagon

Made by the McKee Glass Company of Jeanette, PA, each piece of this very attractive table set (creamer missing) is marked "PRES CUT." As you can see, the handles and finials are clear while the rest of each piece is well iridized. Often found in crystal, this is the first time I've encountered pieces in carnival.

### Pretty Panels

This is a marked Northwood tumbler and as such is quite a sight for tumbler collectors. The color is a very bold frosty green, and the enameled cherry design is above average. It is found in marigold also.

### Primrose

This well-conceived Millersburg pattern is much neglected and certainly shouldn't be. It is found only on fair-sized bowls in marigold, clambroth, amethyst, green, and a very rare blue. The exterior pattern is always Fine Cut Hearts, and the two are very compatible.

### Primrose and Fishnet (#2475)

This unusual Imperial pattern has two kissin' cousins, also in red carnival; one showing grapes, the other roses. The floral design is on one side only, and the fishnet covers the remainder of the glass. While red is the only reported color in iridized glass, all three patterns are known in crystal. The Primrose and Fishnet vase stands 6" tall. Needless to say, they are quite scarce.

*Primrose*

*Primrose and
Fishnet (#2475)*

*Primrose Ribbon Shade*

*Prism and Daisy Band*

## Primrose Ribbon Shade

Except for the small panel lines that run from top to bottom, and the very subtle ribbon of flowers around the edge, this very pretty shade relies on rich color for its show. The bell shape turns in at the edge. It measures 5½" tall and is nearly 5" wide.

## Prism and Cane

This very scarce product of Sowerby has an interior pattern of Embossed Scroll variant, and, as you can see, the base is ground. Apparently it is a sauce dish or jam dish as it measures 5" across the rim and stands 2¼" tall.

## Prism and Daisy Band

Apparently one of Imperial's late designs in carnival glass and intended for a cheap mass sale, Prism and Daisy Band can be found only in marigold in berry sets, breakfast sets, a stemmed compote, and a vase shape. The coloring is adequate but not superior.

## Prism Panels

This large 9" bowl is 3" tall and rather undistinguished in design. The coloring is quite good and the iridescence super. It looks European but I have no proof of its origin. This example came from England some time ago.

*Prism and Cane*

*Prism Panels*

*Prisms*

*Propeller*

*Pulled Loop*

*Pulled Husk Corn Vase*

210

*Standard Encyclopedia of*
*Carnival*
*Glass*

## Prisms

Found mainly on a stemmed, two-handled nappy, this Westmoreland pattern measures 7¼" across the handles and is 2½" tall. There is however, a one-handled whimsey known in green. Colors found on the nappy are marigold, green, and amethyst. The pattern is all exterior and intaglio with an ornate star in the base.

## Propeller

Besides the usual small compote found in this Imperial pattern, I'm very happy to show the rare 7½" stemmed vase in the Propeller pattern. The coloring is a good rich marigold, but others may exist since the compote is seen in marigold, green, and amethyst.

## Pulled Husk Corn Vase

Apparently Harry Northwood wasn't quite satisfied with this very rare example of a corn vase, for few of these are around in comparison with the regular corn vase. Known in two sizes, the Pulled Husk vase has been seen in green and purple, and some are pulled more grotesquely than others.

## Pulled Loop

This rather simple Dugan vase design is found quite often, mostly in marigold, blue, or amethyst, but it is known in a beautiful green, as well as an occasional peach opalescent finish. The size may vary from 8" to 16", but the finish is usually very heavily lustered.

*Puzzle*

# Puzzle

Found in stemmed bonbons and compotes, Dugan's Puzzle is an appealing pattern. The allover design is well balanced and the stippling adds interest. Colors known are marigold, purple, green, blue, white, and peach opalescent.

# Quarter Block

After seeing a jelly dish complete with a wire frame and spoon attached, I'm convinced this pattern is English. It is found primarily in table set pieces, and I've seen the open sugar, creamer, covered butter, and the jelly piece. Color is usually a good marigold. The creamer stands 3½" tall and measures 5" across from lip to handle.

# Queen's Jewel

I know very little about this interesting stemmed goblet except that the coloring is light flashing and the design, while busy, gives an interesting cover to the entire bowl area as well as the flared base. I suspect it is from Europe.

# Queen's Lamp

While only a handful of these kerosene lamps exist in carnival glass and all in a deep green, sometimes with light iridescence, they are also found in crystal with a matching shade. They are large with a base diameter of 7" and stand 9" to the top of the font.

*Quarter Block*

*Queen's Jewel*

*Queen's Lamp*

211

*Question Marks*

*Quill*

*Quilted Diamond*

## Question Marks

Here is a simple Dugan pattern found on the interiors of bonbons and occasionally compotes like the one shown. Again the exterior is usually plain, and the colors are peach opalescent, marigold, purple, and white. Both the compote and the bonbon are footed; the compote is one of the small size, measuring 4½" tall and 4" across the highly ruffled edge. The exterior occasionally has a pattern called Georgia Belle.

## Quill

Once again we show a pattern of which shards were found in the Dugan diggings, and I truly believe Quill was indeed a Dugan Glass Company pattern. The pitcher is some 10" tall and has a base diameter of 4½". The colors are marigold and amethyst, and the iridescence is usually above average. Quill is a scarce pattern and apparently small quantities were made, again pointing toward the Dugan company as the manufacturer. The water set is the only shape.

## Quilted Diamond

Certainly one of Imperial's best exterior designs, this pattern is found as a companion to the Pansy pattern on one-handled nappies, dresser trays, and pickle dishes. Just why Imperial didn't use it more is a mystery for it is beautifully done and very pleasing to the eye.

**Radiance**

# R adiance
The very name says it all on this rare and attractive enameled water set. Both the tumblers and the pitcher have six creased panels around the perimeter with the latter having a flaring base while the tumbler's base is flat and heavy. Coloring is light and extends only to the neck on the pitcher.

# R agged Robin
Just why more of these Fenton bowls weren't produced is a mystery, but the fact remains these are quite hard to find today. Found only on average size bowls often with a ribbon candy edge. Colors reported are amethyst, marigold, blue, green, and white with blue most available.

# R ainbow (Northwood)
Similar to the Northwood Raspberry compote or the one with only a Basketweave exterior, this one is completely plain with iridescence on the inside only. The luster swirls around the glass in layers, just like a rainbow, thus the name.

# R aindrops
Here is another of the dome-footed bowls available in peach opalescent like so many offered by the Dugan company. Remember, I said earlier that I felt Dugan was responsible for at least 90% of the peach carnival, and a close study of these bowls will support this belief. Raindrops is found without stippling. It has the Keyhole pattern as an exterior companion and has four mold marks. All in all, it is a nice pattern to own, especially if you like the peach opalescent glass. Also found in amethyst.

**Ragged Robin**

**Rainbow (Northwood)**

**Raindrops**

213

*Rambler Rose*

*Ranger*

*Raspberry*

# R ambler Rose

Until quite recently, I'd always felt Rambler Rose was a Fenton product, but upon examining a large shard of this pattern from the Dugan dump site, I'm compelled to admit my mistake. This water set has a bulbous pitcher with a ruffled top. The flowers are well designed and clearly molded. The colors are marigold, purple, blue, and green. Perhaps research in the years ahead will add more information about this pattern.

# R anger

Known in breakfast sets, water sets, a milk pitcher, and table sets, this pattern, often confused with the Australian Blocks and Arches pattern, is found only in marigold. It is an Imperial product, but one version of the tumbler is known to have been produced by Cristales de Mexico and is so marked.

# R aspberry

Even without the famous trademark, this pattern would be recognized as a Northwood product, for it includes the basketweave so often found on that company's designs. Available in water sets, table sets, berry sets, and a milk pitcher. Raspberry has long been a favorite with collectors. The colors are marigold, green, purple, ice blue, and ice green with the richly lustered purple most prevalent.

*Rays*

# Rays

If you look closely at this Dugan pattern you will detect an inner ring of pointed rays before the veins fan out toward the outer edges, distinguishing the simple design from similar ones. It was made in all the Dugan colors, and this one has a Jeweled Heart exterior.

# Rays and Ribbon

Each of the makers of carnival glass seems to have had a try at a pattern using stippled rays. The Millersburg version is quite distinctive because of the bordering of ribbon-like design, resembling a fleur-de-lis design. Most of the bowls are not radium finish and usually carry the Cactus pattern on the exterior. Occasionally a plate is found in Rays and Ribbons, but one wonders if this were not produced as a shallow bowl. Amethyst is the usual color, followed by green, marigold, and vaseline in that order.

# Regal Flower

What a stately vase this is! It stands nearly 14" tall and the coloring blends from a clear-to-slightly-green base to a very rich marigold at the top. The enameling is very fine, much like several Dugan items that have surfaced in an experimental line that dates to 1905 – 1910. A quick comparison of this enameling and that on the standard pieces in carnival glass reveals striking superiority.

*Rays and Ribbon*

*Regal Flower*

*Rib and Panel*

*Ribbed Holly*

*Ribbons and Leaves*

*Ribbon Tie*

### Rib and Panel

Found in both the vase shape shown and a spittoon whimsey, Rib and Panel seems to always have a pontil mark on the base, so we can assume it is a blown pattern. Colors are marigold, amethyst, blue, and peach opalescent. Both Fenton and Dugan-Diamond are mentioned as possible makers, but I lean toward the latter.

### Ribbed Holly

Just like the unusual Fenton Holly items, these small, stemmed pieces had the interior ribbing added for some reason. Most are seen in cobalt blue but here is a brilliant cherry red one! These stemmed pieces can be shaped like compotes, deep unruffled compotes, or goblets.

### Ribbons and Leaves

I've known about this pattern for 20 years, but this is the first example I've been able to show. It is an open sugar made by Sowerby, I believe. It measures 6½" across the handles and 2¼" tall. The unusual ribboning and binding around the rim are unique.

### Ribbon Tie

Sometimes called Comet, this well-known Fenton pattern is found chiefly on all sorts of bowls as well as ruffled plates. The colors range from very good to poor in marigold, blue, amethyst, red, and green, and often the luster is only so-so.

*Ribs (Small Basket)*

# Ribs (Small Basket)

When only the soap dish shape was known this pattern was called Small Basket. Now a complete dresser set consisting of a tumbler, ring tree, puffbox, three perfumes, a bud vase, and the soap dish are known in a good marigold. This set was made in Czechoslovakia and has paper labels saying so. I have renamed the set Ribs.

# Rings

Besides the large, 8" vase shown, I've recently seen this pattern on a 6½" covered cookie jar in a pale marigold. This pattern is shown in old Jeanette company ads, and the pattern was still being made in the 1958 – 59 period in pink milk glass, so it must have been a popular pattern.

# Ripple

Ranging in height from 8" to 18", this Imperial glass vase, while easy to find, is always a very attractive item. The pattern of rings around the glass that has been swung or pulled out makes for appeal. Colors are marigold, purple, green, blue, teal, clambroth, smoke, and amber.

*Rings*

*Ripple*

*Rising Sun*

*Robin*

*Rococo*

*Rolled Ribs*

# R *ising Sun*

Made by U.S. Glass, this very distinctive geometric pattern is seldom mistaken for any other. It can be found in water sets with two different pitcher shapes, a rare table set, and a lemonade tray. Colors are mostly cobalt blue with rare examples of marigold known.

# R *obin*

Despite the reproductions of this fine old Imperial pattern, the prices have held up rather well on the old pieces. The water sets, found only in marigold, and the mug, found in smoke, are especially desirable. Apparently the appeal lies in the handsome presentation of the nicely done bird, the flower and branch dividers, and the flowering leaf pattern, so pleasing to the eye.

# R *ococo*

This beautiful little Imperial vase was the first item in smoke I'd ever seen, and I must admit I loved it at first sight! While it may be found on a small bowl shape with a dome base and in marigold as well as smoke, it is the vase most think of whenever Rococo is mentioned. The vase is 5½" tall and shows four mold marks. I have had a green one reported but haven't seen it yet.

# R *olled Ribs*

Apparently a part of the New Martinsville line called Muranese, this very beautiful bowl has a striking marigold iridescence on the outer half of the rim and then turns to a milky opalescence. Muranese ware came in a host of shapes and finishes and one coloring is known as New Martinsville Peachblow. Only some of the finishes were iridized and dates of production were from 1904 to 1907 with the iridized pieces near the end of production.

# Roman Rosette Goblet (Unlisted)

While this pattern is not difficult to find in pressed glass, this is the only reported item in iridized glass to the best of my knowledge. As you can see, it is slightly crooked, but the iridization on the clear glass is unmistakable with beautiful blue and pink coloring. It measures 6" tall and has a base diameter of 2¾".

# Rosalind (Millersburg)

Once called Drape and Tie, this classy design is found as the interior of the famous Dolphin compote as well as on large and small bowls and a rare compote that stands 9" tall. Colors are marigold, amethyst, and green, but occasionally a rare blue is found on all shapes and the 9" bowl is known in a rare aqua.

# Rosalind Variant (Millersburg)

If you look closely at this design and the regular Rosalind shown elsewhere, you will see a good deal of difference, especially in concentric peacock tail sections. For this reason, I'm listing the compote shown as a variant (and expect letters about it). Colors reported in this compote are amethyst and green, but marigold was probably made also.

# Rose and Greek Key Plate

This very beautiful square plate is a sight to behold. Not only is it quite unique, but it is so very well designed that I simply cannot understand why there aren't more of these. But alas, there's only the one known. The coloring is a smoky amber. The plate measures 8½" across, and the roses are deep and hollow on the underside, much like the well-known Rose Show bowls.

*Roman Rosette Goblet (Unlisted)*

*Rosalind Variant (Millersburg)*

*Rosalind (Millersburg)*

*Rose and Greek Key Plate*

219

*Rose Ann Shade*

**Rose Band**

*Rose Column*

*Rose Garden*

# Rose Ann Shade

Rose Presznick named this shade and says it can also be found in other treatments including goofus glass. The one shown is a very rich marigold with good iridescence. There are four panels of design around the piece and the bell is slightly curved inward.

# Rose Band

While the name is somewhat confusing with a similar tumbler pattern called Band of Roses, the name certainly does describe the design. The pattern is typically European, and the tumbler is short at 3¾" tall. The color is good, and the pattern rare.

# Rose Column

This stately Millersburg vase is a real beauty and like several carnival patterns such as the Imperial Grape carafe or the Grape Arbor pitcher, the rows of roses are hollow. This requires great skill by the worker when removing it from the mold, and many must have been broken in doing so. This lovely vase is 10" tall and 5" across the diameter. There are six columns of roses, each topped by a sprig of leaves. The iridescence is top quality, and the colors are marigold, blue, green, and amethyst. The Rose Column vase would make a lovely companion to the People's Vase.

# Rose Garden

Once again we finally have a true maker for a much-disputed pattern, and Rose Garden is now in the list of glass from the Eda Glassworks of Sweden. It is found in many shapes including bowls, round and oblong vases, a pitcher that is rare, a beautiful rose bowl, and a covered butter dish. Colors are marigold and blue only.

# Rose Panels

While this is an interesting pattern, all exterior and found only on large compotes, it has never created much interest by collectors. It is 6½" tall and the bowl measures about 9" across. I've been told the Rose Panels compote is Australian but I have a strong hunch it may just be a Scandinavian pattern. Marigold is the only reported color.

# Roses and Fruit

This beautiful little compote is unique in several ways and is a very hard-to-find Millersburg item. It measures 5¼" from handle to handle and is nearly 4" high. Notice the deep bowl effect (so often used by Millersburg on compotes and bonbons) and the pedestal base. In addition, observe the unusual stippling around the edge of the interior, and, of course, the combination of roses, berries, and pears are quite distinctive. It is found in green and amethyst mostly, but was made in marigold and blue too.

# Roses and Ruffles Lamp (Red)

I'm frankly not too taken with Gone With the Wind Lamps, but the beautifully iridized ones are in a class by themselves. The very few known are simply beautiful. The Roses and Ruffles lamp is 22" tall. It has excellent fittings of brass and is quality all the way. The mold work on the glass is quite beautiful and the luster superior.

# Rose Show

What a handsome piece of glass this is! The design of this Northwood is flawless, heavy, and covering every inch of available space. Yet it isn't in the least bit busy looking. One has the distinct feeling he is looking into a reeded basket of fresh-cut roses and can almost smell the perfume. Found only on bowls and a plate, the beautiful pattern was produced in small amounts in marigold, purple, blue, green, white, ice blue, ice green, peach opalescent, amber, aqua opalescent, and a rare ice green opalescent.

*Rose Panels*

*Roses and Fruit*

*Roses and Ruffles*
*Lamp (Red)*

*Rose Show*

*Rose Show Variant*

*Rose Spray Compote*

*Rose Tree*

*Rosette*

### Rose Show Variant

Over the years, very little has been learned about this plate variant of the Rose Show pattern, but as you can see, it is quite different in both flower and leaf arrangement and number. It is found in a host of colors including marigold, amethyst, green, blue, peach opalescent, aqua opalescent, ice blue, and white.

### Rose Spray Compote

Standing only 4½" at its tallest point, this beautiful compote is a real treasure. The only colors I've heard about are white and the beautiful ice blue and ice green. I suspect this is a Fenton product, but have no verification of this. The rose and leaf spray is on one side of the rim only and is rather faint, much like the Kittens bowl.

### Rose Tree

Make no mistake about it, this is a very scarce and desirable Fenton bowl pattern. I believe this was the Fenton answer to the Imperial Luster Rose, but apparently it was made in small quantities. The colors known are marigold and cobalt blue, and the size is a generous 10" diameter.

### Rosette

Combining several well-known carnival glass patterns, including Stippled Rays and Beads and Prisms, this Northwood pattern isn't the easiest thing to find. In arrangement it reminds one of the Greek Key patterns, but Rosette stands on its own. Found only on generous sized bowls, the colors are blue, marigold, and amethyst. Green may be a possibility but I haven't seen one.

*Rose Windows*

# Rose Windows

I find this tumbler one of the prettiest geometric designs I've ever seen and wish other shapes were known. It has been seen in both a flashed light finish as well as the beautiful marigold shown. It stands 4½" tall, flares at both top and bottom, and is quality all the way.

# Round-Up

As I stated earlier, Round-Up, Fanciful, and Apple Blossoms Twigs all have the same exterior pattern and shards of the latter two were found in the Dugan diggings. Found only on bowls, ruffled plates, and true plates, Round-Up is available in marigold, purple, peach opalescent, blue, amber, white, and a pale shade of lavender. The true plate is quite scarce and always brings top dollar.

# Royal Pineapple

Please compare this attractive 8" vase to the photo of the Thistle vase shown elsewhere and you will see a remarkable similarity. The Royal Pineapple has a neat crowning edge around the top and while the color isn't great, the iridescence is good. These vases were found in the 1930s – 40s in crystal also, mostly in florist shops.

# Royalty

Perhaps one might mistake this for the Fashion pattern at first glance, but with a little concentrated study it becomes obvious they aren't the same. Royalty is a pattern formed from a series of hobstars above a series of diamond panels. Found on punch sets and two-piece fruit bowls, this Imperial pattern is mostly found in marigold, but the fruit bowl set has been reported in smoke.

*Round-Up*

*Royal Pineapple*

*Royalty*

223

**Ruffled Rib Spittoon**

**Ruffles and Rings**

**Rustic**

**Sacic Ashtray**

## Ruffled Rib Spittoon

This little Northwood spittoon could be called Fine Rib or Luster and Clear, I guess, but I feel the name given is more appropriate. At any rate, the coloring is a good rich marigold, and the ribbing is on the interior. The spittoon stands 4" tall and has a rim diameter of 4½" with a collar base diameter of nearly 2".

## Ruffles and Rings

Found in carnival glass as the exterior pattern for Rosette pattern bowls, Ruffles and Rings was originally a Jefferson Glass pattern, made in opalescent glass. Northwood bought this mold and made use of it as a secondary pattern.

## Rustic

I would venture to say Rustic is one of the best known and most common of vase shapes for it is plentiful and found in many sizes and colors including marigold, blue, green, amethyst, aqua, vaseline, amber, white, peach opalescent, and red. It was pulled from the Fenton Hobnail vase shapes and can be found in sizes from 6" to 20".

## Sacic Ashtray

This little ashtray is a real mystery in many ways. It reads: "NARAJA SACIC POMELO." Apparently it was meant to go to Brazil, but why an English glassmaker would mold such an item escapes me. The color is quite good with a touch of amber in marigold.

# Sailboats

Found in small bowls, plates, compotes, goblets, and wines, Sailboats is a well-known Fenton pattern that competes nicely with Imperial's Windmill pattern. Colors I've heard about are marigold, blue, green, vaseline, amber, and red, but not all colors are found in all shapes.

# Sawtooth Band

From the Heisey Company this pretty enameled tumbler is much like others except for the bands just above the base. This same pattern has been seen without the enameling also. All are marigold, and all are rare.

# Sawtooth Prisms

Despite not having a great deal of lustre, this cute jelly jar has a lot of character. It measures just over 3" in diameter and stands 4¼" tall. The sawtooth edges fit the lid and the bottom together nicely. Marigold is the only color reported. It is known in two other sizes also.

# Scale Band

While not too original, this Fenton pattern of smooth rays and bands of scale filler does quite nicely in the shapes chosen: bowls, plates, pitchers, and tumblers. The color most seen is, of course, marigold. However, Scale Band can also be found in green, amethyst, peach opalescent, aqua opalescent (quite rare), white, and red.

*Sailboats*

*Sawtooth Band*

*Sawtooth Prisms*

*Scale Band*

*Scarab Hatpin*

*Scotch Thistle*

*Scottie*

## Scarab Hatpin
I have always avoided showing hatpins or buttons, but the one here is so pretty, I couldn't resist. It is on a very deep amethyst base color and has super luster. It measures 1¾" x 1⅜".

## Scotch Thistle
What a pretty pattern this is for the interior of a compote! As you can see, the exterior is plain like so many compotes, but the edges have a very interesting ruffled effect. Colors I've seen are marigold, blue, green, and amethyst, but others may certainly exist. This pattern was manufactured by Fenton.

## Scottie
Surely there isn't a collector that hasn't seen these in the flea markets in Scotties, poodles, deer, duckies, or rabbits. They are all covered powder jars, all marigold, and made near the end of the carnival glass heyday. Still the coloring is usually respectable, and they are cute little critters.

## Scroll and Flower Panels
I've always been intrigued by this stylish Imperial pattern even though it was reproduced in the 1960s with a flared top. As you can see, the mold work, while very busy, is quite satisfying and the coloring is super. I've seen this vase in marigold and purple, but green is a possibility. The vase stands 10" tall on a collar base with a many-rayed star.

*Scroll and Flower Panels*

*Scroll and Grape (Millersburg)*

## Scroll and Grape (Millersburg)

Nothing pleases me more than showing an unlisted pattern, especially if it is Millersburg! The only example reported of this Multi-Fruits and Flowers punch bowl interior is such a find. From the center four strings of acanthus leaves extend to four clusters of grapes, all topped by a rich scroll. What a shame this wasn't a standard pattern! It's as pretty as anything Millersburg ever made.

## Scroll Embossed (Imperial)

As I said earlier, while this pattern originated at the Imperial factory, it was later produced in England on carnival glass, notably on the Diving Dolphins bowl and on a four-handled sauce dish. The Imperial version is used with the File pattern exterior, on bowls with Eastern Star as an exterior pattern, on large compotes, as well as alone on bowls and smaller compotes. The usual colors are green, marigold, or purple, but smoke does exist. A scarce plate shape is shown.

*(Interior of Scroll and Grape)*

*Scroll Embossed (Imperial)*

227

**Scroll Embossed Variant (English)**

**Seafoam**

**Seacoast Pintray**

**Seagulls Bowl**

## Scroll Embossed Variant (English)

Much like the Imperial pattern it was copied from, the English version is found on small bowls, plates, handled ashtrays, compotes, as well as on the Diving Dolphin pieces. The exterior design is the giveaway; File on Imperial, a vine-like pattern on the English pieces. Colors are marigold, blue, green, and amethyst.

## Seacoast Pintray

Pintrays are not common in carnival glass, and this one from Millersburg is one of the nicest ones. The irregular shaping, the beautiful coloring and fine detail make this an outstanding item. It measures 5½" x 3¾" and rests on an oval-collar base. The colors are marigold, green, amethyst, and a fine deep purple.

## Seafoam

This Dugan-Diamond pattern is actually the same as their S-Repeat pattern and the Seafoam piece is nothing more than a reshaped goblet with an interior pattern called Constellation added. Seafoam is found in white, marigold, peach opalescent, amethyst, and a strange yellow opalescent treatment.

## Seagulls Bowl

If one rarity in this book stands as an example of "scarce but not prized," the Seagulls bowl is that rarity. Certainly there are far fewer of these to be found than many items that bring 10 times the money, but for some strange reason, these cuties are not sought by most collectors. The two bird figures are heavily detailed as is the bowl pattern. The color, while not outstanding, is good and is iridized both inside and out. The diameter of the bowl is 5¾" and the depth is 2⅞". I believe the manufacturer was Dugan.

*Seagulls Vase*

### Seagulls Vase

This rare vase has been traced to the Eda Glassworks of Sweden, adding to their growing importance as a non-American maker of iridized glass. The only color reported is a rich marigold with a good deal of amber hue.

### Seaweed

Can you imagine a more graceful pattern than this one from Millersburg? The curving leaves and snail-like figures seem to be drifting back and forth in the watery depths, and the bubbles of beading add just the right touch. Usually found on fairly large bowls, Seaweed has three mold marks. The colors are marigold, green, and amethyst. Also a rare plate and a rare small bowl have been found.

### Seaweed Lamp

I've heard of four of these lamps in two different base shapes, but all with the Seaweed design circling the body. All were in marigold ranging from quite good to poor. The example shown measures 12" to the top of the font. The maker is unknown, but the lamp is a rare one.

*Seaweed*

*Seaweed Lamp*

**229**

*Serpentine Rose*

*Shanghai*

*Shasta Daisy*

## Serpentine Rose

The owner of this very unusual bowl called it by this name and since I haven't found it listed by any other, I am continuing with it here. The pattern is a series of rose and twisting vine and leaf patterns, three around the bowl. The feet are spatula and clear while the bowl has a very rich marigold finish with great iridescence.

## Shanghai

Certainly not much to brag about in either color or design, the novelty of this short tumbler is in the lettering on the base which says SHANGHAI, CHINA. There is also a small triangle in the center. I suspect this tumbler to date to the 1930s since anything after WWII would say Republic of China. There may be other shapes but I haven't seen them.

## Shasta Daisy

Here is the familiar Zig-Zag water set from Fenton with a painted design that is called Shasta Daisy. It is a fine frosty white and the flowers and leaves are pastel too, showing greens, blues, and reds.

*Shell*

## Shell

I've always felt this was a superior Imperial pattern – simple yet effective. This is especially true on the few plates I've seen. The pattern is a well-balanced one of eight scalloped shells around a star-like pattern. The background may or may not be stippled – I've seen it both ways. The shapes are smallish bowls, plates, and a reported compote I haven't seen. The colors are marigold, green, purple, smoke, and amber.

## Shell and Jewel

Easily found, this Westmoreland pattern was made only in the shapes shown in colors of marigold, amethyst, and green (white has been reported but not confirmed). The pattern is a copy of the Nugget Ware pattern of the Dominion Glass Company of Canada. Shell and Jewel has been reproduced, so buy with caution.

## Shooting Star

Identified in the *Carnival Glass News of Great Britain* (#15) in 1986, this pattern has been seen in the creamer, a covered butter dish, and probably came in a matching open sugar on a stem. The pattern is all intaglio (on the outside of the sugar but on the inside of the butter lid) and the color is quite good.

*Shell and Jewel*

*Shooting Star*

*Shrine Champagne (Rochester)*

*Simplicity Scroll*

*Silver Queen*

*Singing Birds*

## Shrine Champagne (Rochester)

Shown is one of three known stemmed champagnes manufactured by the U.S. Glass Company, to be given away at Shrine conventions (a rare toothpick holder is also known). The 1911 Rochester, NY, champagne has painted scenes of Rochester and Pittsburgh with a gilt decoration. The other champagnes are the 1910 New Orleans and Tobacco Leaf (Louisville, KY – 1909). Each is a premium example of the glassmaker's skill.

## Simplicity Scroll

This very interesting toothpick holder is shown in an old Westmoreland ad along with several Estate pieces and the Miniature Basket with wire bale handle. The toothpick holder is in a smoke over gold finish Westmoreland called their "Antique Iridescent." It stands 2⅞" tall and 2⅝" wide. It is lettered: "Souvenir of Tolley, N.D."

## Silver Queen

While this Fenton pattern has never been one of my favorite enameled water sets, it is certainly not all that easy to find and has good color and finish. It is found only in marigold with the wide silver band and white scroll and only in water sets.

## Singing Birds

Found in custard glass, crystal, and carnival glass, Singing Birds is one of the better known Northwood patterns. The shapes are berry sets, table sets, water sets, and mugs in vivid and pastel colors.

*Single Flower Framed*

# Single Flower Framed

Much like the Single Flower pattern, this one has odd framing of double wavy lines that encircle the flowers. The pattern is exterior, the colors the usual Dugan ones. Shapes are large and small bowls, and the interior of the one shown shows a Fine Rib pattern.

# Six Petals

Nearly always seen in shallow bowls in peach opalescent, Six Petals is occasionally found in a rare plate. The other colors available are purple, green, blue, and white. It is a Dugan product shown in black amethyst in exterior view.

# Six-Sided Candlestick

What a beauty this candlestick is! Not only is the near-cut design quite imaginative, but the workmanship is just super. The Six-Sided candlestick is 7½" tall and has a base diameter of 3¾". It has been seen in a rich marigold, an outstanding purple, smoke, and green. It has been reproduced by Imperial in crystal, so be cautious in your selection!

*Six Petals*

*(Six Petals Exterior)*

*Six-Sided Candlestick*

*Ski Star*

*Slick Willie Vase*

*Slipper (Lady's)*

*Small Basket*

## Ski Star

While this Dugan pattern is found occasionally on small bowls in purple, blue, and green, it is on the larger dome-footed bowls in peach opalescent where the pattern has its "day in the sun." These are found in many variations, some crimped with one side turned down, others with both sides pulled up to resemble a banana bowl. The exterior usually carries the Compass pattern, an interesting geometric design, or is plain.

## Slick Willie Vase

I expect I'll be criticized for this name, but since we already have a Hale Baths and a Hot Springs vase, this was the first name to come to mind. This advertising piece is about 11½" tall and is marked "Hale Baths – Hot Springs, Ark." The design looks like raindrops running down the surface.

## Slipper (Lady's)

Here's another novel miniature from U.S. Glass so ornamental yet appealing. Needless to say, very few of these were ever iridized, so all are rare. The Lady's Slipper is 4½" long and 2¾" high and is a good marigold. The entire piece is covered with stippling.

## Small Basket

Made by Sowerby in England, this handled pintray measures a bit less that 6" across from handle to handle and stands 1½" tall. It is eight-sided and ribbed over each section with pie-shaped sections in the bottom that are also ribbed. Coloring is typically English carnival with a soft marigold.

*Small Rib*

*Smooth Panels*

## Small Rib

The compote shown has been pulled into the rose bowl shape, but versions of the lip opened out are also known. Coloring is much like the Daisy Squares pieces and may have the same common maker.

## Smooth Panels

Since I first showed this vase in marigold iridescence on milk glass, I've seen many sizes and colors. These vases remind one of the Imperial Flute pattern around their base. Found in sizes ranging from 8" tall to 18", the lip is often widened to 7". Colors are marigold, amethyst, green, purple, peach opalescent, amber, teal, red, and several colors over milk glass including marigold, amber, and a beautiful smoke.

## Smooth Rays (Westmoreland)

Like most of the other major manufacturers, Westmoreland had a try at a Smooth Rays pattern in compotes and various size bowls with both flat and dome bases. Here is one of theirs in a beautiful blue milk glass iridized, but these were made in marigold, amethyst, green, marigold milk glass, amber, and teal as well.

*Smooth Rays (Westmoreland)*

235

*Snow Fancy*

*Soda Gold*

*Soda Gold Spears*

### Snow Fancy

Known in small bowls as well as a creamer and sugar breakfast set, this scarce near-cut pattern is one with which many collectors are not familiar. The bowl has been seen in green as well as a frosty white, and the breakfast set is shown in marigold; other colors may exist, but I haven't seen them. It is a McKee product.

### Soda Gold

Much confused with Tree of Life and Crackle shown elsewhere in this book, Imperial's Soda Gold differs from either in that the veins are much more pronounced and are highly raised from the stippled surface. It is found only on short candlesticks, a rare 9" bowl, and beautiful water sets in marigold or smoke.

### Soda Gold Spears

Similar to Tree of Life and Crackle patterns, this all-over design is easy on the eye and a good background to hold iridescence well. The bowl shown is the 8" size, but 5" bowls and plates are known in both marigold and clambroth.

*Soldiers and Sailors (Illinois)*

# Soldiers and Sailors (Illinois)

One of two known such commemorative plates, this is the Illinois version. It features the Soldiers and Sailors Home in Quincy, IL, and measures 7½". On the exterior is found Fenton's Berry and Leaf Circle design. The colors known are marigold, amethyst, and blue.

# Soutache Plate

I've long believed this to be a Northwood pattern, and while I've seen it on both bowls and lamp shades, this is the first footed plate I've run across. It measures 8¾" in diameter and has peach opalescent edging. The foot is a dome base and is of clear glass.

# Sowerby's File and Shell

A rare find, this two-piece candle lamp stands 9½" tall and like the Grape and Cable lamp, has a fitted holder that ties the shade to the candle. It is marked Sowerby and was a very strong marigold until it was tragically put in a dishwasher! The iridescence is now a pastel but still lovely.

*Soutache Plate*

*Sowerby's File and Shell*

*Sowerby Wide Panel*

*Spanish Moss*

*Spearhead and Rib*

*Spiral Candle*

### $S$*owerby Wide Panel*

While there isn't much special about this bowl — a wide panel exterior with a many-rayed star base, it does have very good color and finish and the scalloping around the rim adds a touch of class. It is English and made by Sowerby.

### $S$*panish Moss*

A very pretty little hatpin holder that stands just 5½" tall, this design has it all — enameling, iridescence, and a very nice pattern. The top is uneven in shaping and it reminds one of spanish moss draping from a branch, while the flared base looks like a tree stump.

### $S$*pearhead and Rib*

At first glance, this appears to be a Fine Rib vase, but it is shown in old Fenton ads as their #916 and has a break in the ribbing in the center of the vase as well as the diamond endings in opposing sections at the top of the vase. These diamonds are in rows of four high but due to the stretching, are not all that evident until the vase is studied closely.

### $S$*piral Candle*

Like the Premium candlesticks also made by Imperial, these heavy, practical candlesticks were sold in pairs and were made in green, smoke, and marigold. They measure 8¼" from the base to the top and, as far as I know, did not have a console bowl to match. The smoke coloring is particularly beautiful with many fiery highlights.

**Split Diamond**

## Spiralex

This is the name used in England to describe these lovely vases, so I've continued using it. The colors are marigold, amethyst, green, and blue, and all I've seen are outstanding with very rich iridescence. Sizes range from 8" to 14".

## Split Diamond

I'm very happy to show the complete table set in this Davison pattern, for while the creamer is easily found, the covered butter and sugar are quite scarce in this country. The only color is a good strong marigold with fine luster and superior mold.

## Spring Opening

Made from the standard Millersburg small berry bowl mold, this interesting hand-grip advertising plate is a seldom-seen, always attractive item from the Ohio company. It measures 6½" in diameter, has the typical many-rayed base, and is known only in amethyst. The lettering says: "Campbell & Beesley Co. Spring Opening 1911."

## Springtime

In many ways this pattern is similar to Northwood's Raspberry pattern, especially since both are bordered at the bottom with versions of a basketweave. Springtime, however, is really its own master and bears panels of wheat, flowers, and butterflies above and throughout the basketweave. Found in berry sets, table sets, and very scarce water sets in marigold, green, amethyst, and also in pastels, Springtime is a very desirable pattern.

**Spiralex**

**Spring Opening**

**Springtime**

239

*Square Diamond*
*(Column Flower)*

*S-Repeat*

*Stag and Holly*

## *S*quare Diamond *(Column Flower)*

Sometime after I gave this vase the above name, another author called it Column Flower, so you have a choice. It was made at the Riihimaki Glassworks in Finland and has been seen only in blue.

## *S*-Repeat

Made in crystal, decorated crystal, and gilt glass prior to being made in carnival glass, S-Repeat is found in only a small range of shapes in iridized glass. Besides the punch set shown, there is a rare toothpick that has been widely reproduced, and a handful of marigold tumblers that some believe are questionable. At any rate, in carnival glass, Dugan's S-Repeat is a very scarce item.

## *S*tag and Holly

This is probably the best known animal pattern in all carnival glass other than the Peacock, and certainly it remains one of Fenton's best efforts. Often brought out at Christmas time, the Stag and Holly is found mainly on footed bowls, rare footed plates, and rare rose bowls. Colors are marigold, blue, green, amethyst, aqua, peach opalescent, and red.

## Standard

This very attractive tubular vase is in two parts and stands some 5¼" tall. The top flares to almost 3", matching the bottom diameter of the metal stand. I believe this to be a Dugan-Diamond product and suspect it may have been made in other colors than the very strong marigold shown.

## Star

While there may not be a great deal of inventiveness to this English pattern, it certainly serves a useful purpose and does it with a good deal of attractiveness. The clear center shows off the star on the base quite well, and the two tiny rows of rope edging add a bit of interest. Marigold is the only color I've heard about.

## Star and Fan Cordial Set

This pattern is not the same as the vase with the same name but has a close tie with the other cordial sets like Zipper Stitch which were made in Czechoslovakia. It is a rare grouping and the only complete set known.

## Star and Fan Vase

I've been privileged to see the two Imperial marigold vases shown, but a beautiful cobalt blue example also exists, and it must be something, for the marigold ones are very beautiful examples of the glassmaker's art. The glass itself is thick and very clear. The luster is rich and even, and the design is flawless. Star and Fan is 9½" tall.

*Standard*

*Star*

*Star and Fan Cordial Set*

*Star and Fan Vase*

Star and File

Star and Hobs (Northern Lights)

Starburst

## *Star and File*

Very much like Star Medallion in concept, Imperial's Star and File doesn't have the cane effect, but uses panels of file, hobstars, and sunbursts in a well-balanced design. Found in bowls, breakfast sets, a water set, a wine decanter set, handled vases, a rare rose bowl, and a large compote, Star and File is known in marigold, smoke, purple, and green.

## *Star and Hobs*
## *(Northern Lights)*

This very attractive 9" rose bowl has much to offer in both quality and looks. The color is a deep purple glass with beautiful gold luster, and while the base pattern resembles Ohio Star, I believe this to be a European product.

## *Starburst*

This beautiful and rare spittoon whimsey shape comes from the Riihimaki Glassworks of Finland. It is found mostly in bowls, table set pieces, and a vase shape and has been reported in cobalt blue; however, this is the first spittoon about which I've heard.

*Starburst Lustre*

## Starburst Lustre

While this bowl's exterior has no pressed design, the pattern of spray used in iridizing it gives it a very pretty pattern called Starburst Lustre, similar to the "Rainbow" treatment also used by Northwood. It can be found on bowls and compotes as well as with a few true patterns (see Stippled Mum).

## Star Fish

As you can see, this little compote is a real cutie. The design is strong and interesting, and the quality is top-notch. Star Fish is from the Dugan company and is seen in marigold, green, purple, and the beautiful peach opalescent.

## Starflower

All our years of investigation haven't determined who made this beautiful pitcher (no tumblers have ever shown up). In design, it is outstanding and has been found in two heights! Colors reported to date are marigold, blue, and a very rare white. All are real collector's items and much sought.

## Star Goblet

While I can't verify other shapes in this very pretty pattern, the milk goblet shows just how beautiful the iridescence is. The only designs are the incised, four-pointed stars that circle the goblet's bowl.

*Star Fish*

*Star Goblet*

*Starflower*

243

*Starlyte Shade*

*Star Medallion*

*Star of David*

*Star of David and Bows*

## Starlyte Shade

Imperial made several very attractive light shades, and this is certainly one of them. The Starlyte shade stands 4" tall and has a bell diameter of 8". The pattern is a series of panels containing graduated hobstars on a stippled background. Colors are a rich marigold and clambroth, but I suspect smoke and green are also possibilities.

## Star Medallion

Star Medallion is a much-overlooked but well designed near-cut Imperial pattern. Apparently, it was a very popular pattern in its day for it is found in many shapes, including bowls of all shapes, a table set, a handled celery, a 9" plate, milk pitcher, punch cup, tumbler, goblet, and a very beautiful compote. Colors are a rich marigold, smoke, and occasionally a beautiful helios green.

## Star of David

For some unknown reason, only small amounts of this beautiful Imperial pattern must have been produced, for it is seldom seen today. As you can see, it is simply a Star of David half-stippled on a plain background with smooth ribbing to the edge of the bowl. The example shown measures 8¾" in diameter and is the famous helios green of Imperial with a silver finish, but the pattern is also known in marigold, smoke, and purple. The exterior carries the Arcs pattern.

## Star of David and Bows

The Northwood version of this figure (Imperial also produced a Star of David bowl) is a very attractive dome-footed bowl and is a tribute to the Jewish religion. The star is interlaced and is beaded while a graceful border of flowers, tendrils, and bows edge the stippled center. The exterior is the Vintage pattern, and the colors are marigold, green, and amethyst.

*Star Spray*

# Star Spray

This smallish (7½") Imperial bowl can be found in crystal as well as iridized glass in marigold and smoke. The pattern is all exterior and intaglio and very well done.

# Stippled Acorns

The covered candy dish shown comes rather late in carnival glass production but is still attractive enough to be of interest. It stands 6½" tall on a 3½" footing. I've seen these in marigold, blue, and amethyst. It was made by Jeanette.

# Stippled Diamond Swag

This beautifully designed English compote seems to be the only shape known in this pattern, and while Mrs. Presznick reports green and blue ones, I've seen only the rich marigold shown. The compote is 5" tall and measures 5¾" across the top with a 3½" base.

*Stippled Acorns*

*Stippled Diamond Swag*

*Stippled Flower*

### Stippled Flower

Seen most often in peach opalescent glass, this Dugan-Diamond pattern is really just the much used rayed or ribbed look with a stippled, six-petal flower in the center. The bowl shown is about 8″ in diameter and has a collar base.

### Stippled Mum (Northwood)

Most who see this pattern call it Stippled Rays but it certainly isn't. The mum is only in the center of the bowl and is completely stippled. The bottom center is marked "Northwood" and the rest of the bowl has an iridizing treatment called "Star Burst Lustre," a Northwood treatment that seems to be used by no one else.

### Stippled Petals

While this Dugan pattern isn't uncommon in peach opalescent bowls, the pretty handled basket sets it well above the ordinary. Made from the 9″ bowl, this basket is a large one and has been seen in amethyst as well as the beautiful peach shown.

*Stippled Mum (Northwood)*

*Stippled Petals*

*Stippled Rambler Rose*

# Stippled Rambler Rose

Most trails seem to lead to the Dugan company with this seldom-discussed pattern, but I have no proof they made it. The shape shown is the only one I've seen, and the colors are marigold and blue only.

# Stippled Rays (Fenton)

While Stippled Rays was used by both Northwood and Millersburg too, the Fenton version is perhaps the most commonly known and is available in bowls, bonbons, compotes, plates, creamers, and sugars. The colors found are marigold, amethyst, green, blue, and a rare red.

# Stippled Rays (Imperial)

Only this footed breakfast set has been reported so far in this Imperial version of Stippled Rays. Most have plain interiors, but the one shown has a duplicate pattern inside as well. Colors reported are marigold, cobalt blue, purple, green, amber, and smoke.

*Stippled Rays (Fenton)*

*Stippled Rays (Imperial)*

*Stippled Rays (Northwood)*

*Stippled Strawberry*

*Stork ABC Plate*

## Stippled Rays (Northwood)

The Northwood company had several versions of this pattern, but most are marked and can be easily spotted. On some, the rays are evenly finished some distance from the outer edge while on others, they extend almost to the lip. Mostly on dome-based bowls and compotes, colors are marigold, blue, green, amethyst, white, black amethyst, and rarely smoke.

## Stippled Strawberry

While this pattern has been reported previously in a tumbler only, it obviously wasn't limited to that shape, and it is a real pleasure to show this rare spittoon shape. It stands 3½" tall and measures 4½" across its widest part. The coloring is nothing spectacular but adequate. Along the spittoon's lip is a checkerboard pattern. The manufacturer is the Jenkins company.

## Stork ABC Plate

Long a favorite with collectors, the child's plate known as the Stork ABC plate was a product of the Belmont Glass Company. Advertisements for this 7½" item show it was made in pink, green, frosted green, and the iridized version. It has a raised rim and flat base.

*Stork and Rushes*

*Stork Vase*

## Stork and Rushes

Stork and Rushes is another pattern whose shards were found in the Dugan diggings, and since it has features that are typical of Northwood, I'm afraid it's difficult to state whether Dugan or Northwood made this pattern. At any rate, it is available in berry sets, punch sets, water sets, hats, and mugs. I've seen only marigold, purple, and blue with purple which is probably the hardest color to find.

## Stork Vase

Much like the Swirl vase in concept, the Stork vase was made by Jenkins and is usually found in a pale marigold glass. The Stork is on one side only with stippling covering the other side. The Stork vase stands 7½" tall.

## Strawberry (Fenton)

This little bonbon shape has been seen in all sorts of glass including crystal, custard, milk glass, and carnival glass where the colors range from marigold, cobalt, amethyst, and green to the rare red amberina shown and a good rich all red. The design qualities aren't all that good, but the iridescence is usually adequate and on the whole, the Fenton bonbon comes off nicely.

*Strawberry (Fenton)*

*Strawberry (Millersburg)*

## Strawberry (Millersburg)

Like its close relatives, Grape and Blackberry Wreaths, this beautiful pattern is the culmination of the design. Its detailing is much finer than either of the other patterns, and the glass is exceptional. The coloring is a true grape purple, and the iridescence is a light even gold. Like other Millersburg patterns, the shapes vary, but the deep tri-cornered bowl with candy-ribbon edge is my favorite. A rare compote exists in the usual colors.

## Strawberry (Northwood)

Available in only bowls of various sizes and plates in either flat or hand grip styles, the well-known Northwood pattern comes either plain or stippled. On the stippled version there are three narrow rings around the outer edge; these are absent on the plain pieces. Colors are both vivid and pastel with the purple showing the pattern to its best.

## Strawberry Epergne

The Strawberry Epergne is very much like the Fishnet one also made by Dugan; however, the former is much rarer and has not been reported in peach opalescent yet. As you can see, the bowl exterior is plain, and the base is domed.

*Strawberry (Northwood)*

*Strawberry Epergne*

*Strawberry Intaglio*

## Strawberry Intaglio

I showed this pattern in *Millersburg, The Queen of Carnival Glass* as a questionable Millersburg pattern. Since then we've been able to trace it to the Northwood Company through both a goofus bowl and a gilt decorated one, both bearing the famous trademark. The glass is thick, the design deeply impressed, and the iridescence only so so. I've seen large and small bowls only.

## Strawberry Scroll

Much like the rare Lily of the Valley in design, this rare Fenton water set is a real beauty that can stand along side of the best designs in carnival glass. The shape, like that of the Blueberry set, is very artistic also. Colors reported are marigold and blue, but I suspect amethyst and green are possibilities.

## Stream of Hearts

The same heart shape employed by Fenton on the Heart and Vine, and Heart and Trees designs is found here on the scale fillers swirls that form a peacock's tail. Usually found on the compote shape, often with Persian Medallion as an exterior companion, Stream of Hearts is available on a 10" footed bowl also. Colors are marigold, blue, and white.

*Strawberry Scroll*

*Stream of Hearts*

*Stretch*

**Stretched Diamonds
and Dots**

**Strutting Peacock**

*Studs*

## Stretch

Made with virtually the same process as carnival glass but with an additional step to give it an "onion skin" appearance, stretch glass was made by most of the major companies in the mid-1920s.

## Stretched Diamonds and Dots

Very little information seems to be available on this tumbler. It is 4½" tall, comes from a two part mold, and has an unusual star design in the base. The pattern of diamonds filled with large buttons above stretched diamonds is very attractive, despite the color being rather light.

## Strutting Peacock

The only shapes in this Westmoreland pattern are the creamer and sugar, and the only colors I've heard about are green or amethyst. The design is much like Shell and Jewel, also a Westmoreland product, but beware; these have been reproduced.

## Studs

While this isn't one of the earliest of carnival glass patterns and certainly not the most imaginative, it has a place in the collector's world. It was made by Jeanette Glass in a footed juice tumbler, a milk pitcher, and a large tray with handles. The only color reported is marigold but most pieces have very good coloring and iridescence.

## Stylized Flower Center

While the plate shown is obviously an Orange Tree design, the center pattern is called Stylized Flower Center and is found only on plates and some bowls. Just why Fenton used this extra design in such a limited manner is hard to understand, but it makes a beautiful plate even nicer.

## Sunflower

Sunflower must have been a very popular pattern in its day, for numerous examples have survived to the present time. It's quite easy to see why it was in demand. It's a pretty, well-designed Northwood pattern that holds iridescence beautifully. The bowl is footed and carries the very pleasing Meander pattern on the exterior. It is also found, rarely, on a plate. The colors are marigold, green, amethyst, and a rare teal blue.

## Sunflower and Diamond

Long felt to be a Jenkins pattern, this well-done vase is now known to be of Swedish origin, and an example in blue has been reported. The usual color is a good marigold. The pattern is all intaglio and very deep.

## Sunflower Pintray

Like its companion piece, the Seacoast Pintray, this Millersburg item joins the list of a select few. It is 5¼" long and 4½" wide and also rests on a collar base. The most unique feature is, of course, the open handle, and the colors are marigold, purple, amethyst, and a rich green.

*Stylized Flower Center*

*Sunflower*

*Sunflower and Diamond*

*Sunflower Pintray*

**Sun-Gold Epergne**

**Sunken Hollyhock**

### *S*un-Gold Epergne

Although I question the origin of this beautiful epergne, I don't for one minute doubt its desirability. The base is of highly polished pierced brass while the bowl and lily are of an unusual pinkish-marigold carnival glass. The epergne is 12" tall, and the bowl has a 9¼" diameter. The glass is clear and mirror-like and has good even iridescence.

### *S*unken Hollyhock

Probably found more readily than the other Gone With the Wind lamps, Sunken Hollyhock can be found in marigold (often with a caramel coloring) and a very rare red. The lamp stands an impressive 25" tall and certainly is a show stopper.

### *S*unray Compote

These small compotes, found on marigold over milk glass, are very pretty in their own plain way. Fenton made many such items, and I strongly feel this compote came from that company also.

**Sunray Compote**

*Superb Drape*

*Sun Punch*

## Superb Drape

For years only one example of this rare and beautiful vase was known, an aqua opalescent finish over a nearly opaque glass. Now a second one in the same coloring on a lighter base glass and the recently discovered green example shown have appeared. These pieces are mold blown, squat, with a 7" top diameter, 4½" base diameter, and are 6¼" tall. Most experts feel Northwood is the maker of this fine rarity.

## Sun Punch

This very unusual bottle is 8" tall, stippled, with three ball shapes sitting one on top the other to make up the shape. A diagonal band says "Sun Punch" and in addition, there are suns and rays above and below the lines of zig-zagging! The coloring is only average but the iridescence isn't bad and after all, isn't the design enough to make this collectible?

## Sweetheart

Besides the rare and beautiful covered cookie jar shown, this Cambridge pattern is known in a very rare tumbler shape in marigold. The cookie jar has been seen in marigold, green, and amethyst, and as you can see, the mold work and finish are superior.

*Sweetheart*

*Swirl (Imperial)*

*Swirl (Northwood)*

*Swirl Candlestick*

*Swirled Flute Vase*

## Swirl (Imperial)

This 7" vase is shown in old Imperial catalogs, and I've heard of it in marigold, smoke, green, and white. The design is nothing outstanding, but the useful shape and the iridescence are adequate.

## Swirl (Northwood)

I've seen this pattern on a beautiful tankard water set and the mug shape in marigold. The tumbler is shown in the Owens book in green and is known in amethyst. While the tumblers are often marked, the mug isn't. Now and then, the tankard pitcher is found with enameled flowers added. Naturally, the pitcher is scarce, and the mug is considered rare.

## Swirl Candlestick

This very attractive candlestick is the same pattern as the rare mug I showed in previous books and was apparently a product of either Northwood or Dugan. While other colors may exist, I haven't heard of any. The luster is top-notch, and the glass is quality all the way.

## Swirled Flute Vase

This little Fenton vase is a real charmer for such simplistic design. The wide panel is quite pronounced at the base and the color and iridescence are quite good. These little vases average about 9" in height and are found in red, marigold, green, amethyst, blue, and white.

## Swirled Threads

What a very pretty piece of glass this stemmed goblet is. The coloring is dark and rich, and the stem ending in a ball shape gives it a nice touch. The threadings are all interior. I'd guess it came from Europe but can't be sure.

## Swirl Hobnail

This is a little Millersburg jewel in either the rose bowl or the lady's spittoon, and once you own either piece, wild horses couldn't drag it away. The glass is simply sparkling and the iridescence outstanding. The spittoon has an irregular scalloped edge opening, and both shapes have a many-rayed base. The usual colors prevail, but the green is extremely difficult to locate. Swirl Hobnail can also be found in a vase shape.

## Sydney

While this Fostoria pattern is known in other shapes in crystal, the tumbler and smaller champagne glass are the only shapes reported in carnival glass. The color is an amber-like marigold that is well iridized. The tumbler is nearly 4" tall, and the champagne measures 3¼".

## Taffeta Lustre Candlesticks

These very rare Fostoria candlesticks were manufactured in 1916 or 1917 (according to an old Fostoria catalog) in colors of amber, blue, green, crystal, or orchid. They were part of a flower set which included a centerpiece bowl 11" in diameter. The candlesticks themselves came in 2", 4", 6", 9", and 12" sizes, and as you can see, these shown still have the original paper labels on the bottom. When held to the light, the ultraviolet color is fantastic, and the iridescence is heavy and rich. Fostoria made very small amounts of iridized glass, and certainly these examples of their Taffeta Lustre line are quite rare.

*Swirled Threads*

*Swirl Hobnail*

*Sydney*

*Taffeta Lustre Candlesticks*

257

*Target Vase*

**Thin and Wide Rib Vase**

*Tall Hat*

### *Tall Hat*

Like the Pastel Hat pieces, this taller version is usually found in pastel blue with a pink top. However, I've also seen marigold examples of this same piece. The example shown is a little over 7″ and the lip is turned down on three sides and up on the back side almost like a jack-in-the-pulpit vase.

### *Target Vase*

This seldom seen vase pattern is from the Dugan-Diamond Glass Company. It can be found in marigold, amethyst, blue, peach opalescent, and a smoky blue. The example shown has a very unusual butterscotch hue to the peach coloring and is heavy with opalescence on both the hobnail-like projections and the panels, as well as flames on the top edges.

### *Ten Mums*

Found on beautiful water sets, large impressive bowls, and rare plates, Fenton's Ten Mums is a very realistic pattern. The mold work is unusually fine, especially on the bowl shape. Colors are marigold, cobalt blue, green, peach opalescent, and white, but not all shapes are found in all colors.

### *Thin and Wide Rib Vase*

This Northwood vase pattern is usually dismissed as just another "rib" pattern, but it is quite distinct from either the Fine Rib, Thin Rib, or any others. It has one wide rib bordered on either side by two thinner ribs. The example shown is a rare ice green example with very strong, fiery highlights.

*Ten Mums*

*Thin Rib (Northwood)*

# Thin Rib (Northwood)

Here is an exterior pattern every one must know, for besides the famous basketweave, it is found on some of Northwood's best known bowl patterns, including Good Luck and Strawberry. It is simple enough, but held to the light, it adds greatly to the design.

# Thin Rib and Drape

While this pretty little vase is much like many coming from American makers, we now know this to be an English product from Sowerby. The ribbing is on the outside while the draping is interior. Colors are marigold, amethyst, and green, and sizes range in height from 4" to 12".

# Thistle

Fairly typical of many Fenton bowl patterns, Thistle is artistically true with the thistles and leaves realistic and graceful. Found on bowls, plates, and a rare compote, the colors seen are marigold, green, blue, and occasionally amethyst. Now and then a bowl appears with advertising on the base.

*Thin Rib and Drape*

*Thistle*

259

*Thistle and Thorn*

*Thistle Banana Boat*

*Thistle Vase*

*Three Fruits*

## *T*histle and Thorn

British in origin, this nicely designed pattern is found on a variety of shapes, all footed, including bowls, sugars, creamers, plates, and nut bowls. Colors are usually marigold, but I've had blue reported.

## *T*histle Banana Boat

This beautiful Fenton banana boat is another of the underrated patterns in carnival glass. Massive in concept, bold in design with the thistle on the interior and cattail and waterlily outside, the four-footed banana boat is usually found in marigold, amethyst, green, or cobalt blue. The iridescence is quite heavy, usually with much gold.

## *T*histle Vase

What a pretty little vase this is. Standing 6" tall with a soft amber shading to the glass, the Thistle vase is a well-designed bit of color for vase lovers. The maker is unknown.

## *T*hree Fruits

So very close in design to the Northwood Fruits and Flowers pattern shown earlier in this book, the two substantial differences are the absence of the small flowers and the addition of an extra cluster of cherries to this pattern. Found in bowls of all sizes, including flat and footed ones, and average size plates. Northwood's Three Fruits is available in all vivid colors as well as pastels.

*Three Fruit Medallion*

## Three Fruits Medallion

The difference between this and the other examples of Northwood's Three Fruits patterns is a center medallion of leaves rather than the usual fruit center. The exterior can be either the Meander pattern or Basketweave. The first is always footed while the latter is collar based. Colors are green, marigold, amethyst, black amethyst, blue, horehound, and aqua opalescent.

## Three Fruits Variant

If you'll compare this beautiful 9" plate with the Northwood version, you'll see a good deal of similarities and some obvious differences. While this version has been credited to Fenton, I strongly suspect it was a Dugan product.

*Three-in-One*

## Three-in-One

Originally called Number One in the crystal line, this well-known Imperial bowl pattern (plates also exist) is always easy to spot because of the two rows of near-cut diamond designs, separated by a center area of flutes. I've seen bowls in 4½", 7½", 8¾" sizes and in colors of deep marigold, green, purple, and smoke. The iridescence is usually quite good and the glass heavy, clear, and sparkling.

*Three Fruits Variant*

## Three-in-One Variant

This beautifully made toothpick holder has been iridized on only the center sections and is exactly like the Three-In-One pattern except for the file work within the top and bottom row of diamonds. Beyond any question, it is an old one.

*Three-in-One Variant*

261

*Three Monkeys Bottle*

*Three Roll Tumble Up*

*Three Row Vase*

*Thumbprint and Oval*

## Three Monkeys Bottle

I'm not sure how many of these are around, but not many I'd guess. The one shown is the reported example in all the previous pattern books, so it may have only a few brothers. The Three Monkeys bottle is of clear glass with good iridescence, stands 8" tall, and bears the words "Patent Pending – 8 oz." on the base. It is a rare find for bottle lovers.

## Three Roll Tumble Up

Another of those European patterns that are rather nondescript, the Three Roll items shown, both parts of a tumble-up or bedroom set, have a good lustre but tend to appear a bit glossy. I suspect other shapes may well exist in this pattern but so far haven't seen any. Amethyst is also a possibility for color but hasn't been reported.

## Three Row Vase

I was very impressed when I saw this beautiful Imperial rarity. The color was truly fabulous and the iridescence fine enough to rival the Farmyard bowl. I have heard of only this one piece in beautiful purple, but others may exist. It is 8" tall and 4½" wide, and the mold work is quite deep and sharp. There is also a variant called Two Row vase which is quite similar.

## Thumbprint and Oval

Standing only 5½" tall, this well-molded Imperial pattern is known in marigold and purple. Either color is scarce, and Thumbprint and Oval is much sought.

*Thunderbird (Shrike)*

# Thunderbird (Shrike)

Called Thunderbird in America, the bird shown in actually a shrike. The flora is, of course, wattle. This Australian pattern can be found in both large and small bowls in marigold or purple.

# Tiered Thumbprint

Again here is a pattern with thin iridization but a very nice pattern that fills the glass much like Moonprint; Tiered Thumbprint may well be a British pattern too, but I can't be sure. It has been seen in two sizes of bowls also and certainly other shapes may exist.

*Tiered Thumbprint*

# Tiger Lily

It really is a shame this well done Imperial pattern was used only on the water set. It would have been quite effective on any number of other shapes including table sets and punch sets. The mold work is some of Imperial's best, all intaglio, and very sharp and precise. Tiger Lily is found in marigold, green, and rarely purple. It has been reproduced in pastels, so beware!

# Tiny Covered Hen

The Imperial novelty item shown is a really well-conceived miniature that until recently had not been reproduced; however, I saw one of these in a gift shop in blue glass (not carnival) not long ago. At any rate, the one shown is old and rare. The coloring is a very nice clambroth, richly iridized with a fiery finish. It measures 3½" long and 3¼" tall.

*Tiger Lily*

*Tiny Covered Hen*

*Tiny Hobnail Lamp*

*Tobacco Leaf (U.S.)*

*Tomahawk*

*Tornado*

# *Tiny Hobnail Lamp*

In all my years in collecting I've seen just two of these miniature oil lamps even though they do come late in carnival glass history. The base is 3" high and has a diameter of 2¼". The shade, which matches, is clear. I haven't a notion as to the maker, but they are scarce and cute as can be.

# *Tobacco Leaf (U.S.)*

Here is another souvenir champagne, but the one shown is a real rarity. Please note that the finish is gold, not the usual clear iridized! As the owner says, this must have been for someone very special at the convention.

# *Tomahawk*

This lovely miniature (7¼" long and 2" wide) is a real "show stopper." Now known to have been a product of the Cambridge Glass Company, the rare Tomahawk is a very deep cobalt blue with heavy iridescence. It has been seen in pieces other than carnival glass and has been reproduced in aqua and vaseline glass, but as far as I know, no iridized reproductions were made.

# *Tornado*

Perhaps because it is one of the most unusual vases in all of carnival glass, Northwood's Tornado is always a favorite with collectors. Available in both plain and ribbed, the size may vary considerably, and I've seen a mini-version in marigold. The colors are marigold, green, purple, white, and ice blue. The Northwood trademark is found on the inside of the vase.

# Tornado Variant

This extremely rare variant is one inch taller that the regular Tornado vase. The base closely resembles that of Northwood's Corn vase, and the top is tightly crimped. The only color reported is a deep rich marigold, iridized both inside and out.

*Tornado Variant*

# Town Pump

Certainly there isn't one collector of carnival glass who isn't familiar with this very famous pattern. The Town Pump is almost 7" tall and is mostly on purple, although marigold and green are found in limited quantities. The design is simple but very pleasing – ivy twining over a stippled background with a crude tree bark spout and handle. No carnival glass collection would be complete without this pattern, and certainly it deserves a prominent place in any Northwood collection.

*Town Pump*

# Tracery

This pattern comes as quite a surprise to many Millersburg fans because of its delicate patterning, but Millersburg it certainly is. It is found on bonbons of rather deep, oval shape and is usually seen in green or amethyst. It measures 7½" long and 5½" wide. The base is 3" in diameter and has a many-rayed center. The exterior is plain and has two mold marks.

*Tracery*

# Tree Bark

As you can see, this is a simplistic pattern, turned out as a giveaway or inexpensive item. The only color is marigold, usually of a deep, rich hue. While it certainly does not show the artistry the Imperial company was known for, Tree Bark does fulfill its purpose of being an available bit of color for the average housewife's table.

*Tree Bark*

*Tree Bark Variant*

*Tree of Life*

*Tree Trunk*

*Triands (and Towers Vase)*

# Tree Bark Variant

The main difference in this pattern and the regular Tree Bark are the even spacings of the bark lines rather than being randomly done. Shapes I know about are a water set, planter, an ornate candle holder on a brass cherub and marble base, as well as a vase shape. This pattern was made by Jeanette.

# Tree of Life

There has always been a great deal of confusion surrounding this pattern and Crackle and Soda Gold patterns, because they are so similar, but there is really no need for the confusion. As you can see, Tree of Life has no stippling whatsoever, thus the filler area is plain. The pitcher shown is a scarce shape in this pattern, and as you can see, the iridescence is thin and light. The shapes known are water sets, plates, and perfume bottles.

# Tree Trunk

Simple but effective is the bark-like pattern for this popular Northwood vase. Apparently it was a well-liked pattern when it was being manufactured for many examples exist in sizes from 8" to tall 20" ones. The colors are marigold, blue, purple, green, white, and aqua opalescent.

# Triands (and Towers Vase)

Triands is a product of Sowerby and is found in a covered butter dish, creamer, sugar, celery, and spooner (both shown). The only color reported is a good rich marigold. The other small hat shape shown is called Towers and is a vase pattern also from Sowerby.

*Tropicana Vase*

# Tropicana Vase

The maker of this intriguing vase is unknown, but I suspect it may be English. It stands 9" tall and has a very rich marigold coloring.

# Trout and Fly

Of course, this is a companion piece to the Big Fish pattern and except for the added fly and a few changes in the water lilies and blossoms, is much the same. The bowls usually measure about 9¼" in diameter and have a wide panel exterior. The detail is good, and the coloring excellent. The shape may vary and even square bowls and a rare plate shape have been found in this Millersburg pattern.

*Trout and Fly*

# Tulip (Millersburg)

This beautiful and rare compote is exactly like the Flowering Vine one shown elsewhere except it has no interior design. It stands about 9" tall, and the bowl measures roughly 6" across. The only colors I've seen are marigold and amethyst, but green was more than likely made. In addition to this size, a 7" variant is known in amethyst.

# Tulip and Cane (Imperial)

Seldom found, this old Imperial pattern is seen in iridized glass only on two sizes of wine goblets, a claret goblet and a rare 8 oz. goblet in marigold and smoke.

*Tulip (Millersburg)*

*Tulip and Cane (Imperial)*

267

*Tulip Scroll (Millersburg)*

*Twelve Rings*

*Twigs*

*Twins*

## Tulip Scroll (Millersburg)

Only a few of these attractive Millersburg vases seem to show up from time to time, mostly in amethyst, but once in a while in green or the quite rare marigold. I've seen them as tall as 11", but most are about 7" and less stretched out. They are always quickly snatched up and are a popular vase pattern.

## Twelve Rings

Much like the Tiered Thumbprint candlestick, this one has a series of overlying rings from top to bottom. The color is a bit weak but the iridescence is adequate. I suspect this is another European pattern but can't be sure. It is 9" tall with a 4½" base diameter.

## Twigs

A kissing cousin to the Beauty Bud vase shown earlier, the Twigs vase has small branch-like stems growing from the base to the body of the vase. These little gems can be found in all sizes from 3" to 12" tall and are mostly seen in marigold or purple. These, like the Beauty, were made by Dugan-Diamond Glass.

## Twins

Like Imperial's Fashion pattern, Twins is another geometric design manufactured in large quantities in berry sets, a rare bride's basket, and the familiar fruit bowl and stand. Pieces have been found in a good rich marigold and a very beautiful smoke, and the berry set has been found in green, as shown. Needless to say, a purple fruit bowl and stand would be a treasure!

*Two Flowers*

## Two Flowers

Once again the scale filler, water lilies, and blossoms are used by Fenton to form an artistic presentation. Known in footed and flat bowls of various sizes and a scarce bowl shape, Two Flowers is seen in blue, marigold, amethyst, red, green, and occasionally white.

## Two Fruits

Once this Fenton pattern was felt to be an Imperial product, but we know from old advertisements that it came from Fenton. The background is Fenton's Stippled Rays and, as you can see, there are four sections to the divided bonbon. Each section contains one fruit – either a pear or an apple. Colors I've heard about are marigold, blue, and amethyst, but certainly green may exist.

*Two Fruits*

## Universal Home Bottle

While I normally shy away from utility bottles, this one is a bit special. It has very rich color and an interesting side panel of measurements by ounces and centimeters. It is a one quart bottle and is impressed "Universal Home Bottle." The maker is unknown as is what it originally held.

*Universal Home Bottle*

*Unshod*

*Venetian*

*Victorian*

## U*nshod*

The owner says this pitcher came with tumblers in the Unshod pattern, so we've listed the pitcher as that pattern. If anyone knows differently, I'm sure I'll hear about it. The styling looks very much like the Millersburg Cherry, but that's only an observation.

## U*rn Vase*

This unusually shaped vase has been seen in white as well as marigold carnival glass and is a product of the Imperial Company. It stands 9" tall and has a finely grained stippling over the surface.

*Urn Vase*

## V*enetian*

While credited to the Cambridge Company, there is evidence that this pattern was iridized at the Millersburg factory. It is shown in old Cambridge ads, however, and the vase was used as a lamp base. Colors are green and a scarce marigold. The base design is quite similar to the Hobstar and Feather rose bowl. A rare lidded sugar bowl is shown in marigold.

## V*ictorian*

This impressively large bowl is another pattern from the Dugan factory in Indiana, PA, and is both rich and desirable. Mostly found in a rich purple, one example in a rare peach opalescent has turned up and rates with the best of bowls.

# Vineyard

Here is another pattern whose shards I catalogued from the Dugan diggings, but actually it didn't come as too much of a surprise. The same design was made in 1905 in crystal, opaque glass, and opalescent ware under the name, Grape and Leaf. Known in iridescent glass, in a water set only, the colors are marigold, purple, and rarely peach opalescent. Often the tumblers are poorly formed, and the glass tends toward being bubbled.

# Vineyard Harvest (Australian Grape)

It now appears this tumbler, like so many to be encountered in the last ten years, is a product of Czechoslovakia. It was first publicized by Muriel Triplett, and at that time she called it Australian Grape. It stands 5½" tall and measures 3⅝" across the top. Found only in marigold, it is considered rare.

# Vining Leaf

There are two variants of the English pattern – one with small berries along portions of the stylized leaves. The examples shown, a rather small bud vase and an ample lady's spittoon, give us the pattern nicely. Please note the frosted effect around the leaves.

# Vintage (Fenton)

Here is the Fenton premier grape pattern, and it is just as well done as Northwood's. It can be found in bowls, plates, rose bowls, compotes, punch sets, small ferneries, and a one-lily epergne. Colors are marigold, blue, green, amethyst, amber, pastel marigold, amberina, red, and reverse amberina.

**Vineyard Harvest
(Australian Grape)**

**Vineyard**

**Vining Leaf**

**Vintage (Fenton)**

*Vintage (Millersburg)*

*Vintage Banded*

*Vintage Leaf (Fenton)*

## *V*intage (Millersburg)

What makes Vintage unique is the hobnail exterior (the hobnail and the honeycomb seem to have been patterns used as standard fillers by Millersburg). It has a many-rayed star in the base and is usually seen on the medium size, shallow bowls. The Millersburg Vintage pattern is a scarce one and is certainly a credit to any collection. Colors are green, marigold, amethyst, and blue. And both 9" and 5" bowls are known.

## *V*intage Banded

Often seen in the mug shape, this Dugan pattern is rather scarce in the footed pitcher shape, and the tumbler is rare and much sought. Please note the grapes are almost identical to those found on the Golden Grape pattern, and the banding is quite similar to that found in the Dugan pattern called Apple Blossoms.

## *V*intage Leaf (Fenton)

Over the years, I've never been able to accept this design with the center leaf as the standard Fenton Vintage pattern, so I've given in to my conscience and given it a name all its own. It is found in bonbon and berry sets in marigold, green, blue, and amethyst and is Fenton, not Millersburg, despite the radium finish.

## *V*iolet Baskets

Here are two of the dainty little baskets designed to hold small bouquets like violets. One has its own glass handle, while the other fits into a handled sleeve. The File pattern in the glass is much like that on some Stork and Rushes pieces, and I suspect both of these baskets come from the Dugan company.

*Violet Baskets*

# Virginia Blackberry

Known to be a variant of a U.S. Glass pattern called Virginia or Galloway, this small pitcher has turned up on a child's water set in crystal without the berries. The example shown in blue carnival is the only reported one that is iridized, making it a very rare item indeed.

# Votive Light

Also bearing the strange "M-inside-a-C" mark like Oklahoma, this very hard-to-find novelty has a beautiful marigold finish. It stands 4¼" tall and is a candle vase. The side shown is the Bleeding Heart of Jesus. On the opposite side is a raised cross measuring nearly 2" tall.

# Waffle Block

This Imperial pattern was originally made in many shapes. The pitcher is hard to come by and, of course, the tumblers are rather rare, but other shapes, including a handled basket, rose bowl, punch set, vases, bowls, parfait glass, and shakers are known. Colors are marigold, clambroth, aqua, and amethyst.

# Washboard

Also called Diamonds and Petals, this pattern has been found in a small creamer shape, and I suspect there is a matching sugar, possibly a stemmed open compote type. The tumbler is tall, some 4⅞" with a flared top opening of 3". The pattern is known in crystal, but iridized pieces are rare.

**Virginia Blackberry**

**Votive Light**

**Waffle Block**

**Washboard**

273

*Water Lily*

*Water Lily and Cattails (Fenton)*

*Water Lily and Cattails (Northwood)*

# Water Lily

This very well done Fenton pattern is found on bonbons, flat and footed berry sets, and the very rare large footed plate shape. The pattern is made up of water lilies, leaves, lotus-like flowers, and other flora. Colors are marigold, blue, green, amethyst, amber, white, and red.

# Water Lily and Cattails (Fenton)

While both Fenton and Northwood had versions of this pattern, the Fenton one is best known and is available in more shapes, including water sets, table sets, berry sets, and a rare spittoon whimsey. Colors are marigold and amethyst, but certainly blue or green may exist but have not been reported.

# Water Lily and Cattails (Northwood)

Here is a pattern used in different degrees by both the Northwood and Fenton companies, and at times it's rather hard to tell who made what. The obvious Fenton rendition is the exterior pattern used on the Thistle banana boat, but it is believed they made other shapes in Water Lily and Cattails, including a whimsey toothpick. This is the Northwood water set.

**Water Lily and Dragonfly**

## Water Lily and Dragonfly

This large (10½") shallow bowl and matching frog is called a flower set and was used much like an epergne. A large flannel flower is under the frog. In Australia these are also called "float bowls."

## Webbed Clematis

I apologize for the weak photo of this huge vase (12½" tall), but it was the only one available. I suspect the vase is Scandinavian, and it reminds me of several others from that area. The color is light marigold.

## Weeping Cherry

The Dugan-Diamond Company must have made small amounts of this pattern for few are found today, despite being made in both footed and collar-based bowls. Colors are marigold, amethyst, peach opalescent, and white.

**Webbed Clematis**

**Weeping Cherry**

*Western Thistle*

*Wheat*

*Whirling Leaves*

# Western Thistle

From Finland the Western Thistle is a very pretty pattern, deeply intaglio with rows of diamonds below a band of thistle flowers and leaves. It has been seen in both amethyst and marigold and is just a tad over 4" tall.

# Wheat

Make no mistake about it, this is a very rare Northwood pattern, known in only a covered sweetmeat (two known) and a single covered bowl in colors of green and amethyst. Surfacing in carnival glass circles only in the last 10 years, these rarities have caused much excitement and brought astonishing prices where they've been shown. The sweetmeat is the same shape as the Northwood Grape pattern. What a pity we don't have more of this truly important pattern.

# Whirling Leaves

What a simple but effective pattern for large bowls! Four flowing leaves and four star-like blossoms – what could be simpler? Please note that the flowers are very much like those found on the Little Stars bowls. This pleasing pattern is not especially difficult to find and does not sell for nearly as much as most Millersburg patterns, but it is worth owning.

# Whirling Star

While this Imperial pattern has never brought many raves, it is a nice, well-planned design found on punch sets, bowls, and an attractive compote. Colors are mostly marigold, but an occasional piece in green is found.

*Whirling Star*

*White Oak*

# White Oak

After years of doubt about the maker of this rare tumbler (no pitcher known), I'm half convinced it was a Dugan product. The bark-like background and the general shape are much like the Vineyard tumbler. Of course, I could be wrong.

# Wickerwork (English)

Sometimes only the bowl without the base of these is found, but here is the complete set. The bowl measures 8½" in diameter. The only color I've seen is the marigold. Apparently, this was a cookie or sandwich tray.

*Wickerwork (English)*

# Wide Panel (Fenton)

Shown is the typical Fenton Wide Panel bowl exterior found on so many patterns. Like the rest, it has a beginning and an end and doesn't just drift away at the bowl's edge. The example shown is on the back of a green vintage bowl and is beautifully iridized.

# Wide Panel (Imperial)

Like the other major carnival glass companies, Imperial produced a Wide Panel pattern. These are found primarily in goblets of two sizes and a covered candy jar. Colors known are marigold, ice blue, ice green, vaseline white, pink, and red. Most have a stretch effect around the edge.

*Wide Panel (Fenton)*

*Wide Panel (Imperial)*

*Wide Paneled Cherry*

*Wide Panel Epergne*

# Wide Paneled Cherry

Unlisted until now, this very interesting pattern is similar to the Stippled Strawberry spittoon I showed in *Rarities of Carnival Glass* some years ago. The shape is a very small pitcher, possibly used for syrup or cream and to date I've heard of no matching pieces.

# Wide Panel Epergne

This beauty is the most stately epergne in carnival glass and is a product of the Northwood factory. Colors are white, marigold, green, amethyst, and ultra-rare aqua opalescent.

# Wide Panels Shade

Shown is one of the most beautiful light shades I've run across. The emerald green coloring is spectacular as is the iridescence. The owner says she was told it came from the Northwood Company which certainly is possible, since they made many fine shades, both marked and unmarked.

*Wide Panels Shade*

# Wide Panel Variant

Rather plain for a Northwood product, this water set relies on symmetry and grace for its charm. It can be found in marigold and white as well as enameled in both colors and a beautiful Persian blue.

*Wide Panel Variant*

# Wide Rib

Most companies had a try at similar vases that had a wide rib configuration but the example shown happens to be the Northwood example, in a scarce green. It was from this mold that the Northwood version of a jester's cap type vase was also made. Colors in the Wide Rib include marigold, amethyst, green, blue, aqua opalescent, ice blue, ice green, amber, horehound, smoke, and white. Rare examples in vaseline (iridized) and iridized custard have also been reported, as well as a beautiful teal blue.

*Wide Rib*

# Wide Rib Vase

While several glass companies produced these wide rib vases, the one shown came from the Dugan factory. Colors I've seen are marigold, green, blue, amethyst, smoke, white, amber, peach opalescent, and aqua opalescent.

# Wild Blackberry

Very much in design like the other Fenton Blackberry patterns, this is strictly a bowl pattern easily identified by the four center leaves and the wheat-like fronts around the outer edges. Colors are marigold, blue, green, and amethyst. The exterior has the wide panel pattern.

*Wild Blackberry*

*Wide Rib Vase*

*Wild Flower (Millersburg)*

*Wild Flower (Northwood)*

*Wild Grape*

*Wild Loganberry (Dewberry)*

## W*ild Flower (Millersburg)*

This deeply cupped, clover-based compote is just over 6" tall and is 4½" wide. The very graceful pattern of four large leaves, four small leaves, and eight blossoms is quite effective. The iridescence is found only on the inside of the compote and has the usual radium finish. This is not an easy compote to find, and anyone having one should be proud. This Millersburg pattern is found in marigold, green, amethyst, and a rare vaseline.

## W*ild Flower (Northwood)*

Found only on the compote shape as an exterior pattern, this very fine pattern can have a plain interior or bear the pretty Blossomtime one. The stem is unusual in that it is shaped like a large screw. Colors are marigold, amethyst, green, or blue.

## W*ild Grape*

I recently encountered this pattern for the first time and at first glance thought it to be a Palm Beach bowl, but as you can clearly see, it isn't. The color is weak, but the design is good, and the dome base looks like many Dugan bowls.

## W*ild Loganberry (Dewberry)*

Since I first showed this Westmoreland pattern in the pitcher and announced the existence of wine and goblets, other shapes have turned up including a covered compote, creamer, sugar, and an open compote. All except the marigold wine have been iridized milk glass, but other colors may exist.

# **W**ild Rose

This well-known Northwood pattern is used on the exterior of an unusual footed bowl, rather small, with an edge of open work in fan-like figures. Certainly, the intricacy of this open work took much care and skill. The colors are marigold, amethyst, green, and occasionally pastels.

# **W**ild Rose Lamp

Long felt to be a Millersburg product, this scarce to rare lamp can be found in three sizes and three colors besides the crystal version. The pattern is a primrose-like flower and leaves that wind around the base above a filler of sunken dots. Occasionally, the large size can be found with three medallions with busts of women on the underside. Colors are green, amethyst, and marigold.

# **W**ild Rose Shade

Rose Presznick called this shade Wild Rose, and I will honor that name despite so many other patterns with the same name. The shade is a strong marigold and has a series of stippled panels, separated by beading with each panel holding a spray of leaves, stems, and a flower that forms the outer edge of the shade.

# **W**ild Rose Syrup

Seen only in marigold of rich color and adequate lustering, the Wild Rose syrup is very attractive. The maker is thus far unknown, but the mold work is quite similar to that of many of Harry Northwood's products. Measuring 6½" tall, the syrup holds 12 fluid ounces and has a metal top.

*Wild Rose*

*Wild Rose Lamp*

*Wild Rose Shade*

*Wild Rose Syrup*

*Wild Rose Wreath
(Miniature Intaglio)*

*Wild Strawberry*

# Wild Rose Wreath (Miniature Intaglio)

The Butler Brothers ad showing this rare and desirable miniature calls it a "stemmed almond," so we know it was intended as a nut cup and was made by U.S. Glass. It stands 2½" tall and is usually about 3" across the top. The design is intaglio, and the only color reported is marigold.

# Wild Strawberry

One might think of this as the "grown-up" version of the regular Northwood Strawberry, since it is much the same. The primary difference is the addition of the blossoms to the patterning and, of course, the size of the bowl itself, which is about 1½" larger in diameter.

# Windflower

Not one, but two shards of this pattern were excavated at the Dugan site including a marigold bit and a sizeable chunk of an ice blue nappy with a portion of the handle attached. To the best of my knowledge, this pattern has not been reported previously in pastels. Windflower is an uncomplicated, well-balanced design with the background stippled and a geometric bordering device. The exterior is plain. Windflower is found on bowls, plates, and handled nappies. The colors are marigold, cobalt, ice blue, and ice green.

*Windflower*

*Windmill*

# Windmill

Again, here is one of the best-selling Imperial patterns, reproduced in the 1960s. It is still rather popular with collectors of old carnival glass, especially in the darker colors. Originally, Windmill was made in a wide range of shapes, including berry sets, water sets, fruit bowls, pickle dishes, dresser trays, and milk pitchers. The colors were marigold, green, purple, clambroth, and smoke.

# Wine and Roses

Please note the similarities between this scarce Fenton cider set, the well-known Lotus and Grape pattern shown elsewhere in this book, and the very rare water set called Frolicking Bears. Wine and Roses can be found in marigold in both pitcher and wine, and the wine is known in blue and the rare aqua.

# Wishbone

I personally feel that this Northwood pattern is one of the most graceful in carnival glass. The lines just flow, covering much of the allowed space. Found on very scarce water sets, flat and footed bowls, plates, and a very stately one-lily epergne, Wishbone is usually accompanied by the basketweave pattern on the exterior. My favorite color is the ice blue, but Wishbone is available in marigold, green, purple, blue, white, and ice green. There is also a variant to this pattern.

*Wine and Roses*

*Wishbone*

*Wishbone and Spades*

*Wishbone Flower Arranger*

*Wisteria*

## Wishbone and Spades

I've always had misgivings about attributing this pattern, and I'm listing it here as a Dugan one. As you can see, the design is a good one, well balanced and artistically sound. The shapes are berry sets, and large and small plates and colors include peach opalescent, purple, and green.

## Wishbone Flower Arranger

Similar in many ways to the Windsor Flower Arranger, for years I confused the two until one collector was kind enough to point out the differences. The Wishbone has an open top and none of the points touch while this isn't true with the Windsor.

## Wisteria

What a beautiful pattern this is, a first cousin to the Grape Arbor pattern in carnival and the Lattice and Cherry one in other types of glass. Wisteria is found only on water set pieces, with both pitchers and tumblers found in white and ice blue, and only tumblers found in ice green. There is a very rare whimsey vase made from the pitcher in green also (one known).

*Wooden Shoe*

# Wooden Shoe

It seems as if good things come in bunches, and that's how it's been with miniatures in this book. However, one could never tire of seeing them, and they are so rare, so here is another. The Wooden Shoe is 4½" long and 3" high. Its coloring is a light, watery amber, and the glass is heavy.

# Woodlands Vase

Once again I show a rare vase that is very impressive even though it measures only 5½" tall. The coloring is a rich marigold with heavy luster, and the pattern is all smooth and raised. The design has a simple, well-balanced attractiveness that raises it above the everyday. And, of course, not many are known.

*Woodlands Vase*

# Woodpecker Vase

The Woodpecker vase is 8¼" long and measures 1⅝" across the top. The only color I've run into is marigold, usually of good color. Perhaps this is strictly a Dugan pattern, and if so, it would explain the lack of other colors or shapes. These vases were usually hung in doorways or used as auto vases and were quite popular in their day.

*Woodpecker Vase*

# Wreathed Cherry

For many years collectors have been puzzled by certain pieces of this pattern turning up with the Diamond Glass Company trademark, notably the covered butter. Now, since the Dugan shards have been catalogued, it becomes apparent this was a Dugan pattern. Known in berry sets consisting of oval bowls, table sets, water sets, and a scarce toothpick holder, the colors are marigold, fiery amethyst, purple, and white (often with gilt). The toothpick has been widely reproduced in cobalt, white, and marigold, so beware! The only color in the old ones is amethyst.

*Wreathed Cherry*

285

*Wreath of Roses (Fenton)*

*Wreath of Roses*
*Rose Bowl (Dugan)*

*Wreath of Roses Variant*
*(Dugan)*

## Wreath of Roses (Fenton)

Known in bonbons with or without stems, compotes, bowls, and the punch sets shown. Fenton's Wreath of Roses is a beautifully executed pattern. Two interior patterns are known. Colors are marigold, green, blue, amethyst, peach opalescent, and white. The luster is very fine and the mold work excellent.

## Wreath of Roses Rose Bowl (Dugan)

Apparently one of the inexpensive, mass-produced patterns made for wide sales, this Dugan pattern is found only on the small rose bowl shapes and ruffled bowl shapes from the same mold. The only colors I've seen are amethyst, marigold, lavender, and a rare amber in the spittoon whimsey shape.

## Wreath of Roses Variant (Dugan)

While Northwood, Fenton, and Dugan all made similar patterns with this name, the Dugan is least known and valued. It hasn't all that much going for it, since the design is weak and doesn't fill the space to advantage. Colors are amethyst, blue, and marigold – at least the ones I've seen, but white, green, and peach opal may exist.

*Zig-Zag (Millersburg)*

### Zig-Zag (Fenton)

I suspect the same mold shape was used for this nicely done Fenton water set and the Fluffy Peacock pattern. The Zig-Zag was brought along in the enameled carnival period and can be found in marigold, blue, green, amethyst, ice green, and white. The floral work may vary slightly from piece to piece.

### Zig-Zag (Millersburg)

This lovely Millersburg bowl pattern is an improved version of a stippled ray theme but with a twist, resulting in a beautiful sunburst effect. This, coupled with a curious star and fan design on the exterior base, creates a unique and intriguing pattern. Colors are green, marigold, and amethyst.

### Zippered Heart

Recent evidence that this is an Imperial pattern is a catalog from the company illustrating the Zippered Heart pattern in crystal in many shapes, including table sets, vases, compotes, rose bowls, a milk pitcher, punch sets, and water sets. However, in iridized glass the shapes I've seen are a berry set and the famous queen's vase. While a beautiful purple is most encountered, marigold is known. Shown is a rare 5" vase.

*Zig-Zag (Fenton)*

*Zippered Heart*

*Zipper Loop*

*Zipper Stitch*

*Zipper Variant*

## Zipper Loop

While the Zipper Loop lamp is the most frequently encountered of all the kerosene lamps, it is a scarce item in itself. Known in four sizes, including a small hand lamp, the Zipper Loop is found in a good rich marigold color as well as a sparkling smoke finish. It has been reproduced in the former in the large size, so be cautious when buying.

## Zipper Stitch

This attractive piece shown is the tray for a lovely cordial set consisting of a decanter, six stemmed cordials, and the tray. These were made in Czechoslovakia and are known only in marigold.

## Zipper Variant

I suspect this nicely done covered sugar is of British origin but can't be sure. The color is quite good as is the mold work. Note the interesting finial on the lid.

# A Few Words about Price Guides

Price guides are a terrible burden to place on a research writer but most of us accept them as a necessary evil and try to avoid controversy. From the moment that first price is put down it becomes inaccurate and this is just something we have to live with.

When I first began compiling a price guide to go with my books on glass, I avoided auction prices completely, knowing they are seldom a true picture of value; however, I soon learned many considered my prices too low and I was made aware of this often and loudly. When I factored in auction prices, the same voices now said prices were suddenly unreasonably high! The truth is, price guides are not the major influence in shaping prices, either in auctions or from dealers. Auction prices are chiefly shaped by heated bidding; by a buyer who doesn't want to lose a bid; by an especially fine item being auctioned. Dealers' prices are mostly affected by two things: **auction prices** and **antique periodical reporting of auction prices**. How many times have you seen a weekly trade paper with headlines saying, "Carnival pitcher tops sales at $12,000.00?" Dealers read these headlines too and react accordingly!

Anyone who credits my price guides with forcing dealer prices to rise dramatically just doesn't know the facts of the game. My price guide is written after the fact and usually prints prices that have actually been realized. The exceptions are rare items that seldom appear for sale and must be speculated about to show what a current market price *might* be.

Finally, I wish everyone that is so quick to criticize *any* price guide would try to write a better one. It isn't an easy task and it is always a thankless one.

Bill Edwards

# Color Code

M—Marigold
PL—Pearl Opalescent
A—Amethyst or Purple
AB—Amberina
B—Blue
RA—Reverse Amberina
G—Green
LV—Lavender
PO—Peach Opalescent
IC—Iridized Custard
AO—Aqua Opalescent
VO—Vaseline Opalescent
BO—Blue Opalescent
PM—Pastel Marigold
IG—Ice Green
W—White
IB—Ice Blue
TL—Teal
SM—Smoke

PeB—Persian Blue
CL—Clear
CeB—Celeste Blue
CM—Clambroth
AP—Apricot
V—Vaseline
BA—Black Amethyst
R—Red
LG—Lime Green
Pas—Pastel
RG—Russet Green (olive)
AQ—Aqua
PK—Pink
AM—Amber
MO—Milkglass Opalescent
IM—Iridized Moonstone
LO—Lime Opalescent
HO—Horehound
RS—Red Slag

RenB—Renniger Blue
WS—Wisteria
PH—Pastel Horehound
CHP—Champagne
HA—Honey Amber
NG—Nile Green
CT—Citrene
MC—Marigold Custard
EB—Electric Blue
SMG—Smoke Milkglass
EmG—Emerald Green
CRAN—Cranberry Flash
AMT-O—Amethyst Opalescent
WO—White Opalescent
MMG—Marigold Milk Glass
SA—Saphire Blue
ALS—Alaskan (Marigold Over Green)
ICG—Iridized Chocolate Glass
MAO—Marigold Opalescent

\* Denotes a speculative price for an item that is rare and hasn't been on the market recently.

Note: While many prices have had an explosion of growth, especially on Northwood plates, red carnival and pastels, certain items after many years of growth have declined slightly or have remained constant. This price guide reflects these changes as well as is possible with today's ever-changing market. Please remember it takes months to print a price guide such as this, and in that time carnival glass sales do not remain static. While I have tried to allow for this passage of time from compilation to print, I cannot guess the future. Still, with over 33,000 price listings, this remains the most complete price source for carnival glass in the world, and I'm proud of the results. Finally, please note mini-vases (4"–7") have become very popular and now command high prices.

Acanthus (Imperial)

African Shield (English)

Apple and Pear Intaglio (Northwood)

Art Deco (English)

| | M | A | G | B | PO | AO | Pas | R |
|---|---|---|---|---|---|---|---|---|
| **ACANTHUS (IMPERIAL)** | | | | | | | | |
| Bowl, 8"-9½" ..................... | 65 | 90 | 110 | 90 | | | 75SM | |
| Plate, 10"...................... | 200 | | | | | | 275SM | |
| **ACORN (FENTON)** | | | | | | | | |
| Bowl, 7"-8½" ..................... | 65 | 140 | 85 | 55 | 290 | 750 | 250AQ | 850 |
| Plate, 9", Scarce ................. | | 600 | | 575 | | | | |
| **ACORN (MILLERSBURG)** | | | | | | | | |
| Compote, Rare.................... | 3,000 | 1,800 | 1,900 | | | | 2,850V | |
| **ACORN (US GLASS)** | | | | | | | | |
| Vase, handled, Rare.............. | | | 3,000 | | | | | |
| **ACORN BURRS (NORTHWOOD)** | | | | | | | | |
| Bowl, Flat, 10"................... | 90 | 150 | 175 | | | | 500 | |
| Bowl, Flat, 5".................... | 30 | 40 | 50 | | | | 100 | |
| Punch Bowl and Base......... | 550 | 700 | 850 | 2,000 | | 37,000 | 4,500W | |
| Punch Cup ....................... | 45 | 90 | 100 | 75 | | 2,500 | 160IG | |
| Covered Butter ................. | 300 | 400 | 950 | | | | 700 | |
| Covered Sugar .................. | 225 | 300 | | | | | 450 | |
| Creamer or Spooner ........... | 200 | 260 | | | | | 390 | |
| Water Pitcher.................... | 500 | 600 | 1,000 | | | | | |
| Tumbler ......................... | 90 | 80 | 100 | | | | | |
| Whimsey Vase, Rare ........... | 3,000 | 3,500+ | | | | | | |
| **ACORN AND FILE** | | | | | | | | |
| Ftd Compote, Rare.............. | | | | | | | 1,500V | |
| **ADAM'S RIB (DUGAN/DIAMOND)** | | | | | | | | |
| Candlestick, pr. ................. | 130 | | | | | | 100IG | |
| Pitcher.............................. | 160 | | | | | | 210IG | |
| Tumbler ............................ | 40 | | | | | | 65IG | |
| Fan vase............................ | 45 | | | | | | 80IG | |
| **A DOZEN ROSES (IMPERIAL)** | | | | | | | | |
| Bowl, Footed, 8½"-10", Rare. | 650 | 750 | 850 | | | | | |
| **ADVERTISING ASHTRAY** | | | | | | | | |
| Various Designs.................... | 60+ | | | | | | | |
| **AFRICAN SHIELD (ENGLISH)** | | | | | | | | |
| Toothpick Holder (or | | | | | | | | |
| Bud Holder)........................ | 115 | | | | | | | |
| **AGE HERALD (FENTON)** | | | | | | | | |
| Bowl, 9¼", Scarce ............... | | 1,700 | | | | | | |
| Plate, 10", Scarce................. | | 2,400 | | | | | | |
| **AMARYLLIS (NORTHWOOD)** | | | | | | | | |
| Small Compote .................... | 500 | 300 | | 275 | | | 450W | |
| Whimsey (Flattened) ............ | | 700 | | | | | | |
| **AMERICAN (FOSTORIA)** | | | | | | | | |
| Tumbler, Rare .................... | 95 | | 125 | | | | | |
| Rose Bowl......................... | 395 | | | | | | | |
| **ANGELA** | | | | | | | | |
| Perfume............................. | 50 | | | | | | | |
| **APOTHECARY JAR** | | | | | | | | |
| Small Size ......................... | 60 | | | | | | | |
| **APPLE AND PEAR INTAGLIO (NORTHWOOD)** | | | | | | | | |
| Bowl, 10"........................... | 115 | | | | | | | |
| Bowl, 5"............................ | 60 | | | | | | | |
| **APPLE BLOSSOM (ENAMELED) (NORTHWOOD)** | | | | | | | | |
| Tumbler ............................ | | | | 90 | | | | |
| **APPLE BLOSSOMS (DUGAN)** | | | | | | | | |
| Bowl, 7½" .......................... | 40 | 58 | 70 | | 175 | | 150W | |
| Plate, 8¼" .......................... | 250 | 275 | | | 260 | | 300W | |
| **APPLE BLOSSOM TWIGS (DUGAN)** | | | | | | | | |
| Bowl.................................. | 40 | 165 | 170 | | 190 | | 150W | |
| Plate.................................. | 200 | 375 | 300 | 190 | 425 | | 225W | |
| **APPLE PANELS (ENGLISH)** | | | | | | | | |
| Creamer ............................ | 35 | | | | | | | |
| Sugar (open) ...................... | 35 | | | | | | | |
| **APPLE TREE (FENTON)** | | | | | | | | |
| Water Pitcher...................... | 350 | | | 500 | | | 350W | |
| Tumbler ............................ | 45 | | | 65 | | | 175W | |
| Pitcher, Vase Whimsey, Rare . | 1,800 | | | 2,000 | | | | |
| **APRIL SHOWERS (FENTON)** | | | | | | | | |
| Vase ................................. | 55 | 110 | 150 | 130 | | | 200 | |
| **ARCADIA BASKETS** | | | | | | | | |
| Plate, 8".............................. | 50 | | | | | | | |
| **ARCADIA LACE** | | | | | | | | |
| Rose Bowl.......................... | 155 | | | | | | | |
| **ARCHED FLEUR-DE-LIS (HIGBEE)** | | | | | | | | |
| Mug, Rare .......................... | 250 | | | | | | | |
| **ARCHED PANELS** | | | | | | | | |
| Tumbler ............................ | 85 | | | | | | | |
| **ARCHES AND SAND** | | | | | | | | |
| Tumbler ............................ | 205 | | | | | | | |
| **ARCS (IMPERIAL)** | | | | | | | | |
| Bowls, 8½"........................... | 40 | 60 | 50 | | | | 175W | |
| Compote............................ | 65 | 90 | | | | | | |
| **ART DECO (ENGLISH)** | | | | | | | | |
| Bowl, 4"............................. | 38 | | | | | | | |

Asters

Autumn Acorns (Fenton)

Balloons (Imperial)

Banded Drape (Fenton)

| | M | A | G | B | PO | AO | Pas | R |
|---|---|---|---|---|---|---|---|---|
| **ASTERS** | | | | | | | | |
| Bowl | 60 | | | | | | | |
| Compote | 90 | | | | | | | |
| **ASTRAL** | | | | | | | | |
| Shade | 55 | | | | | | | |
| **AUGUST FLOWERS** | | | | | | | | |
| Shade | 42 | | | | | | | |
| **AURORA PEARLS** | | | | | | | | |
| Bowl, 2 Sizes Decorated | 400 | 700 | | | | | 950IM | |
| **AUSTRALIAN (CRYSTAL)** | | | | | | | | |
| Flower set, 2 pcs | 150 | 195 | | | | | | |
| **AUSTRALIAN DIAMOND (CRYSTAL)** | | | | | | | | |
| Sugar | 70 | 85 | | | | | | |
| Creamer | 60 | 80 | | | | | | |
| **AUSTRALIAN PANELS (CRYSTAL)** | | | | | | | | |
| Creamer | 50 | 70 | | | | | | |
| Sugar | 60 | 75 | | | | | | |
| **AUSTRALIAN SWAN (CRYSTAL)** | | | | | | | | |
| Bowl, 5" | 170 | 140 | | | | | | |
| Bowl, 9" | 225 | 450 | | | | | | |
| **AUTUMN ACORNS (FENTON)** | | | | | | | | |
| Bowl, 8¼" | 55 | 75 | 80 | 70 | | | 220VAS | 4,800 |
| Plate, Rare | | 1,000 | 1,000 | 1,500 | | | | |
| **AZTEC (McKEE)** | | | | | | | | |
| Pitcher, Rare | 1,300 | | | | | | | |
| Tumbler, Rare | 650 | | | | | | | |
| Creamer | 250 | | | | | | 250CM | |
| Sugar | 250 | | | | | | 250CM | |
| Rosebowl | | | | | | | 400CM | |
| **BABY BATHTUB (U.S. GLASS)** | | | | | | | | |
| Miniature Piece | | | | | | | 500 | |
| **BABY'S BOUQUET** | | | | | | | | |
| Child's Plate, Scarce | 115 | | | | | | | |
| **BAKER'S ROSETTE** | | | | | | | | |
| Ornament | 75 | 90 | | | | | | |
| **BALL AND SWIRL** | | | | | | | | |
| Mug | 120 | | | | | | | |
| **BALLARD-MERCED, CA. (NORTHWOOD)** | | | | | | | | |
| Plate | | 1,375 | | | | | | |
| Bowl | | 950 | | | | | | |
| **BALLOONS (IMPERIAL)** | | | | | | | | |
| Cake Plate | 85 | | | | | | 110SM | |
| Compote | 65 | | | | | | 90SM | |
| Perfume Atomizer | 60 | | | | | | 90SM | |
| Vase, 3 Sizes | 75 | | | | | | 100SM | |
| **BAMBI** | | | | | | | | |
| Powder Jar w/lid | 30 | | | | | | | |
| **BAMBOO BIRD** | | | | | | | | |
| Jar, Complete | 800 | | | | | | | |
| **BAND (DUGAN)** | | | | | | | | |
| Violet Hat | 30 | 40 | | | 75 | | | |
| **BAND OF ROSES** | | | | | | | | |
| Pitcher | 250 | | | | | | | |
| Tumbler | 150 | | | | | | | |
| Tray | 75 | | | | | | | |
| Tumble-up, 2 pcs. | 200 | | | | | | | |
| **BANDED BASKETWEAVE** | | | | | | | | |
| Hatpin | | 265 | | | | | | |
| **BANDED CRIS CROSS** | | | | | | | | |
| Hatpin | | 160 | | | | | | |
| **BANDED DIAMONDS (CRYSTAL)** | | | | | | | | |
| Water Pitcher, Rare | 900 | 1,250 | | | | | | |
| Tumbler, Rare | 500 | 400 | | | | | | |
| Bowl, 10" | 100 | 125 | | | | | | |
| Bowl, 5" | 50 | 75 | | | | | | |
| **BANDED DIAMONDS & BARS (FINLAND)** | | | | | | | | |
| Decanter, Complete | 175 | | | | | | | |
| Tumbler, 4" tall | 550 | | | | | | | |
| Tumbler, 2¼" tall | 550 | | | | | | | |
| **BANDED DIAMOND AND FAN (ENGLISH)** | | | | | | | | |
| Toothpick Holder | 80 | | | | | | | |
| **BANDED DRAPE (FENTON)** | | | | | | | | |
| Water Pitcher | 200 | | 500 | 400 | | | 750W | |
| Tumbler | 40 | | 75 | 50 | | | 95W | |
| **BANDED GRAPE (FENTON)** | | | | | | | | |
| Mini creamer | 75 | | | | | | | |
| **BANDED GRAPE AND LEAF (ENGLISH)** | | | | | | | | |
| Water Pitcher, Rare | 650 | | | | | | | |
| Tumbler, Rare | 100 | | | | | | | |
| **BANDED KNIFE AND FORK** | | | | | | | | |
| One Shape | 75 | | | | | | | |
| **BAND OF ROSES** | | | | | | | | |
| Pitcher | 250 | | | | | | | |

Barbella (Northwood)

Basket (Northwood)

Basketweave and Cable
(Westmoreland)

Beaded Basket (Dugan)

| | M | A | G | B | PO | AO | Pas | R |
|---|---|---|---|---|---|---|---|---|
| Tumbler | 150 | | | | | | | |
| Tray | 75 | | | | | | | |
| Tumble-up, 2pcs. | 200 | | | | | | | |
| **BANDED PANELS (CRYSTAL)** | | | | | | | | |
| Open Sugar | 45 | 60 | | | | | | |
| **BANDED PORTLAND (U.S. GLASS)** | | | | | | | | |
| Puff Jar | 80 | | | | | | | |
| **BANDED RIB** | | | | | | | | |
| Tumbler | 25 | | | | | | | |
| Pitcher | 125 | | | | | | | |
| **BANDED ROSE** | | | | | | | | |
| Vase, Small | 175 | | | | | | | |
| **BARBELLA (NORTHWOOD)** | | | | | | | | |
| Bowl | 50 | | | | | | 70 V | |
| Plate | 70 | | | | | | 85TL | |
| Tumbler | | | | | | | 225VAS | |
| **BARBER BOTTLE (CAMBRIDGE)** | | | | | | | | |
| Complete | 575 | 750 | 750 | | | | | |
| **BARBER BOTTLE (CZECH)** | | | | | | | | |
| Cordial Bottle | 60 | | | | | | | |
| Stemmed Cordial | 40 | | | | | | | |
| Tray | 50 | | | | | | | |
| **BASKET (NORTHWOOD)** | | | | | | | | |
| Either Shape, Ftd | 225 | 150 | 475 | 300 | | 500 | 750SM | |
| **BASKET FLOWER** | | | | | | | | |
| Hatpin | 225 | | | | | | | |
| **BASKETWEAVE (FENTON)** | | | | | | | | |
| Hat Shape-Advertising | 50 | | 65 | | | | | |
| Vase Whimsey, Rare | 750 | | 900 | | | | | 1450 |
| Basket-Open Edge Jip | 50 | 180 | 275 | 110 | | | 370IG | |
| Open Edge Plate, 10" | 1,000 | | | 1,600 | | | 2,000IB | |
| Open Edge Bowl, 8" | 140 | 175 | | 190 | | | 290IG | |
| Open Edge Bowl, 5" | 45 | 50 | 55 | 50 | | | 100W | |
| **BASKETWEAVE (NORTHWOOD)** | | | | | | | | |
| Compote | 75 | 85 | 110 | 120 | | | | |
| **BASKETWEAVE AND CABLE (WESTMORELAND)** | | | | | | | | |
| Creamer, Complete | 50 | 75 | 100 | | | | 250W | |
| Sugar, Complete | 50 | 75 | 100 | | | | 250W | |
| Syrup Whimsey | 180 | | | | | | | |
| **BEADED** | | | | | | | | |
| Hatpin | | 45 | | | | | | |
| **BEADED ACANTHUS (IMPERIAL)** | | | | | | | | |
| Milk Pitcher | 95 | | 260 | | | | 170SM | |
| **BEADED BAND AND OCTAGON** | | | | | | | | |
| Kerosene Lamp | 250 | | | | | | | |
| **BEADED BASKET (DUGAN)** | | | | | | | | |
| One shape | 95 | 260 | 280 | 160 | | | 235LG | |
| **BEADED BULL'S EYE (IMPERIAL)** | | | | | | | | |
| Vase, 8"-14" | 47 | 125 | 140 | | | | 130SM | |
| **BEADED CABLE (NORTHWOOD)** | | | | | | | | |
| Rose Bowl | 60 | 95 | 150 | 260 | 9,000 | 325 | 425W | |
| Candy Dish | 50 | 70 | 80 | 185 | | 200 | 200W | |
| **BEADED HEARTS (NORTHWOOD)** | | | | | | | | |
| Bowl | 50 | 85 | 90 | | | | | |
| **BEADED LOOP (OREGON)** | | | | | | | | |
| Vase Whimsey | 95 | | | | | | | |
| **BEADED PANELS (IMPERIAL)** | | | | | | | | |
| Bowl, 8" | 45 | | | | | | | |
| Bowl, 5" | 25 | | | | | | | |
| Powder Jar w/lid | 50 | | | | | | | |
| **BEADED PANELS (WESTMORELAND)** | | | | | | | | |
| Compote | 45 | 55 | | | | 115 | | |
| **BEADED PANELS & GRAPES (CZECH)** | | | | | | | | |
| Tumbler | 275 | | | | | | | |
| **BEADED SHELL (DUGAN)** | | | | | | | | |
| Bowl, Ftd, 9" | 75 | 95 | | | | | | |
| Bowl, Ftd, 5" | 35 | 40 | | | | | | |
| Mug | 200 | 95 | | 175 | | | 450W | |
| Covered Butter | 130 | 150 | | | | | | |
| Covered Sugar | 90 | 110 | | | | | | |
| Creamer or Spooner | 75 | 90 | | | | | | |
| Water Pitcher | 500 | 650 | | | | | | |
| Tumbler | 60 | 70 | | 180 | | | | |
| Mug Whimsey | | 450 | | | | | | |
| **BEADED SPEARS (CRYSTAL)** | | | | | | | | |
| Pitcher, Rare | 490 | 560 | | | | | | |
| Tumbler, Rare | 190 | 200 | | | | | | |
| **BEADED STAR MEDALLION** | | | | | | | | |
| Shade, either | 75 | | | | | | | |
| **BEADED STARS (FENTON)** | | | | | | | | |
| Plate, 9" | 110 | | | | | | | |

Beaded Swirl (English)

Bells and Beads (Dugan)

Big Basketweave (Dugan)

Big Fish (Millersburg)

294

| | M | A | G | B | PO | AO | Pas | R |
|---|---|---|---|---|---|---|---|---|
| Bowl | 40 | | | | 90 | | | |
| Rose Bowl | 60 | | | | | | | |
| Banana Boat | 110 | | | | | | | |
| **BEADED SWIRL (ENGLISH)** | | | | | | | | |
| Compote | 50 | | | 60 | | | | |
| Covered Butter | 70 | | | 85 | | | | |
| Milk Pitcher | 75 | | | 90 | | | | |
| Sugar | 50 | | | 55 | | | | |
| **BEADS (NORTHWOOD)** | | | | | | | | |
| Bowl, 8½" | 45 | 60 | 70 | | | | | |
| **BEADS AND BARS (U.S. GLASS)** | | | | | | | | |
| Spooner | 55 | | | | | | | |
| **BEARDED BERRY (FENTON)** | | | | | | | | |
| Exterior Pattern Only | | | | | | | | |
| **BEAUTY BUD VASE (DUGAN)** | | | | | | | | |
| Regular Size | 40 | 85 | | | | | 80SM | |
| Twig Size, Rare | 150 | 1,000 | | | | | | |
| **BEAUTY BUD VASE VT.** | | | | | | | | |
| No Twigs | 30 | | | | | | 35SM | |
| **BEE** | | | | | | | | |
| Ornament | 75 | | | | | | | |
| **BEETLE ASHTRAY (ARGENTINA)** | | | | | | | | |
| One Size, Rare | | | | 350 | | | | |
| **BEETLE HATPIN** | | | | | | | | |
| Complete | | 85 | | | | | | |
| **BELLAIRE SOUVENIR (IMPERIAL)** | | | | | | | | |
| Bowl, Scarce | 185 | | | | | | | |
| **BELLE** | | | | | | | | |
| Hatpin | | 240 | | | | | | |
| **BELL FLOWER (FUCHSIA)** | | | | | | | | |
| Compote, handled | | | | 2,000 | | | | |
| **BELLS AND BEADS (DUGAN)** | | | | | | | | |
| Bowl, 7½" | 45 | 90 | 115 | 120 | 90 | | | |
| Nappy | 60 | 95 | | | 100 | | | |
| Plate, 8" | | 170 | | | | | | |
| Hat Shape | 40 | 60 | | | | | | |
| Compote | 70 | 75 | | | | | | |
| Gravy Boat, Handled | 55 | 70 | | | 140 | | | |
| **BERNHEIMER (MILLERSBURG)** | | | | | | | | |
| Bowl, 8¾", Scarce | | | | 1,900 | | | | |
| **BERRY BASKET** | | | | | | | | |
| One Size | 55 | | | | | | | |
| Matching Shakers, Pair | 75 | | | | | | | |
| **BIG BASKETWEAVE (DUGAN)** | | | | | | | | |
| Vase, 6"-14" | 90 | 120 | | | 140 | 275 | 150W | |
| Basket, Small | 45 | 60 | | | | | | |
| Basket, Large | 95 | | | | | | | |
| **BIG CHIEF** | | | | | | | | |
| One Shape | | 95 | | | | | | |
| **BIG FISH (MILLERSBURG)** | | | | | | | | |
| Bowl, Various Shapes | 500 | 600 | 650 | | | | 6,500V | |
| Banana Bowl, Rare | | 2,000 | 2,000 | | | | | |
| Bowl, Tri-Cornered | 1,050 | 2,000 | 2,000 | | | | 2,000V | |
| Rose Bowl, Very Rare | | | | | | | 7,500V | |
| Square Bowl, Very Rare | 900 | 1,500 | 1,500 | | | | 6,000V | |
| **BIG THISTLE (MILLERSBURG)** | | | | | | | | |
| Punch Bowl and Base Only, Rare | | 10,000 | | | | | | |
| **BIRD OF PARADISE (NORTHWOOD)** | | | | | | | | |
| Bowl, Advertising | | 395 | | | | | | |
| Plate, Advertising | | 450 | | | | | | |
| Hatpin, Rare | | 1,300 | | | | | | |
| **BIRDS AND CHERRIES (FENTON)** | | | | | | | | |
| Bon-bon | 45 | 65 | 65 | 65 | | | 90 | |
| Bowl, 9½", Rare | 200 | 325 | | 375 | | | | |
| Bowl, 5", Rare | 65 | 90 | | | | | | |
| Compote | 45 | 60 | 65 | 60 | | | 95 | |
| Plate, 10", Rare | 1,200 | | 1,600 | 1,500 | | | | |
| **BIRD WITH GRAPES (COCKATOO)** | | | | | | | | |
| Wall Vase | 75 | | | | | | | |
| **BLACKBERRY (FENTON)** | | | | | | | | |
| Open Edge Hat | 40 | 45 | 50 | 40 | | 175 | 80 | 475 |
| Spittoon Whimsey, Rare | 3,200 | | | 3,600 | | | | |
| Vase Whimsey, Rare | 750 | | | 900 | | | 700W | |
| Plate, Rare | 800 | | | 400 | | | | |
| **BLACKBERRY (NORTHWOOD)** | | | | | | | | |
| Compote | 55 | 65 | | 75 | | | 150W | |
| Bowl, Ftd, 9" | 50 | 60 | | | | | | |
| **BLACKBERRY BANDED (FENTON)** | | | | | | | | |
| Hat Shape | 35 | | 55 | 45 | 90 | | | |
| **BLACKBERRY BARK** | | | | | | | | |
| Vase, Rare | | 1,900* | | | | | | |
| **BLACKBERRY BLOCK (FENTON)** | | | | | | | | |
| Pitcher | 450 | 1,250 | 1,500 | 1,250 | | | 6,500V | |
| Tumbler | 50 | 150 | 85 | 75 | | | 300V | |

Blackberry Wreath (Millersburg)

Blossom and Palm (Northwood)

Booker

Border Plants (Dugan)

| | M | A | G | B | PO | AO | Pas | R |
|---|---|---|---|---|---|---|---|---|
| **BLACKBERRY BRAMBLE (FENTON)** | | | | | | | | |
| Bowl | | | | 60 | | | | |
| Compote | 40 | 50 | 70 | 55 | | | | |
| **BLACKBERRY, MINIATURE (FENTON)** | | | | | | | | |
| Compote, Small | 125 | 150 | 200 | 175 | | | 590W | |
| Stemmed Plate, Rare | | | | 450 | | | | |
| **BLACKBERRY RAYS** | | | | | | | | |
| Compote | 500 | 350 | | | | | | |
| **BLACKBERRY SPRAY (FENTON)** | | | | | | | | |
| Bon-bon | 35 | 45 | 50 | 45 | | | | |
| Compote | 40 | 50 | 55 | 50 | | | | |
| Hat Shape | 45 | 55 | 200 | 40 | | 1,700JIP | 600AMT-O | 485 |
| **BLACKBERRY WREATH (MILLERSBURG)** | | | | | | | | |
| Plate, 10", Rare | 4,700 | 5,000 | | | | | | |
| Plate, 6", Rare | 2,250 | 2,700 | 2,900 | | | | | |
| Bowl, 5" | 50 | 70 | 75 | | | | 90CM | |
| Bowl, 7"-9" | 65 | 90 | 90 | 975 | | | | |
| Bowl, 10", Ice Cream | 100 | 600 | 650 | 1,100 | | | | |
| Spittoon Whimsey, Rare | | | 3,800 | | | | | |
| Plate, 8" Rare | | | 4,200 | | | | | |
| **BLACK BOTTOM (FENTON)** | | | | | | | | |
| Candy Jar | 60 | | | | | | 60 | |
| **BLAZE** | | | | | | | | |
| Bowl, 8"-10" | 75 | | | | | | | |
| **BLOCKS AND ARCHES** | | | | | | | | |
| Creamer | 42 | | | | | | | |
| **BLOCKS AND ARCHES (CRYSTAL)** | | | | | | | | |
| Pitcher, Rare | 100 | 140 | | | | | | |
| Tumbler, Rare | 75 | 90 | | | | | | |
| **BLOSSOM AND PALM (NORTHWOOD) Also known as Blossom and Shell.** | | | | | | | | |
| Bowl, 9" | 50 | 65 | 70 | | | | 150ALS | |
| **BLOSSOM AND SPEARS** | | | | | | | | |
| Plate, 8" | 52 | | | | | | | |
| **BLOSSOMS AND BAND (IMPERIAL)** | | | | | | | | |
| Bowl, 10" | 38 | 45 | | | | | | |
| Bowl, 5" | 20 | 30 | | | | | | |
| Wall Vase, Complete | 15 | | | | | | | |
| **BLOSSOMTIME (NORTHWOOD)** | | | | | | | | |
| Compote | 450 | 310 | 650 | | | | | |
| **BLOWN CANDLESTICKS** | | | | | | | | |
| One Size, Pair | 90 | | | | | | | |
| **BLUEBERRY (FENTON)** | | | | | | | | |
| Pitcher, Scarce | 500 | | | 900 | | | | |
| Tumbler, Scarce | 60 | | | 100 | | | 140W | |
| **BOGGY BAYOU (FENTON)** | | | | | | | | |
| Vase 7"-11" | 110 | 140 | 160 | 150 | | | | |
| Vase 12"-15" | 115 | 145 | 170 | 160 | | | | |
| **BOOKER** | | | | | | | | |
| Cider pitcher | 600 | | | | | | | |
| Mug | 160 | | | | | | | |
| **BOOT** | | | | | | | | |
| One Shape | 150 | | | | | | | |
| **BO PEEP (WESTMORELAND)** | | | | | | | | |
| ABC Plate, Scarce | 550 | | | | | | | |
| Mug, Scarce | 160 | | | | | | | |
| **BORDER PATH** | | | | | | | | |
| Hatpin | | 175 | | | | | | |
| **BORDER PLANTS (DUGAN)** | | | | | | | | |
| Bowl, Flat, 8½" | | 125 | | | 180 | | | |
| Bowl, Ftd, 8½" | | 600 | | | 250 | | | |
| Handgrip Plate | 350 | | | | 365 | | | |
| **BOUQUET (FENTON)** | | | | | | | | |
| Pitcher | 285 | | | 550 | | | 750W | |
| Tumbler | 37 | 80 | | 55 | | | 90W | |
| **BOUQUET AND LATTICE** Various Shapes from $15.00 each, Late Carnival | | | | | | | | |
| **BOUQUET TOOTHPICK HOLDER** | | | | | | | | |
| One Size | 75 | | | | | | | |
| **BOUTONNIERE (MILLERSBURG)** | | | | | | | | |
| Compote | 280 | 275 | 270 | | | | | |
| **BOW AND ENGLISH HOB (ENGLISH)** | | | | | | | | |
| Nut Bowl | 50 | | | 60 | | | | |
| **BOW AND KNOT** | | | | | | | | |
| Perfume | 45 | | | | | | | |
| **BOXED STAR** | | | | | | | | |
| One Shape, Rare | | | | | | | 110 | |

Brocaded Acorns (Fostoria)

Brocaded Palms

Brooklyn

Butterflies (Fenton)

| | M | A | G | B | PO | AO | Pas | R |
|---|---|---|---|---|---|---|---|---|
| **BRIAR PATCH** | | | | | | | | |
| Hat Shape | 40 | 50 | | | | | | |
| **BRIDLE ROSETTE** | | | | | | | | |
| One Shape | 85 | | | | | | | |
| **BROCADED ACORNS (FOSTORIA)** | | | | | | | | |
| **BROCADED DAFFODILS** | | | | | | | | |
| **BROCADED DAISIES** | | | | | | | | |
| **BROCADED PALMS** | | | | | | | | |
| **BROCADED POPPIES** | | | | | | | | |
| **BROCADED ROSES** | | | | | | | | |
| **BROCADED SUMMER GARDENS** | | | | | | | | |
| All Related Patterns in Similar Shapes and Colors | | | | | | | | |
| Wine | | | | | | | 170 | |
| Bowls, Various Sizes | | | | | | | 185 | |
| Center Bowl, Ftd. | | | | | | | 220 | |
| Dome Bowl | | | | | | | 95 | |
| Handled Bowl | | | | | | | 75 | |
| Rose Bowl | | | | | | | 170 | |
| Bon-bon | | | | | | | 165 | |
| Cake Tray | | | | | | | 210 | |
| Ice Bucket | | | | | | | 200 | |
| Covered Box | | | | | | | 195 | |
| Tray | | | | | | | 200 | |
| Plate | | | | | | | 85 | |
| Cake Plate, Center Handle | | | | | | | 210 | |
| Vase | | | | | | | 220 | |
| Flower Set, 3 Pieces | | | | | | | 290 | |
| **BROCKER'S (NORTHWOOD)** | | | | | | | | |
| Advertising Plate | | 1,700 | | | | | | |
| **BROKEN ARCHES (IMPERIAL)** | | | | | | | | |
| Bowl, 8½"-10" | 45 | 50 | 75 | | | | | |
| Punch Bowl and Base | 365 | 595 | | | | | | |
| Punch Cup | 30 | 30 | | | | | | |
| **BROOKLYN** | | | | | | | | |
| Bottle w/stopper | 75 | 95 | | | | | | |
| **BROOKLYN BRIDGE (DUGAN)** | | | | | | | | |
| Bowl, Scarce | 350 | | | | | | | |
| Unlettered Bowl, Rare | 1,200 | | | | | | | |
| **BUBBLE BERRY** | | | | | | | | |
| Shade | | | | | | | 75 | |
| **BUBBLES** | | | | | | | | |
| Hatpin | | 65 | | | | | | |
| Lamp Chimney | | | | | | | 50 | |
| **BUDDHA (ENGLISH)** | | | | | | | | |
| One Shape, Rare | 900 | | | | | | 1,100IB | |
| **BULLDOG** | | | | | | | | |
| Paperweight | 1,250 | | | | | | | |
| **BULL'S EYE (U.S. GLASS)** | | | | | | | | |
| Oil Lamp | 210 | | | | | | | |
| **BULL'S EYE AND LEAVES (NORTHWOOD)** | | | | | | | | |
| Bowl, 8½" | 40 | 55 | 50 | | | | | |
| **BULL'S EYE AND LOOP (MILLERSBURG)** | | | | | | | | |
| Vase, 7"-11", Rare | 400 | 400 | 500 | | | | | |
| **BULL'S EYE AND SPEARHEAD** | | | | | | | | |
| Wine | 90 | | | | | | | |
| **BUMBLEBEES** | | | | | | | | |
| Hatpin | | 70 | | | | | | |
| **BUNNY** | | | | | | | | |
| Bank | 35 | | | | | | | |
| **BUTTERFLIES (FENTON)** | | | | | | | | |
| Bon-bon | 60 | 70 | 75 | 65 | | | 90 | |
| Card Tray | 55 | | | 60 | | | | |
| **BUTTERFLIES AND BELLS (CRYSTAL)** | | | | | | | | |
| Compote | 220 | 245 | | | | | | |
| **BUTTERFLIES AND WARATAH (CRYSTAL)** | | | | | | | | |
| Cake Plate, 8" Rare | 450 | | | | | | | |
| Compote, Large | 220 | 300 | | | | | | |
| **BUTTERFLY** | | | | | | | | |
| Hatpin | | 100 | | | | | | |
| Pintray | 40 | | | | | | 50 | |
| **BUTTERFLY (FENTON)** | | | | | | | | |
| Ornament, Rare | 190 | 220 | 225 | 200 | | | 300W | |
| **BUTTERFLY (NORTHWOOD)** | | | | | | | | |
| Bon-bon, Regular | 65 | 90 | 100 | 325 | | | | |
| Bon-bon, Ribbed Exterior | | 250 | | | | | 575IB | |
| **BUTTERFLY (U.S. GLASS)** | | | | | | | | |
| Tumbler, Rare | 5,800 | | 6,000 | | | | | |

Butterfly and Corn (Northwood)

Canada Dry

Cane (Imperial)

Captive Rose (Fenton)

| | M | A | G | B | PO | AO | Pas | R |
|---|---|---|---|---|---|---|---|---|
| **BUTTERFLY AND BERRY (FENTON)** | | | | | | | | |
| Bowl, Ftd, 10" | 100 | 200 | 250 | 225 | | | 750W | |
| Bowl, Ftd, 5" | 35 | 40 | 145 | 140 | | | 95W | 1,200 |
| Covered Butter | 150 | 240 | 300 | 225 | | | | |
| Covered Sugar | 100 | 160 | 200 | 175 | | | | |
| Covered Creamer | 100 | 150 | 200 | 170 | | | | |
| Nut Bowl Whimsey | | 700 | | | | | | |
| Spooner | 90 | 125 | 190 | 160 | | | | |
| Hatpin Holder | | | | | | | | |
| Whimsey | 1,350 | | | | | | | |
| Pitcher | 350 | 500 | | 490 | | | 1,200W | |
| Tumbler | 40 | 70 | 80 | 70 | | | 100W | |
| Hatpin Holder, Rare | 1,200 | | | 650 | | | | |
| Vase, Rare | 70 | 95 | 200 | 50 | | | 500W | 700 |
| Spittoon Whimsey, 2 Types | | 2,600 | | 2,600 | | | | |
| Bowl Whimsey (Fernery) | 850 | 1,200 | | 1,400 | | | | |
| Plate, Ftd (Whimsey) | | | | 1,500 | | | | |
| **BUTTERFLY AND CORN (NORTHWOOD)** | | | | | | | | |
| Vase, Rare | | | | | | | 4,000V | |
| **BUTTERFLY AND FERN (FENTON)** | | | | | | | | |
| Pitcher | 395 | 575 | 650 | 485 | | | | |
| Tumbler | 80 | 60 | 85 | 65 | | | | |
| **BUTTERFLY AND TULIP (DUGAN)** | | | | | | | | |
| Bowl, Ftd, 10½", Scarce | 320 | 4,000 | | | | | | |
| Bowl, Whimsey Shape, Rare | 900 | 1,500 | | | | | | |
| **BUTTERFLY BOWER (CRYSTAL)** | | | | | | | | |
| Compote | 115 | 200 | | | | | | |
| Cake Plate, Stemmed | | 200 | | | | | | |
| **BUTTERFLY BUSH (CRYSTAL)** | | | | | | | | |
| Compote, Large | 300 | 375 | | | | | | |
| **BUTTERFLY LAMP** | | | | | | | | |
| Oil Lamp | 1,500 | | | | | | | |
| **BUTTERMILK, PLAIN (FENTON)** | | | | | | | | |
| Goblet | 60 | 70 | 80 | | | | | |
| **BUTTON AND FAN** | | | | | | | | |
| Hatpin | | 60 | | | | | | |
| **BUTTONS AND DAISY (IMPERIAL)** | | | | | | | | |
| Hat (Old Only) | | | | | | | 70CM | |
| Slipper (Old Only) | | | | | | | 80CM | |
| **BUTTRESS (U.S. GLASS)** | | | | | | | | |
| Pitcher, Rare | 400 | | | | | | | |
| Tumbler, Rare | 300 | | | | | | | |
| **BUTTRESS MIRROR** | | | | | | | | |
| Hatpin | | 100 | | | | | | |
| **BUZZ SAW** | | | | | | | | |
| Shade | 45 | | | | | | | |
| **BUZZ SAW (CAMBRIDGE)** | | | | | | | | |
| Cruet, Small 4", Rare | | | 575 | | | | | |
| Cruet, Large 6", Rare | 550 | | 675 | | | | | |
| **CACTUS (MILLERSBURG)** | | | | | | | | |
| Exterior Pattern | | | | | | | | |
| **CAMBRIDGE HODSTAR (CAMBRIDGE)** | | | | | | | | |
| Napkin Ring | 50 | | | | | | | |
| **CANADA DRY** | | | | | | | | |
| Bottle – 2 sizes | 55 | | | | | | 65CL | |
| **CANDLE LAMP (FOSTORIA)** | | | | | | | | |
| One Size | 110 | | | | | | 150AM | |
| **CANDLE VASE** | 55 | | | | | | | |
| **CANE (IMPERIAL)** | | | | | | | | |
| Bowl, 7½"-10" | 40 | | | | | | 50 | |
| Pickle Dish | 32 | | | | | | 46 | |
| Wine | 65 | | | | | | 75 | |
| Compote | 80 | | | | | | 115 | |
| **CANE AND DAISY CUT (JENKINS)** | | | | | | | | |
| Vase | 150 | | | | | | | |
| Basket, Handled, Rare | 220 | | | | | | 250 | |
| **CANE AND SCROLL (SEA THISTLE) (ENGLISH)** | | | | | | | | |
| Rose Bowl | 55 | | | 75 | | | | |
| Creamer or Sugar | 45 | | | | | | | |
| **CANNONBALL VT.** | | | | | | | | |
| Pitcher | 240 | | | 285 | | | 400W | |
| Tumbler | 50 | | | 65 | | | 90W | |
| **CANOE (U.S. GLASS)** | | | | | | | | |
| One Size | 150 | | | | | | | |
| **CAPITOL (WESTMORELAND)** | | | | | | | | |
| Mug, Small | 140 | | | | | | | |
| Bowl, Ftd, Small | | 70 | | 70 | | | | |
| **CAPTIVE ROSE (FENTON)** | | | | | | | | |
| Bowl, 8½"-10" | 95 | 90 | 90 | 80 | | | 250BA | |
| Compote | 65 | 80 | 90 | 160 | | | 140W | |

297

Carolina Dogwood (Westmoreland)

Caroline (Dugan)

Cathedral (Sweden)

Chatelaine (Imperial)

| | M | A | G | B | PO | AO | Pas | R |
|---|---|---|---|---|---|---|---|---|
| Plate, 7".................. | 140 | 190 | 210 | 200 | | | 550 | |
| Plate, 9".................. | 225 | 410 | 500 | 400 | | | | |
| Bon-bon .................. | 95 | | 110 | 85 | | | 160 | |
| **CARNATION (NEW MARTINSVILLE)** | | | | | | | | |
| Punch Cup .............. | 57 | | | | | | | |
| **CARNIVAL BEADS** | | | | | | | | |
| Various Strands.................. | 30+ | | | | | | | |
| **CARNIVAL BELL** | | | | | | | | |
| One Size ............................ | 425 | | | | | | | |
| **CARNIVAL HONEYCOMB (IMPERIAL)** | | | | | | | | |
| Bon-bon .................. | 40 | 55 | 60 | | | | 75AM | |
| Creamer or Sugar ................ | 35 | | | | | | | |
| Plate, 7".................. | | 95 | | | | | | |
| Bowl, Handles, 6" .............. | 30 | | | | | | | |
| **CAROLINA DOGWOOD (WESTMORELAND)** | | | | | | | | |
| Bowl, 8½" .......................... | 80 | 110 | | | 260MO | 500 | | |
| Plate, Rare.......................... | | | | | 320MO | | | |
| **CAROLINE (DUGAN)** | | | | | | | | |
| Bowl, 7"-10" ...................... | 70 | | | | 190 | | | |
| Banana Bowl ...................... | | | | | 210 | | | |
| Basket, Scarce.................... | | | | | 275 | | | |
| **CARRIE (ANCHOR-HOCKING)** | | | | | | | | |
| One Size ............................ | 60 | | | | | | | |
| **CARTWHEEL #411 (HEISEY)** | | | | | | | | |
| Compote............................ | 50 | | | | | | | |
| Goblet ................................ | 75 | | | | | | | |
| **CATHEDRAL (SWEDEN)** (Also know as Curved Star) | | | | | | | | |
| Chalice, 7".......................... | 125 | | | 190 | | | | |
| Pitcher, Rare........................ | | | | 3,700 | | | | |
| Bowl, 10".............................. | 50 | | | | | | | |
| Flower Holder ...................... | 75 | | | | | | | |
| Epergne, Scarce.................... | 245 | | | | | | | |
| Compote, 2 Sizes ................ | 60 | | | 80 | | | | |
| Creamer, Ftd ...................... | 60 | | | | | | | |
| Butterdish, 2 Sizes .............. | 240 | | | | | | | |
| **CATHEDRAL ARCHES (ENGLISH)** | | | | | | | | |
| Punch Bowl, 1 Piece ............ | 350 | | | | | | | |
| **CATTAILS** | | | | | | | | |
| Hatpin................................ | | 90 | | | | | | |
| **CENTRAL SHOE STORE (NORTHWOOD)** | | | | | | | | |
| Bowl, 6"-7" .......................... | | 1,200 | | | | | | |
| **CHAIN AND STAR (FOSTORIA)** | | | | | | | | |
| Tumbler, Rare ..................... | 900 | | | | | | | |
| Covered Butter, Rare ........... | 1,500 | | | | | | | |
| **CHARIOT** | | | | | | | | |
| Compote, large .................... | 120 | | | | | | | |
| **CHATELAINE (IMPERIAL)** | | | | | | | | |
| Pitcher, Rare........................ | | 3,700 | | | | | | |
| Tumbler, Rare ..................... | | 510 | | | | | | |
| **CHATHAM (U.S. GLASS)** | | | | | | | | |
| Compote............................ | 75 | | | | | | | |
| Candlesticks, Pair................ | 90 | | | | | | | |
| **CHECKERBOARD (WESTMORELAND)** | | | | | | | | |
| Cruet, Rare.......................... | | | | | | | 750CL | |
| Pitcher, Rare........................ | | 3,800 | | | | | | |
| Tumbler, Rare .................... | 750 | 550 | | | | | | |
| Goblet, Rare ........................ | 350 | 425 | | | | | | |
| Punch Cup .......................... | 90 | | | | | | | |
| Wine, Rare.......................... | 295 | | | | | | | |
| Vase .................................... | | 2,700 | | | | | | |
| **CHECKERBOARD BOUQUET** | | | | | | | | |
| Plate, 8".............................. | | 85 | | | | | | |
| **CHECKERBOARD PANELS (ENGLISH)** | | | | | | | | |
| Bowl................................... | 70 | | | | | | | |
| **CHECKERS** | | | | | | | | |
| Ashtray ............................... | 47 | | | | | | | |
| Bowl, 4"............................... | 28 | | | | | | | |
| Bowl, 9"............................... | 40 | | | | | | | |
| Butter, 2 Sizes .................... | 200 | | | | | | | |
| Plate, 7"............................... | 90 | | | | | | | |
| **CHERRY (DUGAN)** | | | | | | | | |
| Bowl, Flat, 5"...................... | 40 | 50 | | | 90 | | | |
| Bowl, Flat, 8"...................... | 65 | 70 | | | 210 | | | |
| Bowl, Ftd, 8½" .................... | 210 | 310 | | | 400 | | | |
| Plate, 6"............................... | | 400 | | | 410 | | | |
| Cruet, Rare.......................... | | | | | | | 650W | |
| **CHERRY (FENTON)** (See Mikado Compote) | | | | | | | | |

Cherry (Millersburg)

Christmas Compote (Dugan)

Circle Scroll (Dugan)

Classic Arts (Czech)

| | M | A | G | B | PO | AO | Pas | R |
|---|---|---|---|---|---|---|---|---|
| **CHERRY (MILLERSBURG)** | | | | | | | | |
| Bowl, 4" | 60 | 85 | 90 | 1,100 | | | | |
| Bowl, 5", Hobnail | | | | | | | | |
| Exterior Rare | | | | 900 | | | | |
| Bowl, 7", Rare | 135 | 95 | 130 | | | | | |
| Bowl, 9", Scarce | 90 | 125 | 150 | | | | | |
| Bowl, Ice Cream, 10" | 250 | 375 | 350 | 1,800 | | | | |
| Bowl, 9", Hobnail | | | | | | | | |
| Exterior Rare | 900 | 1,250 | | 2,700 | | | | |
| Compote, Large, Rare | 1,250 | 1,495 | 1,600 | 4,000 | | | 5,000V | |
| Banana Compote, Rare | | 4,000 | | | | | | |
| Milk Pitcher, Rare | 1,700 | | | | | | | |
| Plate, 6", Rare | 1,050 | | | | | | | |
| Plate, 7½", Rare | 800 | 3,000 | 4,300 | | | | | |
| Plate, 10", Rare | 4,600 | | | | | | | |
| Powder Jar, Rare | | | 1,950 | | | | | |
| Covered Butter | 250 | 375 | 450 | | | | | |
| Covered Sugar | 170 | 300 | 325 | | | | | |
| Creamer or Spooner | 150 | 275 | 275 | | | | | |
| Pitcher, Scarce | 1,150 | 1,000 | 1,450 | | | | | |
| Tumbler, 2 Variations | 145 | 190 | 210 | | | | | |
| **CHERRY AND CABLE (NORTHWOOD)** | | | | | | | | |
| Pitcher, Rare | 1,450 | | | | | | | |
| Tumbler, Rare | 425 | | | | | | | |
| Bowl, 5", Scarce | 75 | | | | | | | |
| Butter, Rare | 450 | | | | | | | |
| Sugar, Creamer, | | | | | | | | |
| Spooner, Each, Rare | 210 | | | 500 | | | | |
| Bowl, 9", Scarce | 125 | | | | | | | |
| **CHERRY AND CABLE INTAGLIO (NORTHWOOD)** | | | | | | | | |
| Bowl, 10" | 75 | | | | | | | |
| Bowl, 5" | 50 | | | | | | | |
| **CHERRY AND DAISIES (FENTON)** | | | | | | | | |
| Banana Boat | 950 | | | 1,050 | | | | |
| **CHERRY BLOSSOMS** | | | | | | | | |
| Pitcher | | | | 150 | | | | |
| Tumbler | | | | 40 | | | | |
| **CHERRY CHAIN (FENTON)** | | | | | | | | |
| Bon-bon | 50 | 60 | 65 | 60 | | | | |
| Bowl, 6½"-10" | 50 | 90 | 90 | 95 | | | | |
| Plate, 7"-9" | 125 | | | 140 | | | | |
| **CHERRY CIRCLES (FENTON)** | | | | | | | | |
| Bon-bon | 50 | 65 | | 75 | | | | 7,400 |
| Bowl, 8" | 50 | 65 | | 70 | | | | |
| Compote | 70 | 80 | | 80 | | | 130W | |
| Plate, 9", Rare | 550 | | | 210 | | | 210W | |
| **CHERRY SMASH (U.S. GLASS)** | | | | | | | | |
| Bowl, 8" | 65 | | | | | | | |
| Butter | 150 | | | | | | | |
| Tumbler | 190 | | | | | | | |
| **CHERRY STIPPLED** | | | | | | | | |
| Tumbler | 110 | | | | | | | |
| **CHERRY VT (MILLERSBURG)** | | | | | | | | |
| Plate, 11"–rare | | 7,000* | | | | | | |
| **CHERUB** | | | | | | | | |
| Lamp, Rare | | | | | | | 150 | |
| **CHERUBS** | | | | | | | | |
| Mini Toothpick Holder | 200 | | | | | | | |
| **CHIPPENDALE SOUVENIR** | | | | | | | | |
| Creamer or Sugar | 65 | 80 | | | | | | |
| **CHRISTMAS COMPOTE (DUGAN)** | | | | | | | | |
| Large Compote, Rare | 5,500 | 4,800 | | | | | | |
| **CHRYSANTHEMUM (FENTON)** | | | | | | | | |
| Bowl, Flat, 9" | 130 | 60 | 95 | 80 | | | | 5,700 |
| Bowl, Ftd, 10" | 80 | 95 | 310 | 220 | | | 600BA | |
| **CHRYSANTHEMUM DRAPE** | | | | | | | | |
| Oil Lamp, Rare | | | | | | | 900 | |
| **CIRCLE SCROLL (DUGAN)** | | | | | | | | |
| Compote, Scarce | | 150 | | | | | | |
| Bowl, 10" | 65 | 80 | | | | | | |
| Bowl, 5" | 40 | 45 | | | | | | |
| Pitcher, Rare | 2,000 | 2,800 | | | | | | |
| Tumbler, Rare | 400 | 600 | | | | | | |
| Hat Shape, Rare | 60 | 100 | | | | | | |
| Creamer or Spooner | 150 | 225 | | | | | | |
| Vase Whimsey, Rare | 135 | 160 | | | | | | |
| Butter or Sugar | 375 | 425 | | | | | | |
| **CLASSIC ARTS (CZECH)** | | | | | | | | |
| Vase, 7" (Egyptian) | 700 | | | | | | | |
| Powder Jar | 575 | | | | | | | |
| Rose Bowl | 525 | | | | | | | |
| Vase, 10", Rare | 750 | | | | | | | |
| **CLEOPATRA** | | | | | | | | |
| Bottle | 110 | | | | | | | |

Coin Spot (Dugan)

Columbia (Imperial)

Columbia VT (Imperial)

Concave Flute

| | M | A | G | B | PO | AO | Pas | R |
|---|---|---|---|---|---|---|---|---|
| **CLEVELAND MEMORIAL (MILLERSBURG)** | | | | | | | | |
| Ashtray, Rare | 6,000 | 8,000 | | | | | | |
| **CLUSTER OF GRAPES** | | | | | | | | |
| Hatpin | | 250 | | | | | | |
| **COAL BUCKET (U.S. GLASS)** | | | | | | | | |
| One Size | 200 | | 350 | | | | | |
| **COBBLESTONES (DUGAN)** | | | | | | | | |
| Bowl, 9" | 65 | 150 | | | | | | |
| Bowl, 5" | 40 | 80 | | | | | | |
| **COBBLESTONES (IMPERIAL)** | | | | | | | | |
| Bowl, 5" | 35 | 40 | 50 | | | | | |
| Bowl, 8½" | 75 | 275 | 115 | | | | | |
| Bon-bon | 45 | 75 | 70 | | | | 95AM | |
| Plate, Rare | | 1,300 | | | | | | |
| **COIN DOT (FENTON)** | | | | | | | | |
| Bowl, 6"-10" | 35 | 40 | 40 | 65 | | 260 | 100LV | 1,200 |
| Plate, 9", Rare | 200 | 250 | 275 | 260 | | | | |
| Pitcher, Rare | 350 | 500 | 550 | 525 | | | | |
| Tumbler, Rare | 190 | 250 | 265 | 225 | | | | |
| Basket Whimsey, Rare | 75 | | 100 | | | | | |
| Rose Bowl | 90 | | | | | | | 1,600 |
| **COIN DOT VT. (WESTMORELAND)** | | | | | | | | |
| Compote | 60 | | | | 175MO | 270 | 350IBO | |
| Rose Bowl | 40 | 75 | 60 | | | | 320TL | |
| Bowl | 40 | 60 | 70 | | | | 90 | |
| **COIN SPOT (DUGAN)** | | | | | | | | |
| Compote | 45 | 60 | 70 | 65 | 200 | 375 | | |
| Goblet, Rare | | | | | | | 390IG | |
| **COLOGNE BOTTLE (CAMBRIDGE)** | | | | | | | | |
| One Size, Rare | 600 | | 850 | | | | | |
| **COLONIAL (IMPERIAL)** | | | | | | | | |
| Lemonade Goblet | 75 | | | | | | | |
| Vase | 40 | 60 | | | | | | |
| Toothpick Holder | 60 | 110 | 95 | | | | | |
| Open Sugar or Creamer | 47 | | | | | | | |
| Candlesticks, Pair | 200 | | | | | | | |
| **COLONIAL LADY (IMPERIAL)** | | | | | | | | |
| Vase, Rare | 1,000 | 1,150 | | | | | 110W | 225 |
| **COLONIAL VT** | | | | | | | | |
| Pitcher | 150 | | | | | | | |
| Tumbler | 25 | | | | | | | |
| **COLUMBIA (IMPERIAL)** | | | | | | | | |
| Vase | 45 | 55 | 50 | | | | | |
| Cake Plate, Rare | 150 | 180 | 200 | | | | 170AM | |
| Compote | 60 | 75 | 65 | | | | | |
| **COLUMBIA VT (IMPERIAL)** | | | | | | | | |
| Compote, scarce | 100 | | | | | | | |
| **COLUMBUS** | | | | | | | | |
| Plate, 8" | 45 | | | | | | | |
| **COMPASS (DUGAN)** | | | | | | | | |
| (Exterior Pattern Only) | | | | | | | | |
| **COMPOTE VASE** | | | | | | | | |
| Stemmed Shape | 50 | 65 | 72 | 76 | | | | |
| **CONCAVE DIAMOND** | | | | | | | | |
| Pitcher w/lid | | | 450RG | | | | 550V | |
| Tumbler | | | 425RG | | | | 190V | |
| Pickle Castor, Ornate Holder | 475 | | | | | | 395CeB | |
| Tumble-Up, Complete, Rare | | | | | | | 230V | |
| Coaster, Not Iridized | | | | | | | 420V | |
| Vase | | | | | | | 100CeB | |
| **CONCAVE FLUTE (WESTMORELAND)** | | | | | | | | |
| Banana bowl, Rare | | 150 | | | | | 200AM | |
| Bowl | 70 | 90 | 85 | | | | | |
| Rose Bowl | 50 | | 65 | | | | | |
| Vase | 40 | 65 | 65 | | | | | |
| **CONCORD (FENTON)** | | | | | | | | |
| Bowl, 9", Scarce | 200 | 300 | 450 | 250 | | | 350AM | |
| Plate, 10", Rare | 1,800 | 3,600 | 6,800 | | | | 1,000AM | |
| **CONE AND TIE (IMPERIAL)** | | | | | | | | |
| Tumbler, Rare | | 950 | | | | | | |
| **CONNIE (NORTHWOOD)** | | | | | | | | |
| Pitcher | | | | | | | 750W | |
| Tumbler | | | | | | | 125W | |
| **CONSTELLATION (DUGAN)** | | | | | | | | |
| Compote | 150 | 60 | | | 200 | | 175V | |
| **CONTINENTAL BOTTLE** | | | | | | | | |
| 2 Sizes | 45 | | | | | | | |
| **COOLEEMEE, NC (FENTON)** | | | | | | | | |
| Advertising Plate, Rare (Heart and Vine) | 1,500 | | | | | | | |
| **COOLIE HAT** | | | | | | | | |
| Hatpin | | 100 | | | | | | |

Corn Bottle (Imperial)

Corn Vase (Northwood)

Cosmos and Cane

Country Kitchen

| | M | A | G | B | PO | AO | Pas | R |
|---|---|---|---|---|---|---|---|---|
| **CORAL (FENTON)** | | | | | | | | |
| Bowl, 9" | 200 | | 300 | 400 | | | 500W | |
| Compote, Rare | 450 | | 500 | | | | 650W | |
| Plate, 9½", Rare | 1,500 | | 1,200 | 1,200 | | | | |
| **CORINTH (DUGAN)** | | | | | | | | |
| Bowl, 9" | 40 | 50 | | | 200 | | | |
| Banana Dish | 55 | 75 | | | 300 | | | |
| **CORINTH (WESTMORELAND)** | | | | | | | | |
| Vase | 30 | 50 | 75 | 450BO | 150 | | 60TL | |
| Bowl | 40 | 60 | | | | | 75TL | |
| **CORN BOTTLE (IMPERIAL)** | | | | | | | | |
| One Size | 285 | | 250 | | | | 400SM | |
| **CORN CRUET** | | | | | | | | |
| One Size, Rare | | | | | | | 1,100W | |
| **CORNING (CORNING)** | | | | | | | | |
| Insulator | 35+ | | | | | | | |
| **CORNUCOPIA (FENTON)** | | | | | | | | |
| Candlestick, pair, 5" | 80 | | | | | | 190W | |
| Vase, 5" | 70 | | | | | | 110W | |
| Candle Holder, 6½" | | | | | | | 110W | |
| **CORN VASE (NORTHWOOD)** | | | | | | | | |
| Regular Mold | 1,700 | 800 | 900 | 2,200 | | 7,800 | 475SM | |
| Pulled Husk, Rare | | 14,000 | 14,000 | | | | | |
| Fancy Husk, Rare (Dugan) | 1,100 | | | | | | | |
| **CORONA** | | | | | | | | |
| Hatpin | | 175 | | | | | | |
| **CORONATION (ENGLISH)** | | | | | | | | |
| Vase, 5" (Victoria Crown Design) | 250 | | | | | | | |
| **COSMOS (MILLERSBURG)** | | | | | | | | |
| Bowl, 5" | | | 70 | | | | | |
| **COSMOS AND CANE** | | | | | | | | |
| Bowl, 10" | 75 | | | | | | 190W | |
| Bowl, 5" | 40 | | | | | | 145W | |
| Compote, Tall, Rare | 350 | | | | | | 300W | |
| Butter, Covered | 200 | | | | | | 300W | |
| Covered Sugar or Creamer | 135 | | | | | | 200W | |
| Flat Tray, Rare | | | | | | | 275W | |
| Spooner | 100 | | | | | | 195W | |
| Stemmed Dessert | | | | | | | 150W | |
| Pitcher, Rare | 750 | | | | | | 1,450W | |
| Tumbler, Rare | 315 | | | | | | 250W | |
| Advertising Tumbler, Rare | | | | | | | 210AM | |
| Rose Bowl, Large | 1,275 | 1,500 | | | | | 2,000AM | |
| Rose Bowl Whimsey | 1,700 | | | | | | | |
| Spittoon Whimsey, Rare | | | | | | | 4,200W | |
| Chop Plate, Rare | 1,450 | | | | | | 1,600W | |
| Breakfast Set, 2 Pieces | | | | | | | 500W | |
| **COSMOS & HOBSTAR** | | | | | | | | |
| Bowl (on metal stand) | 450 | | | | | | | |
| **COSMOS VT. (FENTON)** | | | | | | | | |
| Bowl, 9"-10" | 40 | 65 | | 75 | | | 75V | 485 |
| Plate, 10", Rare | 175 | 210 | | | 400 | | | |
| **COUNTRY KITCHEN (MILLERSBURG)** | | | | | | | | |
| Bowl, 9", Rare | 595 | | | | | | | |
| Bowl, 5", Rare | 90 | | | | | | | |
| Spittoon Whimsey, Rare | | 4,600 | | | | | | |
| Covered Butter, Rare | 650 | 750 | | | | | | |
| Sugar, Creamer or Spooner | 400 | 500 | 800 | | | | 900V | |
| Vase Whimsey, Rare | 600 | 700 | | | | | | |
| **COURTHOUSE (MILLERSBURG)** | | | | | | | | |
| Lettered (Round or Ruffled), Scarce | | 950 | | | | | | |
| Unlettered, Rare | | 2,800 | | | | | | |
| **COVERED FROG (COOPERATIVE FLINT)** | | | | | | | | |
| One Size | 375 | 450 | 500 | 275 | | | 650 | |
| **COVERED HEN (ENGLISH)** | | | | | | | | |
| One Size | 110 | | | 145 | | | | |
| **COVERED LITTLE HEN (TINY)** | | | | | | | | |
| Miniature, 3½", Rare | | | | | | | 90CM | |
| **COVERED MALLARD (U.S. GLASS)** | | | | | | | | |
| One Shape | | | | | | | 450CM | |
| **COVERED SWAN (ENGLISH)** | | | | | | | | |
| One Size | 240 | 350 | | 325 | | | | |
| **CR (ARGENTINA)** | | | | | | | | |
| Ash Tray | 90 | | | 135 | | | | |
| **CRAB CLAW (IMPERIAL)** | | | | | | | | |
| Bowl, 5" | 25 | 37 | 40 | | | | | |
| Bowl, 10" | 50 | 65 | 65 | | | | 70SM | |
| Fruit Bowl w/base | 110 | | | | | | | |
| Pitcher, Scarce | 650 | | | | | | | |
| Tumbler, Scarce | 140 | | | | | | | |
| Cruet, Rare | 950 | | | | | | | |

Crackle (Imperial)

Cut Arcs (Fenton)

Cut Grecian Gold (Fenton)

Dahlia (Dugan)

| | M | A | G | B | PO | AO | Pas | R |
|---|---|---|---|---|---|---|---|---|
| **CRACKLE (IMPERIAL)** | | | | | | | | |
| Auto Vase | 30 | 35 | 35 | | | | | |
| Bowl, 9" | 25 | 30 | 30 | | | | | |
| Bowl, 5" | 15 | 18 | 18 | | | | | |
| Candy Jar w/lid | 30 | | | | | | | |
| Candlestick, 3½" | 25 | | | | | | | |
| Candlestick, 7" | 30 | | | | | | | |
| Plate | 45 | 55 | 60 | | | | | |
| Plate, 6" | 25 | | | | | | | |
| Punch Bowl and Base | 55 | | | | | | | |
| Punch Cup | 10 | | | | | | | |
| Pitcher, Dome Base | 90 | 150 | 160 | | | | | |
| Spittoon, Large | 45 | | | | | | | |
| Tumbler, Dome Base | 20 | 30 | 30 | | | | | |
| Wall Vase | 40 | | | | | | | |
| Window Planter, Rare | 110 | | | | | | | |
| **CROCUS VT.** | | | | | | | | |
| Tumbler | 45 | 65 | | | | | | |
| **CRUCIFIX (IMPERIAL)** | | | | | | | | |
| Candlestick, Rare, Each | 650 | | | | | | | |
| **CRYSTAL CUT (CRYSTAL)** | | | | | | | | |
| Compote | 75 | | | | | | | |
| **CUBA (McKee)** | | | | | | | | |
| Goblet, Rare | 45 | | | | | | | |
| **CURTAIN OPTIC (FENTON)** | | | | | | | | |
| Pitcher | | | | | | | 450VAS | |
| Tumbler | | | | | | | 150VAS | |
| Guest Set (tumble-up) | | | | | | | 350VAS | |
| **CURVED STAR** | | | | | | | | |
| **CUT ARCHES (ENGLISH)** | | | | | | | | |
| Banana Bowl | 80 | | | | | | | |
| **CUT ARCS (FENTON)** | | | | | | | | |
| Bowl, 7½"-10" | 40 | | 120 | | | | 250V | |
| Compote | 55 | 60 | | 55 | | | | |
| Vase Whimsey (From Bowl) | 40 | 50 | 150 | 50 | | | 80W | |
| **CUT COSMOS (MILLERSBURG)** | | | | | | | | |
| Tumbler, Rare | 450 | | | | | | | |
| **CUT CRYSTAL (U.S. GLASS)** | | | | | | | | |
| Compote, 5½" | 110 | | | | | | | |
| Water Bottle | 185 | | | | | | | |
| **CUT FLOWERS (JENKINS)** | | | | | | | | |
| Vase, 10" | 200 | | | | | | | |
| **CUT GRECIAN GOLD (FENTON)** | | | | | | | | |
| Lamp Font | 85 | | | | | | | |
| **CUT OVALS (FENTON)** | | | | | | | | |
| Candlesticks, pair | 175 | | | | | | 210 | 700 |
| Bowl, 7"-10" | 60 | | | | | | 75 | 425 |
| **CUT SPRAYS** | | | | | | | | |
| Vase, 9" | 45 | | | 75 | | | | |
| **DAHLIA (DUGAN)** | | | | | | | | |
| Bowl, Ftd, 10" | 95 | 125 | | | | | 290W | |
| Bowl, Ftd, 5" | 40 | 50 | | | | | 190W | |
| Butter | 120 | 155 | | | | | 350W | |
| Sugar | 90 | 100 | | | | | 250W | |
| Creamer or Spooner | 75 | 90 | | | | | 220W | |
| Pitcher, Rare | 500 | 950 | | | | | 800W | |
| Tumbler, Rare | 90 | 145 | | | | | 170W | |
| **DAHLIA (FENTON)** | | | | | | | | |
| Twist Epergne, One Lily | 250 | | | | | | 300W | |
| **DAHLIA AND DRAPE (FENTON)** | | | | | | | | |
| Tumble-Up, Complete | 150 | | | | | | 190IB | |
| **DAINTY BUD VASE** | | | | | | | | |
| One Size | 55 | | | | | | | |
| **DAISY (FENTON)** | | | | | | | | |
| Bon-bon, Scarce | 250 | | | 300 | | | | |
| **DAISY AND CANE (ENGLISH)** | | | | | | | | |
| Vase | 75 | | | | | | | |
| Decanter, Rare | 90 | | | | | | | |
| Spittoon, Rare | | | | 250 | | | | |
| **DAISY AND DRAPE (NORTHWOOD)** | | | | | | | | |
| Vase | 300 | 375 | 2,200 | 1,250 | | 600 | 3,000IB | |
| **DAISY AND PLUME (NORTHWOOD – DUGAN)** | | | | | | | | |
| Rose Bowl, 2 – Ftd | 75 | 100 | 105 | 110 | 175 | 2,000 | 550 | |
| Compote –Stemmed or Ftd | 60 | 110 | 90 | 100 | 160 | | | |
| Candy Dish – Ftd | 70 | 90 | 90 | 100 | 165 | | | |
| **DAISY BASKET (IMPERIAL)** | | | | | | | | |
| One Size | 65 | | | | | | 85SM | |
| **DAISY BLOCK (ENGLISH)** | | | | | | | | |
| Rowboat, Scarce | 250 | 250 | | | | | 300AQ | |
| **DAISY CHAIN** | | | | | | | | |
| Shade | 50 | | | | | | | |
| **DAISY CUT BELL (FENTON)** | | | | | | | | |
| One Size, Rare | 500 | | | | | | | |

Daisy Squares

Dance of the Veils (Fenton)

Dart

Delta Base

| | M | A | G | B | PO | AO | Pas | R |
|---|---|---|---|---|---|---|---|---|
| **DAISY DEAR (DUGAN)** | | | | | | | | |
| Bowl........................... | 40 | 48 | | | 55 | | 70W | |
| **DAISY IN OVAL PANELS (U.S. GLASS)** | | | | | | | | |
| Creamer or Sugar, Each ...... | 55 | | | | | | | |
| **DAISY SQUARES** | | | | | | | | |
| Rose Bowl.................... | 600 | | 675 | | | | 650IG | |
| Goblet, Rare ................. | 700 | 900 | | | | | 800AM | |
| Compote, Rare................ | 775 | | | | | | 700AM | |
| **DAISY WEB (DUGAN)** | | | | | | | | |
| Hat, Rare ................... | 400 | 1,800 | | | 750 | | | |
| **DAISY WREATH (WESTMORELAND)** | | | | | | | | |
| Bowl, 8"-10" .................. | | 250 | | | 250MMG | 600 | 500MO | |
| **DANCE OF THE VEILS (FENTON)** | | | | | | | | |
| Vase, Rare ................... | 3,000 | | | | | | | |
| **DANDELION (NORTHWOOD)** | | | | | | | | |
| Mug........................ | 500 | 300 | 600 | 500 | | 550 | 750BO | |
| Pitcher...................... | 395 | 620 | 1,700 | 900 | | | 7,500IB | |
| Tumbler ..................... | 75 | 90 | 200 | 250 | | | 475IG | |
| Vase Whimsey, Rare ........... | | 850 | | | | | | |
| **DART** | | | | | | | | |
| Oil lamp, Rare .................... | 500* | | | | | | | |
| **DAVISON'S SOCIETY CHOCOLATES (NORTHWOOD)** | | | | | | | | |
| Plate, Handgrip.................. | | 795 | | | | | | |
| **DECO LILY** | | | | | | | | |
| Bulbous Vase ...................... | 140 | | | | | | | |
| **DEEP GRAPE (MILLERSBURG)** | | | | | | | | |
| Compote, Rare..................... | 1,700 | 1,500 | 2,100 | 3,000 | | | | |
| Compote, Ruffled Top, Rare... | | 2,400 | | | | | | |
| Rose Bowl, Stemmed .......... | | | 8,000 | | | | | |
| **DELORES** | | | | | | | | |
| Perfume........................ | 60 | | | | | | | |
| **DELTA BASE** | | | | | | | | |
| Candlesticks, pr............ | 150 | | | | | | | |
| **DeVILBISS** | | | | | | | | |
| Atomizer, Complete............. | 65+ | | | | | | | |
| Perfumer ..................... | 60+ | | | | | | | |
| **DIAMOND AND DAISY CUT (U.S. GLASS)** | | | | | | | | |
| Vase, Square, 10" ............... | 225 | | | | | | | |
| Compote ...................... | 55 | 70 | | 75 | | | | |
| Pitcher, Rare...................... | 400 | | | 450 | | | | |
| Tumbler, Rare ................... | 50 | | | 60 | | | | |
| **DIAMOND AND DAISY CUT VT (JENKINS)** | | | | | | | | |
| Punch Bowl/Base, Rare....... | 600 | | | | | | | |
| **DIAMOND AND FAN (MILLERSBURG) Exterior pattern only.** | | | | | | | | |
| **DIAMOND AND FILE** | | | | | | | | |
| Banana Bowl...................... | 65 | | | | | | | |
| Bowl, 7"-9" ....................... | 50 | | | | | | 70 | |
| **DIAMOND AND RIB (FENTON)** | | | | | | | | |
| Vase, 7"-12"......................... | 45 | 100 | 90 | 80 | | | 70SM | |
| Funeral Vase, 17"-22" ......... | 700 | 900 | 1,000 | 1,000 | | | 800W | |
| Vase Whimsey ..................... | | | 900 | | | | | |
| **DIAMOND AND SUNBURST (IMPERIAL)** | | | | | | | | |
| Bowl, 8"............................ | 50 | 55 | 55 | | | | 50AM | |
| Decanter ............................ | 110 | 150 | 150 | | | | | |
| Wine................................. | 55 | 60 | 60 | | | | | |
| Oil Cruet, Rare ................................ | | 900* | | | | | | |
| **DIAMOND BAND (CRYSTAL)** | | | | | | | | |
| Open Sugar ....................... | 45 | 60 | | | | | | |
| Float Set............................ | 400 | 550 | | | | | | |
| **DIAMOND BAND AND FAN (ENGLISH)** | | | | | | | | |
| Cordial Set, Complete, Rare... | 900 | | | | | | | |
| **DIAMOND CHECKERBOARD** | | | | | | | | |
| Cracker Jar ........................ | 85 | | | | | | | |
| Butter ............................... | 90 | | | | | | | |
| Bowl, 9".............................. | 40 | | | | | | | |
| Bowl, 5".............................. | 25 | | | | | | | |
| Tumbler ............................ | 100 | | | | | | | |
| **DIAMOND DAISY** | | | | | | | | |
| Plate, 8"............................. | 95 | | | | | | | |
| **DIAMOND FLUTES (U.S. GLASS)** | | | | | | | | |
| Creamer ............................ | 45 | | | | | | | |
| Parfait .............................. | 55 | | | | | | | |
| **DIAMOND FOUNTAIN (HIGBEE)** | | | | | | | | |
| Cruet, Rare......................... | 750* | | | | | | | |
| **DIAMOND LACE (IMPERIAL)** | | | | | | | | |
| Bowl, 10"-11" ..................... | 65 | 110 | | | | | | |

Diamond Ovals (English)

Diamond Pinwheel (English)

Diamond Points (Northwood)

Double Dolphins (Fenton)

| | M | A | G | B | PO | AO | Pas | R |
|---|---|---|---|---|---|---|---|---|
| Bowl, 5" | 30 | 40 | | | | | | |
| Pitcher | | 325 | | | | | | |
| Tumbler | 190 | 55 | | | | | 250W* | |
| **DIAMOND OVALS (ENGLISH)** | | | | | | | | |
| Compote (Open Sugar) | 40 | | | | | | | |
| Creamer | 40 | | | | | | | |
| Stemmed Plate | 150 | | | | | | | |
| **DIAMOND PINWHEEL (ENGLISH)** | | | | | | | | |
| Compote | 45 | | | | | | | |
| Butter | 75 | | | | | | | |
| **DIAMOND POINT** | | | | | | | | |
| Rose Bowl | 700 | | | | | | | |
| Basket, Rare | 1,350 | 2,000 | | 2,300 | | | | |
| **DIAMOND POINT COLUMNS (IMPERIAL – FENTON)** | | | | | | | | |
| Bowl, 4½" | 20 | | | | | | | |
| Compote | 30 | | | | | | 40 | |
| Plate, 7" | 35 | | | | | | | |
| Vase | 40 | 55 | | | | | 55 | |
| Butter | 70 | | | | | | | |
| Creamer, Sugar or Spooner, Each | 40 | | | | | | | |
| Powder Jar w/lid | 40 | | | | | | | |
| Milk Pitcher | 35 | | | | | | | |
| **DIAMOND POINTS (NORTHWOOD)** | | | | | | | | |
| Vase, 7"-14" | 45 | 90 | 95 | 140 | 300 | 500 | 350SM | |
| **DIAMOND PRISMS (ENGLISH)** | | | | | | | | |
| Compote | 58 | | | | | | | |
| **DIAMOND RING (IMPERIAL)** | | | | | | | | |
| Rose Bowl, Rare | 400* | 650* | | | | | 450*SM | |
| Bowl, 9" | 40 | 50 | | | | | 55SM | |
| Bowl, 5" | 25 | 30 | | | | | 32SM | |
| Fruit Bowl, 9½" | 65 | 90 | | | | | 60SM | |
| **DIAMONDS (MILLERSBURG)** | | | | | | | | |
| Pitcher | 285 | 395 | 350 | | | | 490AQ | |
| Tumbler | 70 | 100 | 85 | | | | 190AQ | |
| Punch Bowl and Base, Rare | 2,800 | 2,300 | 2,500 | | | | | |
| Pitcher Oddity (No Spout) | | 550 | 550 | | | | | |
| Spittoon Whimsey, Very Rare | 7,500 | | | | | | | |
| **DIAMOND SPEARHEAD** | | | | | | | | |
| Hatpin | 145 | | | | | | | |
| **DIAMOND STAR** | | | | | | | | |
| Mug, 2 sizes | 120+ | | | | | | | |
| Vase, 8" | 80 | | | | | | | |
| **DIAMOND TOP (ENGLISH)** | | | | | | | | |
| Creamer | 40 | | | | | | | |
| Spooner | 40 | | | | | | | |
| **DIAMOND VANE (ENGLISH)** | | | | | | | | |
| Creamer, 4" | 35 | | | | | | | |
| **DIMPLES AND BRILLIANTS** | | | | | | | | |
| Hatpin | 400 | | | | | | | |
| **DIVING DOLPHINS (ENGLISH)** | | | | | | | | |
| Bowl, Ftd, 7" | 200 | 425 | 450 | 270 | | | | |
| **DOG** | | | | | | | | |
| Ashtray | 85 | | | | | | | |
| **DOGWOOD SPRAYS (DUGAN)** | | | | | | | | |
| Compote | 270 | | | | 360 | | | |
| Bowl, 9" | 250 | 270 | | | 370 | | | |
| **DOLPHINS (MILLERSBURG)** | | | | | | | | |
| Compote, Rare | | 1,850 | 2,000 | 6,000 | | | | |
| **DOROTHY** | | | | | | | | |
| Perfume | 50 | | | | | | | |
| **DORSEY AND FUNKENSTEIN (NORTHWOOD)** | | | | | | | | |
| Plate | | 600 | | | | | | |
| **DOTS AND CURVES** | | | | | | | | |
| Hatpin | | 55 | | | | | | |
| **DOTTED DAISIES** | | | | | | | | |
| Plate, 8" | 90 | | | | | | | |
| **DOTTED DIAMONDS & DAISIES** | | | | | | | | |
| Tumbler | 90 | | | | | | | |
| **DOUBLE DIAMONDS** | | | | | | | | |
| Cologne | 115 | | | | | | | |
| Pin Tray | 60 | | | | | | | |
| Ring Tree | 85 | | | | | | | |
| Puff Box | 50 | | | | | | | |
| **DOUBLE DOLPHINS (FENTON)** | | | | | | | | |
| Bowl, Ftd, 9"-11" | | | | | | | 115 | |
| Cake Plate, Center Handle | | | | | | | 85 | |
| Candlesticks, pair | | | | | | | 90 | |
| Compote | | | | | | | 70 | |
| Fan Vapse | | | | | | | 70 | |
| Covered Candy Dish, Stemmed | | | | | | | 80 | |
| Bowl, 8"-10", Flat | | | | | | | 65 | |

Double Dutch (Imperial)

Double Stem Rose (Dugan)

Drapery (Northwood)

Dugan Stipple Rays

| | M | A | G | B | PO | AO | Pas | R |
|---|---|---|---|---|---|---|---|---|
| **DOUBLE DUTCH (IMPERIAL)** | | | | | | | | |
| Bowl, 9", Ftd. | 50 | 75 | 75 | | | | 85SM | |
| **DOUBLE LOOP (NORTHWOOD)** | | | | | | | | |
| Creamer | 155 | 160 | 170 | 425 | | 275 | | |
| Sugar | 155 | 160 | 170 | 190 | | 290 | | |
| **DOUBLE SCROLL (IMPERIAL)** | | | | | | | | |
| Bowl | 45 | 55 | 55 | | | | 65 | 210 |
| Candlesticks, pair | 75 | 80 | 80 | | | | 80 | 260 |
| Punch Cup | 25 | | | | | | | |
| **DOUBLE STAR (CAMBRIDGE)** | | | | | | | | |
| Pitcher, Scarce | 750 | 650 | 500 | | | | | |
| Tumbler, Scarce | 280 | 240 | 60 | | | | | |
| Spittoon Whimsey, Rare | | | 3,000 | | | | | |
| Bowl, 9", Rare | | | 400 | | | | | |
| **DOUBLE STEM ROSE (DUGAN)** | | | | | | | | |
| Bowl, Dome Base, 8½" | 100 | 90 | 115 | 100 | 190 | | 600CeB | |
| Plate, Ftd. | | | | | | | 165W | |
| **DOUGHNUT BRIDLE ROSETTE** | | | | | | | | |
| One Size | | 95 | | | | | | |
| **DRAGON AND LOTUS (FENTON)** | | | | | | | | |
| Bowl, Flat, 9" | 185 | 150 | 195 | 115 | 450 | 2,400 | 875AM | 4,800 |
| Bowl, Ftd, 9" | 180 | 195 | 175 | 190 | 200 | | 85LV | 4,500 |
| Plate, 9½", Rare | 2,800 | 1,350 | | 1,600 | 1,100 | | 1200 | 0,000 |
| **DRAGON AND STRAWBERRY (FENTON)** | | | | | | | | |
| Bowl, Flat, 9", Scarce | 450 | 1,500 | 900 | 950 | | 2,300 | | |
| Bowl, Ftd, 9", Scarce | 400 | | 1,100 | 795 | | | | |
| Plate (Absentee Dragon), Rare | 3,700 | | | | | | | |
| **DRAGON'S TONGUE (FENTON)** | | | | | | | | |
| Bowl, 11", Scarce | 950 | | | | | | | |
| Shade | 40 | | | | 115 | | | |
| **DRAGON VASE** | | | | | | | | |
| Square Vase | | 250 | | | | | | |
| **DRAGONFLY** | | | | | | | | |
| Shade | | | | | | | 65 | |
| **DRAGONFLY LAMP** | | | | | | | | |
| Oil Lamp, Rare | | | | | | | 1,800 | |
| **DRAPE AND TASSEL** | | | | | | | | |
| Shade | 45 | | | | | | | |
| **DRAPERY (NORTHWOOD)** | | | | | | | | |
| Vase | 45 | 235 | 110 | 225EB | | 250 | 250IG | |
| Rose Bowl | 240 | 135 | 170 | 120 | | 700 | 600W | |
| Candy Dish | 65 | 140 | 200 | 110 | | 550 | 200AQ | |
| **DRAPERY VT. (FENTON)** | | | | | | | | |
| Pitcher, Rare | 510 | | | | | | | |
| Tumbler, Scarce | 190 | | | | | | | |
| **DREIBUS PARFAIT SWEETS (NORTHWOOD)** | | | | | | | | |
| Plate, Handgrip, 6" | | 550 | | | | | | |
| **DUCKIE** | | | | | | | | |
| Powder Jar w/lid | 40 | | | | | | | |
| **DUGAN FAN (DUGAN)** | | | | | | | | |
| Sauce, 5" | 40 | 55 | | | 145 | | | |
| Gravy Boat, Ftd | 65 | 175 | | | 210 | | 100 | |
| **DUGAN'S MANY RIBS** | | | | | | | | |
| Vase | 60 | 80 | | 75 | 110 | | | |
| Hat Shape | 50 | 70 | | 60 | 100 | | | |
| **DUGAN STIPPLE RAYS** | | | | | | | | |
| Bowl | 35 | 45 | 50 | | | | | |
| Hat | 40 | 47 | 52 | | | | | |
| **DUNCAN (NATIONAL GLASS)** | | | | | | | | |
| Cruet | 600 | | | | | | | |
| **DURAND (FENTON)** | | | | | | | | |
| Bowl - Grape and Cable | | | | | 1,575 | | | |
| **DUTCH MILL** | | | | | | | | |
| Plate, 8" | 50 | | | | | | | |
| Ashtray | 65 | | | | | | | |
| **DUTCH PLATE** | | | | | | | | |
| One Size, 8" | 55 | | | | | | | |
| **DUTCH TWINS** | | | | | | | | |
| Ashtray | 50 | | | | | | | |
| **EAGLE FURNITURE (NORTHWOOD)** | | | | | | | | |
| Plate | | 800 | | | | | | |
| **E.A. HUDSON FURNITURE (NORTHWOOD)** | | | | | | | | |
| Plate | | 1,000 | | | | | | |
| **EAT PARADISE SODA (NORTHWOOD)** | | | 595 | | | | | |
| **EBON** | | | | | | | | |
| Vase | | 110BA | | | | | | |
| **EGG AND DART** | | | | | | | | |
| Candlestick, pr. | 90 | | | | | | | |
| **ELEGANCE** | | | | | | | | |
| Bowl, 8¼", Rare | 2,800 | | | | | | 3,200IB | |

Enameled Panel

Encore

Estate (Westmoreland)

Etched Vine

| | M | A | G | B | PO | AO | Pas | R |
|---|---|---|---|---|---|---|---|---|
| Plate, Rare | | | | | | | 3,500IB | |
| **ELEPHANT** | | | | | | | | |
| Paperweight | 1,250 | | | | | | | |
| Vase, 3 sizes | 750+* | | | | | | | |
| **ELKS (DUGAN)** | | | | | | | | |
| Nappy, Very Rare | | 4,200 | | | | | | |
| **ELKS (FENTON)** | | | | | | | | |
| Detroit Bowl, Scarce | 1,300 | 1,000 | 750 | 700 | | | | |
| Parkersburg Plate, Rare | | | 1,450 | 1,000 | | | | |
| Atlantic City Plate, Rare | | | 1,800 | 1,300 | | | | |
| Atlantic City Bowl | | | | 1,325 | | | | |
| 1911 Atlantic City Bell, Rare | | | | 1,800 | | | | |
| 1917 Portland Bell, Rare | | | | 15,000* | | | | |
| 1914 Parkersburg Bell, Rare | | | | 2,300 | | | | |
| **ELKS (MILLERSBURG)** | | | | | | | | |
| Bowl, Rare | | 1,750 | | | | | | |
| Paperweight, Rare | | 1,500 | 1,700 | | | | | |
| **EMBROIDERED MUMS (NORTHWOOD)** | | | | | | | | |
| Bowl, 9" | 475 | 500 | 585 | 525 | | 3,900 | 1,950IG | |
| Stemmed Bon-bon | | | | | | | 1,250W | |
| Plate | 600 | 550 | 695 | 650 | | | 2,500IG | |
| **EMU (CRYSTAL)** | | | | | | | | |
| Bowl, 5", Rare | 175 | | | | | | | |
| Bowl, 10", Rare | 1,000 | | | | | | 1550AM | |
| **ENAMELED GRAPE (NORTHWOOD)** | | | | | | | | |
| Pitcher | | | | 400 | | | | |
| Tumbler | | | | 45 | | | | |
| **ENAMELED PANEL** | | | | | | | | |
| Goblet | 190 | | | | | | | |
| **ENAMELED PRISM BAND** | | | | | | | | |
| **ENAMELED SWALLOW** | | | | | | | | |
| Pitcher | 150 | | | | | | | |
| Tumbler | 75 | | | | | | | |
| **ENCORE** | | | | | | | | |
| Bottle (late) | 40 | | | | | | | |
| **ENGLISH BUTTON BAND (ENGLISH)** | | | | | | | | |
| Creamer | 45 | | | | | | | |
| Sugar | 45 | | | | | | | |
| **ENGLISH HOB AND BUTTON (ENGLISH)** | | | | | | | | |
| Bowl, 7"-10" | 60 | 80 | 95 | 70 | | | | |
| Epergne (metal base), Rare | 125 | | | 145 | | | | |
| **ENGLISH HOBSTAR** | | | | | | | | |
| Oval Bowl, 6" in holder | 150* | | | | | | | |
| **ENGRAVED DAISY & SPEARS** | | | | | | | | |
| Goblet, 4½" | 75 | | | | | | | |
| **ENGRAVED FLORAL (FENTON)** | | | | | | | | |
| Tumbler | | | 95 | | | | | |
| **ENGRAVED GRAPES (FENTON)** | | | | | | | | |
| Vase, 8" | 65 | | | | | | 75 | |
| Candy Jar w/lid | 85 | | | | | | | |
| Juice Glass | 30 | | | | | | | |
| Pitcher, Squat | 120 | | | | | | | |
| Tumbler | 30 | | | | | | | |
| Pitcher, Tall | 145 | | | | | | | |
| Tumble-Up | 150 | | | | | | | |
| **ENGRAVED ZINNIA** | | | | | | | | |
| **ESTATE (WESTMORELAND)** | | | | | | | | |
| Mug, Rare | 75 | | | | | | | |
| Perfume | | | | | | | 1,100SM | |
| Creamer or Sugar | 55 | | | | 90 | 290BO | 110AQ | |
| Bud Vase, 6" | 50 | | | | | | 65 | |
| **ESTATE, STIPPLED (WESTMORELAND)** | | | | | | | | |
| Vase, 3" | | | | | 190 | | 200 | |
| **ETCHED DECO** | | | | | | | | |
| Plate, ftd. 8" | 60 | | | | | | | |
| **ETCHED VINE** | | | | | | | | |
| Tumbler | 40 | | | | | | | |
| **EVELYN (FOSTORIA)** | | | | | | | | |
| Bowl (1940's) | | 1,000* | | | | | | |
| **EXCHANGE BANK (NORTHWOOD)** | | | | | | | | |
| Plate, 6" | | 500 | | | | | | |
| **EYE CUP** | | | | | | | | |
| One Size | 90 | | | | | | | |
| **FACETED OVALS** | | | | | | | | |
| Hatpin | | 155 | | | | | | |
| **FACETED SPEARHEAD** | | | | | | | | |
| Hatpin | | 150 | | | | | | |
| **FACETED DOME** | | | | | | | | |
| Hatpin | | 195 | | | | | | |

Fan Star (Millersburg)

Feather and Heart (Millersburg)

Feathers (Northwood)

Feather Stitch (Fenton)

| | M | A | G | B | PO | AO | Pas | Red |
|---|---|---|---|---|---|---|---|---|
| **FAMOUS** | | | | | | | | |
| Puff box | 75 | | | | | | | |
| **FANCIFUL (DUGAN)** | | | | | | | | |
| Bowl, 8½" | 90 | 350 | | 295 | 250 | | 175W | |
| Plate, 9" | 275 | 550 | | 850 | 650 | | 250W | |
| **FANCY (NORTHWOOD)** | | | | | | | | |
| (Interior on some "Fine Cut and Roses" Rose Bowls) | | | | | | | | |
| **FANCY CUT (ENGLISH)** | | | | | | | | |
| Miniature Pitcher, Rare | 225 | | | | | | | |
| Miniature Tumbler | 60 | | | | | | | |
| **FANCY FLOWERS (IMPERIAL)** | | | | | | | | |
| Compote | 120 | | 175 | | | | | |
| **FANS (ENGLISH)** | | | | | | | | |
| Pitcher | 185 | | | | | | | |
| Cracker Jar (metal lid) | 150 | | | | | | | |
| Tumbler | 150 | | | | | | | |
| **FAN STAR (MILLERSBURG)** | | | | | | | | |
| Exterior pattern only. | | | | | | | | |
| **FAN-TAIL (FENTON)** | | | | | | | | |
| Bowl, Ftd, 5" | 80 | | | 220 | | | 145 | |
| Bowl, Ftd, 9" | 110 | | | 275 | | | 180 | |
| Compote | 90 | | | 195 | | | | |
| Plate, Ftd, Rare | 5,700 | | | 1,600 | | | | |
| **FARMYARD (DUGAN)** | | | | | | | | |
| Bowl, 10", Rare | | 5,500 | 8,500 | | 10,000 | | | |
| Plate, 10½", Very Rare | | 18,000 | | | | | | |
| **FASHION (IMPERIAL)** | | | | | | | | |
| Creamer or Sugar | 42 | 125 | | | | | 50 | |
| Fruit Bowl and Base | 70 | | | | | | 75 | |
| Punch Bowl and Base | 85 | 195 | | | | | 90 | |
| Punch Cup | 24 | 40 | | | | | 30 | |
| Pitcher | 250 | 1,000 | | | | | 600SM | |
| Tumbler | 20 | 225 | | | | | 100SM | |
| Bowl, 9" | 40 | | 90 | | | | 55SM | |
| Bride's Basket | 125 | | | | | | 140 | |
| Butter | 75 | 200 | | | | | | |
| Rose Bowl, Rare | 450 | 1,300 | 950 | | | | | |
| **FEATHER AND HEART (MILLERSBURG)** | | | | | | | | |
| Pitcher, Scarce | 600 | 750 | 850 | | | | 14,500V | |
| Tumbler, Scarce | 95 | 150 | 200 | | | | | |
| Spitton Whimsey | 7,000 | | | | | | | |
| **FEATHERED ARROW (ENGLISH)** | | | | | | | | |
| Bowl, 8½" | 50 | | | | | | | |
| **FEATHERED FLOWERS** | | | | | | | | |
| (Exterior Pattern) | | | | | | | | |
| **FEATHERED SERPENT (FENTON)** | | | | | | | | |
| Bowl, 5" | 30 | 40 | 45 | 42 | | | | |
| Bowl, 10" | 90 | 75 | 90 | 65 | | | | |
| Spittoon Whimsey, Rare | | 4,000 | | | | | | |
| **FEATHERS (NORTHWOOD)** | | | | | | | | |
| Vase, 7"-12" | 60 | 85 | 95 | 105 | | | | |
| **FEATHER STITCH (FENTON)** | | | | | | | | |
| Bowl, 8½"-10" | 90 | 80 | 90 | 80 | | | | |
| **FEATHER SWIRL (U.S. GLASS)** | | | | | | | | |
| Vase | 65 | | | | | | | |
| Butter | 165 | | | | | | | |
| **FELDMAN BROTHERS (NORTHWOOD)** | | | | | | | | |
| Bowl | | 550 | | | | | | |
| **FENTONIA** | | | | | | | | |
| Bowl, Ftd, 9½" | 60 | 85 | 75 | 70 | | | | |
| Bowl, Ftd, 5" | 30 | 50 | 40 | 40 | | | | |
| Fruitbowl, 10" | 85 | | | 90 | | | | |
| Butter | 115 | | | 185 | | | | |
| Creamer, Sugar or Spooner | 75 | | | 85 | | | | |
| Pitcher | 390 | | | 600 | | | | |
| Tumbler | 50 | | | 75 | | | | |
| **FENTONIA FRUIT (FENTON)** | | | | | | | | |
| Bowl, Ftd, 6" | 45 | | | 55 | | | | |
| Bowl, Ftd, 10" | 120 | | | 160 | | | | |
| Pitcher, Rare | 575 | | | 700 | | | | |
| Vase Whimsey, Rare | 140 | | | 160 | | | | |
| Tumbler, Rare | 150 | | | 200 | | | | |
| **FENTON'S ARCHED FLUTE (FENTON)** | | | | | | | | |
| Toothpick Holder | 85 | | | 100 | | | 140 | |
| **FENTON'S BASKET (FENTON)** | | | | | | | | |
| Two Row or Three Row (Open Edge) | 45 | | 225+ | 150 | | | 550SM | 600 |
| Advertising | 85 | | | | | | | |
| Plate, Rare | | | | | | | 5,000*SM | |

**307**

| | M | A | G | B | PO | AO | Pas | Red |
|---|---|---|---|---|---|---|---|---|
| **FENTON SMOOTH RAYS** | | | | | | | | |
| Bowl 6"–7" .................. | 35 | 40 | 65 | 45 | | | | |
| **FERN (FENTON)** | | | | | | | | |
| Bowl, 7"-9", Rare ................. | | | | 900* | | | | |
| **FERN (NORTHWOOD)** | | | | | | | | |
| Bowl, 6½"-9" ................ | 50 | 65 | 70 | | | | | |
| Compote...................... | 55 | 70 | 85 | 100 | | | 110 | |
| Hat, Rare ...................... | 90 | 120 | 135 | | | | 160 | |
| **FERN BRAND CHOCOLATES (NORTHWOOD)** | | | | | | | | |
| Plate................................. | | 800 | | | | | | |
| **FERN PANELS (FENTON)** | | | | | | | | |
| Hat............................ | 45 | | 60 | 50 | | | 495 | |
| **FIELD FLOWER (IMPERIAL)** | | | | | | | | |
| Pitcher, Scarce.................. | 165 | 350 | 365 | 400 | | | 360AM | |
| Tumbler, Scarce ................ | 35 | 60 | 70 | 150 | | | 90AM | 1,500 |
| Milk Pitcher, Rare .............. | 180 | 200 | 220 | | | | 225AM | |
| **FIELD THISTLE (U.S. GLASS)** | | | | | | | | |
| Plate, 6", Rare.................... | 180 | | | | | | | |
| Plate, 9" Rare..................... | 350 | | | | | | | |
| Butter, Rare...................... | 125 | | | | | | | |
| Sugar, Creamer or Spooner, Rare ............... | 80 | | | | | | | |
| Compote, Large .................. | 190 | | | | | | | |
| Pitcher, Scarce.................. | 160 | | | | | | | |
| Tumbler, Scarce ................ | 45 | | | | | | | |
| Breakfast Set, 2 Pc, Rare ..... | | | | | | | 350IB | |
| Bowl, 6"-10" .................... | 45 | | | | | | 290LG | |
| Vase .................................. | 565 | | | | | | | |
| **FILE (IMPERIAL AND ENGLISH)** | | | | | | | | |
| Pitcher, Rare.................... | 265 | 445 | | | | | | |
| Tumbler, Scarce ................ | 150 | | | | | | | |
| Bowl, 5"........................... | 30 | 40 | | | | | | |
| Bowl, 7"-10" .................... | 45+ | 50 | | | | | 60 | |
| Compote........................... | 40 | 50 | | | | | 60 | |
| Vase ................................ | 75 | | | | | | | |
| Butter ............................. | 190 | | | | | | | |
| Creamer or Spooner ........... | 100 | | | | | | | |
| Sugar ............................. | 120 | | | | | | | |
| **FILE AND FAN** | | | | | | | | |
| Bowl, Ftd, 6"...................... | 40 | | | | 160 | | | |
| Compote............................ | | | | | | 200BO | 175MMG | |
| **FILIGREE (DUGAN)** | | | | | | | | |
| Vase, rare .......................... | | 1,350* | | | | | | |
| **FINE BLOCK (IMPERIAL)** | | | | | | | | |
| Shade.............................. | | | 45 | | | | | |
| **FINE CUT AND ROSES (NORTHWOOD)** | | | | | | | | |
| Rose Bowl, Ftd ................... | 100 | 200 | 200 | 220 | | 1,500 | 1,000IG | |
| Candy Dish, Ftd ................. | 85 | 90 | 170 | 185 | | 450 | 260W | |
| (Add 25% for Fancy Interior) | | | | | | | | |
| **FINE CUT AND STAR** | | | | | | | | |
| Banana Boat, 5" ................. | 150 | | | | | | | |
| **FINE CUT FLOWERS AND VT. (FENTON)** | | | | | | | | |
| Compote............................ | 50 | | 75 | | | | | |
| Goblet ............................... | 50 | | 75 | | | | | |
| **FINE CUT HEART (MILLERSBURG)** | | | | | | | | |
| (Primrose Bowl Exterior Pattern) | | | | | | | | |
| **FINE CUT OVALS (MILLERSBURG)** | | | | | | | | |
| (Whirling Leaves Exterior Pattern) | | | | | | | | |
| **FINE CUT RINGS (ENGLISH)** | | | | | | | | |
| Oval Bowl........................... | 140 | | | | | | | |
| Vase ................................ | 150 | | | | | | | |
| Celery................................ | 160 | | | | | | | |
| Butter ............................... | 170 | | | | | | | |
| Creamer ............................ | 145 | | | | | | | |
| Stemmed Sugar.................. | 145 | | | | | | | |
| Stemmed Cake Stand .......... | 175 | | | | | | | |
| Round Bowl........................ | 135 | | | | | | | |
| Jam Jar w/lid ..................... | 165 | | | | | | | |
| **FINE CUT RINGS VT (ENGLISH)** | | | | | | | | |
| Celery Vase........................ | 150 | | | | | | | |
| Cakestand, ftd.................... | 195 | | | | | | | |
| **FINE PRISMS AND DIAMONDS (ENGLISH)** | | | | | | | | |
| Vase, 7"-14"........................ | | | | | | | 90AM | |
| **FINE RIB (NORTHWOOD, FENTON AND DUGAN)** | | | | | | | | |
| Bowl, 9"-10" ........................ | 50 | 60 | 75 | | | | | |
| Bowl, 5".............................. | 30 | 35 | 40 | | | | | |
| Plate, 9"............................. | 80 | 90 | 135 | | | | | |
| Vase, 7"-15", 2 Types ........... | 40 | 85 | 190 | 80 | | 390 | 165AM | 500 |
| Compote............................. | | | | | 165 | | | |
| **FIREFLY (MOTH)** | | | | | | | | |
| Candlesticks, pr................. | 90 | | | | | | | |

Fern (Northwood)

Filigree (Dugan)

Fine Block (Imperial)

Fine Cut and Roses

Flora (English)

Floral and Grape VT. (Fenton)

Floral and Optic

Florentine (Imperial)

| | M | A | G | B | PO | AO | Pas | Red |
|---|---|---|---|---|---|---|---|---|
| **FIRESTONE** | | | | | | | | |
| Ashtray, advertising, various | | | | 375 | | | | |
| **FISHERMAN'S MUG (DUGAN)** | | | | | | | | |
| One Size | 240 | 150 | | 550 | 1,450 | | 255LV | |
| **FISH NET (DUGAN)** | | | | | | | | |
| Epergne | | 450 | 240 | | 360 | | | |
| **FISHSCALES AND BEADS (DUGAN)** | | | | | | | | |
| Bowl, 6"-8" | 35 | 45 | | | 150 | | 80W | |
| Bride's Basket, Complete | | | | | 140 | | | |
| Plate, 7" | 50 | 200 | | | 185 | | 140W | |
| **FISH VASE (CZECH)** | | | | | | | | |
| One shape, Marked "Jain" | 450 | 400 | 500 | 450 | | | | |
| **FIVE HEARTS (DUGAN)** | | | | | | | | |
| Bowl, Dome Base, 8¾" | 95 | 110 | | | 165 | | | |
| **FIVE LILY EPERGNE** | | | | | | | | |
| Complete, Metal Fittings | 175 | 250 | | | | | | |
| **FIVE PANEL** | | | | | | | | |
| Candy Jar, Stemmed | 70 | | | | | | | |
| **FLANNEL FLOWER (CRYSTAL)** | | | | | | | | |
| Compote, Large | 120 | 155 | | | | | | |
| Cake Stand | 140 | 195 | | | | | | |
| **FLARED PANEL** | | | | | | | | |
| Shade | | | | | 75MO | | | |
| **FLARED WIDE PANEL** | | | | | | | | |
| Atomizer, 3½" | 90 | | | | | | | |
| **FLEUR-DE-LIS (CZECH)** | | | | | | | | |
| Vase | 650 | | | | | | | |
| Bowl, 8", Rare | 350* | | | | | | | |
| **FLEUR-DE-LIS (MILLERSBURG)** | | | | | | | | |
| Bowl, Flat, 8½" | 240 | 500 | 300 | | | | 240CM | |
| Bowl, Ftd, 8½" | 260 | 370 | 400 | | | | | |
| Compote, Very Rare | | | 5,000* | | | | | |
| Rose Bowl, Either Base, Rare | | 2,750 | | | | | | |
| **FLICKERING FLAMES** | | | | | | | | |
| Shade | | | | | | | 50 | |
| **FLORA (ENGLISH)** | | | | | | | | |
| Float Bowl | | | | 175 | | | | |
| Vase | 95 | | | 120 | | | | |
| **FLORABELLE** | | | | | | | | |
| Pitcher | | | | | | | 600IG | |
| Tumbler | | | | | | | 200IG | |
| **FLORAL** | | | | | | | | |
| Hatpin | | | | | | | 75AM | |
| **FLORAL FAN** | | | | | | | | |
| Etched Vase | 57 | | | | | | | |
| **FLORAL AND GRAPE (DUGAN)** | | | | | | | | |
| Pitcher | 145 | 200 | | 270 | | | 450W | |
| Tumbler | 20 | 30 | | 35 | | | 50W | |
| Hat, Whimsey | 40 | | | | | | | |
| **FLORAL AND GRAPE VT. (FENTON)** | | | | | | | | |
| Pitcher, 2 Variations | 195 | 285 | 290 | 270 | | | | |
| Tumbler | 30 | 35 | 40 | 30 | | | | |
| **FLORAL AND OPTIC (IMPERIAL)** | | | | | | | | |
| Bowl, Ftd, 8"-10" | 35 | | | | 150 | | 140SM | 400 |
| Bowl, Flat, 8"-10" | 30 | | | | | | 120SM | |
| Cake Plate, Ftd | | | | | 180 | | 250SM | 650 |
| Rose Bowl, Ftd | | | | | 190 | | 185AQ | |
| **FLORAL AND SCROLL** | | | | | | | | |
| Shade, Various Shapes | 45 | | | | | | | |
| **FLORAL AND WHEAT (DUGAN)** | | | | | | | | |
| Compote | 40 | 45 | | 45 | 150 | | | |
| Bon-bon, Stemmed | 40 | 45 | | 45 | 155 | | | |
| **FLORAL OVAL (HIG-BEE)** | | | | | | | | |
| Bowl, 8" | 50 | | | | | | | |
| Plate, 7", Rare | 90 | | | | | | | |
| Creamer | 60 | | | | | | | |
| **FLORAL SUNBURST** | | | | | | | | |
| Vase | 175 | | | | | | | |
| **FLORENTINE (FENTON AND NORTHWOOD)** | | | | | | | | |
| Candlesticks, pair | 120 | | 160RG | 150CeB | | | 140IG | 1,050 |
| **FLORENTINE (IMPERIAL)** | | | | | | | | |
| Hat Vase | | | | | | | 95 | |
| **FLOWER AND BEADS** | | | | | | | | |
| Plate, 6 Sided, 7½" | 95 | 115 | | | | | | |
| Plate, Round, 8½" | 95 | | | | | | | |
| **FLOWER BASKET** | | | | | | | | |
| One Size | 50 | | | | | | | |
| **FLOWER BLOCK** | | | | | | | | |
| Various sizes | 20–50 | | | | | | | |
| **FLOWERING DILL (FENTON)** | | | | | | | | |
| Hat | 40 | | 45 | 40 | | | 75 | 550 |

Flower Pot (Fenton)

Flowers and Frames (Dugan)

Footed Prism Panels

Formal (Dugan)

| | M | A | G | B | PO | AO | Pas | Red |
|---|---|---|---|---|---|---|---|---|
| **FLOWERING VINE (MILLERSBURG)** | | | | | | | | |
| Compote, Tall, Very Rare ..... | | 8,500 | 9,000 | | | | | |
| **FLOWER POT (FENTON)** | | | | | | | | |
| One Size, Complete............. | 60 | | | | | | | |
| **FLOWERS AND FRAMES (DUGAN)** | | | | | | | | |
| Bowl, 8"-10" ...................... | 70 | 300 | 285 | | 300 | | 95 | |
| **FLOWERS AND SPADES (DUGAN)** | | | | | | | | |
| Bowl, 10".......................... | 50 | 90 | 85 | | 210 | | | |
| Bowl, 5"............................ | 25 | 40 | 37 | | 80 | | | |
| **FLUTE (BRITISH)** | | | | | | | | |
| Sherbet, Marked "British".... | 50 | | | | | | | |
| **FLUTE (MILLERSBURG)** | | | | | | | | |
| Vase, Rare ........................ | 300 | 400 | 425 | 2,750 | | | | |
| Bowl, 4" (Variant)................ | | 45 | | | | | | |
| Compote, 6" (Marked "Krystol," Very Rare)............. | 450 | 500 | | | | | | |
| Punch Bowl and Base, Rare. | 265 | 320 | | | | | | |
| Punch Cup ........................ | 27 | 30 | | | | | | |
| Bowl, 10".......................... | 65 | 90 | | | | | | |
| Bowl, 5"............................ | 25 | 40 | | | | | | |
| **FLUTE (NORTHWOOD)** | | | | | | | | |
| Creamer or Sugar ............... | 75 | 85 | 95 | | | | | |
| Salt Dip, Ftd...................... | 32 | | | | | | 75V | |
| Sherbet ........................... | 35 | 50 | 45 | | | | 55CeB | |
| Pitcher, Rare...................... | 395 | | 600 | | | | | |
| Tumbler, 3 Varieties............. | 50 | | | | | | | |
| Ringtree, Rare ................... | 175 | | | | | | | |
| Bowl, 10".......................... | 45 | 55 | | | | | | |
| Bowl, 5"............................ | 25 | 30 | | | | | | |
| Butter .............................. | 135 | 170 | 185 | | | | | |
| **FLUTE #3 (IMPERIAL)** | | | | | | | | |
| Covered Butter ................... | 180 | 240 | 210 | | | | | |
| Sugar, Creamer or Spooner.. | 90 | 105 | 95 | | | | | |
| Celery, Rare....................... | | 390 | | | | | | |
| Punch Bowl and Base.......... | 295 | 500 | 470 | | | | | |
| Punch Cup ........................ | 25 | 40 | 38 | | | | | |
| Pitcher............................. | 300 | 595 | 510 | 450 | | | | |
| Tumbler ........................... | 40 | 195 | 185 | 100 | | | 300AQ | 300 |
| Handled Toothpick Holder ... | 85 | | | | | | | |
| Toothpick Holder, Regular ... | 270 | 165 | 175 | 595 | | | 300AQ | |
| Bowl, 10".......................... | | 225 | | | | | | |
| Bowl, 5"............................ | 30 | 70 | | | | | | |
| Custard Bowl, 11" .............. | | 300 | 300 | | | | | |
| Cruet............................... | 90 | | | | | | | |
| **FLUTE AND CANE (IMPERIAL)** | | | | | | | | |
| Pitcher, Stemmed, Rare ....... | 400 | | | | | | | |
| Wine................................ | 50 | | | | | | | |
| Champagne, Rare................ | 135 | | | | | | | |
| Milk Pitcher....................... | 115 | | | | | | | |
| Punch Cup ........................ | 25 | | | | | | | |
| Tumbler, Rare .................... | 450 | | | | | | | |
| **FLUTE AND HONEYCOMB (MILLERSBURG)** | | | | | | | | |
| Bowl, 5" rare ..................... | | 75 | | | | | | |
| **FLUTED SCROLLS (DUGAN)** | | | | | | | | |
| Rose Bowl, Ftd, Very Rare.... | | 975 | | | | | | |
| **FLYING BAT** | | | | | | | | |
| Hatpin, Scarce................... | 195 | 200 | 200 | | | | 350 | |
| **FOLDING FAN (DUGAN)** | | | | | | | | |
| Compote............................ | | 75 | | 85 | 135 | 295 | | |
| **FOOTED DRAPE (WESTMORELAND)** | | | | | | | | |
| Vase ................................ | 50 | | | | | | 55W | |
| **FOOTED PRISM PANELS (ENGLISH)** | | | | | | | | |
| Vase ................................ | 85 | | 120 | 100 | | | | |
| **FOOTED RIB (NORTHWOOD)** | | | | | | | | |
| Vase ................................ | 50 | 80 | 90 | 75 | | 190 | 110 | |
| Vase, Advertising ................ | | | | | | 250 | 150 | |
| **FOOTED SHELL (WESTMORELAND)** | | | | | | | | |
| Large, 5"............................ | 40 | 50 | 55 | 55 | | | 75AM | |
| Small, 3" ........................... | 45 | 55 | 60 | 60 | 100MO | | 70AM | |
| **FORGET-ME-NOT (FENTON)** | | | | | | | | |
| Pitcher............................. | 165 | 285 | 300 | 320 | | | 350W | |
| Tumbler ........................... | 30 | 40 | 50 | 45 | | | 55W | |
| **FORKS (CAMBRIDGE)** | | | | | | | | |
| Cracker Jar, Rare ............... | | | 500 | | | | | |
| **FORMAL (DUGAN)** | | | | | | | | |
| Hatpin Holder, Rare............ | 800 | 950 | | | | | | |
| Vase, Jack-In-Pulpit, Rare ... | 700 | 600 | | | | | 850 | |
| **FOSTORIA #600 (FOSTORIA)** | | | | | | | | |
| Napkin Ring ...................... | 75 | | | | | | | |

| | M | A | G | B | PO | AO | Pas | Red |
|---|---|---|---|---|---|---|---|---|
| **FOSTORIA #1231 (FOSTORIA)** | | | | | | | | |
| Rose Bowl........................ | | | | | | | 145 | |
| **FOSTORIAL #1299 (FOSTORIA)** | | | | | | | | |
| Tumbler ........................... | 150* | | | | | | | |
| **FOUNTAIN (ENGLISH)** | | | | | | | | |
| Epergne, Silver Fittings, Various............................ | 250 | | | | | | | |
| Lamp, Complete, Scarce ...... | 290 | | | | | | | |
| **FOUR FLOWERS** | | | | | | | | |
| Plate, 6½" ........................ | | 210 | 200 | | 150 | | | |
| Plate, 9"-10½" .................... | | 700 | 350 | | 650 | | | |
| Rose Bowl, Rare ................. | | 850* | | | | | | |
| Bowl, 6¼" ........................ | | 45 | 50 | 70 | 190 | | | |
| Bowl, 10" ........................ | | 180 | 185 | 190 | 220 | | | |
| **FOUR FLOWERS VT.** | | | | | | | | |
| Bowl, 9"-11" ..................... | 70 | 75 | 70 | | 210 | | 170LV | |
| Bowl, Ftd, 8½" ................... | | 80 | 90 | | | | | |
| Plate, 10½", Rare ............... | | 450 | 470 | | | | 400TL | |
| Bowl on Metal Base, Rare .... | 350LV | | | | 300 | | 350TL | |
| **FOUR PILLARS (NORTHWOOD AND DUGAN)** | | | | | | | | |
| Vase ............................... | 50 | 60 | 75 | 60 | 110 | 175 | 400SA | |
| **474 (IMPERIAL)** | | | | | | | | |
| Bowl, 8"-9" ...................... | 60 | | 85 | | | | | |
| Punch Bowl and Base.......... | 220 | 700 | 600 | | | | | |
| Cup ................................. | 30 | 40 | 35 | | | | | |
| Covered Butter ................... | 100 | 150 | 125 | | | | | |
| Creamer, Sugar or Spooner.. | 65 | 90 | 85 | | | | | |
| Milk Pitcher, Scarce............ | 225 | | 275 | | | | 600LV | |
| Pitcher, 2 Sizes, Scarce........ | 210 | 510 | 480 | | | | 610PK | |
| Tumbler, Scarce ................. | 35 | 80 | 65 | | | | 120PK | |
| Goblet ............................. | 50 | 90 | 65 | | | | | |
| Wine, Rare........................ | 105 | | | | | | | |
| Cordial, Rare ..................... | 90 | 210 | | | | | | |
| Vase, 7", Rare .................... | | | | | | | | 3,200 |
| Vase, 14", Rare .................. | 950 | | 1,100 | | | | | |
| **474 VARIENT (SWEDEN)** | | | | | | | | |
| Compote, 7"...................... | | | 90 | | | | | |
| **49'ER** | | | | | | | | |
| Atomizer ........................... | 90 | | | | | | | |
| Tumbler ........................... | 75 | | | | | | | |
| Wine................................ | 80 | | | | | | | |
| Decanter ........................... | 125 | | | | | | | |
| Perfume, 3 sizes ................. | 80+ | | | | | | | |
| Pin Box............................ | 60 | | | | | | | |
| Pin Tray, 2 sizes ................. | 45 | | | | | | | |
| Pitcher, Squat..................... | 210 | | | | | | | |
| Powder Box ....................... | 70 | | | | | | | |
| Ring Tray .......................... | 70 | | | | | | | |
| **FRENCH GRAPE** | | | | | | | | |
| Bowl, 4"............................ | 175 | | | | | | | |
| **FRENCH KNOTS (FENTON)** | | | | | | | | |
| Hat.................................. | 40 | 50 | 50 | 45 | | | | |
| **FRINGED BEADS** | | | | | | | | |
| Hatpin.............................. | | 275 | | | | | | |
| **FROLICKING BEARS (U.S. GLASS)** | | | | | | | | |
| Pitcher, Rare...................... | | | 10,000 | | | | | |
| Tumbler, Rare .................... | | | 8,000 | | | | | |
| **FROSTED BLOCK (IMPERIAL)** | | | | | | | | |
| Bowl, 6½"-7½".................... | 30 | | | | | | 35CM | |
| Bowl, 9"............................ | 35 | | | | | | 40CM | |
| Celery Tray........................ | 40 | | | | | | | |
| Covered Butter ................... | 70 | | | | | | | |
| Creamer or Sugar ............... | 50 | | | | | | | |
| Rose Bowl......................... | 50 | | | | | | 75CM | |
| Compote............................ | 85 | | | | | | 120CM | |
| Milk Pitcher, Rare............... | 90 | | | | | | | |
| Pickle Dish, Handled, Rare .. | 60 | | | | | | 65CM | |
| Bowl, Square, Rare.............. | 50 | | | | | | 60CM | |
| Plate, 7½" .......................... | 70 | | | | | | 65CM | |
| Plate, 9".......................... | | | | | | | 170CM | |
| Vase, 6" ............................ | | | | | | | 100SM | |
| 25% More if Marked "Made in USA" | | | | | | | | |
| **FROSTED BUTTONS (FENTON)** | | | | | | | | |
| Bowl, Ftd, 10"..................... | | | | | | | 175 | |
| **FROSTED OXFORD** | | | | | | | | |
| Bobeche, each .................... | 65 | | | | | | | |
| **FROSTED RIBBON** | | | | | | | | |
| Pitcher............................. | 85 | | | | | | | |
| Tumbler ........................... | 30 | | | | | | | |
| **FROSTY** | | | | | | | | |
| Bottle .............................. | 30 | | | | | | | |
| **FRUIT AND BERRIES (ENGLISH)** | | | | | | | | |
| Bean Pot, Covered, Rare ...... | 385 | | | 425 | | | | |

Four Pillars (Northwood and Dugan)

French Knots (Fenton)

Frolicking Bears (U.S. Glass)

Frosted Oxford

Garden Mums (Northwood)

Gay 90's (Millersburg)

Golden Flowers

Golden Honeycomb

| | M | A | G | B | PO | AO | Pas | Red |
|---|---|---|---|---|---|---|---|---|
| **FRUIT AND FLOWERS (NORTHWOOD)** | | | | | | | | |
| Bowl, 9"........... | 100 | 150 | 140 | | | | 250 | |
| Bowl, 5"........... | 40 | 50 | 55 | | | | 75 | |
| Fruit Bowl, 10".... | 110 | 170 | 250 | | | | 780IG | |
| Banana Plate, 7", Rare........ | | 350 | 325 | | | | | |
| Bon-bon, Stemmed.......... | 100 | 100 | 185 | 275 | | 500 | 650IG | |
| Plate, 7"............ | 185 | 250 | 195 | 240 | | | | |
| Plate, 9½"......... | 235 | 270 | 260 | | | | 385 | |
| **FRUIT BASKET (MILLERSBURG)** | | | | | | | | |
| Compote, Handled, Rare...... | | 1,950 | | | | | | |
| **FRUIT JAR (BALL)** | | | | | | | | |
| One Size.......... | 65 | | | | | | | |
| **FRUIT LUSTRE** | | | | | | | | |
| Tumbler............ | 40 | | | | | | | |
| **FRUIT SALAD (WESTMORELAND)** | | | | | | | | |
| Punch Bowl and Base, Rare ... | 600 | 700 | | | 3,900 | | | |
| Cup, Rare........... | 30 | 40 | | | 60 | | | |
| **GAMBIER, MT, (CRYSTAL)** | | | | | | | | |
| Mug............ | 95 | | | | | | | |
| **GARDEN MUMS (NORTHWOOD)** | | | | | | | | |
| Bowl, 8½"-10"........ | 60 | 75 | 80 | 85 | | | 110 | |
| Plate, Regular or Handgrip, 7"........ | 180 | 575 | 225 | 240 | | | 250 | |
| Shallow Bowl, 5"..... | 200 | | | | | | | |
| **GARDEN PATH (DUGAN)** | | | | | | | | |
| Bowl, 5"............ | | | | | 60 | | | |
| Bowl, 8½"-10"........ | 60 | 85 | | | 140 | | | |
| Fruit Bowl, 10"...... | 90 | 115 | | | | | | |
| Hatpin............ | | 150 | | | | | | |
| Compote, Rare........ | 200 | 365 | | | | | 500 | |
| Plate, 6", Rare....... | 430 | 585 | | | 985 | | 650W | |
| **GARDEN PATH VT. (DUGAN)** | | | | | | | | |
| Bowl, 9"............ | | | | | 175 | | | |
| Fruit Bowl, 10"...... | | 375 | | | 410 | | | |
| Plate, 11", Rare..... | 3,200 | 5,200 | | | 3,300 | | | |
| Rose Bowl, Rare....... | 400 | | | | | | | |
| **GARLAND (FENTON)** | | | | | | | | |
| Rose Bowl, Ftd....... | 85 | 170 | | 360 | | | 280AM | |
| **GAY 90'S (MILLERSBURG)** | | | | | | | | |
| Pitcher, Rare........ | | 8,500 | 9,500 | | | | | |
| Tumbler, Rare........ | 1,250 | 1,150 | | | | | | |
| **GEM DANDY** | | | | | | | | |
| Butter churn (age?)........ | 500 | | | | | | | |
| **GEO. GETZ PIANOS (NORTHWOOD)** | | | | | | | | |
| Plate................ | | 2,000 | | | | | | |
| **GEORGIA BELLE (DUGAN)** | | | | | | | | |
| Compote, Ftd......... | 65 | 75 | 85 | | 140 | | | |
| Card Tray, Ftd, Rare........ | 75 | 80 | 95 | | 175 | | | |
| **GERMAN STEINS** | | | | | | | | |
| Various sizes........175–295 | | | | | | | | |
| **GERVUTZ BROTHERS (NORTHWOOD)** | | | | | | | | |
| Bowl................ | | 750 | | | | | | |
| **GIBSON GIRL** | | | | | | | | |
| Toothpick Holder........ | 60 | | | | | | | |
| **GOD AND HOME (DUGAN)** | | | | | | | | |
| Pitcher, Rare........ | | | | 2,000 | | | | |
| Tumbler, Rare........ | | | | 275 | | | | |
| **GODDESS (CZECH)** | | | | | | | | |
| Vase, 8½," Rare....... | 1000* | | | | | | | |
| **GODDESS ATHENA** | | | | | | | | |
| Epergne, Rare........ | | | 2,000 | | | | 2,000AM | |
| **GODDESS OF HARVEST (FENTON)** | | | | | | | | |
| Bowl, 9½", Rare....... | 6,000 | 6,900 | | 6,500 | | | | |
| Plate, Very Rare........ | | 7,800 | | | | | | |
| **GOLD FISH** | | | | | | | | |
| Bowl................ | 145 | | | | | | | |
| **GOLDEN CUPIDS** | | | | | | | | |
| Bowl, 9", Rare........ | | | | | | | 500 | |
| Bowl, 5", Rare........ | | | | | | | 225 | |
| **GOLDEN FLOWERS** | | | | | | | | |
| Vase, 7½"........... | 95 | | | | | | | |
| **GOLDEN GRAPES (DUGAN)** | | | | | | | | |
| Bowl, 7"............ | 35 | 45 | 60 | | | | 50 | |
| Rose Bowl, Collar Base........ | 85 | | | | | | | |
| **GOLDEN HARVEST (U.S. GLASS)** | | | | | | | | |
| Decanter w/stopper........ | 125 | 250 | | | | | | |
| Wine................ | 25 | 35 | | | | | | |
| **GOLDEN HONEYCOMB (IMPERIAL)** | | | | | | | | |
| Bowl, 5"............ | 25 | | | | | | | |

312

| | M | A | G | B | PO | AO | Pas | Red |
|---|---|---|---|---|---|---|---|---|
| Plate, 7" | 55 | | | | | | | |
| Compote | 50 | | | | | | | |
| Creamer or Sugar | 35 | | | | | | | |
| Bon-bon | 45 | 55 | 60 | | | | 60AM | |
| **GOLDEN OXEN** | | | | | | | | |
| Mug | 90 | | | | | | | |
| **GOLDEN THISTLE** | | | | | | | | |
| Tray, 5," Rare | | | | | | | 350* | |
| **GOLDEN WEDDING** | | | | | | | | |
| Bottle, Various Sizes | 40+ | | | | | | | |
| **GOOD LUCK (NORTHWOOD)** | | | | | | | | |
| Bowl, 8¼" | 235 | 400 | 475 | 450 | | 1,900 | 1,600TL | |
| Plate, 9" | 425+ | 700+ | 850+ | 1,100+ | | | 5000IB | |
| **GOOD LUCK VT. (NORTHWOOD)** | | | | | | | | |
| Bowl, 8¼", Rare | 300 | 400 | 450 | | | | 600 | |
| **GOODYEAR** | | | | | | | | |
| Ashtray in Tire | 60 | | | | | | | |
| **GOOSEBERRY SPRAY** | | | | | | | | |
| Bowl, 10" | 55 | 85 | 90 | 90 | | | 120 | |
| Bowl, 5" | | 110 | 125 | 125 | | | 155 | |
| Compote, Rare | | 225 | 260 | 250 | | | 260 | |
| **GOTHIC ARCHES** | | | | | | | | |
| Vase, 8"-12", Rare | 45 | 70 | 85 | 95 | | | 95SM | |
| **GRACEFUL (NORTHWOOD)** | | | | | | | | |
| Vase | 60 | 100 | 120 | 135 | | | 200W | |
| **GRACEFUL TUMBLER** | | | | | | | | |
| Tumbler | | | | 800 | | | 500AMB | |
| **GRAND THISTLE (FINLAND)** | | | | | | | | |
| Pitcher, Rare | | | | 700 | | | 750AM | |
| Tumbler, Rare | | | | 120 | | | 350AM | |
| **GRAPE (FENTON'S GRAPE AND CABLE)** | | | | | | | | |
| Ftd. Bowl, 7¼" | 110 | 115 | 125 | 135 | | | 1,000CeB | |
| Bowl, 9" (Spatula Footed) | 120 | 130 | 145 | 400 | | | | |
| Orange Bowl, Ftd | 110 | 220 | 240 | 200 | | | 265 | |
| Orange Bowl, Advertising, Very Rare | 1,900 | | | 2,200 | | | | |
| Bowl, Ftd, 8¾" | 65 | 80 | 95 | 775 | | | | |
| Bowl, Flat, 8" | 50 | 60 | 80 | 70 | | 850 | 600 | 900 |
| Plate, Ftd, 9" | 145 | 350 | 200 | | | | | 1,600 |
| Orange Basket, Very Rare | | 3,800 | | | | | | |
| Spittoon Whimsey, Rare | 1,150 | | | | | | | |
| **GRAPE (IMPERIAL)** | | | | | | | | |
| Bowl, 10" | 40 | 80 | 65 | | | | 135AM | |
| Bowl, 5" | 25 | 40 | 30 | | | | 40SM | |
| Fruit Bowl, 8¾" | 40 | 60 | 55 | 2,200 | | | | 305 |
| Compote | 50 | 60 | 60 | | | | 275SM | |
| Cup and Saucer | 70 | 155 | 50 | | | | | |
| Nappy | 30 | | 40 | | | | 35SM | |
| Tray, Center Handle | 45 | | | | | | 65HA | |
| Goblet, Rare | 40 | 75 | 65 | | | | 70AM | |
| Plate, 7"-12" | 90 | 290 | 175 | 1,750 | | | 150AM | |
| Plate, Ruffled, 8½" | 45 | 65 | 50 | 55 | | | 70SM | |
| Pitcher | 100 | 350 | 175 | | | | 270SM | |
| Tumbler | 25 | 45 | 30 | | | | 40SM | |
| Punch Bowl and Base | 135 | 390 | 275 | | | | 300SM | |
| Cup | 20 | 45 | 35 | | | | 30AM | |
| Water Bottle, Rare | 125 | 250 | 165 | | | | 270CM | |
| Milk Pitcher | 260 | 350 | 300 | | | | 190CM | |
| Basket, Handled, Rare | 75 | | 90 | | | | 130SM | |
| Rose Bowl, Rare | 175 | 225 | 190 | | | | | |
| Decanter w/stopper | 135 | 270 | 170 | | | | 150 | |
| Wine | 30 | 40 | 35 | | | | 90SM | |
| Spittoon Whimsey | 1,100 | | 2,250 | | | | | |
| **GRAPE (NORTHWOOD'S GRAPE AND CABLE)** | | | | | | | | |
| Bowl, Flat, 9"-10" | 200 | 75 | 85 | 75 | | 3,200 | 275BA | |
| Bowl, Flat, 5½" | | | | | | | 75W | |
| Scalloped Bowl, 5½"-11½" | 80+ | 75+ | 100+ | 120 | | | 750IG | |
| Bon-bon | 65 | 58 | 105 | 100 | | | 350W | |
| Banana Boat, Ftd | 250 | 300 | 400 | 425 | | | 700IB | |
| Bowl, Ftd | 60 | 80 | 105 | 90 | | | | |
| Ice Cream Bowl, 11" | 150 | 325 | 350 | 500 | | 1700 | 400IB | |
| Orange Bowl, Ftd | | 250 | | 450 | | | | |
| Breakfast Set, 2 pcs | 140 | 250 | 200 | | | | | |
| Candlelamp, Complete | 800 | 475 | 500 | | | | | |
| Compote, Covered | 2,500 | 350 | | | | | | |
| Compote, Open | 500 | 375 | 1,100 | | | | 750 | |
| Sweetmeat w/lid | 1,850 | 165 | | 2,000 | | | | |
| Sweetmeat Whimsey | 400 | 325 | | | | | | |
| Cookie Jar w/lid | 350 | 500 | | | | 9,000 | 2,350IG | |
| Centerpiece Bowl, Ftd | 300 | 595 | 1,100 | 1,250 | | | 1,100IG | |
| Cup and Saucer, Rare | 400 | 425 | | | | | | |
| Cologne w/stopper | 180 | 195 | 220 | | | | 600IB | |
| Perfume w/stopper | 375 | 650 | | | | | | |
| Dresser Tray | 175 | 250 | 295 | | | | 550IB | |
| Pin Tray | 395 | 195 | 250 | | | | 250IC | |

Golden Oxen

Golden Thistle

Gothic Arches

Grape (Imperial)

Grape and Cherry (English)

Grape Delight (Dugan)

Grape Leaves (Northwood)

Grape Wreath (Millersburg)

| | M | A | G | B | PO | AO | Pas | Red |
|---|---|---|---|---|---|---|---|---|
| Hatpin Holder | 275 | 300 | 275 | 900 | | 12,000 | 2,000W | |
| Powder Jar w/lid | 100 | 150 | 180 | 200 | | | | |
| Nappy | 85 | 100 | 135 | 165 | | | | |
| Fernery, Rare | 1,250 | 950 | 1,000 | | | | 1,200W | |
| Hat | 40 | 50 | 50 | | | | 90 | |
| Ice Cream Sherbet | 40 | 50 | 60 | | | | 90 | |
| Plate, Flat, 6"–9½" | 150 | 200 | 250 | 750 | | | 2,000TL | |
| Plate, Handgrip | 140 | 200 | 220 | | | | 240 | |
| Plate, Ftd | 65 | 95 | 110 | 135 | | | 1,200IG | |
| Plate, 2 Sides Up | 200 | 170 | 375 | | | | | |
| Shade | 200 | 180 | | | | | | |
| Punch Bowl and Base (Standard) | 380 | 500 | 500 | 900 | | | 900 | |
| Punch Bowl and Base (Small) | 300 | 600 | 700 | 850 | | | 10,000IB | |
| Plate, Advertising | | | 450 | | | | | |
| Punch Bowl and Base (Banquet) | 2,000 | 2,300 | 3,000 | 4,200 | | | 16,000IB | |
| Cup | 25 | 27 | 50 | 60 | | | 80W | |
| Butter | 175 | 220 | 225 | | | | 300 | |
| Sugar w/lid | 70 | 85 | 85 | | | | 150 | |
| Creamer or Spooner | 45 | 85 | 75 | | | | | |
| Tobacco Jar w/lid | 350 | 525 | | 1,350 | | | 550SM | |
| Pitcher, Standard | 270 | 250 | 300 | | | | 2,000IG | |
| Pitcher, Tankard | 700 | 800 | 3,300 | | | | 2,600IG | |
| Tumbler, Jumbo | 60 | 75 | 90 | | | | | |
| Tumbler, Regular | 50 | 60 | 75 | | | | 500IG | |
| Decanter w/stopper | 650 | 700 | | | | | | |
| Shot Glass | 125 | 285 | | | | | | |
| Spittoon, Rare | 6,000 | 7,800 | 7,500 | | | | | |
| Candlesticks, ea | 160 | 200 | 210 | | | | | |
| Orange Bowl, Blackberry Interior, Rare | | 1,800 | | | | | | |
| Hatpin Holder Whimsey, Rare | | 3,500 | 4,000 | | | | | |

**GRAPE AND CHERRY (ENGLISH)**

| | M | A | G | B | PO | AO | Pas | Red |
|---|---|---|---|---|---|---|---|---|
| Bowl, 8½", Rare | 75 | | | 180 | | | | |

**GRAPE AND GOTHIC ARCHES (NORTHWOOD)**

| | M | A | G | B | PO | AO | Pas | Red |
|---|---|---|---|---|---|---|---|---|
| Bowl, 10" | 80 | 120 | 90 | 80 | 150PL | | | |
| Bowl, 5" | 25 | 40 | 40 | 35 | 45PL | | | |
| Butter | 100 | 140 | 140 | 125 | 420PL | | | |
| Sugar w/lid | 75 | 120 | 110 | 90 | 125PL | | | |
| Creamer or Spooner | 55 | 85 | 75 | 70 | 125PL | | | |
| Pitcher | 200 | 385 | 400 | 360 | 750PL | | | |
| Tumbler | 35 | 80 | 70 | 50 | 170PL | | 160CM | |

**GRAPE ARBOR (DUGAN)**

| | M | A | G | B | PO | AO | Pas | Red |
|---|---|---|---|---|---|---|---|---|
| Bowl, Ftd, 9½"-11" | 150 | 400 | | | | | 150W | |

**GRAPE ARBOR (NORTHWOOD)**

| | M | A | G | B | PO | AO | Pas | Red |
|---|---|---|---|---|---|---|---|---|
| Pitcher | 320 | 650 | | 3,000 | | | 800W | |
| Tumbler | 45 | 70 | | 375 | | | 150W | |
| Hat | 75 | | | 175 | | | 350IG | |

**GRAPE DELIGHT (DUGAN)**

| | M | A | G | B | PO | AO | Pas | Red |
|---|---|---|---|---|---|---|---|---|
| Rose Bowl, Ftd, 6" | 65 | 80 | | 70 | | | 70W | |
| Nut Bowl, Ftd, 6" | 65 | 120 | | 180 | | | 80W | |

**GRAPE FIEZE (NORTHWOOD)**

| | M | A | G | B | PO | AO | Pas | Red |
|---|---|---|---|---|---|---|---|---|
| Bowl, 10½", Rare | | | | | | | 600IC | |

**GRAPE, HEAVY (DUGAN)**

| | M | A | G | B | PO | AO | Pas | Red |
|---|---|---|---|---|---|---|---|---|
| Bowl, 5", Rare | 160 | 185 | | 395 | | | | |
| Bowl, 10" | 240 | 295 | | 600 | | | | |

**GRAPE, HEAVY (IMPERIAL)**

| | M | A | G | B | PO | AO | Pas | Red |
|---|---|---|---|---|---|---|---|---|
| Bowl, 9" | 100 | 265 | | | | | | |
| Bowl, 5" | 25 | 30 | | | | | | |
| Nappy | 45 | 55 | | | | | | |
| Plate, 8" | 65 | 185 | 190 | | | | 200AM | |
| Plate, 6" | 52 | 160 | 170 | | | | 90 | |
| Plate, 11" | 265 | 375 | | | | | 300AM | |
| Fruit Bowl w/base | 295 | | | | | | | |
| Custard Cup | 20 | 35 | 35 | | | | | |
| Punch Bowl w/base | 210 | 510 | 450 | | | | | |

**GRAPE LEAVES (MILLERSBURG)**

| | M | A | G | B | PO | AO | Pas | Red |
|---|---|---|---|---|---|---|---|---|
| Bowl, 10", Rare | 600 | 800 | 900 | | | | 850V | |

**GRAPE LEAVES (NORTHWOOD)**

| | M | A | G | B | PO | AO | Pas | Red |
|---|---|---|---|---|---|---|---|---|
| Bowl, 8¼" | 65 | 80 | 85 | 90 | | | 200BA | |
| Brides Basket, Complete | | 300 | | | | | | |

**GRAPEVINE LATTICE (DUGAN)**

| | M | A | G | B | PO | AO | Pas | Red |
|---|---|---|---|---|---|---|---|---|
| Bowl, 8½" | 42 | 60 | 52 | 65 | | | 80W | |
| Plate, 7"-9 | 275 | 295 | | 290 | | | 150W | |
| Bowl, 5" | 30 | | | | | | 60W | |
| Hat Shape, Jip | 75 | | | | | | | |

**GRAPEVINE LATTICE (FENTON)**

| | M | A | G | B | PO | AO | Pas | Red |
|---|---|---|---|---|---|---|---|---|
| Pitcher, Rare | 325 | 600 | | 650 | | | 850W | |
| Tumbler, Rare | 55 | 75 | | 95 | | | 100W | |

**GRAPE WREATH (MILLERSBURG)**

| | M | A | G | B | PO | AO | Pas | Red |
|---|---|---|---|---|---|---|---|---|
| Bowl, 5" | 40 | 55 | 320 | | | | | |
| Bowl, 7½"-9 | 60 | 75 | 80 | 420 | | | | |
| Bowl, Ice Cream, 10" | 120 | 175 | 175 | | | | | |
| Spittoon Whimsey, Rare | 3,200 | | 3,800 | | | | | |

Grecian Urn

Halloween

Hamilton Souvenir

Hammered Bell Chandelier

| | M | A | G | B | PO | AO | Pas | Red |
|---|---|---|---|---|---|---|---|---|
| **GRAPE WREATH MULTI-STAR VT** | | | | | | | | |
| Bowl, 5" | 50 | 60 | 70 | | | | | |
| Bowl, 7½" | 70 | 80 | 90 | | | | | |
| Bowl, 9" | 90 | 90 | 95 | | | | | |
| Bowl, 10" ice cream | 130 | 145 | 160 | | | | | |
| **GRAPE WREATH VT (MILLERSBURG)** | | | | | | | | |
| Bowl, 5" | 40 | 65 | 70 | | | | | |
| Bowl, 7½" | 50 | 75 | 80 | | | | | |
| Bowl, 9" | 55 | 90 | 100 | | | | | |
| Bowl, 10" ice cream | 70 | 120 | 135 | | | | | |
| **GRECIAN URN** | | | | | | | | |
| Perfume, 6" | 45 | | | | | | | |
| **GREEK KEY (NORTHWOOD)** | | | | | | | | |
| Bowl, 7"-8½" | 250 | 120 | 150 | 375 | | | | |
| Plate, 9"-11", Rare | 5,800 | 850 | 1,200 | 2,900 | | 1,750* | | |
| Pitcher, Rare | 750 | 900 | 1,650 | | | | | |
| Tumbler, Rare | 120 | 295 | 350 | | | | | |
| **GREEK KEY AND SCALES (NORTHWOOD)** | | | | | | | | |
| Bowl, ftd. | 75 | 90 | 85 | | | | | |
| **GREEK KEY VT.** | | | | | | | | |
| Hatpin | | 90 | | | | | | |
| **GREENGARD FURNITURE (MILLERSBURG)** | | | | | | | | |
| Bowl, Rare | | 1,295 | | | | | | |
| **HAIR RECEIVER** | | | | | | | | |
| Complete | 75 | | | | | | | |
| **HALLOWEEN** | | | | | | | | |
| Pitcher, 2 sizes | 485 | | | | | | | |
| Tumbler, 2 sizes | 175 | | | | | | | |
| Spittoon | 600 | | | | | | | |
| **HAMILTON SOUVENIR** | | | | | | | | |
| Vase, 6¼" | 70 | | | | | | | |
| **HAMMERED BELL CHANDELIER** | | | | | | | | |
| Complete, 5 Shades | | | | | | | 600W | |
| Shade, Each | | | | | | | 95W | |
| **HAND VASE (CZECH)** | | | | | | | | |
| One Shape, 5½"-8" | 280 | 380 | | | | | | 1450* |
| **HANDLED TUMBLER** | | | | | | | | |
| One Size | 55 | | | | | | | |
| **HANDLED VASE (IMPERIAL)** | | | | | | | | |
| One Shape | 47 | | | | | | | |
| **HARVEST FLOWER (DUGAN)** | | | | | | | | |
| Pitcher, Rare | 1,250 | | | | | | | |
| Tumbler | 105 | 300 | 365 | | | | | |
| **HARVEST POPPY** | | | | | | | | |
| Compote | 320 | 450 | 400 | 450 | | | 500AM | |
| **HATCHET (U.S. GLASS)** | | | | | | | | |
| One Shape | 150 | | | | | | | |
| **HATTIE (IMPERIAL)** | | | | | | | | |
| Bowl | 47 | 115 | | | | | | |
| Rose Bowl | 95 | | | | | | 250AM | |
| Plate, Rare | 875 | 1,100 | 500 | | | | 900 | |
| **HAWAIIAN LEI (HIGBEE)** | | | | | | | | |
| Sugar | 75 | | | | | | | |
| Creamer | 75 | | | | | | | |
| **HAWAIIAN MOON** | | | | | | | | |
| Pitcher | 200 | | | | | | 250CRAN | |
| Tumbler | 75 | | | | | | 90CRAN | |
| **HEADDRESS** | | | | | | | | |
| Bowl, 9", 2 Varieties | 47 | | 60 | 52 | | | | |
| Compote | 58 | | 75 | 60 | | | | |
| **HEART AND HORSESHOE (FENTON)** | | | | | | | | |
| Bowl, 8½" | 900 | | | | | | | |
| Plate, 9", Rare | 1,150 | | | | | | | |
| **HEART AND TREES (FENTON)** | | | | | | | | |
| Bowl, 8¾" | 165 | | 215 | 200 | | | | |
| **HEART AND VINE (FENTON)** | | | | | | | | |
| Bowl, 8½" | 80 | 150 | 115 | 120 | | | 70LV | |
| Plate, 9", Rare | 300 | 475 | 365 | 600 | | | | |
| Spector Plate, Advertising, Rare | 900 | | | | | | | |
| **HEART BAND** | | | | | | | | |
| One Shape (Salt) | 45 | | | | | | | |
| **HEART BAND SOUVENIR (McKEE)** | | | | | | | | |
| Mug, Small | 85 | | 140 | | | | 115AQ | |
| Mug, Large | 90 | | 165 | | | | 127AQ | |
| **HEARTS AND FLOWERS (NORTHWOOD)** | | | | | | | | |
| Bowl, 8½" | 525 | 450 | 750 | 650 | | | 800IG | |
| Compote | 300 | 550 | 1,650 | 500 | | 800 | 2,100IG | |
| Plate, 9", Rare | 1,000 | 1,150 | 2,500 | 550 | | 2,300 | 6,000IB | |

Heavy Banded Diamonds (Crystal)

Heisey Colonial (Heisey)

Heron (Dugan)

Hobnail Soda Gold (Imperial)

| | M | A | G | B | PO | AO | Pas | Red |
|---|---|---|---|---|---|---|---|---|
| **HEAVY BANDED DIAMONDS (CRYSTAL)** | | | | | | | | |
| Bowl, 9" | | 135 | | | | | | |
| Bowl, 5" | | 60 | | | | | | |
| **HEAVY DIAMOND** | | | | | | | | |
| Nappy | 40 | | | | | | | |
| **HEAVY DIAMOND (IMPERIAL)** | | | | | | | | |
| Bowl, 10" | 45 | | | | | | | |
| Creamer | 30 | | | | | | | |
| Sugar | 35 | | | | | | | |
| Vase | 50 | | 65 | | | | 85SM | |
| Compote | 45 | | 55 | | | | | |
| **HEAVY HEART (HIGBEE)** | | | | | | | | |
| Tumbler | 150 | | | | | | | |
| **HEAVY HOBNAIL (FENTON)** | | | | | | | | |
| Vase, Rare | | 550 | | | | | 465W | |
| **HEAVY HOBS** | | | | | | | | |
| Lamp (Amber Base Glass) | | | | | 300 | | | |
| **HEAVY PRISMS (ENGLISH)** | | | | | | | | |
| Celery Vase, 6" | 85 | 115 | | 95 | | | | |
| **HEAVY SHELL (FENTON)** | | | | | | | | |
| Bowl, 8¼" | | | | | | | 150 | |
| Candleholder, Each | | | | | | | 100 | |
| **HEAVY VINE** | | | | | | | | |
| Lamp | 250 | | | | | | | |
| Atomizer | 85 | | | | | | | |
| **HEAVY WEB (DUGAN)** | | | | | | | | |
| Bowl, 10", Rare | | | | | 1,300 | | | |
| Plate, 11", Rare | | | | | 1,800 | | | |
| **HEINZ** | | | | | | | | |
| Bottle | | | | | | | 58 | |
| **HEISEY** | | | | | | | | |
| Breakfast Set | | | | | | | 290 | |
| **HEISEY CARTWHEEL** | | | | | | | | |
| Compote | | | | | | | 85 | |
| **HEISEY COLONIAL (HEISEY)** | | | | | | | | |
| Compote | 80 | | | | | | | |
| Juice Tumbler | 65 | | | | | | | |
| Perfume (Cologne) | 90 | | | | | | | |
| Puff Box | 120 | | | | | | | |
| Hair Receiver | 135 | | | | | | | |
| Dresser Tray | 100 | | | | | | | |
| **HEISEY FLORAL SPRAY** | | | | | | | | |
| Stemmed Candy w/lid, 11" | | | | | | | 85IB | |
| **HEISEY FLUTE** | | | | | | | | |
| Punch Cup | 35 | | | | | | | |
| Toothpick Holder | 100 | | | | | | | |
| **HEISEY SET** | | | | | | | | |
| Creamer and Tray | 150 | | | | | | 195 | |
| **HEISEY #357** | | | | | | | | |
| Water Bottle | 190 | | | | | | | |
| Tumbler | 65 | | | | | | | |
| **HERON (DUGAN)** | | | | | | | | |
| Mug, Rare | 1,000 | 375 | | | | | | |
| **HERRINGBONE AND BEADED OVAL** | | | | | | | | |
| Compote, Rare | 600* | | | | | | | |
| **HERRINGBONE AND MUMS (JEANETTE)** | | | | | | | | |
| Tumbler, very rare | 600 | | | | | | | |
| **HEXAGON AND CANE (IMPERIAL)** | | | | | | | | |
| Covered Sugar | 90 | | | | | | | |
| **HEX BASE** | | | | | | | | |
| Candlesticks, pair | 75 | 125 | 110 | | | | 175SM | |
| **HEX-OPTIC (JEANETTE)** | | | | | | | | |
| Pitcher | | | | | | | 135CL | |
| Tumbler | | | | | | | 50CL | |
| **HICKMAN** | | | | | | | | |
| Castor Set, 4 pc | 250 | | | | | | 450 | |
| **HOBNAIL (FENTON)** | | | | | | | | |
| Vase, 5"–11" | | | | | | | 95+W | |
| **HOBNAIL (MILLERSBURG)** | | | | | | | | |
| Hat Whimsey, Rare | 1,700 | | | | | | | |
| Pitcher, Rare | 1,800 | 1,900 | 2,200 | 1,600 | | | | |
| Tumbler, Rare | 775 | 500 | 1,000 | 950 | | | | |
| Rose Bowl, Scarce | 200 | 395 | 595 | | | | | |
| Spittoon, Rare | 900 | 1,000 | 1,800 | | | | | |
| Butter, Rare | 500 | 600 | 650 | 800 | | | | |
| Sugar w/lid, Rare | 350 | 500 | 575 | 800 | | | | |
| Creamer or Spooner, Rare | 275 | 375 | 450 | 500 | | | | |
| **HOBNAIL, MINIATURE** | | | | | | | | |
| Tumbler, 2½" | 50 | | | | | | | |
| Pitcher 6", Rare | 250 | | | | | | | |
| **HOBNAIL PANELS (McKEE)** | | | | | | | | |
| Vase, 8¾" | | | | | | | 70CM | |
| **HOBNAIL SODA GOLD (IMPERIAL)** | | | | | | | | |
| Spittoon, Large | 50 | | 75 | | | | 60W | |

Hobstar (Imperial)

Hobstar Flower (Northwood)

Hobstar Panels (English)

Hocking Mixing Bowl

| | M | A | G | B | PO | AO | Pas | Red |
|---|---|---|---|---|---|---|---|---|
| **HOBNAIL VT. (MILLERSBURG)** | | | | | | | | |
| Vase Whimsey, Rare | 600 | 750 | 750 | | | | | |
| Rose Bowl, Rare | 900 | | | | | | | |
| Jardinere, Rare | | 950 | | 1,100 | | | | |
| **HOBSTAR (IMPERIAL)** | | | | | | | | |
| Bowl, Berry, 10" | 40 | | | | | | 50 | |
| Bowl, Berry, 5" | 25 | | | | | | 35 | |
| Bowls, Various | | | | | | | | |
| Shapes, 6"-12" | 30 | | | | | | 40 | |
| Fruit Bowl w/base | 50 | 85 | 75 | | | | | |
| Cookie Jar w/lid | 65 | | 100 | | | | | |
| Butter | 80 | 195 | 185 | | | | 90CM | |
| Sugar w/lid | 65 | 100 | 90 | | | | 60CM | |
| Creamer or Spooner | 45 | 85 | 75 | | | | 50CM | |
| Pickle Castor, Complete | 750 | | | | | | | |
| Bride's Basket, Complete | 75 | | | | | | | |
| Vase, Flared | 350 | 200 | | | | | | |
| **HOBSTAR AND ARCHES (IMPERIAL)** | | | | | | | | |
| Bowl, 9" | 50 | 75 | 60 | | | | 60SM | |
| Fruit Bowl w/base | 60 | 90 | 75 | | | | | |
| **HOBSTAR AND CUT TRIANGLES (ENGLISH)** | | | | | | | | |
| Rose Bowl | 45 | 55 | 70 | | | | | |
| Bowl | 30 | 40 | 60 | | | | | |
| Plate | 70 | 100 | 110 | | | | | |
| **HOBSTAR AND DIAMONDS** | | | | | | | | |
| Tumbler, very rare | 500 | | | | | | | |
| **HOBSTAR AND FEATHER (MILLERSBURG)** | | | | | | | | |
| Punch Bowl and Base (Open), Rare | 1,800 | | 3,800 | | | | | |
| Punch Bowl and Base (Tulip), Rare | | 3,500 | | | | | | |
| Punch Cup, Scarce | 30 | 40 | | 275* | | | | |
| Rose Bowl, Giant, Rare | 3,000* | 2,000 | 2,000 | | | | | |
| Vase Whimsey, Rare | | 5,000 | 5,000 | | | | | |
| Punch Bowl Whimsey, Rare | | | 7,500 | | | | | |
| Compote Whimsey (From Rose Bowl), Rare | | 5,500 | | | | | | |
| Bowl, Round, 5", Rare | | 450 | | | | | | |
| Bowl, Diamond, 5", Rare | 400 | | | | | | | |
| Bowl, Heart, 5", Rare | 350 | | | | | | | |
| Butter, Rare | 1,500 | 1,800 | 1,800 | | | | | |
| Sugar w/lid, Rare | 900 | 1,000 | 1,000 | | | | | |
| Creamer, Rare | 700 | 800 | 800 | | | | | |
| Spooner, Rare | 700 | 800 | 800 | | | | | |
| Dessert, Stemmed, Rare | 650 | | | | | | | |
| Compote, 6" Rare | 1,500 | | | | | | | |
| Stemmed Whimsey Tray-Ftd, 4½", Very Rare | 750 | | | | | | | |
| **HOBSTAR AND FILE** | | | | | | | | |
| Pitcher, Rare | 1,700 | | | | | | | |
| Tumbler, Rare | 200 | | | | | | | |
| **HOBSTAR AND FRUIT (WESTMORELAND)** | | | | | | | | |
| Bowl, 6", Rare | | | | | 100 | 300 | | |
| Bowl, 10", Rare | | | | | 195 | | | |
| Plate, 10½", Rare | | | | | | | 400IB | |
| **HOBSTAR AND SHIELD** | | | | | | | | |
| Pitcher | 195 | | | | | | | |
| Tumbler | 100 | | | | | | | |
| **HOBSTAR AND WAFFLE BLOCK (IMPERIAL)** | | | | | | | | |
| Basket | 150 | | | | | | 175SM | |
| **HOBSTAR BAND (IMPERIAL)** | | | | | | | | |
| Celery | 85 | | | | | | | |
| Compote, Rare | 100 | | | | | | | |
| Bowl, Rare | 90 | | | | | | | |
| Pitcher, 2 Shapes, Rare | 275 | | | | | | | |
| Tumbler, 2 Shapes, Rare | 70 | | | | | | | |
| **HOBSTAR FLOWER (NORTHWOOD)** | | | | | | | | |
| Compote, Scarce | 155 | 165 | 270 | 280 | | | | |
| **HOBSTAR PANELS (ENGLISH)** | | | | | | | | |
| Creamer | 45 | | | | | | | |
| Sugar, Stemmed | 45 | | | | | | | |
| **HOBSTAR REVERSED (ENGLISH)** | | | | | | | | |
| Spooner | 45 | | | | | | | |
| Butter | 55 | 75 | 70 | | | | | |
| Frog and Holder | 50 | | | | | | | |
| **HOBSTAR WHIRL (WHIRLAGIG)** | | | | | | | | |
| Compote, 4½" | 50 | 60 | 60 | | | | | |
| **HOCKING MIXING BOWL** | | | | | | | | |
| 3 sizes, each | 60–100 | | | | | | | |
| **HOLIDAY** | | | | | | | | |
| Bottle | | | | | | | 75 | |

317

|  | M | A | G | B | PO | AO | Pas | Red |
|---|---|---|---|---|---|---|---|---|
| **HOLIDAY (NORTHWOOD)** | | | | | | | | |
| Tray, 11", Rare ................. | 375 | | | | | | | |
| **HOLLY (FENTON)** | | | | | | | | |
| Bowl, 8"-10" ..................... | 75 | 80 | 180 | 100 | | | 150W | 2,150 |
| Compote, 5".................... | 45 | 150 | 225 | 50 | | | 85AM | 1,600 |
| Goblet ............................ | 40 | 60 | | 260 | | | 90W | 1,450 |
| Hat ................................. | 35 | 40 | 150 | 140 | | | 75LG | 750 |
| Plate, 9".......................... | 280 | 750 | 1,450 | 345 | | | 850BA | 2,800 |
| Rose Bowl........................ | 400 | | 900* | 500 | | | | |
| **HOLLY AND BERRY (DUGAN)** | | | | | | | | |
| Bowl, 7"-9" ....................... | 40 | 47 | 50 | 50 | 70 | | | |
| Nappy.............................. | 45 | 55 | 60 | 55 | 70 | | | |
| Gravy Boat, Handled ........... | | 65 | | 65 | 140 | | | |
| **HOLLY, PANELLED (NORTHWOOD)** | | | | | | | | |
| Bowl................................ | | 75 | 70 | | | | | |
| Bon-bon, Ftd ..................... | 60 | 90 | 75 | | | | | |
| Creamer or Sugar ............... | 90 | | | | | | | |
| Pitcher, Rare..................... | | 12,000* | | | | | | |
| Spooner........................... | 50 | | | | | | | |
| **HOLLY SPRIG OR WHIRL (MILLERSBURG)** | | | | | | | | |
| Deep Sauce, Rare ............... | 175 | 275 | 350 | | | | | |
| Nappy, Tri-Cornered, Rare... | 85 | 115 | 120 | | | | | |
| Bon-bon (Plain)................... | 155 | 160 | 160 | | | | | |
| Bon-bon (Isaac Benesch), Rare ................................. | 125 | | | | | | | |
| Bowl, Round or Ruffled, 7"-10" ................ | 50 | 65 | 60 | | | | 60CM | |
| Compote, Very Rare ............ | 450 | 625 | | | | | 1,000V | |
| Rose Bowl Whimsey, Rare.... | | | | | | | 1,250V | |
| Bowl, Tri-Cornered, 7"-10"... | 325 | 200 | 190 | | | | | |
| Card Tray, hdld................... | 90 | 135 | 145 | | | | | |
| **HOLLY SPRIG VT. (MILLERSBURG)** | | | | | | | | |
| Bowl, Scarce...................... | 290 | 320 | 350 | | | | | |
| **HOLLY WREATH MULTI-STAR VT (MILLERSBURG)** | | | | | | | | |
| Bowl, 7"............................ | 90 | 140 | 130 | | | | | |
| Bowl, 9"............................ | 120 | 170 | 160 | | | | | |
| Ice Cream Bowl, 10" ............ | 160 | 190 | 180 | | | | | |
| **HOLM SPRAY** | | | | | | | | |
| Atomizer, 3" ....................... | 65 | | | | | | | |
| **HOMESTEAD** | | | | | | | | |
| Shade.............................. | 50 | | | | | | | |
| **HONEYBEE (JEANETTE)** | | | | | | | | |
| Pot ................................. | | | 180 | | | | 85 | |
| **HONEYCOMB (DUGAN)** | | | | | | | | |
| Rose Bowl.......................... | 90 | | | | 250 | | | |
| **HONEYCOMB AND CLOVER (FENTON)** | | | | | | | | |
| Bon-bon ........................... | 40 | 60 | 60 | 50 | | | 70AM | |
| Compote............................ | 35 | 50 | 60 | 50 | | | | |
| Spooner, Rare..................... | 95 | | | | | | | |
| **HONEYCOMB AND HOBSTAR (MILLERSBURG)** | | | | | | | | |
| Vase, 8¼", Rare.................. | | 7,000 | | 7,500 | | | | |
| **HONEYCOMB ORNAMENT** | | | | | | | | |
| Hatpin............................... | | 80 | | 90 | | | | |
| **HONEYCOMB PANELS** | | | | | | | | |
| Tumbler ............................ | | 175* | | | | | | |
| **HORN OF PLENTY** | | | | | | | | |
| Bottle ............................... | 60 | | | | | | | |
| **HORN, POWDER (CAMBRIDGE)** | | | | | | | | |
| Candy Holder ...................... | 200 | | | | | | | |
| **HORSES' HEADS (FENTON)** | | | | | | | | |
| Bowl, Flat, 7½" ................... | 175 | | 300 | 250 | | | 290W | 1,200 |
| Bowl, Ftd, 7"-8" .................. | 195 | | 400 | 270 | | | 295W | 1,200 |
| Plate, 6½"-8½".................... | 500 | 1,000 | | 800 | | | | |
| Rose Bowl, Ftd ................... | 170 | | | 400 | | | 800V | |
| Nut Bowl, Rare ................... | | 250 | | | | | 750SM | |
| **HORSESHOE** | | | | | | | | |
| Shot Glass.......................... | 50 | | | | | | | |
| **HOT SPRINGS SOUVENIR** | | | | | | | | |
| Vase, 9⅞", Rare.................. | 115* | | | | | | | |
| **HOURGLASS** | | | | | | | | |
| Bud Vase ........................... | 50 | | | | | | | |
| **HOWARD ADVERTISING (NORTHWOOD)** | | | | | | | | |
| Vase (Four Pillers)............... | | 95 | | | | | | |
| **HUMPTY-DUMPTY** | | | | | | | | |
| Mustard Jar ....................... | 75 | | | | | | | |
| **HYACINTH** | | | | | | | | |
| Lamp................................ | 1,900 | | | | | | | |
| **ICE CRYSTALS** | | | | | | | | |
| Bowl, Ftd........................... | | | | | | | 85 | |

Holly (Fenton)

Holly and Berry (Dugan)

Homestead

Howard Advertising (Northwood)

318

| | M | A | G | B | PO | AO | Pas | Red |
|---|---|---|---|---|---|---|---|---|
| Candlesticks, pair................ | | | | | | | 160 | |
| Salt, Ftd .......................... | | | | | | | 65 | |
| **IDYLL (FENTON)** | | | | | | | | |
| Vase, Rare ....................... | 550 | 750 | | 850 | | | | |
| **ILLINOIS DAISY (ENGLISH)** | | | | | | | | |
| Bowl, 8"............................ | 40 | | | | | | | |
| Cookie Jar w/lid................ | 60 | | | | | | | |
| **ILLUSION (FENTON)** | | | | | | | | |
| Bon-bon ........................... | 55 | | | 85 | | | | |
| Bowl............................... | 60 | | | 90 | | | | |
| **IMPERIAL BASKET (IMPERIAL)** | | | | | | | | |
| One Shape, Rare ............... | 65 | | | | | | 80 | |
| **IMPERIAL DAISY (IMPERIAL)** | | | | | | | | |
| Shade.............................. | 45 | | | | | | | |
| **IMPERIAL GRAPE (IMPERIAL)** | | | | | | | | |
| Shade.............................. | 85 | | | | | | | |
| **IMPERIAL PAPERWEIGHT (IMPERIAL)** | | | | | | | | |
| Advertising Weight, Rare...... | | 1,050 | | | | | | |
| **IMPERIAL #5 (IMPERIAL)** | | | | | | | | |
| Bowl, 8"............................ | 40 | | | | | | 50AM | |
| Vase, 6", Rare .................. | 95 | | | | | | | |
| **IMPERIAL #9 (IMPERIAL)** | | | | | | | | |
| Compote........................... | 40 | | | | | | | |
| **IMPERIAL #284** | | | | | | | | |
| Vase, 6–14"........................ | 95+ | 185+ | 150+ | | | | | |
| **INCA (CZECH)** | | | | | | | | |
| Vase, 7", Rare ................... | 900 | 950 | | | | | | |
| Bottle .............................. | 175* | | | | | | | |
| **INDIANA GOBLET (INDIANA GLASS)** | | | | | | | | |
| One Shape, Rare ................ | | | | | | | 800AM | |
| **INDIANA STATEHOUSE (FENTON)** | | | | | | | | |
| Plate, Rare....................... | 16,000 | | | 3,500 | | | | |
| **INDIAN CANOE** | | | | | | | | |
| Novelty Boat Shape............. | 100 | | | | | | | |
| **INSULATOR (VARIOUS MAKERS)** | | | | | | | | |
| Various Sizes...................... | 35+ | | | | | | | |
| **INTAGLIO DAISY (ENGLISH)** | | | | | | | | |
| Bowl, 7½" ......................... | 50 | | | | | | | |
| Bowl, 4½" ......................... | 30 | | | | | | | |
| **INTAGLIO FEATHERS** | | | | | | | | |
| Cup.................................. | 25 | | | | | | | |
| **INTAGLIO OVALS (U.S. GLASS)** | | | | | | | | |
| Bowl, 7"............................ | | | | | | 70 | | |
| Plate, 7½".......................... | | | | | | 90 | | |
| **INTAGLIO STARS** | | | | | | | | |
| Tumbler, Rare .................... | 600 | | | | | | | |
| **INTERIOR FLUTE** | | | | | | | | |
| Creamer ........................... | 50 | | | | | | | |
| Sugar ............................... | 60 | | | | | | | |
| **INTERIOR PANELS** | | | | | | | | |
| Decanter ........................... | 65 | | | | | | | |
| Mug................................. | 75 | | | | | | | |
| **INTERIOR POINSETTIA (NORTHWOOD)** | | | | | | | | |
| Tumbler, Rare .................... | 485 | | | | | | | |
| **INTERIOR RAYS** | | | | | | | | |
| Sherbet ............................ | 35 | | | | | | | |
| **INTERIOR RAYS (WESTMORELAND)** | | | | | | | | |
| Covered Butter ................... | 65 | | | | | | | |
| Sugar, Creamer or Jam Jar, Each............................ | 40 | | | | | | | |
| **INTERIOR RIB** | | | | | | | | |
| Vase ................................. | 50 | | | | | | 50SM | |
| **INTERIOR SWIRL** | | | | | | | | |
| Vase, Ftd, 9" ...................... | 40 | | | | | | | |
| Spittoon ............................ | | | | | 95 | | | |
| **INTERIOR SWIRL AND WIDE PANEL** | | | | | | | | |
| Squat Pitcher...................... | 75 | | | | | | | |
| **INVERTED COIN DOT (NORTHWOOD-FENTON)** | | | | | | | | |
| Pitcher.............................. | 325 | 450 | | 400 | | | | |
| Tumbler ............................ | 75 | 95 | | 85 | | | | |
| Bowl................................. | 40 | 50 | 70 | 50 | | | 70 | |
| Rose Bowl.......................... | 50 | | 60 | | | | 85 | |
| **INVERTED FEATHER (CAMBRIDGE)** | | | | | | | | |
| Bon-bon Whimsey (from cracker jar)...................... | | | 1,600* | | | | | |
| Cracker Jar w/lid ............... | | 1,000 | 395 | | | | | |
| Covered Butter, Rare .......... | 450 | 500 | | | | | | |
| Sugar, Creamer or | | | | | | | | |

Imperial Basket (Imperial)

Imperial #284

Inca (Czech)

Interior Panels

Inverted Prisms (English)

Jack-in-the-Pulpit (Dugan)

Jackman

Jelly Jar

| | M | A | G | B | PO | AO | Pas | Red |
|---|---|---|---|---|---|---|---|---|
| Spooner, Rare ...................... | 400 | 325 | | | | | | |
| Pitcher, Tall, Rare ............... | 4,500 | | | | | | | |
| Tumbler, Rare .................... | 500 | | 600 | | | | | |
| Compote........................... | 85 | | | | | | | |
| Punch Bowl w/base, Rare.... | 3,000 | | 4,000 | | | | | |
| Cup, Rare........................... | 60 | | | | | | | |
| Wine, Rare......................... | 200 | | | | | | | |
| Squat Pitcher, Rare.............. | 1,200 | | | | | | | |
| **INVERTED PRISMS (ENGLISH)** | | | | | | | | |
| Creamer ............................ | 70 | | | | | | | |
| Suger, Open ...................... | 60 | | | | | | | |
| **INVERTED STRAWBERRY** | | | | | | | | |
| Bowl, 9"-10½" ..................... | 190 | 300 | 295 | 350 | | | | |
| Bowl, 5".............................. | 40 | 55 | 50 | | | | | |
| Sugar, Creamer or Spooner, Rare, Each ............... | 525 | | | 150 | | | | |
| Covered Butter .................... | 850 | 1,050 | | | | | | |
| Candlesticks, Rare, Pair ...... | 300 | 425 | 600 | | | | | |
| Compote, Large, Rare ......... | 350 | 500 | 450 | | | | | |
| Compote, Small, Rare ......... | 400 | | | 350 | | | | |
| Cruet Whimsey, Very Rare ... | 1,500* | | | | | | | |
| Powder Jar, Rare ................. | 195 | | | | | | | |
| Ladies Spittoon, Rare .......... | 900 | 1,000 | 1,000 | | | | | |
| Milk Pitcher, Rare ............... | | 1,850 | | | | | | |
| Pitcher, Rare...................... | 2,200 | 3,200 | 3,000 | | | | | |
| Tumbler, Rare .................... | 300 | 250 | 350 | | | | | |
| Table Set, 2 pcs, Rare (Stemmed) ......................... | | 1,275 | | | | | | |
| Celery, Rare....................... | | 1,300 | 1,300 | 1,300 | | | | |
| Compote Whimsey, Rare...... | 500 | | | | | | | |
| **INVERTED, THISTLE (CAMBRIDGE)** | | | | | | | | |
| Bowl, 9", Rare..................... | | 350 | 350 | | | | | |
| Spittoon, Rare .................... | | 4,000 | | | | | | |
| Covered Box, Rare .............. | | | | 400 | | | | |
| Pitcher, Rare...................... | 3,800 | 3,500 | | | | | | |
| Tumbler, Rare .................... | 425 | 300 | 275 | | | | | |
| Butter, Rare....................... | 500 | 600 | 700 | | | | | |
| Sugar, Creamer or Spooner, Rare ............................. | 350 | 400 | 500 | | | | | |
| Chop Plate, Rare.................. | | 2,600 | | | | | | |
| Milk Pitcher, Rare ............... | | 2,850 | | | | | | |
| Bowl, 5", Rare..................... | | 200 | 200 | | | | | |
| **IOWA** | | | | | | | | |
| Small Mug, Rare.................. | 95 | | | | | | | |
| **IRIS (FENTON)** | | | | | | | | |
| Compote............................ | 50 | 60 | 60 | 75 | | | 275W | |
| Buttermilk Goblet, Scarce.... | 55 | 65 | 65 | 160 | | | 80AM | |
| **IRIS, HEAVY (DUGAN)** | | | | | | | | |
| Pitcher.............................. | 400 | 750 | | | 1,000 | | 1,450W | |
| Tumbler ............................ | 90 | 80 | | | | | 255W | |
| **IRIS HERRINGBONE (JEANETTE)** | | | | | | | | |
| Various Shapes, Prices range from $10.00 to $35.00 each in this late pattern. | | | | | | | | |
| **ISAAC BENESCH** | | | | | | | | |
| Advertising Bowl, 6½" .......... | | 350 | | | | | | |
| Misspelled Version, Rare...... | | 1050* | | | | | | |
| **IVY** | | | | | | | | |
| Stemmed Wine ................... | 75 | | | | | | | |
| Stemmed Claret.................. | 85 | | | | | | | |
| **I.W. HARPER** | | | | | | | | |
| Decanter w/stopper............. | 85 | | | | | | | |
| **JACK-IN-THE-PULPIT (DUGAN)** | | | | | | | | |
| Vase ................................. | 45 | 75 | | 80 | 110 | | | |
| **JACKMAN** | | | | | | | | |
| Whiskey Bottle ................... | 50 | | | | | | | |
| **JACOBEAN RANGER (CZECHOSLOVAKIAN AND ENGLISH)** | | | | | | | | |
| Pitcher.............................. | 350 | | | | | | | |
| Tumbler ............................ | 195 | | | | | | | |
| Juice Tumbler .................... | 180 | | | | | | | |
| Miniature Tumbler ............. | 350 | | | | | | | |
| Decanter w/stopper............. | 250 | | | | | | | |
| Wine................................. | 50 | | | | | | | |
| Bowls, Various Sizes............ | 60+ | | | | | | | |
| **JACOB'S LADDER** | | | | | | | | |
| Perfume............................. | 60 | | | | | | | |
| **JACOB'S LADDER VT. (U.S. GLASS)** | | | | | | | | |
| Rose Bowl.......................... | 90 | | | | | | | |
| **JARDINERE (FENTON)** | | | | | | | | |
| Various Shapes................... | 350 | 500 | 500 | 600 | | | | |
| **JELLY JAR** | | | | | | | | |
| Complete, Rare.................... | 65 | | | | | | | |

Jeweled Heart (Dugan)

Kingfisher and Variant (Australian)

Kittens (Fenton)

Kokomo (English)

| | M | A | G | B | PO | AO | Pas | Red |
|---|---|---|---|---|---|---|---|---|
| **JESTER'S CAP (DUGAN/DIAMOND)** | | | | | | | | |
| Vase | 150 | 195 | | | | | | |
| **JESTER'S CAP (WESTMORELAND)** | | | | | | | | |
| Vase | 140 | 275 | 250 | 200 | 265 | | 275CEB | |
| **JEWEL BOX** | | | | | | | | |
| Ink Well | 150 | | | | | | | |
| **JEWELED HEART (DUGAN)** | | | | | | | | |
| Bowl, 10" | | 95 | | | 135 | | | |
| Bowl, 5" | | 40 | | | 65 | | | |
| Pitcher, Rare | 900 | | | | | | | |
| Tumbler, Rare | 100 | | | | | | 575W | |
| Plate, 6" | 195 | | | | 250 | | | |
| **JEWELS (IMPERIAL — DUGAN)** | | | | | | | | |
| Candlesticks, Pair | 90 | 150 | 180 | 190 | | | 120CeB | 395 |
| Bowls, Various Sizes | | 50 | 150 | 185 | | | 80 | 350 |
| Hat Shape | | 65 | | | | | 90 | 300 |
| Vase | 100 | 150 | 150 | 175 | | | 195AM | 250 |
| Creamer or Sugar | | | | | | | 70 | 235 |
| **JOCKEY CLUB (NORTHWOOD)** | | | | | | | | |
| Bowl, 7" | | 600 | | | | | | |
| **KANGAROO (AUSTRALIAN)** | | | | | | | | |
| Bowl, 9½" | 500 | 650 | | | | | | |
| Bowl, 5" | 75 | 125 | | | | | | |
| **KEYHOLE (DUGAN)** | | | | | | | | |
| Exterior Pattern of Raindrops Bowls | | | | | | | | |
| **KEYSTONE COLONIAL (WESTMORELAND)** | | | | | | | | |
| Compote, 6¼" | | 295 | | | | | | |
| **KINGFISHER AND VARIANT (AUSTRALIAN)** | | | | | | | | |
| Bowl, 5" | 75 | 125 | | | | | | |
| Bowl, 9½" | 175 | 295 | | | | | | |
| **KING'S CROWN** | | | | | | | | |
| Stemmed Wine | 50 | | | | | | | |
| **KITTEN** | | | | | | | | |
| Miniature Paperweight, Rare | 250 | | | | | | | |
| **KITTENS** | | | | | | | | |
| Bottle | | | | | | | 65 | |
| **KITTENS (FENTON)** | | | | | | | | |
| Bowl, 4", Scarce | | | | 775 | | | 500AO | |
| Bowl, 2 Sides Up, Scarce | 175 | 500 | | 625 | | | 500LV | |
| Cup and Saucer, Scarce | 250 | | | 1,400 | | | | |
| Spooner, 2½", Rare | 175 | | | 450 | | | 250V | |
| Plate, 4½", Scarce | 175 | | | 500 | | | 275SM | |
| Cereal Bowl, Scarce | 275 | | | 700 | | | | |
| Vase or Toothpick holder, 3" | 175 | | | 400 | | | 300V | |
| Spittoon Whimsey, Rare | 1,200 | | | 1,600* | | | | |
| **KIWI (AUSTRALIAN)** | | | | | | | | |
| Bowl, 10", Rare | 350 | 1,100BA | | | | | | |
| **KNIGHT TEMPLAR (NORTHWOOD)** | | | | | | | | |
| Advertising Mug, Rare | 600 | | | | | | 700IB | |
| **KNOTTED BEADS (FENTON)** | | | | | | | | |
| Vase, 4"-12" | 30+ | | 40+ | 40+ | | | 85V | |
| **KOKOMO (ENGLISH)** | | | | | | | | |
| Rose Bowl, Ftd | 45 | | 60 | 50 | | | | |
| **KOOKABURRA AND VTS. (AUSTRALIAN)** | | | | | | | | |
| Bowl, 5" | 95 | 135 | | | | | | |
| Bowl, 10" | 180 | 350 | | | | | | |
| **LACY DEWDROP (WESTMORELAND)** | | | | | | | | |
| Pitcher | | | | | | | 650 | |
| Compote, Covered | | | | | | | 450 | |
| Bowl, Covered | | | | | | | 280 | |
| Banana Boat | | | | | | | 375 | |
| Tumbler | | | | | | | 275 | |
| Goblet | | | | | | | 180 | |
| Creamer | | | | | | | 160 | |
| Sugar | | | | | | | 180 | |
| (Note: All Items Listed Are in Pearl Carnival) | | | | | | | | |
| **LADY'S SLIPPER** | | | | | | | | |
| One Shape, Rare | 250 | | | | | | | |
| **LARGE KANGAROO (AUSTRALIAN)** | | | | | | | | |
| Bowl, 5" | 60 | 75 | | | | | | |
| Bowl, 10" | 295 | 500 | | | | | | |
| **LATE ENAMELED BLEEDING HEARTS** | | | | | | | | |
| Tumbler | 175 | | | | | | | |
| **LATE ENAMELED GRAPE** | | | | | | | | |
| Goblet | 90 | | | | | | | |

321

Lattice and Leaves

LBJ Hat

Leaf Rays (Dugan)

Leaf Swirl and Flower (Fenton)

| | M | A | G | B | PO | AO | Pas | Red |
|---|---|---|---|---|---|---|---|---|
| LATE ENAMELED STRAWBERRY | | | | | | | | |
| Tumbler, tall........................ | 175 | | | | | | | |
| LATE ENAMELED | | | | | | | | |
| LATE WATERLILY | | | | | | | | |
| Pitcher............................... | 50 | | | | | | | |
| Tumbler.............................. | 20 | | | | | | | |
| LATTICE (DUGAN) | | | | | | | | |
| Bowl, Various Sizes ............. | 60 | 70 | | | | | 85 | |
| LATTICE AND DAISY (DUGAN) | | | | | | | | |
| Bowl, 9".............................. | 60 | | | | | | | |
| Bowl, 5".............................. | 30 | | | | | | | |
| Pitcher............................... | 225 | | | 285 | | | 325 | |
| Tumbler.............................. | 30 | 60 | | 50 | | | 60 | |
| LATTICE AND GRAPE (FENTON) | | | | | | | | |
| Pitcher............................... | 260 | 425 | 485 | 410 | 2,200 | | 850W | |
| Tumbler ............................. | 38 | 45 | 55 | 40 | 500 | | 300W | |
| Spittoon Whimsey, Rare ...... | 2,600 | | | | | | | |
| LATTICE AND LEAVES | | | | | | | | |
| Vase, 9½"............................ | 275 | | | 295 | | | | |
| LATTICE AND POINTS (DUGAN) | | | | | | | | |
| Vase ................................... | 40 | 45 | | | | | 65W | |
| LATTICE AND PRISMS | | | | | | | | |
| Cologne w/stopper ............. | 65 | | | | | | | |
| LATTICE AND SPRAYS | | | | | | | | |
| Vase, 10½"........................... | 50 | | | | | | | |
| LATTICE HEART (ENGLISH) | | | | | | | | |
| Bowl, 10"............................. | 50 | 75 | | 70 | | | | |
| Bowl, 5".............................. | 30 | | | 40 | | | | |
| Compote.............................. | 60 | 90 | | 85 | | | | |
| LAUREL | | | | | | | | |
| Shade................................. | 40 | | | | | | 50 | |
| LAUREL BAND | | | | | | | | |
| Tumbler .............................. | 40 | | | | | | | |
| LAUREL AND GRAPE | | | | | | | | |
| Vase, 6" .............................. | 120 | | | | | | | |
| LAUREL LEAVES (IMPERIAL) | | | | | | | | |
| Plate.................................. | 40 | 55 | | | | | 60SM | |
| LBJ HAT | | | | | | | | |
| Ashtray ............................... | 35 | | | | | | | |
| LEA AND VT. (ENGLISH) | | | | | | | | |
| Bowl, Ftd............................ | 40 | | | | | | | |
| Pickle Dish, Handled ........... | 45 | | | | | | | |
| Creamer, Ftd ...................... | 45 | 50 | | | | | | |
| LEAF AND BEADS (NORTHWOOD-DUGAN) | | | | | | | | |
| Bowl, 9".............................. | 150 | 275 | 700 | | | 275 | | |
| Plate Whimsey ..................... | 495* | | | | | | | |
| Candy Dish, Ftd ................. | 80 | 110 | 115 | | | 575 | 425 | |
| Rose Bowl, Ftd .................... | 90 | 120 | 125 | 190 | | 450 | 500W | |
| Nut Bowl, Rare .................... | | | | | | 1,200 | | |
| (Note: Add 25% for Patterned Interior) | | | | | | | | |
| LEAF AND LITTLE FLOWERS (MILLERSBURG) | | | | | | | | |
| Compote, Miniature, Rare.... | 450 | 495 | 475 | | | | | |
| LEAF CHAIN (FENTON) | | | | | | | | |
| Bon-bon ............................. | 60 | 55 | 60 | 150 | | | | |
| Bowl, 7"–9" ......................... | 60 | 80 | 90 | 140 | | 1,400 | 145AQ | 1,250 |
| Plate, 7½" ........................... | 195 | 3,000 | 1,500 | 1,500 | | | | |
| Plate, 9¼" ........................... | 460 | 150 | 175 | 135 | | 2,350 | 225W | |
| LEAF COLUMN (NORTHWOOD) | | | | | | | | |
| Vase ................................... | 30 | 45 | 45 | | 150 | | 190IB | |
| Shade................................. | | | | | | | 90 | |
| LEAF RAYS (DUGAN) | | | | | | | | |
| Nappy, Either Exterior ......... | 30 | 40 | | 375 | 50 | | 60W | |
| LEAF SWIRL (WESTMORELAND) | | | | | | | | |
| Compote.............................. | 55 | 75 | | 65TL | | | 70AM | |
| LEAF SWIRL AND FLOWER (FENTON) | | | | | | | | |
| Vase ................................... | 55 | | | | | | 65W | |
| LEAF TIERS (FENTON) | | | | | | | | |
| Bowl, Ftd, 10"...................... | 60 | | | | | | | |
| Bowl, Ftd, 5"........................ | 30 | | | | | | | |
| Butter, Ftd........................... | 175 | | | | | | | |
| Sugar, Ftd .......................... | 90 | | | | | | | |
| Creamer, Spooner, Ftd......... | 85 | | | | | | | |
| Pitcher, Ftd, Rare ................ | 475 | 650 | 650 | 695 | | | | |
| Tumbler, Ftd, Rare .............. | 75 | 90 | 90 | 95 | | | | |
| Banana Bowl Whimsey ........ | 200 | | | | | | | |
| LEVERNE | | | | | | | | |
| Perfume.............................. | 40 | | | | | | | |
| LIBERTY BELL | | | | | | | | |
| Bank .................................. | 50 | | | | | | | |
| LIGHTNING FLOWER | | | | | | | | |
| Nappy, Rare .:..................... | 250 | | | | | | | |

Lined Lattice (Dugan)

Little Stars (Millersburg)

Loganberry (Imperial)

Lotus and Grape (Fenton)

| | M | A | G | B | PO | AO | Pas | Red |
|---|---|---|---|---|---|---|---|---|
| **LILY OF THE VALLEY (FENTON)** | | | | | | | | |
| Pitcher, Rare | | | | 3,900 | | | | |
| Tumbler, Rare | 700 | | | 260 | | | | |
| **LINED LATTICE (DUGAN)** | | | | | | | | |
| Vase, 5"-14" | 140 | 175 | 190 | 180 | 160 | | 275MAO | |
| **LINCOLN DRAPE** | | | | | | | | |
| Mini Lamp, rare | 1,000 | | | | | | | |
| **LION (FENTON)** | | | | | | | | |
| Bowl, 7", Scarce | 150 | | | 360 | | | | |
| Plate, 7½", Rare | 1,100 | | | | | | | |
| **LITTLE BARREL (IMPERIAL)** | | | | | | | | |
| One Shape | 175 | | 195 | | | | 210AM | |
| **LITTLE BEADS** | | | | | | | | |
| Bowl, 8" | 22 | | | | 45 | | | |
| Compote, Small | 30 | | | | 50 | 95 | 40AQ | |
| **LITTLE DAISIES (FENTON)** | | | | | | | | |
| Bowl, 8"–9½", Rare | 1,100 | | | 1,350 | | | | |
| **LITTLE DAISY** | | | | | | | | |
| Lamp, Complete, 8" | | | | | | | 500 | |
| **LITTLE DARLING** | | | | | | | | |
| Bottle | 60 | | | | | | | |
| **LITTLE FISHES (FENTON)** | | | | | | | | |
| Bowl, Flat or Ftd, 10" | 250 | | 340 | 365 | | | 1,100W | |
| Bowl Flat or Ftd, 5½", | 75 | 290 | 280 | 185 | | | 350W | |
| Plate, 10½", Rare | | | | 850 | | | 1,050W | |
| **LITTLE FLOWERS (FENTON)** | | | | | | | | |
| Bowl, 9¼" | 90 | 135 | 150 | 160 | | | 140AM | 11,000 |
| Bowl, 5½", Rare | 40 | 80 | 70 | 90 | | | 80V | |
| Plate, 7", Rare | 245 | | | | | | | |
| Plate, 10", Rare | 795 | | | | | | | |
| **LITTLE JEWEL** | | | | | | | | |
| Finger Lamp, Rare | 650 | | | | | | | |
| **LITTLE MERMAID** | | | | | | | | |
| One Shape | | | | | | | 90 | |
| **LITTLE OWL** | | | | | | | | |
| Hatpin, Rare | 450* | | 1,100 | 1,200 | | | 800LV | |
| **LITTLE STARS (MILLERSBURG)** | | | | | | | | |
| Bowl, 4", Rare | | 800 | 450 | | | | | |
| Bowl, 7", Scarce | 110 | 125 | 135 | 1,400 | | | 120CM | |
| Bowl, 9", Rare | 900 | 550 | 575 | | | | 400CM | |
| Bowl, 10½", Rare | 600 | 700 | 750 | | | | | |
| Plate, 7⅝", Rare | | | 1,200 | | | | | |
| **LITTLE SWAN** | | | | | | | | |
| Miniature, 2" | | | | | | | 75 | |
| **LOG** | | | | | | | | |
| Paperweight, 3" x 1¼", Rare | 150 | | | | | | | |
| **LOGANBERRY (IMPERIAL)** | | | | | | | | |
| Vase, Scarce | 225 | 525 | 395 | | | | 1,000AM | |
| Whimsey Vase | | 2,400 | | | | | | |
| **LONG HOBSTAR** | | | | | | | | |
| Bowl, 8½" | 45 | | | | | | | |
| Bowl, 10½" | 60 | | | | | | | |
| Compote | 65 | | | | | | | |
| Punch Bowl and Base | 125 | | | | | | 135CM | |
| **LONG HORN** | | | | | | | | |
| Wine | 60 | | | | | | | |
| **LONG LEAF (DUGAN)** | | | | | | | | |
| Bowl, Ftd | | | | | 165 | | | |
| **LONG PRISMS** | | | | | | | | |
| Hatpin | | 75 | | | | | | |
| **LONG THUMBPRINT (DUGAN)** | | | | | | | | |
| Vase, 7"-11" | 30 | 35 | 40 | 40 | 150 | | | |
| Bowl, 8¼" | 30 | 40 | | | | | | |
| Compote | 35 | 40 | 40 | | | | | |
| Creamer, Sugar, ea | 40 | | | | | | 50SM | |
| Butter | 70 | | | | | | | |
| **LOTUS AND GRAPE (FENTON)** | | | | | | | | |
| Absentee Bowl, Rare | | | | 1,750 | | | | |
| Bon-bon | 145 | 165 | 170 | 160 | | | 195AQ | 950 |
| Bowl, Flat, 7" | 50 | 50 | 55 | 60 | | | 600PeB | |
| Bowl, Ftd, 7" | 55 | 60 | | 70 | | | | |
| Plate, 9½", Rare | 295 | 2,800 | 2,100 | 1,500 | | | | |
| **LOTUS LAND (NORTHWOOD)** | | | | | | | | |
| Bon-bon | 1,500 | | | | | | | |
| **LOUISA (WESTMORELAND)** | | | | | | | | |
| Rose Bowl | 55 | 65 | 70 | 67 | | | 150HO | |
| Candy Dish, Ftd | 50 | 60 | 65 | | | | 80AQ | |
| Bowl, Ftd | | | 50 | 50RG | | | 70AQ | |
| Nut Bowl, Rare | | 350 | | | | | | |
| Plate, Ftd, 8", Rare | | 155 | | | | | 190AG | |
| Mini-Banana Boat (old only) | 40 | 65 | | | | | | |
| **LOVEBIRDS** | | | | | | | | |
| Bottle w/stopper | 575 | | | | | | | |
| **LOVELY (NORTHWOOD)** | | | | | | | | |
| Ftd. Bowl | | 750 | 900 | | | | | |

Luster Rose (Imperial)

Maize (Libby)

Mallard Duck

Maple Leaf (Dugan)

| | M | A | G | B | PO | AO | Pas | Red |
|---|---|---|---|---|---|---|---|---|
| **LUCILLE** | | | | | | | | |
| Pitcher, Rare | 1,200 | | | 1,300 | | | | |
| Tumbler, Rare | 750 | | | 800 | | | | |
| **LUCKY BANK** | | | | | | | | |
| One Shape | 40 | | | | | | | |
| **LUCKY BELL** | | | | | | | | |
| Bowl, 8¾", Rare | 80 | | | | | | | |
| **LUSTER** | | | | | | | | |
| Tumbler | 45 | | | | | | | |
| **LUSTRE AND CLEAR (FENTON)** | | | | | | | | |
| Fan Vase | 40 | | 60 | 55 | | | 90IG | |
| **LUSTRE AND CLEAR (IMPERIAL)** | | | | | | | | |
| Pitcher | 195 | | | | | | | |
| Creamer or Sugar | 40 | 65 | 150 | | | | 60 | |
| Bowl, 5" | 20 | | | | | | 30 | |
| Bowl, 10" | 40 | | | | | | 50 | |
| Shakers, pair | 70 | | | | | | | |
| Tumbler | 40 | | | | | | | |
| Butter Dish | 75 | | | | | | | |
| Console Set, 3 pcs. | 60 | | | | | | | 325 |
| **LUSTRE AND CLEAR (LIGHTOLIER)** | | | | | | | | |
| Shade | 45 | | | | | | | |
| **LUSTRE AND FLUTE (NORTHWOOD)** | | | | | | | | |
| Bowl, 5½" | 35 | 37 | 37 | | | | | |
| Bowl, 8" | 40 | 55 | 54 | | | | | |
| Bon-bon | | 60 | 60 | | | | | |
| Creamer or Sugar | 40 | 55 | 55 | | | | | |
| Hat | 30 | 40 | 40 | | | | | |
| Compote | | 50 | 45 | | | | | |
| Sherbet | 30 | | | | | | | |
| Nappy | 40 | 45 | 40 | | | | | |
| Punch Bowl and Base | 150 | 165 | 150 | | | | | |
| Cup | 15 | 25 | 20 | | | | | |
| **LUSTRE ROSE (IMPERIAL)** | | | | | | | | |
| Bowl, Flat, 7"–11" | 35 | 45 | 50 | | | | 60CM | |
| Bowl, Ftd, 9"–12" | 40 | 55 | 60 | | | | 75 | 3,200 |
| Fernery | 50 | 60 | 65 | 145 | | | 275AM | |
| Plate, 6"–9" | 58 | 70 | 75 | | | | 140AM | |
| Butter | 60 | 75 | 70 | | | | 100AM | |
| Sugar | 40 | 55 | 55 | | | | 80AM | |
| Creamer or Spooner | 40 | 55 | 55 | | | | 70AM | |
| Berry Bowl, 8"–9" | 40 | 40 | 48 | | | | 40 | |
| Berry Bowl, 5" | 20 | 25 | 30 | | | | 20 | |
| Pitcher | 85 | 100 | 110 | | | | 100AM | |
| Tumbler | 25 | 90 | 40 | | | | 50AM | |
| Milk Pitcher | 60 | | | | | | 120AM | |
| Plate Whimsey, Ftd | 50 | | | | | | 65CM | |
| **LUTZ (McKEE)** | | | | | | | | |
| Mug, Ftd | 60 | | | | | | | |
| **MAGNOLIA DRAPE** | | | | | | | | |
| Pitcher | 275 | | | | | | | |
| Tumbler | 55 | | | | | | | |
| **MAGPIE (AUSTRALIAN)** | | | | | | | | |
| Bowl, 6"-10" | 245 | 560 | | | | | | |
| **MAIZE (LIBBEY)** | | | | | | | | |
| Vase, Celery, Rare | | | | | | | 185CL | |
| Syrup, (cruet), Rare | | | | | | | 235CL | |
| **MAJESTIC (McKEE)** | | | | | | | | |
| Tumbler, Rare | 500 | | | | | | | |
| **MALAGA (DUGAN)** | | | | | | | | |
| Bowl, 9" Scarce | 160 | 185 | | | | | | |
| Plate, 10", Rare | | 650 | | | | | 375 | |
| **MALLARD DUCK** | | | | | | | | |
| One Shape | | | | | | | 600* | |
| **MANHATTAN (U.S. GLASS)** | | | | | | | | |
| Decanter | 250* | | | | | | | |
| Wine | 40* | | | | | | | |
| **MANY FRUITS (DUGAN)** | | | | | | | | |
| Punch Bowl w/base | 450 | 900 | | | | | 1,400W | |
| Cup | 25 | 30 | 40 | 45 | | | 60W | |
| **MANY PRISMS** | | | | | | | | |
| Perfume w/stopper | 75 | | | | | | | |
| **MANY STARS (MILLERSBURG)** | | | | | | | | |
| Bowl, Ruffled, 9", Scarce | 475 | 675 | 850 | 2,700 | | | 1,850V | |
| Bowl, Round, 9½", Rare | 500 | 1,000 | 900 | 2,800 | | | | |
| Tri-cornered Bowl, Rare | | 1,650 | | | | | | |
| **MAPLE LEAF (DUGAN)** | | | | | | | | |
| Bowl, Stemmed, 9" | 70 | 115 | | 95 | | | | |
| Bowl, Stemmed, 4½" | 30 | 35 | 50 | 30 | | | | |
| Butter | 110 | 130 | | 120 | | | | |
| Sugar | 75 | 85 | | 75 | | | | |
| Creamer or Spooner | 50 | 65 | | 60 | | | | |
| Pitcher | 185 | 350 | | 300 | | | | |
| Tumbler | 30 | 50 | | 40 | | | | |

Martha

Mayflower

Mexican Bell

Miniature Loving Cup

| | M | A | G | B | PO | AO | Pas | Red |
|---|---|---|---|---|---|---|---|---|
| **MARIE (FENTON)** | | | | | | | | |
| Rustic Vase Interior | | | | | | | | |
| Base Pattern | | | | | | | | |
| **MARILYN (MILLERSBURG)** | | | | | | | | |
| Pitcher, Rare...................... | 750 | 1,000 | 1,350 | | | | | |
| Tumbler, Rare ................... | 150 | 275 | 400 | | | | | |
| **MARTEC (McKEE)** | | | | | | | | |
| Tumbler, Rare ................... | 500 | | | | | | | |
| **MARTHA** | | | | | | | | |
| Compote, 7½" ...................... | 295 | | | | | | | |
| **MARY ANN (DUGAN)** | | | | | | | | |
| Vase, 2 Varieties, 7" ............ | 140 | 275 | | | | | | |
| Loving Cup, 3 Handles, | | | | | | | | |
| Rare ..................................... | 800 | | | | | | | |
| **MASSACHUSETTS (U.S. GLASS)** | | | | | | | | |
| Vase ..................................... | 175* | | | | | | | |
| **MAYAN (MILLERSBURG)** | | | | | | | | |
| Bowl, 8½"-10" ...................... | 2,500* | | 125 | | | | | |
| **MAY BASKET (ENGLISH)** | | | | | | | | |
| Basket, 7½" ......................... | 40 | | 95 | | | | | |
| Bowl, 9", Rare..................... | | | 160 | | | | | |
| **MAYFLOWER** | | | | | | | | |
| Bowl, 7½" ............................ | 30 | 40 | | | 160 | | 50 | |
| Compote............................... | 40 | 50 | | | | | 60 | |
| Shade.................................... | 35 | | | | | | | |
| Hat....................................... | 40 | 50 | | | 150 | | 60 | |
| **MAYFLOWER (MILLERSBURG)** | | | | | | | | |
| Exterior Pattern on Grape | | | | | | | | |
| Leaves Bowls | | | | | | | | |
| **MAYPOLE** | | | | | | | | |
| Vase, 6¼".............................. | 45 | 55 | 60 | | | | | |
| **MEANDER (NORTHWOOD)** | | | | | | | | |
| (Exterior Pattern Only) | | | | | | | | |
| **MELON RIB (IMPERIAL)** | | | | | | | | |
| Candy Jar w/lid .................. | 30 | | | | | | | |
| Pitcher................................ | 60 | | | | | | | |
| Tumbler .............................. | 20 | | | | | | | |
| Powder Jar w/lid ................ | 35 | | | | | | | |
| Shakers, Pair....................... | 35 | | | | | | | |
| Decanter ............................. | 90 | | | | | | | |
| **MEMPHIS (NORTHWOOD)** | | | | | | | | |
| Bowl, 10"............................. | 100 | 400 | 200 | | | | | |
| Bowl, 5"............................... | 35 | 45 | 50 | | | | | |
| Fruit Bowl w/base................ | 450 | 550 | 600 | 2,300 | | | 3,750IG | |
| Punch Bowl w/base.............. | 400 | 500 | 575 | | | | 5,600IB | |
| Cup...................................... | 30 | 40 | 45 | | | | 110IB | |
| Sugar or Creamer ................ | | 70 | | | | | | |
| **MEXICAN BELL** | | | | | | | | |
| Goblet, Flashed .................... | 40 | | | | | | | |
| **MIKADO (FENTON)** | | | | | | | | |
| Compote, Large ................... | 295 | 1,200 | 2,400 | 400 | | | 750W | 7,000* |
| **MILADY (FENTON)** | | | | | | | | |
| Pitcher................................. | 500 | 700 | 800 | 975 | | | | |
| Tumbler ............................... | 95 | 140 | 150 | 160 | | | | |
| **MILLER FURNITURE (FENTON)** | | | | | | | | |
| Open Edge Basket ............... | 50 | | 65 | | | | | |
| Hat....................................... | 40 | | 50 | | | | | |
| **MINIATURE BATHTUB** | | | | | | | | |
| One Shape............................ | 150 | | | | | | | |
| **MINIATURE BELL** | | | | | | | | |
| Paperweight, 2½" ................. | 60 | | | | | | | |
| **MINIATURE CANDELABRA** | | | | | | | | |
| **(CAMBRIDGE)** | | | | | | | | |
| One Size.............................. | 250 | | | | | | | |
| **MINIATURE FLOWER BASKET** | | | | | | | | |
| **(WESTMORELAND)** | | | | | | | | |
| One Shape............................ | 75 | | | | 150 | | 300BO | |
| **MINIATURE HOBNAIL** | | | | | | | | |
| Cordial Set, Rare ................ | 1,250 | | | | | | | |
| **MINIATURE INTAGLIO** | | | | | | | | |
| **(WESTMORELAND)** | | | | | | | | |
| Nut Cup, Stemmed, Rare..... | 585 | | | | | | 700W | |
| (Note: Also Known as "Wild | | | | | | | | |
| Rose Wreath") | | | | | | | | |
| **MINIATURE LOVING CUP** | | | | | | | | |
| One Size.............................. | 60 | | | | | | | |
| **MINIATURE ROSE BOWL** | | | | | | | | |
| One Shape, 4" ...................... | 30 | | | | | | | |
| **MINIATURE SANDAL** | | | | | | | | |
| One Shape............................ | 200 | | | | | | | |
| **MINIATURE SHELL** | | | | | | | | |
| Candleholder, Each ............. | | | | | | | 75CL | |
| **MINIATURE URN** | | | | | | | | |
| One Shape............................ | 40 | | | | | | | |
| **MINNESOTA (US GLASS)** | | | | | | | | |
| Mug...................................... | 100 | | | | | | | |
| Toothpick Holder ................ | 60 | | | | | | | |

Morning Glory (Imperial)

Moxie

Mt. Gambier

Multi-fruits and Flowers
(Millersburg)

| | M | A | G | B | PO | AO | Pas | Red |
|---|---|---|---|---|---|---|---|---|
| **MIRRORED LOTUS (FENTON)** | | | | | | | | |
| Bon-bon | 85 | | 100 | 95 | | | | |
| Bowl, 7"–8½" | 60 | | 90 | 80 | | | 900CeB | |
| Plate, 7½", Rare | 400 | | | 550 | | | 3,000CeB | |
| Rose Bowl, Rare | 375 | | | 480 | | | 1,100W | |
| **MIRRORED PEACOCKS** | | | | | | | | |
| Tumbler, Rare | 400 | | | | | | | |
| **MITERED DIAMOND AND PLEATS (ENGLISH)** | | | | | | | | |
| Bowl, 4½" | 25 | | | 30 | | | | |
| Bowl, 8½", Shallow | 40 | | | 45 | | | | |
| **MITERED OVALS (MILLERSBURG)** | | | | | | | | |
| Vase, Rare | 7,000 | 7,500 | 6,700 | | | | | |
| **MODERNE** | | | | | | | | |
| Cup | 35 | | | | | | | |
| Saucer | 30 | | | | | | | |
| **MOIRE BEETLE** | | | | | | | | |
| Hatpin | | 75 | | | | | | |
| **MOON AND STAR (WESTMORELAND)** | | | | | | | | |
| Compote (Pearl Carnival) | | | | | | | 385 | |
| **MOONPRINT (ENGLISH)** | | | | | | | | |
| Bowl, 8¼" | 45 | | | | | | | |
| Candlesticks, Rare, Each | 50 | | | | | | | |
| Compote | 50 | | | | | | | |
| Jar w/lid | 60 | | 85 | | | | | |
| Vase | 50 | | | | | | | |
| Cheese Keeper, Rare | 145 | | | | | | | |
| Sugar, Stemmed | 50 | | | | | | | |
| Banana Boat, Rare | 135 | | | | | | | |
| Creamer | 45 | | | | | | | |
| Butter | 100 | | | | | | | |
| Bowl, 14" | 80 | | | | | | | |
| Milk Pitcher, Scarce | 150 | | | | | | | |
| **MORNING GLORY (IMPERIAL)** | | | | | | | | |
| Vase, 5"-16" | 150+ | 190+ | 180+ | | | | 125SM | |
| Funeral Vase | 185 | 300 | 350 | | | | 180SM | |
| **MORNING GLORY (MILLERSBURG)** | | | | | | | | |
| Pitcher, Rare | 9,100 | 9,400 | 10,000 | | | | | |
| Tumbler, Rare | 1,100 | 1,400 | 1,000 | | | | | |
| **MOXIE** | | | | | | | | |
| Bottle, Rare | | | | | | | 90 | |
| **MT. GAMBIER** | | | | | | | | |
| Mug | | | | | | | | |
| **MULTI-FRUITS AND FLOWERS (MILLERSBURG)** | | | | | | | | |
| Dessert, Stemmed, Rare | | 1,050 | 1,050 | | | | | |
| Punch Bowl w/base, Rare | 2,000 | 2,300 | 2,600 | 3,700 | | | | |
| Cup, Rare | 50 | 75 | 90 | 175 | | | | |
| Pitcher, Rare (Either Base) | 3,400 | 3,600 | 4,000* | | | | | |
| Tumbler, Rare | 900 | 1,250 | 1,400 | | | | | |
| **MUSCADINE** | | | | | | | | |
| Tumbler, Rare | 450 | | | | | | | |
| **MY LADY** | | | | | | | | |
| Powder Jar w/lid | 150 | | | | | | | |
| **MYSTERY** | | | | | | | | |
| Perfume | 40 | | | | | | | |
| **MYSTIC (CAMBRIDGE)** | | | | | | | | |
| Vase, Ftd, Rare | 165 | | | | | | | |
| **NAPOLEON** | | | | | | | | |
| Bottle | | | | | | | 85 | |
| **NARCISSUS AND RIBBON (FENTON)** | | | | | | | | |
| Wine Bottle w/stopper, Rare | 1,150 | | | | | | | |
| **NAUTILUS (DUGAN-NORTHWOOD)** | | | | | | | | |
| Lettered, Rare | | 285 | | | 250 | | | |
| Unlettered | | 200 | | | 170 | | | |
| Giant Compote, Rare | 3,000* | | | | | | | |
| Vase Whimsey, Rare | 1,750* | 1,750* | | | | | | |
| **NEAR CUT (CAMBRIDGE)** | | | | | | | | |
| Decanter w/stopper, Rare | | | 3,500 | | | | | |
| **NEAR CUT SOUVENIR (CAMBRIDGE)** | | | | | | | | |
| Mug, Rare | 190 | | | | | | | |
| Tumbler, Rare | 260 | | | | | | | |
| **NEAR CUT WREATH (MILLERSBURG)** | | | | | | | | |
| Exterior Pattern Only | | | | | | | | |
| **NELL (HIGBEE)** | | | | | | | | |
| Mug | 75 | | | | | | | |
| **NESTING SWAN (MILLERSBURG)** | | | | | | | | |
| Rose Bowl, Rare | 3,000 | | | | | | | |

326

| | M | A | G | B | PO | AO | Pas | Red |
|---|---|---|---|---|---|---|---|---|
| Bowl, Scarce, Round or Ruffled, 10" | 250 | 395 | 500 | 2,800* | | | 2,650V* | |
| Spittoon Whimsey, Rare | | 5,000* | 5,000* | | | | | |
| Bowl, Tri-Cornered, Rare | 500 | 1,200 | 1,200 | 3,500 | | | 750CM | |
| **NEW ORLEANS SHRINE (U.S. GLASS)** | | | | | | | | |
| Champagne | | | | | | | 150CL | |
| **NIGHT STARS (MILLERSBURG)** | | | | | | | | |
| Bon-bon, Rare | 800 | 600 | 500 | | | | | |
| Card Tray, Rare | | 700 | | | | | | |
| Nappy, Tri-Cornered, Very Rare | | 1,000 | | | | | | |
| **NIPPON (NORTHWOOD)** | | | | | | | | |
| Bowl, 8½" | 250 | 220 | 325 | 350 | | | 850IG | |
| Plate, 9" | 400 | 550 | 650 | 700 | | | 1,350W | |
| **NOLA (SCANDANAVIAN)** | | | | | | | | |
| Squat pitcher | 350* | | 450* | | | | | |
| Tumbler, 2 Shapes | 150* | | 180* | | | | | |
| **NORRIS N. SMITH (NORTHWOOD)** | | | | | | | | |
| Advertising Plate, 5¾" | | 1,800 | | | | | | |
| **NORTHERN STAR (FENTON)** | | | | | | | | |
| Card Tray, 6" | 40 | | | | | | | |
| Bowl, 6"-7" | 30 | | | | | | | |
| Plate, 6½", Rare | 90 | | | | | | | |
| **NORTHWOOD JACK-IN THE PULPIT** | | | | | | | | |
| Vase, Various Sizes | 40 | 50 | 45 | 50 | 90 | 225 | 85 | |
| **NORTHWOOD'S NEARCUT** | | | | | | | | |
| Compote | 85 | 130 | | | | | | |
| Goblet, Rare | 195 | 140 | | | | | | |
| Pitcher, Rare | 1,500* | | | | | | | |
| **NORTHWOOD'S POPPY** | | | | | | | | |
| Bowl, 7"-8¾" | 100 | 135 | | 140 | 350* | 595 | | |
| Pickle Dish, Oval | 180 | 175 | 225 | 275 | | 750 | 450IB | |
| Tray, Oval, Rare | | 300 | | 375 | | | | |
| **NORTHWOOD'S REGAL (NORTHWOOD)** | | | | | | | | |
| Sauce | | | | | 250 | | | |
| **NU-ART (HOMESTEAD) (IMPERAL)** | | | | | | | | |
| Plate, Scarce | 850 | 950 | 3,000 | 5,500 | | | 1,200W | |
| Shade | 90 | | | | | | | |
| **NU-ART CHRYSANTHEMUM (IMPERIAL)** | | | | | | | | |
| Plate, Rare | 950 | 1,100 | 3,800 | 5,400 | | | 1,500AM* | |
| **NU-ART DRAPE (IMPERIAL)** | | | | | | | | |
| Shade | 60 | | | | | | | |
| **NUGGET BEADS** | | | | | | | | |
| Beads | | 125 | | | | | | |
| **NUMBER 270 (WESTMORELAND)** | | | | | | | | |
| Compote | | 90 | 140RG | | 75MMG | | 140AQ | |
| **NUMBER 600 (FOSTORIA)** | | | | | | | | |
| Toothpick Holder | 45 | | | | | | | |
| **NUMBER 2176 (SOWERBY)** | | | | | | | | |
| Lemon Squeezer | 55 | | | | | | | |
| **NUMBER 2351 (CAMBRIDGE)** | | | | | | | | |
| Bowl, 9", Rare | | | 350* | | | | | |
| Punch Cup | | 65 | 65 | | | | | |
| Punch Bowl/Base, Very Rare | 1,500* | | | | | | | |
| **OCTAGON (IMPERIAL)** | | | | | | | | |
| Bowl, 8½" | 40 | | 50 | | | | 80 | |
| Bowl, 4½" | | 35 | | | | | | |
| Goblet | 65 | | | | | | | |
| Butter | 90 | | 475 | | | | | |
| Sugar | 60 | | 75 | | | | | |
| Creamer or Spooner | 55 | | 65 | | | | | |
| Toothpick Holder, Rare | 170 | 485 | | | | | | |
| Pitcher | 120 | 400 | 240 | | | | 200 | |
| Tumbler | 30 | 40 | 35 | | | | 45 | |
| Decanter, Complete | 90 | 200 | 750 | | | | | |
| Wine | 25 | 40 | 70 | | | | | |
| Vase, Rare | 90 | 140 | 125 | | | | | |
| Milk Pitcher, Scarce | 150 | 200 | 170 | | | | 150 | |
| Cordial | | | | | | | 70 | |
| Shakers, Pair, Old Only | | 500 | | | | | | |
| **OCTET (NORTHWOOD)** | | | | | | | | |
| Bowl, 8½" | 100 | 150 | | | | | 190W | |
| **O'HARA (LOOP)** | | | | | | | | |
| Pitcher | 120 | | | | | | | |
| Goblet | 25 | | | | | | | |
| **OHIO STAR (MILLERSBURG)** | | | | | | | | |
| Vase, Rare | 1,300 | 1,500 | 1,400 | | | 13,000* | 4,000W* | |
| Compote, Rare | 1,100 | | | | | | | |
| Vase Whimsey, Rare | | 1,800* | 1,800* | | | 12,000* | | |
| Plate, Tri-cornered, Rare | 6,000* | | | | | | | |

New Orleans Shrine (U.S. Glass)

Night Stars (Millersburg)

Nu-Art (Homestead) (Imperial)

Nu-Art Drape (Imperial)

| | M | A | G | B | PO | AO | Pas | Red |
|---|---|---|---|---|---|---|---|---|
| **OKLAHOMA (MEXICAN)** | | | | | | | | |
| Decanter | 850 | | | | | | | |
| Tumble-Up, Complete | 200 | | | | | | | |
| Pitcher, Rare | 500* | | | | | | | |
| Tumbler, Rare | 500 | | | | | | | |
| Shade, Various Sizes, Rare | | | | | | | 95CL | |
| **OLYMPIC (MILLERSBURG)** | | | | | | | | |
| Compote, Small, Rare | | 4,600* | 4,500* | | | | | |
| **OLYMPUS** | | | | | | | | |
| Shade | 60 | | | | | | | |
| **OMNIBUS** | | | | | | | | |
| Tumbler, Rare | 275 | | 795 | 795 | | | | |
| **OPEN FLOWER (DUGAN)** | | | | | | | | |
| Bowl, Flat or Ftd, 7" | 35 | 45 | 50 | | 85 | | | |
| **OPEN ROSE (IMPERIAL)** | | | | | | | | |
| Fruit Bowl, 7"-10" | 40 | 65 | | | | | 70 | |
| Bowl, Ftd, 9"-12" | 65 | 45 | | | | | 95 | |
| Bowl, Flat, 9" | 45 | 40 | | 50 | | | 165SM | |
| Bowl, Flat, 5½" | 20 | 40 | | | | | 45 | |
| Plate, 9" | 75 | 180 | 185 | | | | 250LG | |
| Rose Bowl | 50 | 60 | 85 | | | | 110TL | |
| **OPTIC (IMPERIAL)** | | | | | | | | |
| Bowl, 9" | | 75 | | | | | | |
| Bowl, 6" | | 50 | | | | | | |
| **OPTIC AND BUTTONS (IMPERIAL)** | | | | | | | | |
| Bowls, 5"-8" | 30 | | | | | | | |
| Bowl, Handled, 12" | 45 | | | | | | | |
| Pitcher, Small, Rare | 185 | | | | | | | |
| Plate, 10½" | 70 | | | | | | | |
| Salt Cup | 850 | | | | | | | |
| Tumbler, 2 Shapes, Rare | 110 | | | | | | | |
| Goblet | 60 | | | | | | | |
| Cup and saucer, Rare | 185 | | | | | | | |
| **OPTIC FLUTE (IMPERIAL)** | | | | | | | | |
| Bowl, 10" | 45 | 80 | | | | | 55SM | |
| Bowl, 5" | 30 | 45 | | | | | 30SM | |
| Compote | 55 | | | | | | | |
| **OPTIC VT.** | | | | | | | | |
| Bowl 6" | | 65 | | | | | | |
| **OPTIC 66 (FOSTORIA)** | | | | | | | | |
| Goblet | 47 | | | | | | | |
| **ORANGE PEEL (WESTMORELAND)** | | | | | | | | |
| Punch Bowl w/base | 200 | 225 | | | | | 225TL | |
| Cup | 20 | 30 | | | | | 35TL | |
| Custard Cup, Scarce | 25 | | | | | | | |
| Dessert, Stemmed, Scarce | 45 | 65 | 70RG | | | | 75TL | |
| **ORANGE TREE (FENTON)** | | | | | | | | |
| Butter | 400 | | | 350 | | | 340W | |
| Bowl, Flat, 8"-10" | 55 | | 325 | 95 | | | 500IM | 3,450 |
| Bowl, Ftd, 9"-11" | 100 | | 140 | 130 | | | 120W | |
| Ice Cream, w/stem, Small | 30 | | | 35 | | | | |
| Bowl, Ftd, 5½" | 40 | | 45 | 48 | | | 900CeB | |
| Breakfast Set, 2 Pieces | 180 | | 230 | 220 | | | 250W | |
| Plate, 8"-9½" | 335 | | 2,600 | 450 | | | 400CM | |
| Powder Jar w/lid | 175 | | 500 | 95 | | | 130W | |
| Mug, 2 Sizes | 90 | 80 | 800 | 130 | | | | 650 |
| Loving Cup | 260 | 450 | 550 | 350 | 4,500* | 5,500* | 500W | |
| Punch Bowl w/base | 200 | | 300 | 275 | 1,000MO* | | 400W | |
| Cup | 30 | | 36 | 32 | | | 38W | |
| Compote, Small | 50 | 60 | 90 | 50 | | | 450TL | |
| Goblet, Large | 90 | | | | | | 85AQ | |
| Wine | 25 | | 295 | 150 | 75 | | 70SM | |
| Sugar | 65 | | | 75 | | | 150W | |
| Pitcher, 2 Designs | 220 | | | 325 | | | 9,000LO* | |
| Tumbler | 35 | | | 42 | | | 75W | |
| Creamer or Spooner | 45 | | | 65 | | | 120W | |
| Rose Bowl | 55 | 65 | 70 | 65 | | | 275W | 1,900 |
| Hatpin Holder | 425 | | 350 | 290 | | | 300W | |
| Hatpin Holder Whimsey, Rare | | | | 2,600 | | | | |
| Centerpiece Bowl, Rare | 900 | | 1,200 | 1,600 | | | | |
| Cruet Whimsey, Rare | | | | 1,250 | | | | |
| Orange Bowl Whimsey, 12" | | | 650 | | | | | |
| Vase, Whimsey, Rare | | | | 2,300* | | | | |
| **ORANGE TREE AND SCROLL (FENTON)** | | | | | | | | |
| Pitcher | 495 | | 600 | 900 | | | | |
| Tumbler | 50 | | 85 | 90 | | | | |
| **ORANGE TREE ORCHARD (FENTON)** | | | | | | | | |
| Pitcher | 400 | 500 | 550 | 600 | | | 650W | |
| Tumbler | 40 | 50 | 55 | 90 | | | 120W | |
| **ORCHID** | | | | | | | | |
| Hatpin, rare | | 950 | | | | | | |

Omnibus

Optic and Buttons (Imperial)

Orange Tree (Fenton)

Orange Tree Orchard (Fenton)

Ostrich (Australian)

Painted Pansy

Palm Beach (U.S. Glass)

Panelled Tree Trunk (Dugan)

| | M | A | G | B | PO | AO | Pas | Red |
|---|---|---|---|---|---|---|---|---|
| **ORIENTAL POPPY (NORTHWOOD)** | | | | | | | | |
| Bowl, Rare, 11" | 1,700* | | | | | | | |
| Pitcher | 500 | 800 | 950 | 3,200 | | | 1,000W | |
| Tumbler | 40 | 55 | 55 | 350 | | | 140W | |
| **OSTRICH (AUSTRALIAN)** | | | | | | | | |
| Compote, Large, Rare | 150 | 200 | | | | | | |
| Cake Stand, Rare | 275 | 350 | | | | | | |
| **OVAL AND ROUND (IMPERIAL)** | | | | | | | | |
| Plate, 10" | 65 | 75 | 80 | | | | 90AM | |
| Bowl, 4" | 20 | 30 | 30 | | | | | |
| Bowl, 7" | 30 | 36 | 40 | | | | 45AM | |
| Bowl, 9" | 35 | 45 | 50 | | | | 60AM | |
| **OVAL PRISMS** | | | | | | | | |
| Hatpin | | 75 | | | | | | |
| **OVAL STAR AND FAN (JENKINS)** | | | | | | | | |
| Rose Bowl | 50 | 60 | | | | | | |
| **OWL BANK** | | | | | | | | |
| One Size | 40 | | | | | | | |
| **OWL BOTTLE** | | | | | | | | |
| One Shape | | | | | | | 65CL | |
| **OXFORD** | | | | | | | | |
| Mustard Pot w/lid | 70 | | | | | | | |
| **PACIFICA (U.S. GLASS)** | | | | | | | | |
| Tumbler | 400 | | | | | | | |
| **PAINTED CASTLE** | | | | | | | | |
| Shade | 65 | | | | | | | |
| **PAINTED PANSY** | | | | | | | | |
| Fan Vase | 50 | | | | | | | |
| **PALM BEACH (U.S. GLASS)** | | | | | | | | |
| Vase Whimsey | 785 | 125 | | | | | 140W | |
| Bowl, 9" | 55 | | | | | | 75 | |
| Bowl, 5" | 30 | | | | | | 90AM | |
| Butter | 120 | | | | | | 250 | |
| Creamer, Spooner, Sugar, Ea. | 75 | | | | | | 125 | |
| Pitcher | 300 | | | | | | 600W | |
| Tumbler | 180 | | | | | | 140W | |
| Plate, 9", Rare | 175 | 250 | | | | | 225 | |
| Banana Bowl | 100 | 200 | | | | | 150AM | |
| Rose Bowl Whimsey, Rare | 90 | | | | | | 300W | |
| **PALM LEAF** | | | | | | | | |
| Handgrip plate, 6" | 225 | | | | | | | |
| **PANAMA (U.S. GLASS)** | | | | | | | | |
| Rose Bowl | 575 | | | | | | | |
| Spittoon | 750 | | | | | | | |
| Goblet, Rare | 135 | | | | | | | |
| **PANELLED CRUET** | | | | | | | | |
| One Size | 95 | | | | | | | |
| **PANELLED DANDELION (FENTON)** | | | | | | | | |
| Pitcher | 400 | 700 | 800 | 575 | | | | |
| Tumbler | 50 | 55 | 60 | 70 | | | | |
| Candle Lamp Whimsey, Rare. | | | | 3,200 | | | | |
| Vase Whimsey, Rare | | | | 3,500* | | | | |
| **PANELLED DIAMOND AND BOWS (FENTON)** | | | | | | | | |
| Vase, 7"–14" | 35 | 140 | 140 | 140 | 185 | | 175 | |
| Also called "Boggy Bayou" | | | | | | | | |
| **PANELLED HOBNAIL (DUGAN)** | | | | | | | | |
| Vase, 5"–10" | 40 | 60 | 75 | | 85 | | 95 | |
| **PANELLED PALM (U.S. GLASS)** | | | | | | | | |
| Mug, Rare | 95 | | | | | | | |
| **PANELLED PRISM** | | | | | | | | |
| Jam Jar w/lid | 55 | | | | | | | |
| **PANELLED SMOCKING** | | | | | | | | |
| Sugar | 50 | | | | | | | |
| **PANELLED SWIRL** | | | | | | | | |
| Rose Bowl | 65 | | | | | | | |
| **PANELLED THISTLE (HIGBEE)** | | | | | | | | |
| Tumbler | 100 | | | | | | | |
| **PANELLED TREE TRUNK (DUGAN)** | | | | | | | | |
| Vase, 7"–12", Rare | 70 | 90 | 110 | | 150 | | | |
| **PANELS AND BALL (FENTON)** | | | | | | | | |
| Bowl, 11" | 60 | | | | | | 175W | |
| Also Called "Persian Pearl" | | | | | | | | |
| **PANELS AND BEADS** | | | | | | | | |
| Shade | | | | | | | 55VO | |
| **PANSY (IMPERIAL)** | | | | | | | | |
| Bowl, 8¼" | 40 | 195 | 100 | 265 | | | 80AQ | |
| Creamer or Sugar | 25 | 40 | 45 | | | | 50SM | |
| Dresser Tray | 60 | 90 | 80 | | | | 100SM | |
| Pickle Dish, Oval | 30 | 50 | 40 | 195 | | | 60SM | |
| Nappy, Old Only | 20 | | 27 | | | | | |
| Plate, Ruffled, Rare | 80 | 195 | 120 | | | | 100SM | |

Parlor Panels

Parquet

Peacock (Millersburg)

Peacock and Urn and Vts.
(Millersburg)

| | M | A | G | B | PO | AO | Pas | Red |
|---|---|---|---|---|---|---|---|---|
| **PANTHER (FENTON)** | | | | | | | | |
| Bowl, Ftd, 10"........... | 135 | 340 | 900 | 450 | | 5,500NG | 780W | |
| Bowl, Ftd, 5"................. | 55 | 225 | 400 | 150 | | | 350W | 1,450 |
| Whimsey Bowl, 10½"........... | 950 | | | 1,000 | | | | |
| **PAPERWEIGHT** | | | | | | | | |
| Flower–Shaped, | | | | | | | | |
| Rare ................. | | | | | | | 200 | |
| **PARLOR** | | | | | | | | |
| Ashtray ................. | | | | 95 | | | | |
| **PARLOR PANELS** | | | | | | | | |
| Vase, 4"–11" ................ | 50 | 190 | 250 | 2000 | | | 450SM | |
| **PARQUET** | | | | | | | | |
| Creamer ................ | 70 | | | | | | | |
| Sugar ........................ | 80 | | | | | | | |
| **PASTEL HAT** | | | | | | | | |
| Various Sizes................ | 50+ | | | | | | 50+ | |
| **PASTEL PANELS (IMPERIAL)** | | | | | | | | |
| Pitcher................ | | | | | | | 300 | |
| Tumbler ................. | | | | | | | 75 | |
| Mug, Stemmed ................... | | | | | | | 90 | |
| Creamer or Sugar .............. | | | | | | | 65 | |
| **PEACH (NORTHWOOD)** | | | | | | | | |
| Bowl, 9" ................ | | | | | | | 150W | |
| Bowl, 5" ................ | | | | | | | 50W | |
| Butter ................ | | | | | | | 275W | |
| Creamer, Sugar, or | | | | | | | | |
| Spooner, ea ................ | 275* | | | | | | 150W | |
| Pitcher................ | | | | 650 | | | 775W | |
| Tumbler ................ | | | | 85EB | | | 175W | |
| **PEACH AND PEAR (DUGAN)** | | | | | | | | |
| Banana Bowl ................ | 90 | 145 | | | | | | |
| **PEACH BLOSSOM** | | | | | | | | |
| Bowl, 7½" ................ | 60 | 75 | | | | | | |
| **PEACHES** | | | | | | | | |
| Wine Bottle................ | 45 | | | | | | | |
| **PEACOCK (MILLERSBURG)** | | | | | | | | |
| Bowl, 9" ................ | 375 | 550 | 500 | | | | 650CM | |
| Bowl, 5" ................ | 90 | 135 | 240 | 1,000 | | | | |
| Bowl, Vt, 7½" Rare ........... | 500 | 500 | 450 | | | | | |
| Bowl, Vt, 6" Rare ................ | | 150 | | | | | | |
| Ice Cream Bowl, 5" ............. | 60 | 190 | 600 | 390 | | | | |
| Plate, 6", Rare.................... | 900 | 800 | | | | | | |
| Spittoon Whimsey, Rare ...... | 5,600 | 7,000 | | | | | | |
| Proof Whimsey, Rare ........... | 300 | 270 | 300 | | | | | |
| Rose Bowl Whimsey, Rare.... | | 4,600 | | | | | | |
| Bowl, 10", Ice Cream, Rare .. | 500 | 1,000 | 1,000 | | | | | |
| Banana Bowl, Rare.............. | | 3,500 | | | | | | |
| **PEACOCK AND DAHLIA (FENTON)** | | | | | | | | |
| Bowl, 7½" ................ | 50 | | 125 | 100 | | | 150W | |
| Plate, 8½", Rare ................ | 450 | | | 585 | | | | |
| **PEACOCK AND GRAPE (FENTON)** | | | | | | | | |
| Bow, Flat or Ftd, 7¾"–8¾" .... | 50 | 350 | 275 | 150 | 900 | | 450V | 1,700 |
| Plate, 9" (Either Base), Rare. | 550 | 425 | 1,200 | 1,700 | | | 395 | |
| **PEACOCK AND URN (FENTON)** | | | | | | | | |
| Bowl, 8½" ................ | 150 | 325 | 300 | 260 | | | | |
| Plate, 9"................ | 650 | 500 | 900 | 800 | | | 550W | |
| Compote................ | 55 | 90 | 190 | 100 | | | 125W | |
| Goblet, Rare ................ | 70 | 100 | | 85 | | | 110W | |
| **PEACOCK AND URN (NORTHWOOD)** | | | | | | | | |
| Bowl, 9" ................ | 200 | 475 | 650 | | | 500LV | 500LV | |
| Bowl, Ice Cream, 10" ........... | 400 | 500 | 4,790 | 1,100 | | 31,000 | 1,100IG | |
| Bowl, 5" ................ | 75 | 190 | 800 | | | | 185W | |
| Bowl, Ice Cream, 6" ............. | 350 | 160 | 185 | 125 | | 2,700 | 2,400IG | |
| Plate, 11", Rare.................... | 2,100 | 1,200 | | | | | | |
| Plate,6", Rare...................... | 450 | 550 | | | | | | |
| (Add 10% If Stippled) | | | | | | | | |
| **PEACOCK AND URN AND VTS. (MILLERSBURG)** | | | | | | | | |
| Bowl, 9½" ................ | 350 | 400 | 375 | 2,000* | | | | |
| Compote, Large, Rare .......... | 1,350 | 1,500 | 1,350 | | | | | |
| Bowl, Ice Cream, 10" Rare ... | 500 | 1,000 | 2,600 | 2,000* | | | | |
| Bowl, Ice Cream, 6" Rare ..... | 300 | 150 | 290 | 750 | | | | |
| Ruffled Bowl, 6" .................. | 190 | 245 | 210 | | | | | |
| Plate, 10½", Rare ................ | 2,900 | | | | | | | |
| Mystery Bowl, Variant, 8¾" | | | | | | | | |
| Rare ................ | 350 | 450 | 390 | 1,350 | | | | |
| **PEACOCK AT THE FOUNTAIN (DUGAN)** | | | | | | | | |
| Pitcher................ | | | | 600 | | | | |
| Tumbler ................ | | 90 | | 80 | | | | |
| **PEACOCK AT THE FOUNTAIN (NORTHWOOD)** | | | | | | | | |
| Bowl, 9" ................ | 75 | 95 | 145 | 100 | | | 600IG | |
| Bowl, 5"................ | 45 | 60 | 95 | 75 | | | 275W | |

| | M | A | G | B | PO | AO | Pas | Red |
|---|---|---|---|---|---|---|---|---|
| Orange Bowl, Ftd................. | 450 | 650 | 3,500 | 900 | | 10,000 | | |
| Punch Bowl w/base............. | 450 | 1,000 | | 600 | | 30,000 | 5,200W | |
| Cup.................................. | 30 | 45 | | 55 | | 1,400 | 125W | |
| Butter ............................. | 265 | 345 | 400 | 300 | | | | |
| Sugar .............................. | 200 | 300 | 370 | 250 | | | | |
| Creamer or Spooner ............ | 100 | 100 | 300 | 225 | | | | |
| Compote, Rare.................... | 900 | 850 | | 500 | | 3,800 | 1,400IG | |
| Pitcher............................. | 375 | 650 | 2,000 | 700 | | | 800W | |
| Tumbler ........................... | 40 | 50 | 500 | 80 | | | 240W | |
| Spittoon Whimsey, Rare ...... | | 4,200 | | | | | | |

**PEACOCK, FLUFFY (FENTON)**

| | M | A | G | B | PO | AO | Pas | Red |
|---|---|---|---|---|---|---|---|---|
| Pitcher............................. | 500 | 600 | 700 | 800 | | | | |
| Tumbler ........................... | 45 | 155 | 260 | 265 | | | | |

**PEACOCK GARDEN (NORTHWOOD)**

| | M | A | G | B | PO | AO | Pas | Red |
|---|---|---|---|---|---|---|---|---|
| Vase, 8", Rare .................... | 4,200 | | | | | | 5,000WO | |

**PEACOCK LAMP**

| | M | A | G | B | PO | AO | Pas | Red |
|---|---|---|---|---|---|---|---|---|
| Carnival Base..................... | 800 | 450 | 495 | | | | 550W | 750 |

**PEACOCKS (ON FENCE) (NORTHWOOD)*** Note: Stippled pieces add 25%

| | M | A | G | B | PO | AO | Pas | Red |
|---|---|---|---|---|---|---|---|---|
| Bowl, 8¼" ........................... | 300 | 450 | 1,000 | 550 | | 3,300 | 2,300SM | |
| Plate, 9"............................. | 500 | 750 | 1,300 | 1,200EB | | 4,800 | 1,600IB | |

**PEACOCK, STRUTTING (WESTMORELAND)**

| | M | A | G | B | PO | AO | Pas | Red |
|---|---|---|---|---|---|---|---|---|
| Creamer or Sugar w/lid...... | | 65 | 65 | | | | | |

**PEACOCK TAIL (FENTON)**

| | M | A | G | B | PO | AO | Pas | Red |
|---|---|---|---|---|---|---|---|---|
| Bon–bon............................ | 75 | 75 | 90 | 55 | | | | |
| Bowl, 4"–10"........................ | 40 | 50 | 360 | 55 | 650 | | | 1,800 |
| Compote............................ | 35 | 45 | 60 | 50 | | | 55W | |
| Hat.................................. | 30 | 40 | 55 | 50 | | | | |
| Hat, Advertising.................. | 40 | | 50 | | | | | |
| Plate, 9".............................. | 200 | 225 | | 175 | | | | |
| Plate, 6".............................. | 70 | 80 | | 870 | | | | |

**PEACOCK TAIL AND DAISY**

| | M | A | G | B | PO | AO | Pas | Red |
|---|---|---|---|---|---|---|---|---|
| Bowl, Very Rare ............... | 1,500 | 1,850* | | | | 2,200DO* | | |

**PEACOCK TAIL VT. (MILLERSBURG)**

| | M | A | G | B | PO | AO | Pas | Red |
|---|---|---|---|---|---|---|---|---|
| Compote, Scarce.................. | 90 | 320 | 110 | | | | | |

**PEBBLE AND FAN (CZECH)**

| | M | A | G | B | PO | AO | Pas | Red |
|---|---|---|---|---|---|---|---|---|
| Vase, 11¼", Rare.................. | | | | 750* | | | 750AM* | |

**PEARL AND JEWELS (FENTON)**

| | M | A | G | B | PO | AO | Pas | Red |
|---|---|---|---|---|---|---|---|---|
| Basket, 4"........................... | | | | | | | 200W | |

**PEARL LADY (NORTHWOOD)**

| | M | A | G | B | PO | AO | Pas | Red |
|---|---|---|---|---|---|---|---|---|
| Shade................................ | | | | | | | 90PG | |

**PEARL #37 (NORTHWOOD)**

| | M | A | G | B | PO | AO | Pas | Red |
|---|---|---|---|---|---|---|---|---|
| Shade................................ | | | | | | | 100PO | |

**PEBBLES (DUGAN)**

| | M | A | G | B | PO | AO | Pas | Red |
|---|---|---|---|---|---|---|---|---|
| Bowl, 8–9" ........................... | 40 | 45 | 55 | 50 | | | | |

**PENNY**

| | M | A | G | B | PO | AO | Pas | Red |
|---|---|---|---|---|---|---|---|---|
| Match Holder, Rare.............. | | 250 | | | | | | |

**PEOPLE'S VASE (MILLERSBURG)**

| | M | A | G | B | PO | AO | Pas | Red |
|---|---|---|---|---|---|---|---|---|
| Large Vase, either shape, rare ...................................... | 9,000 | 8,000 | 10,000 | 12,000 | | | | |

**PEPPER PLANT (FENTON)**

| | M | A | G | B | PO | AO | Pas | Red |
|---|---|---|---|---|---|---|---|---|
| Hat Shape .......................... | 175 | 250 | 250 | 200 | | | | |

**PERFECTION (MILLERSBURG)**

| | M | A | G | B | PO | AO | Pas | Red |
|---|---|---|---|---|---|---|---|---|
| Pitcher, Rare....................... | 4,000 | 4,000 | 5,000 | | | | | |
| Tumbler, Rare ..................... | 600 | 400 | 650 | | | | | |

**PERSIAN GARDEN (DUGAN)**

| | M | A | G | B | PO | AO | Pas | Red |
|---|---|---|---|---|---|---|---|---|
| Bowl, Ice Cream, 11" .......... | 295 | 1,100 | 500 | 450 | 650 | | 350W | |
| Bowl, Ice Cream, 6" ............ | 140 | 165 | 150 | 135 | 170 | | 105W | |
| Bowl, Berry, 10" .................. | 190 | 220 | | | | | 300 | |
| Bowl, Berry, 5" .................... | 50 | 60 | | | 80 | | 100 | |
| Plate, Chop, 13" Rare........... | | 11,000 | | | 4,800 | | 2,400W | |
| Plate, 6", Rare..................... | 90 | 450 | | | | | 250W | |
| Fruit Bowl, w/base............... | 110 | 420 | | | 500 | | 125W | |

**PERSIAN MEDALLION (FENTON)**

| | M | A | G | B | PO | AO | Pas | Red |
|---|---|---|---|---|---|---|---|---|
| Bon-bon ............................ | 75 | 100 | 160 | 150 | | | 200AQ | 1,000 |
| Compote 2 sizes................... | 100 | 400 | 190 | 85 | | | 650W | |
| Bowl, 10".............................. | 75 | 210 | 400 | 550 | | | | |
| Bowl, 5"............................... | 48 | 55 | 40 | 60 | | | | 1,100 |
| Bowl, 8¾"............................. | 60 | 90 | 200* | | | | | 950 |
| Orange Bowl........................ | 95 | 300 | 2,500 | 275 | | | | |
| Rose Bowl........................... | 60 | 70 | 80 | 70 | | | 90W | |
| Plate, 7".............................. | 50 | 250 | 600 | 225 | | | 700V | |
| Plate, 9½"............................ | | 450 | 550 | 1,000-- | | | 500W | |
| Hair Receiver ...................... | 70 | 90 | | 80 | | | 110 | |
| Punch Bowl/Base............... | 265 | 400 | 500 | 375 | | | | |
| Punch Cup ......................... | 25 | 35 | 40 | 30 | | | | |

**PETAL AND FAN (DUGAN)**

| | M | A | G | B | PO | AO | Pas | Red |
|---|---|---|---|---|---|---|---|---|
| Bowl, 10".............................. | 275 | 525 | 400 | | 340 | | 300W | |
| Bowl, 5"............................... | 35 | 60 | 50 | | 40 | | 60 | |
| Bowl, 8½"............................. | 65 | 95 | | | | | | |
| Plate, Ruffled, 6"................. | | 750 | | | | | | |

Peacock Garden (Northwood)

Peacocks (On Fence) (Northwood)

Pebbles (Dugan)

Petal and Fan (Dugan)

Petal Band

Petals and Prisms (English)

Pinched Swirl (Dugan)

Pineapple Crown

| | M | A | G | B | PO | AO | Pas | Red |
|---|---|---|---|---|---|---|---|---|
| **PETAL BAND** | | | | | | | | |
| Compote Vase, 6" ................. | 85 | | | | | | | |
| **PETALS (DUGAN)** | | | | | | | | |
| Bowl, 8¾" ........................... | 40 | 55 | | | 110 | | 70 | |
| Compote ............................. | 47 | 60 | 175 | | | | 85 | |
| Banana Bowl ....................... | | 90 | | | 110 | | | |
| **PETALS AND PRISMS (ENGLISH)** | | | | | | | | |
| Bowl, 9" .............................. | 60 | | | | | | | |
| Sugar, Ftd., 5" ..................... | 70 | | | | | | | |
| Fruit Bowl, 2 pc. ................... | 90 | | | | | | | |
| Open Sugar ......................... | 65 | | | | | | | |
| **PETER RABBIT (FENTON)** | | | | | | | | |
| Bowl, 9", Rare ..................... | 1,300 | | 1,600 | 1,200 | | | | |
| Plate, 10", Rare ................... | 1,700 | | 2,200 | 1,700 | | | 1,800AM | |
| **PIAZZA** | | | | | | | | |
| Hatpin ................................ | | 450 | | | | | | |
| **PICKLE** | | | | | | | | |
| Paperweight, 4½" ................ | | 65 | | | | | | |
| **PIGEON** | | | | | | | | |
| Paperweight ........................ | 190 | | | | | | | |
| **PILLAR AND DRAPE** | | | | | | | | |
| Shade ................................. | | | | | 70MO | | 90W | 750 |
| **PILLAR AND FLUTE (IMPERIAL)** | | | | | | | | |
| Compote ............................. | 50 | | | | | | 55SM | |
| Rose Bowl ........................... | 60 | | | | | | 75SM | |
| Creamer or sugar ................ | 35 | | | | | | 40SM | |
| Celery Vase ......................... | 60 | 90 | | | | | 85SM | |
| **PILLOW AND SUNBURST (WESTMORELAND)** | | | | | | | | |
| Bowl, 7½"–9" ...................... | 45 | 60 | | | 70 | | 65AM | |
| **PINCHED RIBS** | | | | | | | | |
| Vase ................................... | 85 | | | | 180 | | | |
| **PINCHED SWIRL (DUGAN)** | | | | | | | | |
| Vase ................................... | 90 | | | | 115 | | | |
| Rose Bowl ........................... | 130 | | | | 150 | | | |
| Spittoon Whimsey ............... | 165 | | | | 170 | | | |
| **PINEAPPLE (ENGLISH)** | | | | | | | | |
| Bowl, 7" .............................. | 60 | 70 | | 67 | | | | |
| Bowl, 4" .............................. | 40 | | | | | | | |
| Creamer ............................. | 70 | 100 | | | | | | |
| Sugar, Stemmed or Flat ....... | 75 | | | | | | | |
| Compote ............................. | 50 | 70 | | 58 | | | | |
| Butter ................................ | 85 | | | | | | | |
| Rose Bowl ........................... | 225 | | | | | | | |
| **PINEAPPLE CROWN** | | | | | | | | |
| Oval Bowl, 8" ...................... | 60 | | | | | | | |
| **PINEAPPLE, HEAVY (FENTON)** | | | | | | | | |
| Bowl, Ftd, 10" Rare ............. | 750 | | | 950 | | | 900W | |
| **PINE CONE (FENTON)** | | | | | | | | |
| Bowl, 6" .............................. | 125 | 250 | 350 | 200 | | | 250W | |
| Plate, 6½" ........................... | 150 | 275 | 275 | 225 | | | | |
| Plate, 8", Rare ..................... | | | 450 | 400 | | | 700AM | |
| **PIN–UPS (AUSTRALIAN)** | | | | | | | | |
| Bowl, 8¾", Rare .................. | 110 | 140 | | | | | | |
| **PINWHEEL (DUGAN)** | | | | | | | | |
| Bowl, 6" .............................. | 50 | | | | 85 | | | |
| Plate, 6½" ........................... | 2,000 | | | | | | | |
| **PINWHEEL (ENGLISH)** | | | | | | | | |
| Vase, 6½" ............................ | 100 | 220 | | | | | | |
| Vase, 8" .............................. | 120 | 140 | | | | | | |
| Bowl, 8", Rare ..................... | 50 | | | | | | | |
| (Also Called Derby) | | | | | | | | |
| **PIPE HUMIDOR (MILLERSBURG)** | | | | | | | | |
| Tobacco Jar w/lid, Rare ....... | 5,000 | 7,000 | 6,500 | | | | | |
| **PLAID (FENTON)** | | | | | | | | |
| Bowl, 8¾" ........................... | 120HA | | 350 | 260 | | | 950CeB | 5,000 |
| Plate, 9", Rare ..................... | 350 | | | 450 | | | | 7,900 |
| **PLAIN JANE** | | | | | | | | |
| Paperweight ........................ | 90 | | | | | | | |
| **PLAIN JANE (IMPERIAL)** | | | | | | | | |
| Basket ................................ | 60 | | | | | | 75SM | |
| Bowl ................................... | 38 | 60 | 55 | | | | 60SM | |
| **PLAIN PETALS (NORTHWOOD)** | | | | | | | | |
| Nappy, Scarce ..................... | | 85 | 90 | | | | | |
| (Interior of Leaf and Beads Nappy) | | | | | | | | |
| **PLAIN RAYS** | | | | | | | | |
| Compote ............................. | 45 | 55 | 60 | 70 | | | | |
| Bowl, 9" .............................. | 40 | 45 | 50 | 65 | | | | |
| **PLEATS AND HEARTS** | | | | | | | | |
| Shade ................................. | | | | | | | 90 | |
| **PLUME PANELS** | | | | | | | | |
| Vase, 7"–12" ....................... | 50 | 85 | 110 | 90 | | | 150 | 850 |
| **PLUMS AND CHERRIES (NORTHWOOD)** | | | | | | | | |
| Sugar, Rare ........................ | | | | 1,750 | | | | |

Pony (Dugan)

Poppy Show (Northwood)

Pretty Panels (Northwood)

Prism and Cane (English)

| | M | A | G | B | PO | AO | Pas | Red |
|---|---|---|---|---|---|---|---|---|
| Spooner, Rare...................... | | | | 1,750 | | | | |
| Tumbler ......................... | 3000* | | | 4,000* | | | | |
| **POINSETTIA (IMPERIAL)** | | | | | | | | |
| Milk Pitcher...................... | 170 | 950 | 500 | | | | 450SM | |
| **POINSETTIA (NORTHWOOD)** | | | | | | | | |
| Bowl, Flat or Ftd, 8½".......... | 400 | 575 | 750 | 1,000EB | | 4,000 | 3,500IB | |
| (Also Called Poinsettia | | 800BA | | | | | | |
| & Lattice) | | | | | | | | |
| **POLO** | | | | | | | | |
| Ashtray ......................... | 85 | | | | | | | |
| **POND LILY (FENTON)** | | | | | | | | |
| Bon–bon ......................... | 45 | | 65 | 60 | | | 175W | |
| **PONY (DUGAN)** | | | | | | | | |
| Bowl, 8½"......................... | 120 | 310 | | | | | 1,100IG | |
| Plate, Age Questionable, | | | | | | | | |
| 9", Rare, ......................... | 450* | | | | | | | |
| **POODLE** | | | | | | | | |
| Powder Jar w/lid ................. | 30 | | | | | | | |
| **POOL OF PEARLS** | | | | | | | | |
| Exterior pattern only | | | | | | | | |
| **POPPY (MILLERSBURG)** | | | | | | | | |
| Compote, Scarce.................. | 650 | 695 | 850 | | | | | |
| Salver, Rare ...................... | 1,200 | 1,450 | 1,600 | | | | | |
| **POPPY AND FISH NET (IMPERIAL)** | | | | | | | | |
| Vase, 6", Rare .................... | | | | | | | | 750 |
| **POPPY SHOW (IMPERIAL)** | | | | | | | | |
| Vase, 12", Old Only............... | 450 | 3,500 | 950 | | | | 1,000SM | |
| Hurricane Whimsey ............. | | 2,500 | | | | | 2,500W | |
| Lamp Whimsey .................. | 2,500* | | | | | | | |
| **POPPY SHOW (NORTHWOOD)** | | | | | | | | |
| Bowl, 8½"......................... | 750 | 600 | 900 | 1,700 | | | 1,700IG | |
| Plate, 9", Rare.................... | 1,700 | 1,400 | 3,000 | 3,200 | | | 2,300IB | |
| **POPPY WREATH (NORTHWOOD)** | | | | | | | | |
| (Amaryllis Exterior Pattern) | | | | | | | | |
| **PORTLAND (U.S. GLASS)** | | | | | | | | |
| Bowl, 8½"......................... | | | | | | | 170 | |
| **POTPOURRI (MILLERSBURG)** | | | | | | | | |
| Milk Pitcher, Rare ............... | 2,750 | | | | | | | |
| **PRAYER RUG (FENTON)** | | | | | | | | |
| Bon–bon, Rare.................... | | | | | | | 1,800IC | |
| (Iridized Custard Only) | | | | | | | | |
| Plate, 7", Rare.................... | | | | | | | 7,400IC | |
| **PREMIUM (IMPERIAL)** | | | | | | | | |
| Candlesticks, Pair............... | 60 | 90 | | | | | 180SM | 150 |
| Bowl, 8½".......................... | 45 | 80 | | | | | 80 | 110 |
| Bowl, 12"......................... | 55 | 75 | | | | | 90 | 130 |
| Under Plate, 14" ................. | 50 | 90 | | | | | 120 | 150 |
| **PRESSED HEXAGON (MCKEE)** | | | | | | | | |
| Covered Butter ................... | 150 | | | | | | | |
| Sugar ............................. | 90 | | | | | | | |
| Spooner............................ | 80 | | | | | | | |
| Creamer .......................... | 85 | | | | | | | |
| **PRETTY PANELS (FENTON)** | | | | | | | | |
| Pitcher w/lid ..................... | | | | | | | | 500 |
| Tumbler, Handled............... | 60 | | | | | | | 90IG |
| **PRETTY PANELS (NORTHWOOD)** | | | | | | | | |
| Pitcher............................ | 125 | | 150 | | | | | |
| Tumbler .......................... | 60 | | 70 | | | | | |
| **PRIMROSE (MILLERSBURG)** | | | | | | | | |
| Bowl, Ruffled, 8¾" .............. | 90 | 185 | 175 | 3,000 | | | 160CM | |
| Bowl, Ice Cream, 9", Scarce . | 110 | 190 | 190 | | | | | |
| Bowl, Experimental, | | | | | | | | |
| Goofus Exterior, Rare .......... | | 900 | | | | | | |
| **PRIMROSE AND FISHNET (IMPERIAL)** | | | | | | | | |
| Vase, 6", Rare .................... | | | | | | | | 750 |
| **PRIMROSE AND RIBBON** | | | | | | | | |
| Lightshade ........................ | 90 | | | | | | | |
| **PRIMROSE PANELS (IMPERIAL)** | | | | | | | | |
| Shade................................ | | | | | | | 60 | |
| **PRINCELY PLUMES** | | | | | | | | |
| Candle Holder .................... | | 300 | | | | | | |
| **PRINCESS (U.S. GLASS)** | | | | | | | | |
| Lamp, Complete, Rare ......... | | 950 | | | | | | |
| **PRISM** | | | | | | | | |
| Shakers, Pair..................... | 60 | | | | | | | |
| Tray, 3" ........................... | 50 | | | | | | | |
| Hatpin.............................. | | 75 | | | | | | |
| **PRISM AND CANE (ENGLISH)** | | | | | | | | |
| Bowl, 5", Rare.................... | 45 | 65 | | | | | | |
| **PRISM AND DAISY BAND (IMPERIAL)** | | | | | | | | |
| Vase ................................. | 28 | | | | | | | |
| Compote............................ | 35 | | | | | | | |
| Bowl, 5"............................ | 18 | | | | | | | |

333

| | M | A | G | B | PO | AO | Pas | Red |
|---|---|---|---|---|---|---|---|---|
| Bowl, 8".................... | 30 | | | | | | | |
| Sugar or Creamer, Each ...... | 35 | | | | | | | |
| **PRISM BAND (FENTON)** | | | | | | | | |
| Pitcher, Decorated ............. | 175 | 350 | 395 | 410 | | | 425IG | |
| Tumbler, Decorated ............ | 30 | 50 | 55 | 55 | | | 150W | |
| **PRISM PANELS** | | | | | | | | |
| Bowl, 8–9" ......................... | 60 | | | | | | | |
| **PRISMS (WESTMORELAND)** | | | | | | | | |
| Compote, 5", Scarce ............ | 50 | 90 | 100 | | | | 150TL | |
| Nappy, one handled, Rare.... | | | 375* | | | | | |
| **PROPELLER (IMPERIAL)** | | | | | | | | |
| Bowl, 9½", Rare .................. | 80 | | | | | | | |
| Compote............................ | 135 | | 70 | | | | 55SM | |
| Vase, Stemmed, Rare........... | 90 | | | | | | | |
| **PROUD PUSS (CAMBRIDGE)** | | | | | | | | |
| Bottle .............................. | 85 | | | | | | | |
| **PUMP, HOBNAIL (NORTHWOOD)** | | | | | | | | |
| One Shape, Age Questionable | | | 850 | | | | | |
| **PULLED LOOP (DUGAN)** | | | | | | | | |
| Vase ................................. | 45 | 60 | 50 | 110 | 60 | | 650CeB | |
| **PUMP, TOWN (NORTHWOOD)** | | | | | | | | |
| One Shape, Rare ................. | 2,350 | 1,150 | 2,800 | | | | | |
| **PUPPY** | | | | | | | | |
| Mini Candy Holder.............. | 100 | | | | | | | |
| **PURITAN (MCKEE)** | | | | | | | | |
| Plate, 6," Rare ................... | 80 | | | | | | | |
| **PUZZLE (DUGAN)** | | | | | | | | |
| Compote............................ | 40 | 50 | 75 | 85 | 90 | | 75W | |
| Bon–bon, Stemmed.............. | 40 | 50 | 90 | 125 | 100 | | 100LV | |
| **PUZZLE PIECE** | | | | | | | | |
| One Shape........................... | | | | 100* | | | | |
| **QUARTER BLOCK** | | | | | | | | |
| Creamer ............................ | 60 | | | | | | | |
| Sugar ............................... | 60 | | | | | | | |
| Butter ............................... | 125 | | | | | | | |
| **QUEEN'S JEWEL** | | | | | | | | |
| Goblet ............................... | 55 | | | | | | | |
| **QUEEN'S LAMP** | | | | | | | | |
| One Shape, Rare ................. | | | 2,500 | | | | | |
| **QUESTION MARKS (DUGAN)** | | | | | | | | |
| Bon–bon............................. | 40 | 55 | | | 60 | | 80IG | |
| Compote............................. | 40 | 70 | | | 75 | | 70W | |
| Cake Plate, Stemmed, Rare.. | 150 | 450* | | | | | | |
| **QUILL (DUGAN)** | | | | | | | | |
| Pitcher, Rare...................... | 2,000 | 3,500 | | | | | | |
| Tumbler, Rare ..................... | 400 | 500 | | | | | | |
| **QUILTED DIAMOND** | | | | | | | | |
| **RABBIT BANK** | | | | | | | | |
| Large................................. | 90 | | | | | | | |
| Small.................................. | 90 | | | | | | | |
| **RADIANCE** | | | | | | | | |
| Pitcher............................... | 240 | | | | | | | |
| Tumbler ............................. | 90 | | | | | | | |
| **RAGGED ROBIN (FENTON)** | | | | | | | | |
| Bowl, 8¾", Scarce ............... | 75 | 100 | 100 | 100 | | | 150W | |
| **RAINBOW (NORTHWOOD)** | | | | | | | | |
| Bowl, 8"............................. | | 80 | 95 | | | | | |
| Compote............................. | | 110 | 150 | | | | | |
| Plate, 9"............................. | | 135 | 160 | | | | | |
| **RAINDROPS (DUGAN)** | | | | | | | | |
| Bowl, 9"............................. | 65 | 80 | | | 295 | | | |
| Banana Bowl, 9¾" .............. | | 150 | | | 265 | | | |
| **RAMBLER ROSE (DUGAN)** | | | | | | | | |
| Pitcher............................... | 160 | 250 | 275 | 220 | | | | |
| Tumbler ............................. | 30 | 50 | 55 | 45 | | | | |
| **RANGER (MEXICAN)** | | | | | | | | |
| Creamer ............................ | 40 | | | | | | | |
| Nappy................................ | 90 | | | | | | | |
| Tumbler ............................. | 290 | | | | | | | |
| Milk Pitcher........................ | 175 | | | | | | | |
| Sugar ................................ | 150 | | | | | | | |
| Butter ................................ | 190 | | | | | | | |
| Breakfast Set, 2 Pieces ........ | 175 | | | | | | | |
| Perfume, 5¼" ...................... | 150* | | | | | | | |
| Pitcher, Rare....................... | 600 | | | | | | | |
| Shot Glass, Rare.................. | 450 | | | | | | | |
| **RANGER TOOTHPICK** | | | | | | | | |
| Toothpick Holder ................. | 95 | | | | | | | |
| Vase, 10" ........................... | 50 | | | | | | 65SM | |
| **RASPBERRY (NORTHWOOD)** | | | | | | | | |
| Bowl, 9"............................. | 60 | 70 | 75 | | | | | |
| Bowl, 5"............................. | 30 | 35 | 40 | | | | | |
| Milk Pitcher........................ | 250 | 325 | 375 | | | | 2,000IB | |
| Sauce Boat, Ftd................... | 90 | 150 | 275 | 190 | | | 350TL | |

Prism Panels

Propeller (Imperial)

Pulled Loop (Dugan)

Rainbow (Northwood)

Regal Flower (Dugan/Diamond)

Rib and Panel

Ribbons and Leaves

Ripple (Imperial)

| | M | A | G | B | PO | AO | Pas | Red |
|---|---|---|---|---|---|---|---|---|
| Pitcher | 265 | 375 | 395 | | | | 950W | |
| Tumbler | 45 | 45 | 60 | | | | 700W | |
| Compote | 48 | 56 | 58 | | | | | |
| **RAYS (DUGAN)** | | | | | | | | |
| Bowl, 5" | 40 | 50 | 50 | | 75 | | | |
| Bowl, 9" | 55 | 90 | 90 | | 125 | | | |
| **RAYS AND RIBBONS (MILLERSBURG)** | | | | | | | | |
| Bowl, Round or Ruffled, 8½"–9½" | 65 | 100 | 90 | | | | 300V | |
| Plate, Rare | 1,100 | | | | | | | |
| Banana Bowl, Rare | | | 1,000 | | | | | |
| Bowl, Tri–Cornered or Square | 115 | 140 | 150 | | | | | |
| **RED PANELS (IMPERIAL)** | | | | | | | | |
| Shade | | | | | | | | 200 |
| **REGAL FLOWER (DUGAN/DIAMOND)** | | | | | | | | |
| Decorated vase, 14" tall, Rare | 295* | | | | | | | |
| **REGAL IRIS (CONSOLIDATED GLASS)** | | | | | | | | |
| "Gone With The Wind" Lamp, Rare | 3,700 | | | | | | | 12,000* |
| **REGAL SWIRL** | | | | | | | | |
| Candlestick, Each | 75 | | | | | | | |
| **REX** | | | | | | | | |
| Pitcher | 375 | | | | | | | |
| Tumbler | 60 | | | | | | | |
| **RIB AND PANEL** | | | | | | | | |
| Vase | 50 | 60 | | 65 | 135 | | | |
| Spittoon Whimsey | 250 | | | | | | | |
| **RIBBED ELIPSE (HIGBEE)** | | | | | | | | |
| Mug, Rare | | | | | | | 150HA | |
| **RIBBED HOLLY (FENTON)** | | | | | | | | |
| Compote | 50 | 70 | | 60 | | | | 350 |
| Goblet | 75 | 100 | | 85 | | | | 390 |
| **RIBBED PANELS** | | | | | | | | |
| Toothpick Holder | 295 | | | | | | | |
| Shot Glass | 225 | | | | | | | |
| Mustard Pot | 350 | | | | | | | |
| **RIBBED SWIRL** | | | | | | | | |
| Tumbler | 60 | 80 | | | | | | |
| Bowl, 9" | 55 | 75 | | | | | | |
| **RIBBON AND BLOCK** | | | | | | | | |
| Lamp, Complete | 600 | | | | | | | |
| **RIBBON AND FERN** | | | | | | | | |
| Atomizer, 7" | 90 | | | | | | | |
| **RIBBONS AND LEAVES** | | | | | | | | |
| Sugar, Small | 50 | | | | | | | |
| **RIBBON TIE (FENTON)** | | | | | | | | |
| Bowl, 8¾" | 190 | 260 | 275 | 335 | | | | 5,600 |
| Plate, Ruffled, 9" | | | | 275 | | | | 7,500* |
| Plate, Flat, 9½" | | 225 | | 360 | | | | |
| **RIBS (CZECHOSLOVAKIA)** | | | | | | | | |
| Ringtree | 60 | | | | | | | |
| Puff Box | 95 | | | | | | | |
| Pinbox | 75 | | | | | | | |
| Perfume | 110 | | | | | | | |
| Soap Dish | 60 | | | | | | | |
| Bud Vase | 60 | | | | | | | |
| Tumbler | 85 | | | | | | | |
| **RINGS (JEANETTE)** | | | | | | | | |
| Vase, 8" | 55 | | | | | | | |
| **RIPPLE (IMPERIAL)** | | | | | | | | |
| Vase, Various Sizes | 120 | 130 | 190 | 350 | | | 350TL | |
| **RISING SUN (U.S. GLASS)** | | | | | | | | |
| Butterdish | 175 | | | | | | | |
| Creamer | 90 | | | | | | | |
| Sugar | 125 | | | | | | | |
| Pitcher, 2 Shapes, Rare | 350 | | | 2,000* | | | | |
| Tumbler, Rare | 200 | | | 600 | | | | |
| Tray, Rare | 300 | | | 500 | | | | |
| Juice Tumbler, Rare | 1,000 | | | | | | | |
| **ROBIN (IMPERIAL)** | | | | | | | | |
| Mug, Old Only | 155 | | | | | | 160 | |
| Pitcher, Old Only, Scarce | 300 | | | | | | | |
| Tumbler, Old Only, Scarce | 60 | | | | | | | |
| **ROCK CRYSTAL (McKEE)** | | | | | | | | |
| Punch Bowl w/base | | 600 | | | | | | |
| Cup | | 45 | | | | | | |
| **ROCOCO (IMPERIAL)** | | | | | | | | |
| Bowl, 5" | 40 | | 150 | | | | 160SM | |
| Vase, 5½" | 110 | | 175 | | | | 250SM | |
| **ROLL** | | | | | | | | |
| Tumbler | 40 | | | | | | | |
| Cordial Set, Complete (Decanter, Stopper, 6 Glasses) | 350 | | | | | | | |

Rose Panels (Australian)

Rose Spray (Fenton)

Rose Tree (Fenton)

Royal Pineapple

| | M | A | G | B | PO | AO | Pas | Red |
|---|---|---|---|---|---|---|---|---|
| Pitcher, Rare...................... | | | | | | | 300CL | |
| Shakers, Rare, Each ............ | 45 | | | | | | | |
| **ROLLED RIBS (NEW MARTINSVILLE)** | | | | | | | | |
| Bowl (Marigold Opal) ........... | | | | | | | 150 | |
| **ROMAN ROSETTE (U.S. GLASS)** | | | | | | | | |
| Goblet, 6", Rare .................... | | | | | | | 110CL | |
| **ROOD'S CHOCOLATES (FENTON)** | | | | | | | | |
| Advertising Plate.................. | | 2,000* | | | | | | |
| **ROOSTER** | | | | | | | | |
| Hatpin................................. | | 100 | 130 | 80 | | | | |
| **ROSALIND (MILLERSBURG)** | | | | | | | | |
| Bowl, 10" Scarce .................. | 275 | 450 | 325 | | | | 500AQ | |
| Bowl, 5", Rare...................... | 1,300 | 295 | 575 | | | | | |
| Compote, 6", Rare (Variant).. | | 650 | 500 | | | | | |
| Compote, Ruffled, 8", Rare... | 1,000 | | | | | | | |
| Compote, Jelly, 9", Rare ...... | 1,800 | 2,000 | 2,000 | 22,000 | | | | |
| Plate, 9" Very Rare .............. | | 2,500 | | | | | | |
| **ROSE** | | | | | | | | |
| Bottle ................................. | | | | | | | 130 | |
| **ROSE AND GREEK KEY** | | | | | | | | |
| Square Plate, Rare.............. | | | | | | | 8,000AM* | |
| **ROSE ANN** | | | | | | | | |
| Shade.................................. | 40 | | | | | | | |
| **ROSE BAND** | | | | | | | | |
| Tumbler, Rare ..................... | 700 | | | | | | | |
| **ROSE BOUQUET** | | | | | | | | |
| Creamer ............................. | 60 | | | | | | | |
| Bon–bon, Rare..................... | 75 | | | | | | 400W | |
| **ROSE COLUMN (MILLERSBURG)** | | | | | | | | |
| Vase, Rare .......................... | 2,200 | 3,400 | 3,200 | 8,000 | | | | |
| Experimental Vase, Rare...... | | 4,600 | | | | | | |
| **ROSE GARDEN (SWEDEN)** | | | | | | | | |
| Letter Vase ......................... | 180 | | | 190 | | | | |
| Bowl, 8¾" ........................... | 80 | 80 | | 75 | | | | |
| Vase, Round, 9" ................... | 385 | | | 250 | | | | |
| Pitcher, Communion, Rare... | 600 | | | 1,600 | | | | |
| Bowl, 6", Rare...................... | | 90 | | | | | | |
| Butter, Rare......................... | 450 | | | 445 | | | | |
| Rose Bowl, Small, Rare........ | 900 | | | | | | | |
| Rose Bowl, Large, Rare ........ | | | | 700 | | | | |
| **ROSE PANELS (AUSTRALIAN)** | | | | | | | | |
| Compote, Large ................... | 145 | | | | | | | |
| **ROSE PINWHEEL** | | | | | | | | |
| Bowl, Rare........................... | 1,900 | | 2,200 | | | | | |
| **ROSES AND FRUIT (MILLERSBURG)** | | | | | | | | |
| Bon–bon, Ftd, Rare.............. | 1,000 | 1,000 | 1,100 | 3,000 | | | | |
| **ROSES AND RUFFLES (CONSOLIDATED GLASS)** | | | | | | | | |
| G–W–T–W Lamp, Rare ......... | 2,900 | | | | | | | 10,000 |
| **ROSE SHOW (NORTHWOOD)** | | | | | | | | |
| Bowl, 8¾" ........................... | 500 | 850 | 3,000 | 1,300 | | 1,550 | 1,900IB | |
| Plate................................... | 1,900 | 2,300 | 8,000 | 1,600 | 12,000MC | 6,000 | 750W | |
| **ROSE SHOW VARIANT (NORTHWOOD)** | | | | | | | | |
| Plate, 9".............................. | 1,800 | 1,900 | 2,200 | 3,800RenB | 3,000 | | 2,500IB | |
| Bowl, 8¾" ........................... | 700 | 750 | | 900 | | | 700W | |
| **ROSE SPRAY (FENTON)** | | | | | | | | |
| Compote.............................. | 175 | | | | | | 190Ceb | |
| **ROSE SPRIG** | | | | | | | | |
| Mini Loving Cup ................. | 195 | | | | | | | |
| **ROSETIME** | | | | | | | | |
| Vase ................................... | 100 | | | | | | | |
| **ROSE TREE (FENTON)** | | | | | | | | |
| Bowl, 10", Rare.................... | 1,150 | | | 1,200 | | | | |
| **ROSETTES (NORTHWOOD)** | | | | | | | | |
| Bowl, Dome Base, 9"........... | 50 | 120 | | | | | | |
| Bowl, Ftd, 7"....................... | | 140 | | | | | | |
| **ROSE WINDOWS** | | | | | | | | |
| Tumbler, Rare ..................... | 400 | | | | | | | |
| **ROSE WREATH (Basket of Roses) (NORTHWOOD)** | | | | | | | | |
| Bon–bon, Rare..................... | 275 | 350 | | 350 | | | | |
| (Basketweave Exterior) | | | | | | | | |
| **ROUND–UP (DUGAN)** | | | | | | | | |
| Bowl, 8¾" ........................... | 100 | 180 | | 230 | 300 | | 180W | |
| Plate, 9", Rare...................... | 185 | 225 | | 500 | 350 | | 325W | |
| **ROYAL PINEAPPLE** | | | | | | | | |
| Vase ................................... | 80 | | | | | | | |
| **ROYALTY (IMPERIAL)** | | | | | | | | |
| Punch Bowl w/base.............. | 140 | | | | | | | |
| Cup..................................... | 30 | | | | | | | |
| Fruit Bowl w/stand ............. | 100 | | | | | | 140SM | |
| **RUFFLED RIB (NORTHWOOD)** | | | | | | | | |
| Spittoon Whimsey, Rare ...... | 225 | | | | | | | |

| | M | A | G | B | PO | AO | Pas | Red |
|---|---|---|---|---|---|---|---|---|
| Bowl, 8"–10" ...................... | 50 | 70 | | | | | | |
| Vase, 7"–14" ...................... | 70 | | | | | | | |

**RUFFLES AND RINGS (NORTHWOOD)**
Exterior Pattern Only

| | M | A | G | B | PO | AO | Pas | Red |
|---|---|---|---|---|---|---|---|---|
| Bowl, Scarce...................... | 125 | 150 | | | | | | |

**RUFFLES, RINGS AND DAISY BAND (NORTHWOOD)**

| | M | A | G | B | PO | AO | Pas | Red |
|---|---|---|---|---|---|---|---|---|
| Bowl, Ftd, Rare, 8½" ........... | | | | | 1,000MO | | | |

**RUSTIC (FENTON)**

| | M | A | G | B | PO | AO | Pas | Red |
|---|---|---|---|---|---|---|---|---|
| Vase, Funeral, 15"–20"........ | 625 | 1,500 | 2,000 | 1,200 | | | | |
| Vase, Various Sizes............. | 45 | 55 | 70 | 60 | 1,300 | | 180 | 4,300 |

**SACIC (ENGLISH)**

| | M | A | G | B | PO | AO | Pas | Red |
|---|---|---|---|---|---|---|---|---|
| Ashtray ............................. | 70 | | | | | | | |

**SAILBOATS (FENTON)**

| | M | A | G | B | PO | AO | Pas | Red |
|---|---|---|---|---|---|---|---|---|
| Bowl, 6"............................. | 38 | | 75 | 70 | | | 125AM | 550 |
| Goblet .............................. | 250 | 380 | 275 | 70 | | | 190 | |
| Wine................................. | 35 | | | 100 | | | | |
| Compote............................ | 65 | | | 150 | | | | |
| Plate................................. | 775 | | | 400 | | | 350AM | |

**SAILING SHIP**

| | M | A | G | B | PO | AO | Pas | Red |
|---|---|---|---|---|---|---|---|---|
| Plate, 8".............................. | 40 | | | | | | | |

**SAINT (ENGLISH)**

| | M | A | G | B | PO | AO | Pas | Red |
|---|---|---|---|---|---|---|---|---|
| Candlestick, Each............... | 300 | | | | | | | |

**SALAMANDERS**

| | M | A | G | B | PO | AO | Pas | Red |
|---|---|---|---|---|---|---|---|---|
| Hatpin.............................. | | 75 | | | | | | |

**SALT CUP (VARIOUS MAKERS)**

| | M | A | G | B | PO | AO | Pas | Red |
|---|---|---|---|---|---|---|---|---|
| One Shape, Averaged........... | 45 | 55 | 88RG | | | | 75CeB | |

**SATIN SWIRL**

| | M | A | G | B | PO | AO | Pas | Red |
|---|---|---|---|---|---|---|---|---|
| Atomizer............................ | | | | | | | 75CL | |

**SAWTOOTH BAND**

| | M | A | G | B | PO | AO | Pas | Red |
|---|---|---|---|---|---|---|---|---|
| Tumbler Rare ...................... | 400 | | | | | | | |

**SAWTOOTH PRISMS**

| | M | A | G | B | PO | AO | Pas | Red |
|---|---|---|---|---|---|---|---|---|
| Jelly Jar 3–sizes ................. | 60 | | | | | | | |

**S–BAND (AUSTRALIAN)**

| | M | A | G | B | PO | AO | Pas | Red |
|---|---|---|---|---|---|---|---|---|
| Compote............................. | 70 | 95 | | | | | | |

**SCALE BAND (FENTON)**

| | M | A | G | B | PO | AO | Pas | Red |
|---|---|---|---|---|---|---|---|---|
| Bowl, 6"............................. | 35 | | | | 80 | | 90W | |
| Plate, Flat, 6½" ................... | 45 | | | | | | 85V | 585 |
| Plate, Dome Base, 7" .......... | 50 | | | | | | | 550 |
| Pitcher.............................. | 125 | | | 400 | | | | |
| Tumbler ............................ | 60 | | | 350 | | | | |

**SCALES (WESTMORELAND)**

| | M | A | G | B | PO | AO | Pas | Red |
|---|---|---|---|---|---|---|---|---|
| Bon–bon............................ | 40 | 48 | | | 90 | 300 | 60TL | |
| Bowl, 7"–10" ...................... | | | | | 90IM | 225BO | 46TL | |
| Deep Bowl, 5" ..................... | | 40 | | | | | | |
| Plate, 6"............................ | 45 | 58 | | | | | 65TL | |
| Plate, 9"............................ | | 95 | | | 155MMG | 260 | 140 | |

**SCARAB**

| | M | A | G | B | PO | AO | Pas | Red |
|---|---|---|---|---|---|---|---|---|
| Hatpin.............................. | | 100 | | | | | 150AM | |

**SCOTCH THISTLE (FENTON)**

| | M | A | G | B | PO | AO | Pas | Red |
|---|---|---|---|---|---|---|---|---|
| Compote............................ | 46 | 60 | 100 | 115 | | | | |

**SCOTTIE**

| | M | A | G | B | PO | AO | Pas | Red |
|---|---|---|---|---|---|---|---|---|
| Powder Jar w/lid ................. | 35 | | | | | | | |
| Paperweight, Rare............... | 250 | | | | | | | |

**SCROLL (WESTMORELAND)**

| | M | A | G | B | PO | AO | Pas | Red |
|---|---|---|---|---|---|---|---|---|
| Pin Tray ............................ | 50 | | | | | | | |

**SCROLL AND FLOWER PANELS (IMPERIAL)**

| | M | A | G | B | PO | AO | Pas | Red |
|---|---|---|---|---|---|---|---|---|
| Vase, 10", Old Only.............. | 95 | 250 | | 150 | | | | |

**SCROLL AND GRAPE (MILLERSBURG)**

| | M | A | G | B | PO | AO | Pas | Red |
|---|---|---|---|---|---|---|---|---|
| Punchbowl and Base (Multi–fruits and Flowers ext) very rare............................. | | 7,000* | | | | | | |

**SCROLL EMBOSSED (IMPERIAL)**

| | M | A | G | B | PO | AO | Pas | Red |
|---|---|---|---|---|---|---|---|---|
| Bowl, 8½" ......................... | 40 | 65 | | | | | | 600 |
| Dessert, Round or Ruffled, Rare ................................. | 90 | 275 | 150 | | | | | |
| Plate, 9"............................ | 200 | 325 | 200 | | | | 90TL | |
| Compote, Large .................. | 50 | 160 | | | | | 100AQ | |
| Compote, Small .................. | 40 | 300 | 60 | | | | | |
| Sauce ............................... | 35 | 50 | | | | | | |

**SCROLL EMBOSSED VT. (ENGLISH)**

| | M | A | G | B | PO | AO | Pas | Red |
|---|---|---|---|---|---|---|---|---|
| Handled Ashtray, 5" ............ | 45 | 60 | | | | | | |
| Plate, 7".............................. | 165 | | | | | | | |

**SEACOAST (MILLERSBURG)**

| | M | A | G | B | PO | AO | Pas | Red |
|---|---|---|---|---|---|---|---|---|
| Pin Tray, Rare .................... | 500 | 550 | 425 | | | | 900CM | |

**SEAFOAM (DUGAN)**
Exterior Pattern Only

**SEAGULL (CZECH)**

| | M | A | G | B | PO | AO | Pas | Red |
|---|---|---|---|---|---|---|---|---|
| Vase, Rare .......................... | 1,150 | | | | | | | |

**SEAGULLS (DUGAN)**

| | M | A | G | B | PO | AO | Pas | Red |
|---|---|---|---|---|---|---|---|---|
| Bowl, 6½", Scarce ................ | 180 | | | | | | | |

Ruffles and Rings (Northwood)

Scale Band (Fenton)

Scroll and Flower Panels

Seagulls (Dugan)

Serpentine Rose (English)

Shanghai (China)

Shooting Star (English)

Simplicity Scroll (Westmoreland)

| | M | A | G | B | PO | AO | Pas | Red |
|---|---|---|---|---|---|---|---|---|
| **SEAWEED** | | | | | | | | |
| Lamp, 2 Sizes | 250 | | | | | | | |
| Lamp Vt., 8½", Rare | | | | | | | 395IB | |
| **SEAWEED (MILLERSBURG)** | | | | | | | | |
| Bowl, 5", Rare | 400 | | 470 | | | | | |
| Bowl, 9", Rare | 275 | | 375 | 1,600 | | | | |
| Plate, 10", Rare | 1,000 | 1,100 | 1,000 | | | | 400CM | |
| Bowl, 10½", Ruffled, Scarce | 350 | 400 | 350 | | | | 300CM | |
| Bowl, Ice Cream, 10½", Rare | 400 | 1,600 | 1,000 | | | | | |
| **SERPENT (CZECH)** | | | | | | | | |
| Vase, Rare | 1000* | | | | | | | |
| **SERPENTINE ROSE (ENGLISH)** | | | | | | | | |
| Rose Bowl, ftd. | 90 | | | | | | | |
| **SERRATED RIBS** | | | | | | | | |
| Shaker, Each | 60 | | | | | | | |
| **SHANGHAI (CHINA)** | | | | | | | | |
| Tumbler | 45 | | | | | | | |
| **SHARP** | | | | | | | | |
| Shot Glass | 50 | | | | | | 70SM | |
| **SHASTA DAISY** | | | | | | | | |
| Pitcher | 250 | | | 495 | | | 600W | |
| Tumbler | 30 | | | 60 | | | 90W | |
| **SHELL** | | | | | | | | |
| Shade | | | | | | | 75 | |
| **SHELL (IMPERIAL)** | | | | | | | | |
| Bowl, 7"–9" | 45 | 150 | 75 | | | | 90SM | |
| Plate, 8½" | 190 | 1,175 | 375 | | | | | |
| **SHELL AND BALLS** | | | | | | | | |
| Perfume, 2½" | 65 | | | | | | | |
| **SHELL AND JEWEL (WESTMORELAND)** | | | | | | | | |
| Creamer w/lid | 55 | 65 | 60 | | | | 90W | |
| Sugar w/lid | 55 | 65 | 60 | | | | 90W | |
| **SHERATON (U.S. GLASS)** | | | | | | | | |
| Pitcher | | | | | | | 170 | |
| Tumbler | | | | | | | 50 | |
| Butter | | | | | | | 130 | |
| Sugar | | | | | | | 90 | |
| Creamer or Spooner | | | | | | | 75 | |
| **SHIP AND STARS** | | | | | | | | |
| Plate, 8" | 40 | | | | | | | |
| **SHOOTING STAR (ENGLISH)** | | | | | | | | |
| Creamer | 70 | | | | | | | |
| Sugar, Open | 65 | | | | | | | |
| Covered Butter | 140 | | | | | | | |
| **SHOVEL** | | | | | | | | |
| Mini Novelty | 250 | | | | | | | |
| **SHRINE (U.S. GLASS)** | | | | | | | | |
| Champagne | | | | | | | 180CL | |
| Toothpick Holder | | 650 | | | | | 200CL | |
| **SIGNET (ENGLISH)** | | | | | | | | |
| Sugar w/lid, 6½" | 75 | | | | | | | |
| **SILVER AND GOLD** | | | | | | | | |
| Pitcher | 150 | | | | | | | |
| Tumbler | 50 | | | | | | | |
| **SILVER QUEEN (FENTON)** | | | | | | | | |
| Pitcher | 200 | | | | | | | |
| Tumbler | 70 | | | | | | | |
| **SIMPLICITY SCROLL (WESTMORELAND)** | | | | | | | | |
| Toothpick Holder | | | | | | | 350SM | |
| **SINGING BIRDS (NORTHWOOD)** | | | | | | | | |
| Bowl, 10" | 60 | 75 | 85 | | | | | |
| Bowl, 5 | 30 | 35 | 40 | 85 | | | | |
| Mug | 225 | 250 | 325 | 290 | | 1,200 | 650IB | |
| Butter | 185 | 300 | 325 | | | | | |
| Sugar | 110 | 140 | 150 | | | | | |
| Creamer | 80 | 110 | 125 | | | | | |
| Spooner | 80 | 150 | 125 | | | | | |
| Pitcher | 350 | 375 | 550 | | | | | |
| Tumbler | 45 | 75 | 150 | | | | | |
| Sherbet, Rare | 300 | | | | | | | |
| **SINGLE FLOWER (DUGAN)** | | | | | | | | |
| Bowl, 8" | 35 | 40 | 45 | | 80 | | | |
| Hat | 30 | 40 | 40 | | | | | |
| Handled Basket Whimsey, Rare | 225 | | | | 300 | | | |
| Banana Bowl, 9½", Rare | | | | | 350 | | | |
| **SINGLE FLOWER FRAMED (DUGAN)** | | | | | | | | |
| Bowl, 8¾" | 65 | 90 | 80 | | 130 | | | |
| Bowl, 5" | 40 | 50 | | | 75 | | | |
| Plate | | 275 | | | 250 | | | |
| **SIX PETALS (DUGAN)** | | | | | | | | |
| Bowl, 8½" | 40 | 125 | 70 | 80 | 75 | | 60 | |
| Plate, Rare | 90 | 200 | 150 | | 195 | | | |

| | M | A | G | B | PO | AO | Pas | Red |
|---|---|---|---|---|---|---|---|---|
| Hat................................ | 45 | 50 | 60 | | 80 | | 150BA | |
| **SIX–SIDED (IMPERIAL)** | | | | | | | | |
| Candlestick, Each.............. | 225 | 300 | 250 | | | | 200SM | |
| **SKATER'S SHOE (U.S. GLASS)** | | | | | | | | |
| One Shape......................... | 120 | | | | | | | |
| **SKI–STAR (DUGAN)** | | | | | | | | |
| Bowl, 8"–10".................. | 60 | 95 | | 175 | 150 | | | |
| Bowl, 5"......................... | 40 | 50 | 60 | 55 | 80 | | | |
| Basket, Handled, Rare........ | | | | | 500 | | | |
| Banana Bowl..................... | | 125 | | | 290 | | | |
| Plate, 7½" ...................... | | | | | 260 | | | |
| Hand Grip Bowl, 8"–10"....... | | | | | 140 | | | |
| Rose Bowl, Rare ................. | | | | | 600 | | | |
| **SLICK WILLIE (HALE BATHS)** | | | | | | | | |
| Vase, 13"........................ | 150* | | | | | | | |
| **SMALL BASKET** | | | | | | | | |
| One Shape......................... | 50 | | | | | | | |
| **SMALL BLACKBERRY (NORTHWOOD)** | | | | | | | | |
| Compote............................ | 50 | 60 | 60 | | | | | |
| **SMALL PALMS** | | | | | | | | |
| Shade................................ | 45 | | | | | | | |
| **SMALL RIB (DUGAN)** | | | | | | | | |
| Compote............................ | 40 | 45 | 45 | | | | 55AM | |
| Rose Bowl, Stemmed .......... | 40 | 45 | 50 | | | | 55AM | |
| **SMALL THUMBPRINT** | | | | | | | | |
| Creamer ............................ | 60 | | | | | | | |
| Toothpick Holder ................ | 70 | | | | | | | |
| **SMITH REAL ESTATE** | | | | | | | | |
| Bowl.................................. | 1,400 | | | | | | | |
| **SMOOTH PANELS (IMPERIAL)** | | | | | | | | |
| Bowl, 6½"......................... | 30 | | | | | | 35PM | |
| Plate, 9¼" ....................... | | | | | | | 90CL | |
| Tumbler ............................ | | | | | | | 45PM | |
| Vase ................................. | 40 | | | | | | 250SMG | 250 |
| Pitcher.............................. | 90 | 175 | | | | | | |
| **SMOOTH RAYS (NORTHWOOD)** | | | | | | | | |
| Bon–bon............................ | 30 | | | | | | 25CL | |
| **SMOOTH RAYS (NORTHWOOD–DUGAN)** | | | | | | | | |
| Compote............................ | 40 | 50 | 55 | | | | | |
| Rose Bowl.......................... | 50 | 60 | | | 60 | | | |
| Bowl, 6"–9"....................... | 45 | 90 | | | 80 | | | |
| Plate, 7"–9"....................... | 60 | | | | | | | |
| **SMOOTH RAYS (WESTMORELAND)** | | | | | | | | |
| Compote............................ | | | 75 | | | | 70AM | |
| Bowl, 7"–9", Flat................ | 40 | 55 | 50 | | 75 | | 125BO | |
| Bowl, Dome Base, 5"–7½" .... | | | 55 | | 75 | | 80TL | |
| **SNOW FANCY (McKEE)** | | | | | | | | |
| Bowl, 5"............................ | | | 50 | | | | | |
| Creamer or Sugar ............... | 50 | | | | | | | |
| **SODA GOLD (IMPERIAL)** | | | | | | | | |
| Candlestick, 3½", Each........ | 55 | | | | | | 60SM | |
| Bowl, 9"............................ | 45 | | | | | | 60SM | |
| Pitcher.............................. | 240 | | | | | | 325SM | |
| Tumbler ............................ | 40 | | | | | | 75SM | |
| **SODA GOLD SPEARS (DUGAN)** | | | | | | | | |
| Bowl, 8½" .......................... | 40 | | | | | | 40CL | |
| Bowl, 4½" .......................... | 30 | | | | | | 30CL | |
| Plate, 9"............................ | 50 | | | | | | 160CL | |
| **SOLDIERS AND SAILORS (FENTON)** | | | | | | | | |
| Plate (Illinois), Rare.............. | 2,100 | 1,600 | | 2,600 | | | | |
| Plate (Indianapolis), Rare ....................... | | | | 10,000 | | | | |
| **SOUTACHE (DUGAN)** | | | | | | | | |
| Bowl, 10"........................... | | | | | 200 | | | |
| Plate, 10½", Rare ................ | | | | | 375 | | | |
| Lamp, Complete ................. | 350 | | | | | | | |
| **SOUTHERN IVY** | | | | | | | | |
| Wine, 2 Sizes...................... | 45 | | | | | | | |
| **SOUVENIR BANDED** | | | | | | | | |
| Mug.................................. | 85 | | | | | | | |
| **SOUVENIR BELL (IMPERIAL)** | | | | | | | | |
| One Shape, Lettering .......... | 180 | | | | | | | |
| **SOUVENIR MINIATURE** | | | | | | | | |
| One Shape, Lettering .......... | 50 | | | | | | | |
| **SOUVENIR MUG (McKEE)** | | | | | | | | |
| Any Lettering..................... | 65 | | | | | | | |
| **SOUVENIR PIN TRAY (U.S. GLASS)** | | | | | | | | |
| One Size ............................ | | | | | | | 75 | |
| (Same as Portland Pattern) | | | | | | | | |
| **SOUVENIR VASE (U.S. GLASS)** | | | | | | | | |
| Vase, 6½", Rare................... | 100 | 135 | | | 150 | 400 | | |

Six-sided (Imperial)

Slick Willie (Hale Baths)

Soda Gold Spears (Dugan)

Sowerby File and Shell

Spanish Moss

Spearhead and Rib

Standard

Star (English)

| | M | A | G | B | PO | AO | Pas | Red |
|---|---|---|---|---|---|---|---|---|
| **SOWERBY FILE AND SHELL** | | | | | | | | |
| Candle Lamp, 9¼" | 350* | | | | | | | |
| **SOWERBY FLOWER BLOCK (ENGLISH)** | | | | | | | | |
| Flower Frog | 60 | | | | | | | |
| **SOWERBY WIDE PANEL (SOWERBY)** | | | | | | | | |
| Bowl | 45 | 75BA | | | | | | |
| **SPANISH MOSS** | | | | | | | | |
| Hatpin Holder, 5½" | 95 | | | | | | | |
| **SPEARHEAD AND RIB (FENTON'S #916)** | | | | | | | | |
| Vase, 8–14" | 175 | 250 | 450 | 350 | | | | |
| **SPHINX (ENGLISH)** | | | | | | | | |
| Paperweight, Rare | | | | | | | 595AM | |
| **SPIDERWEB (NORTHWOOD)** | | | | | | | | |
| Candy Dish, covered | | | | | | | 40SM | |
| **SPIDERWEB (NORTHWOOD–DUGAN)** | | | | | | | | |
| Vase, 8" | 50 | | | | | | 80 | |
| **SPIDERWEB AND TREEBARK (DUGAN)** | | | | | | | | |
| Vase, 6" | | | | | | | 65 | |
| **SPIRAL (IMPERIAL)** | | | | | | | | |
| Candlestick, Pair. | 165 | 185 | 195 | | | | 170SM | |
| **SPIRAL DANCE** | | | | | | | | |
| Hatpin | | 135 | | | | | | |
| **SPIRALED DIAMOND POINT** | | | | | | | | |
| Vase, 6" | 90 | | | | | | | |
| **SPIRALEX (ENGLISH)** | | | | | | | | |
| Vase, Various Sizes | 50 | 65 | 70 | 60 | | | 80 | |
| **SPLIT DIAMOND (ENGLISH)** | | | | | | | | |
| Butter, Scarce | 65 | | | | | | | |
| Creamer, Small | 40 | | | | | | | |
| Sugar, Open | 40 | | | | | | | |
| Sauce, Flat | 35 | 70 | | | | | | |
| **SPRING BASKET (IMPERIAL)** | | | | | | | | |
| Handled Basket, 5" | 50 | | | | | | 65SM | |
| **SPRING OPENING (MILLERSBURG)** | | | | | | | | |
| Plate, 6½", Rare | | 1,600 | | | | | | |
| **SPRINGTIME (NORTHWOOD)** | | | | | | | | |
| Bowl, 9" | 80 | 200 | 250 | | | | | |
| Bowl, 5" | 40 | 55 | 75 | | | | | |
| Butter | 375 | 450 | 475 | | | | | |
| Sugar | 300 | 400 | 425 | | | | | |
| Creamer or Spooner | 275 | 350 | 400 | | | | | |
| Pitcher, Rare | 750 | 1,000 | 1,250 | | | | 1,800 | |
| Tumbler, Rare | 75 | 120 | 200 | | | | 300 | |
| **SQUARE DAISY AND BUTTON (IMPERIAL)** | | | | | | | | |
| Toothpick Holder, Rare | | | | | | | 125 | |
| **SQUARE DIAMOND** | | | | | | | | |
| Vase, Rare | | | 750 | | | | | |
| **S–REPEAT (DUGAN)** | | | | | | | | |
| Creamer, Small | | 75 | | | | | | |
| Punch Bowl w/base, Rare | | 1,800 | | | | | | |
| Cup, Rare | | 120 | | | | | | |
| Toothpick Holder (Old Only), Rare | | 85 | | | | | | |
| Tumbler | 300 | 100 | | | | | | |
| Sugar, Rare (Very Light Iridescence) | | 250 | | | | | | |
| **STAG AND HOLLY (FENTON)** | | | | | | | | |
| Bowl, Ftd, 9"–13" | 150 | 350 | 800 | 425 | 1,700 | | 790AQ | 3,000 |
| Rose Bowl, Ftd | 350 | | 1,000 | | | | | |
| Plate, Ftd, 13" | 1,000 | | | | | | | |
| Plate, Ftd, 9" | 700 | 3,250 | | 1,800 | | | | |
| **STANDARD** | | | | | | | | |
| Vase, 5½" | 50 | | | | | | | |
| **STAR** | | | | | | | | |
| Paperweight, Rare | | | | | | | 295 | |
| **STAR** | | | | | | | | |
| Milk Goblet | 50 | | | | | | | |
| **STAR (ENGLISH)** | | | | | | | | |
| Bowl, 8" | 50 | | | | | | | |
| **STAR AND DIAMOND POINT** | | | | | | | | |
| Hatpin | | 75 | | | | | | |
| **STAR AND FAN** | | | | | | | | |
| Vase, 9½", Rare | 250 | | 200 | | | | | |
| (Note: Same as curved Star Pattern) | | | | | | | | |
| **STAR AND FAN (ENGLISH)** | | | | | | | | |
| Cordial Set | 1,500 | | | | | | | |
| (Decanter, 4 Stemmed Cordials and Tray) | | | | | | | | |
| **STAR AND FILE (IMPERIAL)** | | | | | | | | |
| Bowl, 7"–9½" | 35 | | | | | | | |
| Vase, Handled | 50 | | | | | | | |

Starburst Lustre (Northwood)

Star of David (Imperial)

Stippled Flower (Dugan)

Stippled Mum (Northwood)

|  | M | A | G | B | PO | AO | Pas | Red |
|---|---|---|---|---|---|---|---|---|
| Compote | 45 | | | | | | | |
| Creamer or Sugar | 30 | | | | | | | |
| Pitcher | 185 | | | | | | | |
| Decanter w/stopper | 110 | | | | | | | |
| Rose Bowl | 75 | 100 | 115 | | | | 100AM | |
| Wine | 75 | | | | | | 250IG | |
| Spooner | 30 | | | | | | | |
| Sherbet | 35 | | | | | | | |
| Custard Cup | 30 | | | | | | | |
| Plate, 6" | 65 | | | | | | | |
| Pickle Dish | 40 | | | | | | | |
| Tumbler, Rare | 275 | | | | | | | |
| Bon–bon | 35 | | | | | | | |
| **STAR AND HOBS (Northern Star)** | | | | | | | | |
| Rose Bowl, 9", Rare | 250 | | 350 | | | | | |
| **STAR AND NEARCUT** | | | | | | | | |
| Hatpin | | 60 | | | | | | |
| **STAR AND ROSETTE** | | | | | | | | |
| Hatpin | | 75 | | | | | | |
| **STARBRIGHT** | | | | | | | | |
| Vase, 6½" | 40 | 45 | 50 | | | | | |
| **STARBURST** | | | | | | | | |
| Perfume w/stopper | 65 | | | | | | | |
| Spittoon | 650 | | | | | | | |
| **STARBURST LUSTRE (NORTHWOOD)** | | | | | | | | |
| Bowl | 40 | 45 | 55 | | | | | |
| Compote | 50 | 60 | 75 | | | | | |
| **STAR CENTER (IMPERIAL)** | | | | | | | | |
| Bowl, 8½" | 30 | 40 | | | | | 50 | |
| Plate, 9" | 60 | 80 | | | | | 90 | |
| **STARFISH (DUGAN)** | | | | | | | | |
| Bon–bon, Handled, Rare | | 275 | | | 160 | | 850 | |
| Compote | 40 | 265 | 75 | | 175 | | | |
| **STARFLOWER** | | | | | | | | |
| Pitcher, Rare | 3,200 | | | 1,750 | | | 18,000W* | |
| **STARLYTE (IMPERIAL)** | | | | | | | | |
| Shade | 40 | | | | | | | |
| **STAR MEDALLION (IMPERIAL)** | | | | | | | | |
| Bon–bon | 45 | | | | | | | |
| Bowl, 7"–9" | 30 | | | | | | 40 | |
| Compote | 45 | | | | | | | |
| Butter | 100 | | | | | | | |
| Creamer, Spooner or Sugar Ea. | 60 | | | | | | | |
| Milk Pitcher | 80 | | 95 | | | | 80SM | |
| Goblet | 45 | | | | | | 60 | |
| Tumbler | 30 | | 50 | | | | 55 | |
| Plate, 5" | 60 | | | | | | 45 | |
| Plate, 10" | | | | | | | 50 | |
| Handled Celery | 80 | | | | | | 65 | |
| Celery Tray | 60 | | | | | | 50 | |
| Ice Cream, Stemmed, Small | 35 | | | | | | | |
| Pickle Dish | 40 | | | | | | | |
| Vase, 6" | 40 | | | | | | 45 | |
| Custard Cup | 20 | | | | | | | |
| **STAR OF DAVID (IMPERIAL)** | | | | | | | | |
| Bowl, 8¾", Scarce | 70 | 275 | 200 | | | | 100SM | 3,000* |
| **STAR OF DAVID AND BOWS (NORTHWOOD)** | | | | | | | | |
| Bowl, 8½" | 50 | 110 | 75 | | | | 150AM | |
| **STARS AND BARS** | | | | | | | | |
| Rose Bowl | 130 | | | | | | | |
| **STARS AND BARS (CAMBRIDGE)** | | | | | | | | |
| Wine, Rare | 150* | | | | | | | |
| **STARS AND STRIPES (OLD GLORY)** | | | | | | | | |
| Plate, 7½", Rare | 150* | | | | | | | |
| **STAR SPRAY (IMPERIAL)** | | | | | | | | |
| Bowl, 7" | 35 | | | | | | 45SM | |
| Bride's Basket, Complete, Rare | 90 | | | | | | 125SM | |
| Plate, 7½", Scarce | 75 | | | | | | 95SM | |
| **STERLING FURNITURE (NORTHWOOD)** | | | | | | | | |
| Bowl | | 700 | | | | | | |
| **STIPPLED ACORNS** | | | | | | | | |
| Candy dish w/lid, Ftd | 75 | 95 | | 80 | | | | |
| **STIPPLED DIAMOND SWAG (ENGLISH)** | | | | | | | | |
| Compote | 45 | | 65 | 60 | | | | |
| **STIPPLED FLOWER (DUGAN)** | | | | | | | | |
| Bowl, 8½" | | | | | 85 | | | |
| **STIPPLED MUM (NORTHWOOD)** | | | | | | | | |
| Bowl, 9" | 65 | 85 | 95 | 125 | | | | |
| **STIPPLED PETALS (DUGAN)** | | | | | | | | |
| Bowl, 9" | | 75 | | | 90 | | | |

Stippled Rambler Rose (Dugan)

Stippled Rays (Fenton)

Strawberry (Millersburg)

Stream of Hearts

| | M | A | G | B | PO | AO | Pas | Red |
|---|---|---|---|---|---|---|---|---|
| Handled Basket .................. | | 150 | | | 165 | | | |
| **STIPPLED RAMBLER ROSE (DUGAN)** | | | | | | | | |
| Nut Bowl, Ftd ................. | 75 | | | 90 | | | | |
| **STIPPLED RAYS (FENTON)** | | | | | | | | |
| Bon–bon ............................ | 35 | 45 | 55 | 40 | | | | 425 |
| Bowl, 5"–10" ...................... | 40 | 50 | 60 | 50 | | | 85VAS | 450 |
| Compote ............................ | 35 | 45 | 50 | 45 | | | | |
| Creamer or Sugar, Each ...... | 30 | 40 | 45 | 45 | | | | 425 |
| Plate, 7" ............................ | 50 | 50 | 100 | 45 | | | | 560 |
| **STIPPLED RAYS (IMPERIAL)** | | | | | | | | |
| Creamer, Stemmed ............. | 40 | | 50 | | | | 55SM | 500 |
| Sugar, Stemmed ................. | 40 | | 50 | | | | 55SM | 500 |
| Sugar Whimsey, Rare ......... | | | | | | | | 600 |
| **STIPPLED RAYS (NORTHWOOD)** | | | | | | | | |
| Bowl, 8"–10" ...................... | 45 | 55 | 65 | | | | 175BA | |
| Compote ............................ | 50 | 60 | 65 | | | | | |
| **STIPPLED SALT CUP** | | | | | | | | |
| One Size ........................... | 45 | | | | | | | |
| **STIPPLED STRAWBERRY (JENKINS)** | | | | | | | | |
| Tumbler ............................ | 60 | | | | | | | |
| Creamer or Sugar ............... | 35 | | | | | | | |
| Spittoon Whimsey, Rare ...... | 225 | | | | | | | |
| Syrup, Rare ....................... | 250 | | | | | | | |
| Butter .............................. | 85 | | | | | | | |
| Bowl, 9", Rare .................... | 90 | 200 | | | | | | |
| **STORK (JENKINS)** | | | | | | | | |
| Vase ................................. | 60 | | | | | | 90W | |
| **STORK ABC** | | | | | | | | |
| Child's Plate, 7½" ............... | 60 | | | | | | | |
| **STORK AND RUSHES (DUGAN)** | | | | | | | | |
| Butter, Rare....................... | 145 | 165 | | | | | | |
| Creamer or Spooner, Rare.... | 80 | 90 | | | | | | |
| Sugar, Rare ....................... | 90 | 120 | | | | | | |
| Bowl, 10" .......................... | 40 | 50 | | | | | | |
| Bowl, 5" ............................ | 30 | 30 | | | | | | |
| Mug.................................. | 35 | 250 | | 350 | | | | |
| Punch Bowl w/base, Rare.... | 190 | 300 | | 325 | | | | |
| Cup.................................. | 20 | 30 | | 35 | | | | |
| Hat.................................. | 25 | 75 | | 30 | | | | |
| Handled Basket .................. | 60 | | | | | | | |
| Pitcher.............................. | 250 | 225 | | 400 | | | | |
| Tumbler ........................... | 30 | 60 | | 75 | | | | |
| **STRAWBERRY** | | | | | | | | |
| Hatpin.............................. | | | 1500 | | | | | |
| **STRAWBERRY (DUGAN)** | | | | | | | | |
| Epergne, Rare..................... | 1,000 | 900 | | | | | | |
| **STRAWBERRY (FENTON)** | | | | | | | | |
| Bon–bon ............................ | 55 | 50 | 65 | 160 | | | 90V | 450 |
| **STRAWBERRY (MILLERSBURG)** | | | | | | | | |
| Bowl, 6½" .......................... | 90 | 150 | 140 | | | | | |
| Bowl, 8"–10", Scarce ............ | 285 | 450 | 400 | | | | 1,300V | |
| Compote, Rare.................... | 575 | 450 | 450 | | | | 2,050V | |
| Gravy Boat Whimsey, Rare .. | | | | | | | 1,500V | |
| Banana Boat Whimsey, Rare.. | | 2,000* | 2,000* | | | | 2,000V | |
| Bowl, 9½", Tri–Cornered ...... | 390 | 500 | 450 | | | | | |
| **STRAWBERRY (NORTHWOOD)** | | | | | | | | |
| Bowl, 8"–10" ...................... | 175 | 390 | 285 | 290 | | 2,200 | 1,100IG | |
| Bowl, 5" ............................ | 45 | 60 | 70 | 80 | | | | |
| Plate, 9" ............................ | 275 | 450 | 395 | 375 | | 2,600 | 500LV | |
| Plate, Handgrip, 7" ............. | 190 | 250 | 275 | 230 | | | | |
| Stippled Plate, 9" ................ | 1,600 | 1,350 | 1,500 | | | | | |
| **STRAWBERRY INTAGLIO (NORTHWOOD)** | | | | | | | | |
| Bowl, 9½" .......................... | 65 | | | | | | | |
| Bowl, 5½" .......................... | 30 | | | | | | | |
| **STRAWBERRY POINT** | | | | | | | | |
| Tumbler ............................ | 150 | | | | | | | |
| **STRAWBERRY SCROLL (FENTON)** | | | | | | | | |
| Pitcher, Rare....................... | 3,900 | | | 3,500 | | | | |
| Tumbler, Rare .................... | 275 | | | 250 | | | | |
| **STRAWBERRY SPRAY** | | | | | | | | |
| Brooch .............................. | | | | 175 | | | | |
| **STREAM OF HEARTS (FENTON)** | | | | | | | | |
| Bowl, Ftd, 10" ..................... | 80 | | | 110 | | | | |
| Compote, Rare.................... | 165 | | | | | | 135 | |
| Goblet, Rare ....................... | 200 | | | | | | | |
| **STRETCHED DIAMOND (NORTHWOOD)** | | | | | | | | |
| Tumbler, Rare .................... | 175 | | | | | | | |
| **STRETCHED DIAMONDS & DOTS** | | | | | | | | |
| Tumbler ............................ | 175 | | | | | | | |

Studs (Jeanette)

Sunflower and Diamond

Superb Drape (Northwood)

Sun Punch

| | M | A | G | B | PO | AO | Pas | Red |
|---|---|---|---|---|---|---|---|---|
| **STRING OF BEADS** | | | | | | | | |
| One Shape............................ | 35 | | 40 | | | | | |
| **STUDS (JEANETTE)** | | | | | | | | |
| Tray, Large, Round or Oval.. | 65 | | | | | | | |
| Juice, Tumbler .................... | 40 | | | | | | | |
| Milk Pitcher......................... | 75 | | | | | | | |
| **STYLE** | | | | | | | | |
| Bowl, 8".............................. | | 95 | | | | | | |
| **STYLIZED FLOWER CENTER (FENTON)** | | | | | | | | |
| Plate................................... | 200 | 300 | 3,100 | 550 | | | | |
| **SUMMER DAYS (DUGAN)** | | | | | | | | |
| Vase, 6" .............................. | 60 | | 70 | | | | | |
| (Note: This is actually the base for the Stork and Rushes punch set.) | | | | | | | | |
| **SUNFLOWER (MILLERSBURG)** | | | | | | | | |
| Pin Tray, Rare...................... | 450 | 395 | 500 | | | | | |
| **SUNFLOWER (NORTHWOOD)** | | | | | | | | |
| Bowl, 8½" ........................... | 50 | 70 | 65 | 1,195ReB | | | | 1,900IB |
| Plate, Rare........................... | 250 | | 400 | | | | | |
| **SUNFLOWER AND DIAMOND** | | | | | | | | |
| Vase, 2 Sizes........................ | 85 | | | 110 | | | | |
| **SUNGOLD (AUSTRALIAN)** | | | | | | | | |
| Epergne................................ | | | | | | | 450 | |
| **SUNK DIAMOND BAND (U.S. GLASS)** | | | | | | | | |
| Pitcher, Rare........................ | 150 | | | | | | 250W | |
| Tumbler, Rare ..................... | 50 | | | | | | 75W | |
| **SUNKEN DAISY (ENGLISH)** | | | | | | | | |
| Sugar .................................. | 30 | | 40 | | | | | |
| **SUNKEN HOLLYHOCK** | | | | | | | | |
| G–W–T–W Lamp, Rare ......... | 4,000 | | | | | | | 12,000 |
| **SUNRAY** | | | | | | | | |
| Compote............................... | | 40 | | | | 55 | | |
| **SUNRAY (FENTON)** | | | | | | | | |
| Compote (Milk Glass Iridized) | | | | | | 90MO | | |
| **SUPERB DRAPE (NORTHWOOD)** | | | | | | | | |
| Vase, Rare ........................... | | | 3,600* | | | 3,700* | | |
| **SUN PUNCH** | | | | | | | | |
| Bottle .................................. | 30 | | | | | | 35 | |
| **SUNS UP** | | | | | | | | |
| Hatpin................................. | | 425 | | | | | | |
| **SWALLOWS** | | | | | | | | |
| Tumbler, Enameled ............. | 120.00 | | | | | | | |
| **SWAN, PASTEL (DUGAN–FENTON)** | | | | | | | | |
| One Size .............................. | 295 | 300 | 500OG | 190 | 375 | | 550AM | |
| **SWEETHEART (CAMBRIDGE)** | | | | | | | | |
| Cookie Jar w/lid, Rare.......... | 1,550 | | 1,100 | | | | | |
| Tumbler, Rare ...................... | 650 | | | | | | | |
| **SWIRL (IMPERIAL)** | | | | | | | | |
| Mug, Rare ........................... | 90 | | | | | | | |
| Candlestick, Each................. | 35 | | | | | | | |
| Vase .................................... | 40 | | | | | | | |
| **SWIRL (NORTHWOOD)** | | | | | | | | |
| Pitcher................................. | 250 | | 800 | | | | | |
| Tumbler ............................... | 110 | | 150 | | | | | |
| **SWIRLED FLUTE (FENTON)** | | | | | | | | |
| Vase, 7"–12" ........................ | 35 | 40 | 50 | 45 | | | 70W | 485 |
| **SWIRLED RIBS (NORTHWOOD)** | | | | | | | | |
| Pitcher................................. | 165 | | | | | | | |
| Tumbler ............................... | 70 | 75 | | | | | | |
| **SWIRLED THREADS** | | | | | | | | |
| Goblet ................................. | 95 | | | | | | | |
| **SWIRL HOBNAIL (MILLERSBURG)** | | | | | | | | |
| Rose Bowl, Rare ................... | 295 | 375 | 650 | | | | | |
| Spittoon, Rare ..................... | 575 | 750 | 7,000 | | | | | |
| Vase, 7"–10", Rare ............... | 250 | 300 | 300 | 500 | | | | |
| **SWIRL VARIANT (IMPERIAL)** | | | | | | | | |
| Bowl, 7"–8" .......................... | 30 | | | | | | | |
| Epergne................................ | | | 200 | | 45 | | | |
| Vase, 6½"............................. | 35 | | 45 | | 200 | | 65W | |
| Plate, 6"–8¾"........................ | 50 | | 60 | | 60 | | 75 | |
| Pitcher, 7½" ......................... | 100 | | | | | | | |
| Cake Plate ........................... | | | | | | | 85CL | |
| Dessert, Stemmed .............. | 30 | | | | | | | |
| Juice Glass............................ | 40 | | | | | | | |
| **SWORD AND CIRCLE** | | | | | | | | |
| Tumbler, Rare ..................... | 150 | | | | | | | |
| **SYDNEY (FOSTORIA)** | | | | | | | | |
| Tumbler, Rare ...................... | 800 | | | | | | | |
| **TAFFETA LUSTRE (FOSTORIA)** | | | | | | | | |
| Candlestick, Pair, Rare ........ | | 300 | 350 | 400 | | | 450AM | |
| Console Bowl, 11", Rare........ | | 150 | 150 | 175 | | | 180AM | |
| (Add 25% For Old Paper Labels Attached) | | | | | | | | |

| | M | A | G | B | PO | AO | Pas | Red |
|---|---|---|---|---|---|---|---|---|
| Perfume w/stopper .............. | 90 | 125 | | | | | 160LV | |
| **TALL HAT** | | | | | | | | |
| Various Sizes, 4"–10" .......... | 45+ | | | | | | 50PK | |
| **TARGET (FENTON)** | | | | | | | | |
| Vase, 7"–11" ...................... | 45 | 55 | 60 | | 95 | | 115W | |
| **TARTON (GERMANY)** | | | | | | | | |
| Spittoon, Rare ................. | 3,500* | | | | | | | |
| Pitcher, Rare...................... | 1,800* | | | | | | | |
| **TEN MUMS (FENTON)** | | | | | | | | |
| Bowl, Ftd, 9", Rare ............. | 500 | | | | | | | |
| Bowl, 8"–11" ..................... | 95 | 125 | 260 | 325 | | | | |
| Plate, 10", Rare.................. | | | | 975 | | | | |
| Pitcher, Rare...................... | 495 | | | 900 | | | 1,500W | |
| Tumbler, Rare ................... | 70 | | | 80 | | | 340W | |
| **TEXAS** | | | | | | | | |
| Giant Tumbler .................... | | | | 260 | | | | |
| **TEXAS HEADDRESS (WESTMORELAND)** | | | | | | | | |
| Punch Cup ........................ | 45 | | | | | | | |
| **THIN AND WIDE RIB (NORTHWOOD)** | | | | | | | | |
| Vase, Ruffled ..................... | 90 | 130 | 150 | 170 | | | | |
| Vase, Jesters ...................... | 120 | 150 | 175 | 200 | | | | |
| **THIN RIB (FENTON)** | | | | | | | | |
| Candlestick, Pair ............... | 80 | | | | | | | 390 |
| Vase, 7–14"........................ | 40+ | 55+ | 65+ | 75+ | | | 145AM | |
| **THIN RIB AND VTS (NORTHWOOD)** | | | | | | | | |
| Vase, 6"–11" ...................... | 35 | 240 | 250 | 55 | 70 | 235 | 1,700AM | |
| **THIN RIB AND DRAPE (ENGLISH)** | | | | | | | | |
| Vase, 5"–14" ...................... | 140 | 250 | 255 | | | | | |
| **THISTLE (ENGLISH)** | | | | | | | | |
| Vase, 6" ............................. | 45 | | | | | | | |
| **THISTLE (FENTON)** | | | | | | | | |
| Bowl, 8"–10" ...................... | 90 | 140 | 160 | 150 | | | 400AQ | |
| Plate, 9", Rare.................... | 6,700 | 4,100 | 3,800 | | | | | |
| Compote............................ | 60 | | | 70 | | | | |
| Advertising Bowl (Horlacher)... | 125 | 225 | 200 | 200 | | | | |
| **THISTLE** | | | | | | | | |
| Shade................................. | 60 | | | | | | | |
| **THISTLE AND LOTUS (FENTON)** | | | | | | | | |
| Bowl, 7".............................. | 55 | | 75 | 70 | | | | |
| **THISTLE AND THORN (ENGLISH)** | | | | | | | | |
| Bowl, Ftd, 6"....................... | 50 | | | | | | | |
| Creamer or Sugar, Each ...... | 60 | | | | | | | |
| Plate, Ftd, 8½" ................... | 150 | | | | | | | |
| Nut Bowl ............................ | 75 | | | | | | | |
| **THISTLE, FENTON'S (FENTON)** | | | | | | | | |
| Banana Boat, Ftd, Scarce .... | 300 | 400 | 500 | 475 | | | | |
| **THREE DIAMONDS (DUGAN)** | | | | | | | | |
| Vase, 6"–10" ....................... | 45 | 50 | 60 | 60 | 75 | | 60 | |
| **THREE FLOWERS (IMPERIAL)** | | | | | | | | |
| Tray, Center Handle, 12" ..... | 60 | | | | | | 70SM | |
| **THREE FRUITS (NORTHWOOD)** | | | | | | | | |
| Bowl, 9"............................. | 130 | 160 | 150 | 180 | | 850 | 240 | |
| Bowl, 5".............................. | 30 | 40 | 70 | 80 | | 150 | 70 | |
| Bowl, Dome Base, 8⅝" ........ | | 190 | | | | | | |
| Bon–bon, Stemmed.............. | 50 | 65 | 80 | 90 | | 850 | 120 | |
| Plate, Round, 9"................... | 200 | 400 | 475 | 375 | | 4,250 | 900IB | |
| (Add 50% if Stippled) | | | | | | | | |
| Bowl, Stippled, 9" ............... | 150 | 250 | 1,000 | 395 | | 1,400 | | |
| **THREE FRUITS MEDALLION (NORTHWOOD)** | | | | | | | | |
| Bowl, Ftd, 8–10½", Rare....... | 120 | 195 | 240 | 285 | | 1,400 | 500AQ | |
| **THREE FRUITS VT. (DUGAN)** | | | | | | | | |
| Plate, 12–Sided.................... | 150 | 175 | 200 | | | | 160 | |
| **THREE–IN–ONE (IMPERIAL)** | | | | | | | | |
| Bowl, 8¾" ........................... | 30 | 40 | 40 | | | | 45SM | |
| Bowl, 4½" ........................... | 20 | 25 | 25 | | | | 30SM | |
| Plate, 6½" ........................... | 50 | | | | | | 80SM | |
| Rose Bowl, Rare ................. | 200 | | | | | | | |
| Banana Bowl Whimsey ........ | 100 | | | | | | | |
| Toothpick Holder, Rare (Vt.) . | | | 85 | | | | | |
| **THREE MONKEYS** | | | | | | | | |
| Bottle, Rare ......................... | | | | | | | 90 | |
| **THREE ROLL** | | | | | | | | |
| Bedroom Set (Tumble Up) .... | 90 | | | | | | | |
| **THREE ROW (IMPERIAL)** | | | | | | | | |
| Vase, Rare .......................... | 900 | 1,200 | | | | | 1,100SM | |
| **THROW PILLOW** | | | | | | | | |
| Hatpin ................................ | | 100 | | | | | | |
| **THUMBPRINT AND OVAL (IMPERIAL)** | | | | | | | | |
| Vase, 5½", Rare.................... | 600 | 850 | | | | | | |
| **THUMBPRINT AND SPEARS** | | | | | | | | |
| Creamer ............................ | 50 | | 60 | | | | | |

Tall Hat

Ten Mums (Fenton)

Thin and Wide Rib

Thin Rib and Drape

Tornado Vt. (Northwood)

Tree Bark Vt.

Tree of Life (Imperial)

Tree Trunk (Northwood)

| | M | A | G | B | PO | AO | Pas | Red |
|---|---|---|---|---|---|---|---|---|
| **THUNDERBIRD (AUSTRALIAN)** | | | | | | | | |
| Bowl, 9½" | 350 | 395 | | | | | | |
| Bowl, 5" | 60 | 75 | | | | | | |
| **TIERED THUMBPRINT** | | | | | | | | |
| Bowls, 2 Sizes | 45 | | | | | | | |
| Candlestick, Pair | 120 | | | | | | | |
| **TIGER LILY (IMPERIAL)** | | | | | | | | |
| Pitcher | 125 | 350 | 275 | 185 | | | | |
| Tumbler | 35 | 60 | 40 | 350 | | | 90AM | |
| **TINY BERRY** | | | | | | | | |
| Tumbler, 2¼" | | | | 45 | | | | |
| **TINY HOBNAIL** | | | | | | | | |
| Lamp | 110 | | | | | | | |
| **TOBACCO LEAF (U.S. GLASS)** | | | | | | | | |
| Champagne | | | | | | | 160CL | |
| **TOLTEC (McKEE)** | | | | | | | | |
| Butter (Ruby Iridized), Rare | | 375 | | | | | | |
| Pitcher, Tankard, Very Rare | 2,600* | | | | | | | |
| **TOMOHAWK (CAMBRIDGE)** | | | | | | | | |
| One Size, Rare | 400 | | 1,850 | | | | | |
| **TOP HAT** | | | | | | | | |
| Vase | | | | | | | 50 | |
| **TOP O' THE MORNING** | | | | | | | | |
| Hatpin | | 160 | | | | | | |
| **TOP O' THE WALK** | | | | | | | | |
| Hatpin | | 200 | | | | | | |
| **TORNADO (NORTHWOOD)** | | | | | | | | |
| Vase, Plain | 450 | 550 | 500 | 1,200 | | | 1,200W | |
| Vase, Ribbed, 2 Sizes | 495 | 575 | 550 | 1,150 | | | 1,500IB | |
| Vase Whimsey | | | | | | | 1,300WS | |
| **TORNADO VT. (NORTHWOOD)** | | | | | | | | |
| Vase, Rare | 1,450 | | | | | | | |
| **TOWERS (ENGLISH)** | | | | | | | | |
| Hat Vase | 65 | | | | | | | |
| **TOY PUNCH SET (CAMBRIDGE)** | | | | | | | | |
| Bowl Only, Ftd | 60 | | | | | | | |
| **TRACERY (MILLERSBURG)** | | | | | | | | |
| Bon–bon, Rare | | 650 | 650 | | | | | |
| **TREE BARK (IMPERIAL)** | | | | | | | | |
| Pitcher, Open Top | 60 | | | | | | | |
| Pitcher w/lid | 70 | | | | | | | |
| Tumbler, 2 Sizes | 25 | | | | | | | |
| Bowl, 7½" | 20 | | | | | | | |
| Pickle Jar, 7½" | 25 | | | | | | | |
| Candlestick, 7", Pair | 50 | | | | | | | |
| Sauce, 4" | 10 | | | | | | | |
| Candlestick, 4½", Pair | 30 | | | | | | | |
| Candy Jar w/lid | 35 | | | | | | | |
| Vase | 45 | | | | | | 55CM | |
| **TREE BARK VT.** | | | | | | | | |
| Candleholder on stand | 85 | | | | | | | |
| Pitcher | 60 | | | | | | | |
| Tumbler | 20 | | | | | | | |
| Planter | 60 | | | | | | | |
| Juice | 25 | | | | | | | |
| **TREE OF LIFE (IMPERIAL)** | | | | | | | | |
| Bowl, 5½" | 30 | | | | | | | |
| Handled Basket | 30 | | | | | | | |
| Plate, 7½" | 40 | | | | | | | |
| Tumbler | 25 | | | | | | | |
| Pitcher | 60 | | | | | | | |
| Perfumer w/lid | 40 | | | | | | | |
| Vase Whimsey (from pitcher) | | | | | | 150CL | | |
| **TREE TRUNK (NORTHWOOD)** | | | | | | | | |
| Vase, 7"–12" | 275 | 220 | 295 | 300 | | 1,200 | 700TL | |
| Funeral Vase, 15"–20" | 950 | 1,500 | 1,250 | 1,400 | 2,800*MO | 6,500 | 26,000IB | |
| Jardinere Whimsey, Rare | 2,000 | 2,500 | | | | | | |
| **TREFOIL FINE CUT (MILLERSBURG)** | | | | | | | | |
| Plate, 11½", Rare | 12,000* | | | | | | | |
| **TRIAD** | | | | | | | | |
| Hatpin | | 55 | | | | | | |
| **TRIANDS (ENGLISH)** | | | | | | | | |
| Creamer, Sugar or Spooner | 50 | | | | | | | |
| Butter | 65 | | | | | | | |
| Celery Vase | 55 | | | | | | | |
| **TRIPLETS (DUGAN)** | | | | | | | | |
| Bowl, 6"–8" | 35 | 40 | 45 | 55 | | | | |
| Hat | 30 | 35 | 38 | | | | | |
| **TROPICANA (ENGLISH)** | | | | | | | | |
| Vase, Rare | 1,600 | | | | | | | |
| **TROUT AND FLY (MILLERSBURG)** | | | | | | | | |
| Bowl, 8¾", Various Shapes | 600 | 600 | 1,000 | | | | 1,100LV | |
| Plate, 9", Rare | | 7,500 | | | | | | |
| **TROUT AND LILY** | | | | | | | | |
| **TUFTED PILLOW** | | | | | | | | |
| Hatpin | | 95 | | | | | | |

Tulip Scroll (Millersburg)

Twelve Rings

Urn

Vineyard Harvest

| | M | A | G | B | PO | AO | Pas | Red |
|---|---|---|---|---|---|---|---|---|
| **TULIP (MILLERSBURG)** | | | | | | | | |
| Compote, 9", Rare | 750 | 850 | 800 | | | | | |
| **TULIP AND CANE (IMPERIAL)** | | | | | | | | |
| Wine, 2 Sizes, Rare | 85 | | | | | | | |
| Claret Goblet, Rare | 110 | | | | | | | |
| Goblet, 8 oz, Rare | 75 | | | | | | | |
| Compote | 45 | | | | | | | |
| **TULIP PANELS** | | | | | | | | |
| Ginger Jar | 125 | | | | | | | |
| **TULIP SCROLL (MILLERSBURG)** | | | | | | | | |
| Vase, 6"–12", Rare | 325 | 400 | 300 | | | | | |
| **TUMBLE–UP (FENTON–IMPERIAL)** | | | | | | | | |
| Plain, Complete | 85 | | | | | | 90 | |
| Handled, Complete, Rare | 295 | | | | | | 320 | |
| **TURBIN** | | | | | | | | |
| Hatpin | | 100 | | | | | | |
| **TWELVE RINGS** | | | | | | | | |
| Candlestick, ea. | 50 | | | | | | | |
| **TWINS (IMPERIAL)** | | | | | | | | |
| Bowl, 9" | 40 | | 50 | | | | 45 | |
| Bowl, 5" | 25 | | 30 | | | | 35 | |
| Fruit Bowl w/base | 95 | | | | | | | |
| **TWITCH (BARTLETT–COLLINS)** | | | | | | | | |
| Cup | 30 | | | | | | | |
| Creamer | 30 | | | | | | | |
| Sherbet | 35 | | | | | | | |
| **TWO FLOWERS (FENTON)** | | | | | | | | |
| Plate, 13", Rare | 2,900 | | | | | | | 7,000 |
| Bowl, Ftd, 5"–8" | 60 | 70 | 70 | 55 | | | | |
| Bowl, Spatula, 8" | 90 | 110 | 135 | 120 | | | 250W | 2,500 |
| Rose Bowl, Rare | 195 | | 225 | 200 | | | | |
| Bowl, Ftd, 8"–10" | 75 | 400 | 250 | 375 | | | 450AQ | 5,800 |
| Plate, Ftd, 9" | 600 | | 675 | 650 | | | | |
| **TWO FRUITS (FENTON)** | | | | | | | | |
| Divided Bowl, 5½" | | | | | | | | |
| Scarce | 75 | 110 | 190 | 195 | | | 120W | |
| **TWO ROW (IMPERIAL)** | | | | | | | | |
| Vase, Rare | | 1,100 | | | | | | |
| **UMBRELLA PRISMS** | | | | | | | | |
| Small Hatpin | | 45 | | | | | | |
| Large Hatpin | | 70 | | | | | | |
| **UNIVERSAL HOME BOTTLE** | | | | | | | | |
| One Shape | 125* | | | | | | | |
| **UNSHOD** | | | | | | | | |
| Pitcher | 85 | | | | | | | |
| **URN** | | | | | | | | |
| Vase, 9" | 65 | | | | | | | |
| **US DIAMOND BLOCK (U.S. GLASS)** | | | | | | | | |
| Compote, Rare | 65 | | | | 90 | | | |
| Shakers, Pair | 80 | | | | | | | |
| **UTILITY** | | | | | | | | |
| Lamp, 8", Complete | 90 | | | | | | | |
| **VALENTINE** | | | | | | | | |
| Ring Tray | 80 | | | | | | | |
| **VALENTINE (NORTHWOOD)** | | | | | | | | |
| Bowl, 10", Rare | 500 | | | | | | | |
| Bowl, 5", Rare | 125 | 200 | | | | | | |
| **VENETIAN (CAMBRIDGE)** | | | | | | | | |
| Vase, (Lamp Base), 9¼", Rare | 1,500 | | 1,300 | | | | | |
| Creamer, Rare | 550 | | | | | | | |
| Sugar, Rare | 550 | | | | | | | |
| Butter, Rare | 950 | | | | | | | |
| **VICTORIAN** | | | | | | | | |
| Bowl, 10"–12", Rare | | 500 | | | 2,500 | | | |
| **VINEYARD (DUGAN)** | | | | | | | | |
| Pitcher | 90 | 300 | | | 950 | | | |
| Tumbler | 25 | 100 | | | | | 300W | |
| **VINEYARD AND FISHNET (IMPERIAL)** | | | | | | | | |
| Vase, Rare | | | | | | | | 750 |
| **VINEYARD HARVEST (AUSTRALIAN)** | | | | | | | | |
| Tumbler, Rare | 250 | | | | | | | |
| **VINING LEAF AND VT. (ENGLISH)** | | | | | | | | |
| Spittoon, Rare | 350 | | | | | | | |
| Vase, Rare | 225 | | 350 | | | | | |
| Rose Bowl, Rare | 250 | | | | | | | |
| **VINING TWIGS (DUGAN)** | | | | | | | | |
| Bowl, 7½" | 35 | 45 | 50 | | | | 55 | |
| Hat | 40 | 50 | | | | | 60W | |
| Plate, Rare, 7" | | | | | | | 750W | |
| **VINTAGE (DUGAN)** | | | | | | | | |
| Powder Jar w/lid | 70 | 120 | | 150 | | | | |
| Perfume w/stopper | 395 | 650 | | | | | | |
| Dresser Tray, 7" x 11" | 85 | | | | | | | |

Vintage Leaf (Fenton)

Violet

Waffle Block and Hobstar (Imperial)

Washboard

| | M | A | G | B | PO | AO | Pas | Red |
|---|---|---|---|---|---|---|---|---|
| **VINTAGE (FENTON)** | | | | | | | | |
| Epergne, One Lily, 2 Sizes ... | 100 | 135 | 150 | 150 | | | | |
| Fernery, 2 Varieties ............. | 55 | 70 | 100 | 95 | | | 200AM | 980 |
| Bowl, 10" .................. | 45 | 60 | 90 | 125 | | | 85 | 4,800 |
| Bowl, 8" .................. | 40 | 45 | 50 | 50 | | 1,000 | 70 | 3,600 |
| Bowl, 6½" .................. | 30 | 40 | 45 | 45 | | | 60 | 7,750 |
| Bowl, 4½" .................. | 25 | 35 | 40 | 40 | | | 55 | |
| Plate, 7¾" .................. | 300 | 485 | 300 | 130 | | | 45 | |
| Whimsey Fernery ................ | | 200 | | | | | | |
| Card Tray ................ | 40 | | | | | | | |
| Punch Bowl w/base ............. | 275 | 400 | 450 | 465 | | | | |
| (Wreath of Roses Exterior) | | | | | | | | |
| Cup ...................... | 25 | 35 | 37 | 40 | | | | |
| Rose Bowl .................. | 55 | | | 60 | | | | |
| Compote ........................ | 40 | 50 | 55 | 60 | | | | |
| Plate, 7" .................. | 115 | 400 | 325 | 240 | | | | |
| Plate, Ruffled, 11" .............. | 200 | | 275 | 295 | | | | |
| Spittoon Whimsey .............. | 6,500 | | | | | | | |
| **VINTAGE (MILLERSBURG)** | | | | | | | | |
| Bowl, 5", Rare .................. | 800 | | 1,000 | 2,000 | | | | |
| Bowl, 9", Rare .................. | 600 | 900 | 800 | 3,500 | | | | |
| **VINTAGE (NORTHWOOD)** | | | | | | | | |
| Exterior pattern only. | | | | | | | | |
| **VINTAGE (U.S. GLASS)** | | | | | | | | |
| Wine .................. | 40 | 50 | | | | | | |
| **VINTAGE BANDED (DUGAN)** | | | | | | | | |
| Mug ...................... | 35 | | | | | | 45SM | |
| Tumbler, Rare .................... | 600 | | | | | | | |
| Pitcher ...................... | 250 | 550 | | | | | | |
| **VINTAGE LEAF (FENTON)** | | | | | | | | |
| Bon bon .......................... | 55 | 150 | 70 | | | | | |
| Bowl, 7" .................. | 35 | 45 | 50 | 55 | | | | |
| Bowl, 8½" .................. | 50 | 75 | 85 | 70 | | | | |
| Bowl, 5½" .................. | 25 | 35 | 40 | 30 | | | | |
| **VINTAGE VT. (DUGAN)** | | | | | | | | |
| Plate .................. | 800 | 400 | | | | | | |
| Bowl, Ftd, 8½" .................... | | | 100 | | | | 450WS | |
| **VIOLET** | | | | | | | | |
| Basket, either type .............. | 50 | 65 | | 75 | | | | |
| **VIRGINIA BLACKBERRY (U.S. GLASS)** | | | | | | | | |
| Pitcher, Small, Rare ............. | | | | 950 | | | | |
| (Note: Tiny Berry Miniature | | | | | | | | |
| Tumbler May Match This.) | | | | | | | | |
| **VOLTEC (MCKEE)** | | | | | | | | |
| Covered Butter .................... | | 150 | | | | | | |
| **VOTIVE LIGHT (MEXICAN)** | | | | | | | | |
| Candle Vase, 4½", Rare ........ | 450 | | | | | | | |
| **WAFFLE BLOCK (IMPERIAL)** | | | | | | | | |
| Handled Basket, 10" ............ | 50 | | | | | | 165TL | |
| Bowl, 7"–9" .......................... | 40 | | | | | | | |
| Parfait Glass, Stemmed ....... | 30 | | | | | | 45 | |
| Fruit Bowl w/base .............. | | | | | | | 200CM | |
| Vase, 8"–11" ........................ | 40 | | | | | | 55 | |
| Nappy ...................... | | | | | | | 40PM | |
| Pitcher ...................... | 120 | | | | | | 170CM | |
| Tumbler ........................ | 200 | | | | | | 215CM | |
| Rose Bowl, Any Size ............ | 70 | | | | | | | |
| Plate, 10"–12", Any Shape.... | 85 | | | | | | 170SM | |
| Sherbet ...................... | | | | | | | 35CL | |
| Punch Bowl ........................ | 175 | | | | | | 225TL | |
| Cup ...................... | 20 | | | | | | 30TL | |
| Shakers, Pair ...................... | 75 | | | | | | | |
| Creamer ...................... | 60 | | | | | | | |
| Sugar ...................... | 60 | | | | | | | |
| **WAFFLE BLOCK AND HOBSTAR (IMPERIAL)** | | | | | | | | |
| Basket ...................... | 250 | | | | | | 265SM | |
| **WAFFLE WEAVE** | | | | | | | | |
| Inkwell ............................ | 95 | | | | | | | |
| **WAR DANCE (ENGLISH)** | | | | | | | | |
| Compote, 5" ........................ | 120 | | | | | | | |
| **WASHBOARD** | | | | | | | | |
| Creamer, 5½" ...................... | 45 | | | | | | | |
| **WATER LILY (FENTON)** | | | | | | | | |
| Bon–bon .......................... | 40 | 50 | 55 | 50 | | | 60 | |
| Bowl, Ftd, 5" ...................... | 50 | 90 | 300 | 100 | | | 150V | 1,600 |
| Bowl, Ftd, 10" .................... | 90 | 140 | 400 | 250 | | | 175BA | 3,700 |
| Chop Plate 11", Very Rare .... | 4,500* | | | | | | | |
| **WATER LILY AND CATTAILS (FENTON)** | | | | | | | | |
| Toothpick Whimsey ............. | 75 | | | | | | | |
| Bon–bon .......................... | 60 | 85 | | 90 | | | | |
| Pitcher ............................ | 340 | | | 5,500 | | | | |
| Tumbler ............................ | 95 | | | | | | | |
| Butter ............................ | 175 | | | | | | | |

| | M | A | G | B | PO | AO | Pas | Red |
|---|---|---|---|---|---|---|---|---|
| Sugar ..................... | 100 | | | | | | | |
| Creamer or Spooner ........... | 75 | | | | | | | |
| Bowl, 5" ..................... | 35 | 50 | | 50 | | | | |
| Bowl, 7"–9" ................. | 50 | | | 180 | | | | |
| Spittoon Whimsey, Rare ...... | 2,400 | | | | | | | |
| Vase Whimsey ................. | 75 | | | | | | | |
| **WATER LILY AND CATTAILS (NORTHWOOD)** | | | | | | | | |
| Pitcher ..................... | 400 | | | 6,000 | | | | |
| Tumbler ..................... | 110 | 200 | | 2,700* | | | | |
| **WATER LILY AND DRAGONFLY (AUSTRALIAN)** | | | | | | | | |
| Float Bowl, 10½", Complete ... | 150 | 185 | | | | | | |
| **WAVES** | | | | | | | | |
| Hatpin (Iridized chocolate glass.) Rare ..................... | | | | | | | 350ICG | |
| **WAVEY SATIN** | | | | | | | | |
| Hatpin ..................... | | 95 | | | | | | |
| **WEBBED CLEMATIS** | | | | | | | | |
| Vase, 12½" ..................... | 250 | | | | | | | |
| **WEEPING CHERRY (DUGAN)** | | | | | | | | |
| Bowl, Ftd. ..................... | 90 | 130 | | | 220 | | 100 | |
| Bowl, Flat Base .................. | 75 | 110 | | | 190 | | 90 | |
| **WESTERN DAISY (WESTMORELAND)** | | | | | | | | |
| Bowl ..................... | 50 | 60 | | | 200MO | | | |
| Hat ..................... | 45 | 50 | | | | | | |
| **WESTERN THISTLE** | | | | | | | | |
| Cider Pitcher ..................... | | | | 350 | | | | |
| Tumbler, Rare ..................... | 340 | | | 200 | | | | |
| Vase. Rare ..................... | 250 | | | | | | | |
| **WESTMORELAND JESTER'S CAP** | | | | | | | | |
| Vase ..................... | 40 | 50 | 55 | 60 | 75 | 225 | 85 | |
| **WHEAT (NORTHWOOD)** | | | | | | | | |
| Sweetmeat w/lid, Rare ......... | | 9,000 | 9,500 | | | | | |
| Bowl w/lid, Rare .................. | | 8,000 | | | | | | |
| **WHEELS (IMPERIAL)** | | | | | | | | |
| Bowl, 9" ..................... | 50 | | | | | | | |
| **WHIRLING HOBSTAR** | | | | | | | | |
| Punch Bowl w/base .............. | 125 | | | | | | | |
| Cup ..................... | 20 | | | | | | | |
| Pitcher ..................... | 290 | | | | | | | |
| **WHIRLING LEAVES (MILLERSBURG)** | | | | | | | | |
| Bowl, 9"–11", Round or Ruffled.. | 95 | 300 | 350 | | | | 250CM | |
| Bowl, 10", Tri-Cornered ....... | 300 | 500 | 500 | | | | 550V | |
| **WHIRLING STAR (IMPERIAL)** | | | | | | | | |
| Bowl, 9"–11" ..................... | 40 | | | | | | | |
| Compote ..................... | 55 | | 85 | | | | | |
| Punch Bowl w/base ............. | 235 | | | | | | | |
| Cup ..................... | 20 | | | | | | | |
| **WHITE ELEPHANT** | | | | | | | | |
| Ornament, Rare .................. | | | | | | | 350W | |
| **WHITE OAK** | | | | | | | | |
| Tumbler, Rare ..................... | 300 | | | | | | | |
| **WICKERWORK (ENGLISH)** | | | | | | | | |
| Bowl w/base, Complete ....... | 275 | | | | | | | |
| **WIDE PANEL (NORTHWOOD–FENTON–IMPERIAL)** | | | | | | | | |
| Master bowl, 11–12" ........... | 90 | | | | | | 110SM | |
| Bowl, 9" ..................... | 45 | 90 | | | | | 80SM | |
| Compote ..................... | 40 | | | | | | | |
| Epergne, 4 Lily, Rare ........... | 1,000 | 1,600 | 1,700 | 2,000 | | 28,000 | 1,900W | |
| Console Set, 3 Pieces ........... | 110 | | | | | | 135 | |
| Goblet ..................... | 40 | | | | | | | 290 |
| Cake Plate, 12"–15", Rare .... | 150UP | 250UP | | | | | 270UP | 400 |
| Punch Bowl ..................... | 115 | | | | | | | 1,175 |
| Cup ..................... | 20 | | | | | | | 150 |
| Lemonade, Handled .............. | 30 | | | | | | 75W | |
| Compote, Miniature ............. | 40 | | | | | | | |
| Covered Candy ................... | 40 | 60 | | | | | | 390 |
| Spittoon Whimsey .................. | 500 | | | | | | | |
| Vase ..................... | 30 | 40 | 45 | 60 | | | 70 | 700 |
| **WIDE PANEL (U.S. GLASS)** | | | | | | | | |
| Salt ..................... | 50 | | | | | | | |
| **WIDE PANEL (WESTMORELAND)** | | | | | | | | |
| Bowl, 7½" ..................... | | | | | | | 70TL | |
| Bowl, 8¼" ..................... | | | | | | | 75TL | |
| **WIDE PANEL BOUQUET** | | | | | | | | |
| Basket, 3½" ..................... | 75 | | | | | | | |
| **WIDE PANEL CHERRY** | | | | | | | | |
| Small Pitcher ..................... | | | | | | | 195W | |
| **WIDE PANEL SHADE** | | | | | | | | |
| Lightshade ..................... | | | 175 | | | | | |
| **WIDE PANEL VT. (NORTHWOOD)** | | | | | | | | |
| Pitcher, Tankard .................. | 200 | 275 | 300 | | | | | |

Water Lily and Cattails (Northwood)

Weeping Cherry (Dugan)

Wide Panel
(Northwood-Fenton-Imperial)

Wide Panel Cherry

Wide Rib (Dugan)

Wildflower (Millersburg)

Wishbone (Northwood)

Wishbone and Spades (Dugan)

| | M | A | G | B | PO | AO | Pas | Red |
|---|---|---|---|---|---|---|---|---|
| **WIDE RIB (DUGAN)** | | | | | | | | |
| Vase | 55 | 60 | 70 | 70 | 90 | 300 | 85 | |
| **WILD BERRY** | | | | | | | | |
| Jar w/lid | 250 | | | | | | | |
| **WILD BLACKBERRY (FENTON)** | | | | | | | | |
| Bowl, 8½", Scarce | 65 | 115 | 225 | | | | | |
| Bowl, "Maday" Advertising, Rare | | 1,250* | 1,500* | | | | | |
| **WILD FERN (AUSTRALIAN)** | | | | | | | | |
| Compote | 165 | 240 | | | | | | |
| **WILDFLOWER (MILLERSBURG)** | | | | | | | | |
| Compote, Ruffled, Rare | 1,000 | 1,400 | 1,500 | | | | | |
| Compote, Jelly, Rare | | 1,600 | | | | | | |
| **WILDFLOWER (NORTHWOOD)** | | | | | | | | |
| Compote (Plain Interior) | 300 | 350 | 350 | 450 | | | | |
| **WILD GRAPE** | | | | | | | | |
| Bowl, 8¾" | 60 | | | | | | | |
| **WILD LOGANBERRY (WESTMORELAND)** | | | | | | | | |
| Cider Pitcher, Rare | | | | | | | 520IM | |
| Compote, Covered, Rare | | | | | | | 295IM | |
| Creamer, Rare | | | | | | | 150IM | |
| Sugar, Rare | | | | | | | 100IM | |
| Wine | 145 | | | | | | | |
| Goblet | | | | | 150 | | | |
| (Note: Also Known as Dewberry) | | | | | | | | |
| **WILD ROSE (NORTHWOOD)** | | | | | | | | |
| Bowl, Ftd, Open Edge, 6" | 60 | 75 | 85 | | | | | |
| **WILD ROSE (MILLERSBURG)** | | | | | | | | |
| Small Lamp, Rare | 1,000 | 1,200 | 1,100 | | | | | |
| Medium Lamp, Rare | 1,200 | 1,500 | 1,200 | | | | | |
| Lamp, Marked "Riverside," Very Rare | | | 3,000* | | | | | |
| Medallion Lamp, Rare | 2,000 | 2,500 | 2,300 | | | | | |
| **WILD ROSE** | | | | | | | | |
| Syrup, Rare | 700 | | | | | | | |
| **WILD ROSE SHADE** | | | | | | | | |
| Lightshade | 95 | | | | | | | |
| **WILD STRAWBERRY (NORTHWOOD)** | | | | | | | | |
| Bowl, 9"–10½" | 200 | 300 | 300 | | 375 | | | |
| Plate, 7"–9", Rare | 180 | 375 | | | | | | |
| Bowl, 6", Rare | 60 | 140 | | | 140 | | | |
| **WINDFLOWER (DUGAN)** | | | | | | | | |
| Bowl, 8½" | 95 | | | 85 | | | | |
| Plate, 9" | 165 | | | 260 | | | | |
| Nappy, Handled | 85 | 95 | | 185 | | | 150IG | |
| **WINDMILL (IMPERIAL)** | | | | | | | | |
| Bowl, 9" | 35 | 55 | 40 | | | | 140V | |
| Bowl, 5" | 20 | 25 | 25 | | | | | |
| Fruit Bowl, 10½" | 40 | | 40 | | | | | |
| Milk Pitcher | 60 | 170 | 110 | | | | | |
| Pickle Dish | 25 | | 45 | | | | | |
| Tray, Flat | 35 | 150 | 65 | | | | 80 | |
| Pitcher | 170 | 350 | 160 | | | | 425 | |
| Tumbler | 25 | 230 | 45 | | | | 175AM | |
| **WINDSOR (IMPERIAL)** | | | | | | | | |
| Flower Arranger, Rare | 90 | | | | | | 90IB | |
| **WINE AND ROSES (FENTON)** | | | | | | | | |
| Cider Pitcher, Scarce | 665 | | | | | | | |
| Wine | 90 | | | 95 | | 550 | 100V | |
| **WINGED HEAVY SHELL** | | | | | | | | |
| Vase, 3½" | | | | | | | 95 | |
| **WINKEN** | | | | | | | | |
| Lamp | 135 | | | | | | | |
| **WISE OWL** | | | | | | | | |
| Bank | 50 | | | | | | | |
| **WISHBONE (IMPERIAL)** | | | | | | | | |
| Flower Arranger | 90 | | | | | | 90 | |
| **WISHBONE (NORTHWOOD)** | | | | | | | | |
| Bowl, Flat, 8"–10" | 190 | 150 | 160 | 370 | 150 | | 900IB | |
| Bowl, Ftd, 9" | 200 | 170 | 190 | | | | 1,300SM | |
| Epergne, Rare | 400 | 1,550 | 1,850 | | | | 1,700W | |
| Plate, Ftd, 9", Rare | 1,900 | 700 | | | | | | |
| Plate, Flat, 10", Rare | 2,500 | 1,875 | 3,900 | | | | | |
| Pitcher, Rare | 800 | 1,000 | 990 | | | | | |
| Tumbler, Scarce | 95 | 170 | 200 | | | | 400PL | |
| **WISHBONE AND SPADES (DUGAN)** | | | | | | | | |
| Bowl, 8½" | | 395 | | | 200 | | | |
| Bowl, 5" | | 250 | | | 190 | | | |
| Plate, 6", Rare | | 595 | | | 300 | | | |
| Plate, 10½", Rare | | 1,350 | | | 1,350 | | | |
| **WISTERIA (NORTHWOOD)** | | | | | | | | |
| Bank Whimsey, Rare | | | | | | | 2,500W | |

Wooden Shoe

Wreath of Roses (Dugan/Diamond)

Zig Zag (Millersburg)

| | M | A | G | B | PO | AO | Pas | Red |
|---|---|---|---|---|---|---|---|---|
| Pitcher, Rare........................ | | | | | | | 7,500IB | |
| Tumbler, Rare .................... | | | | | | | 900IB | |
| Vase Whimsey, Rare ........... | | | 20,000 | | | | | |
| **WITCHES POT** | | | | | | | | |
| One Shape, Souvenir .......... | 295 | | | | | | | |
| **WOODEN SHOE** | | | | | | | | |
| One Shape, Rare ................ | 175 | | | | | | | |
| **WOODLANDS** | | | | | | | | |
| Vase, 5", Rare .................... | 200 | | | | | | | |
| **WOODPECKER (DUGAN)** | | | | | | | | |
| Wall Vase........................ | 55 | | 90 | | | | 115V | |
| **WOODPECKER AND IVY** | | | | | | | | |
| Vase, Rare ......................... | | | 1,900 | | | | 2,100V | |
| **WREATHED BLEEDING HEARTS (DUGAN)** | | | | | | | | |
| Vase, 5¼".......................... | 110 | | | | | | | |
| **WREATHED CHERRY (DUGAN)** | | | | | | | | |
| Oval Bowl, 10½".................. | 90 | 140 | | 300 | | | 225W | |
| Oval Bowl, 5"...................... | 40 | 40 | | 75 | | | 60W | |
| Butter ............................... | 110 | 160 | | | | | 195W | |
| Sugar ................................ | 70 | 100 | | | | | 110W | |
| Creamer or Spooner ........... | 65 | 95 | | | | | 100W | |
| Toothpick, Old Only............. | | 175 | | | | | | |
| Pitcher............................... | 295 | 425 | | | | | 775W | |
| Tumbler ............................. | 50 | 55 | | | | | 170W | |
| **WREATHED MEDALLION** | | | | | | | | |
| Oil Lamp ........................... | 150 | | | | | | | |
| **WREATH OF ROSES (DUGAN/DIAMOND)** | | | | | | | | |
| Rose Bowl........................... | 50 | 60 | | | | | | |
| Nut Bowl ........................... | 70 | | | | | | | |
| Rose Bowl Whimsey............. | 70 | | | | | | | |
| **WREATH OF ROSES (FENTON)** | | | | | | | | |
| Bon–bon............................. | 40 | 45 | 50 | 45 | | | 65 | |
| Bon–bon, Stemmed.............. | 45 | 50 | 50 | 50 | | | 65 | |
| Compote............................. | 45 | 50 | 50 | 45 | | | | |
| Punch Bowl w/base............. | 2,000 | 350 | 375 | 390 | 2,000 | | | |
| Cup.................................... | 25 | 30 | 35 | 40 | 320 | | | |
| **WREATH OF ROSES VT. (DUGAN)** | | | | | | | | |
| Compote............................. | 55 | 65 | 65 | 60 | | | | |
| **ZIG ZAG (FENTON)** | | | | | | | | |
| Pitcher, Decorated, Rare ...... | 250 | | | 450 | | | 575IG | |
| Tumbler, Decorated ............. | 40 | | | 50 | | | 75IG | |
| **ZIG ZAG (MILLERSBURG)** | | | | | | | | |
| Bowl, Round or Ruffled, 9½" ... | 275 | 420 | 375 | | | | | |
| Bowl, Tri–Cornered, 10"....... | 450 | 575 | 575 | | | | | |
| Card Tray, Rare................... | | | 900 | | | | | |
| **ZIPPERED HEART** | | | | | | | | |
| Bowl, 9".............................. | 70 | 110 | | | | | | |
| Bowl, 5".............................. | 40 | 50 | | | | | | |
| Queen's Vase, Rare.............. | 4,000 | 3,800 | | | | | | |
| Pitcher (Not Confirmed) ....... | 1,000* | 1,500* | | | | | | |
| Tumbler (Not Confirmed) ..... | 120* | 150* | | | | | | |
| **ZIPPER LOOP (IMPERIAL)** | | | | | | | | |
| Hand Lamp, Rare ................ | 1,000 | | | | | | 1,500SM | |
| Medium Lamp, Rare ............ | 600 | | | | | | 600SM | |
| Large Lamp, Rare ................ | 500 | | | | | | 500SM | |
| **ZIPPER STITCH (CZECH)** | | | | | | | | |
| Cordial Set (Tray, Decanter, 4 Cordials), Complete .......... | 1,700 | | | | | | | |
| **ZIPPER VT. (ENGLISH)** | | | | | | | | |
| Sugar w/lid ........................ | 50 | | | | | | | |
| **ZIP ZIP (ENGLISH)** | | | | | | | | |
| Flower Frog Holder .............. | 60 | | | | | | | |

# BOOKS ON COLLECTIBLES

This is only a partial listing of the books on antiques that are available from Collector Books. All books are well illustrated and contain current values. Most of the following books are available from your local bookseller, antique dealer, or public library. If you are unable to locate certain titles in your area, you may order by mail from COLLECTOR BOOKS, P.O. Box 3009, Paducah, KY 42002-3009. Customers with Visa or MasterCard may phone in orders from 7:00–4:00 CST, Monday–Friday, Toll Free 1-800-626-5420. Add $2.00 for postage for the first book ordered and $0.30 for each additional book. Include item number, title, and price when ordering. Allow 14 to 21 days for delivery.

## DOLLS, FIGURES & TEDDY BEARS

| | | |
|---|---|---|
| 2382 | **Advertising Dolls**, Identification & Values, Robison & Sellers | $9.95 |
| 2079 | **Barbie** Doll Fashions, Volume I, Eames | $24.95 |
| 3957 | **Barbie** Exclusives, Rana | $18.95 |
| 3310 | **Black Dolls**, 1820–1991, Perkins | $17.95 |
| 3873 | **Black Dolls**, Book II, Perkins | $17.95 |
| 3810 | **Chatty Cathy** Dolls, Lewis | $15.95 |
| 2021 | Collector's **Male Action Figures**, Manos | $14.95 |
| 1529 | Collector's Encyclopedia of **Barbie** Dolls, DeWein | $19.95 |
| 3727 | Collector's Guide to **Ideal Dolls**, Izen | $18.95 |
| 3728 | Collector's Guide to Miniature **Teddy Bears**, Powell | $17.95 |
| 4506 | **Dolls in Uniform**, Bourgeois | $18.95 |
| 3967 | Collector's Guide to **Trolls**, Peterson | $19.95 |
| 1067 | **Madame Alexander** Dolls, Smith | $19.95 |
| 3971 | **Madame Alexander** Dolls Price Guide #20, Smith | $9.95 |
| 2185 | **Modern Collector's** Dolls I, Smith | $17.95 |
| 2186 | **Modern Collector's** Dolls II, Smith | $17.95 |
| 2187 | **Modern Collector's** Dolls III, Smith | $17.95 |
| 2188 | **Modern Collector's** Dolls IV, Smith | $17.95 |
| 2189 | **Modern Collector's** Dolls V, Smith | $17.95 |
| 3733 | **Modern Collector's** Dolls, Sixth Series, Smith | $24.95 |
| 3991 | **Modern Collector's** Dolls, Seventh Series, Smith | $24.95 |
| 3472 | **Modern Collector's** Dolls Update, Smith | $9.95 |
| 3972 | Patricia Smith's **Doll Values**, Antique to Modern, 11th Edition | $12.95 |
| 3826 | Story of **Barbie**, Westenhouser | $19.95 |
| 1513 | **Teddy Bears & Steiff** Animals, Mandel | $9.95 |
| 1817 | **Teddy Bears & Steiff** Animals, 2nd Series, Mandel | $19.95 |
| 2084 | **Teddy Bears, Annalee's & Steiff** Animals, 3rd Series, Mandel | $19.95 |
| 1808 | **Wonder of Barbie**, Manos | $9.95 |
| 1430 | **World of Barbie** Dolls, Manos | $9.95 |

## TOYS, MARBLES & CHRISTMAS COLLECTIBLES

| | | |
|---|---|---|
| 3427 | **Advertising Character** Collectibles, Dotz | $17.95 |
| 2333 | Antique & Collector's **Marbles**, 3rd Ed., Grist | $9.95 |
| 3827 | Antique & Collector's **Toys**, 1870–1950, Longest | $24.95 |
| 3956 | Baby Boomer **Games**, Identification & Value Guide, Polizzi | $24.95 |
| 1514 | Character **Toys** & Collector's, Longest | $19.95 |
| 1750 | Character **Toys** & Collector's, 2nd Series, Longest | $19.95 |
| 3717 | **Christmas** Collectibles, 2nd Edition, Whitmyer | $24.95 |
| 1752 | **Christmas** Ornaments, Lights & Decorations, Johnson | $19.95 |
| 3874 | Collectible Coca-Cola Toy **Trucks**, deCourtivron | $24.95 |
| 2338 | Collector's Encyclopedia of **Disneyana**, Longest, Stern | $24.95 |
| 2151 | Collector's Guide to **Tootsietoys**, Richter | $16.95 |
| 3436 | **Grist's Big Book of Marbles** | $19.95 |
| 3970 | Grist's Machine-Made & Contemporary **Marbles**, 2nd Ed. | $9.95 |
| 3732 | **Matchbox® Toys**, 1948 to 1993, Johnson | $18.95 |
| 3823 | **Mego** Toys, An Illustrated Value Guide, Chrouch | 15.95 |
| 1540 | **Modern Toys** 1930–1980, Baker | $19.95 |
| 3888 | **Motorcycle** Toys, Antique & Contemporary, Gentry/Downs | $18.95 |
| 3891 | Schroeder's Collectible **Toys**, Antique to Modern Price Guide | $17.95 |
| 1886 | Stern's Guide to **Disney** Collectibles | $14.95 |
| 2139 | Stern's Guide to **Disney** Collectibles, 2nd Series | $14.95 |
| 3975 | Stern's Guide to **Disney** Collectibles, 3rd Series | $18.95 |
| 2028 | **Toys**, Antique & Collectible, Longest | $14.95 |
| 3975 | **Zany Characters** of the Ad World, Lamphier | $16.95 |

## JEWELRY, HATPINS, WATCHES & PURSES

| | | |
|---|---|---|
| 1712 | Antique & Collector's **Thimbles** & Accessories, Mathis | $19.95 |
| 1748 | Antique **Purses**, Revised Second Ed., Holiner | $19.95 |
| 1278 | Art Nouveau & Art Deco **Jewelry**, Baker | $9.95 |
| 3875 | Collecting Antique **Stickpins**, Kerins | $16.95 |
| 3722 | Collector's Ency. of **Compacts, Carryalls & Face Powder Boxes**, Mueller | $24.95 |
| 3992 | Complete Price Guide to **Watches**, #15, Shugart | $21.95 |
| 1716 | Fifty Years of Collector's **Fashion Jewelry**, 1925-1975, Baker | $19.95 |
| 1424 | **Hatpins** & Hatpin Holders, Baker | $9.95 |
| 1181 | 100 Years of Collectible **Jewelry**, Baker | $9.95 |
| 2348 | 20th Century Fashionable Plastic **Jewelry**, Baker | $19.95 |
| 3830 | Vintage **Vanity Bags & Purses**, Gerson | $24.95 |

## FURNITURE

| | | |
|---|---|---|
| 1457 | American **Oak** Furniture, McNerney | $9.95 |
| 3716 | American **Oak** Furniture, Book II, McNerney | $12.95 |
| 1118 | Antique **Oak** Furniture, Hill | $7.95 |
| 2132 | Collector's Encyclopedia of **American** Furniture, Vol. I, Swedberg | $24.95 |
| 2271 | Collector's Encyclopedia of **American** Furniture, Vol. II, Swedberg | $24.95 |
| 3720 | Collector's Encyclopedia of **American** Furniture, Vol. III, Swedberg | $24.95 |
| 1437 | Collector's Guide to **Country** Furniture, Raycraft | $9.95 |
| 3878 | Collector's Guide to **Oak** Furniture, George | $12.95 |
| 1755 | Furniture of the **Depression Era**, Swedberg | $19.95 |
| 3906 | **Heywood-Wakefield** Modern Furniture, Rouland | $18.95 |
| 1965 | **Pine** Furniture, Our American Heritage, McNerney | $14.95 |
| 1885 | **Victorian** Furniture, Our American Heritage, McNerney | $9.95 |
| 3829 | **Victorian** Furniture, Our American Heritage, Book II, McNerney | $9.95 |
| 3869 | **Victorian** Furniture books, 2 volume set, McNerney | $19.90 |

## INDIANS, GUNS, KNIVES, TOOLS, PRIMITIVES

| | | |
|---|---|---|
| 1868 | Antique **Tools**, Our American Heritage, McNerney | $9.95 |
| 2015 | Archaic **Indian** Points & Knives, Edler | $14.95 |
| 1426 | **Arrowheads** & Projectile Points, Hothem | $7.95 |
| 1668 | **Flint Blades** & Projectile Points of the North American Indian, Tully | $24.95 |
| 2279 | **Indian** Artifacts of the Midwest, Hothem | $14.95 |
| 3885 | **Indian** Artifacts of the Midwest, Book II, Hothem | $16.95 |
| 1964 | **Indian** Axes & Related Stone Artifacts, Hothem | $14.95 |
| 2023 | **Keen Kutter** Collectibles, Heuring | $14.95 |
| 3887 | Modern **Guns**, Identification & Values, 10th Ed., Quertermous | $12.95 |
| 2164 | **Primitives**, Our American Heritage, McNerney | $9.95 |
| 1759 | **Primitives**, Our American Heritage, Series II, McNerney | $14.95 |
| 3325 | Standard **Knife** Collector's Guide, 2nd Ed., Ritchie & Stewart | $12.95 |

## PAPER COLLECTIBLES & BOOKS

| | | |
|---|---|---|
| 1441 | Collector's Guide to **Post Cards**, Wood | $9.95 |
| 2081 | Guide to Collecting **Cookbooks**, Allen | $14.95 |
| 3969 | Huxford's **Old Book** Value Guide, 7th Ed. | $19.95 |
| 3821 | Huxford's **Paperback** Value Guide | $19.95 |
| 2080 | Price Guide to **Cookbooks** & Recipe Leaflets, Dickinson | $9.95 |
| 2346 | **Sheet Music** Reference & Price Guide, Pafik & Guiheen | $18.95 |

## OTHER COLLECTIBLES

| | | |
|---|---|---|
| 2280 | Advertising **Playing Cards**, Grist | $16.95 |
| 2269 | Antique **Brass & Copper** Collectibles, Gaston | $16.95 |
| 1880 | Antique **Iron**, McNerney | $9.95 |
| 3872 | Antique **Tins**, Dodge | $24.95 |
| 1714 | **Black** Collectibles, Gibbs | $19.95 |
| 1128 | **Bottle** Pricing Guide, 3rd Ed., Cleveland | $7.95 |
| 3959 | **Cereal Box** Bonanza, The 1950's, Bruce | $19.95 |
| 3718 | Collector's **Aluminum**, Grist | $16.95 |
| 3445 | Collectible **Cats**, An Identification & Value Guide, Fyke | $18.95 |
| 1634 | Collector's Ency. of Figural & Novelty **Salt & Pepper Shakers**, Davern | $19.95 |
| 2020 | Collector's Ency. of Figural & Novelty **Salt & Pepper Shakers**, Vol. II, Davern | $19.95 |
| 2018 | Collector's Encyclopedia of **Granite Ware**, Greguire | $24.95 |
| 3430 | Collector's Encyclopedia of **Granite Ware**, Book II, Greguire | $24.95 |
| 3879 | Collector's Guide to Antique **Radios**, 3rd Ed., Bunis | $18.95 |
| 1916 | Collector's Guide to **Art Deco**, Gaston | $14.95 |
| 3880 | Collector's Guide to **Cigarette Lighters**, Flanagan | $17.95 |
| 1537 | Collector's Guide to **Country Baskets**, Raycraft | $9.95 |
| 3966 | Collector's Guide to **Inkwells**, Identification & Values, Badders | $18.95 |
| 3881 | Collector's Guide to **Novelty Radios**, Bunis/Breed | $18.95 |
| 3729 | Collector's Guide to **Snow Domes**, Guarnaccia | $18.95 |
| 3730 | Collector's Guide to **Transistor Radios**, Bunis | $15.95 |
| 2276 | **Decoys**, Kangas | $24.95 |
| 1629 | **Doorstops**, Identification & Values, Bertoia | $9.95 |
| 3968 | **Fishing Lure** Collectibles, Murphy/Edmisten | $24.95 |
| 3817 | **Flea Market Trader**, 9th Ed., Huxford | $12.95 |
| 3819 | **General Store** Collectibles, Wilson | $24.95 |
| 2215 | Goldstein's **Coca-Cola** Collectibles | $16.95 |
| 3884 | Huxford's Collector's **Advertising**, 2nd Ed. | $24.95 |
| 2216 | **Kitchen Antiques**, 1790–1940, McNerney | $14.95 |
| 1782 | 1,000 **Fruit Jars**, 5th Edition, Schroeder | $5.95 |
| 3321 | Ornamental & Figural **Nutcrackers**, Rittenhouse | $16.95 |
| 2026 | **Railroad** Collectibles, 4th Ed., Baker | $14.95 |
| 1632 | **Salt & Pepper Shakers**, Guarnaccia | $9.95 |
| 1888 | **Salt & Pepper Shakers** II, Identification & Value Guide, Book II, Guarnaccia | $14.95 |
| 2220 | **Salt & Pepper Shakers** III, Guarnaccia | $14.95 |
| 3443 | **Salt & Pepper Shakers** IV, Guarnaccia | $18.95 |
| 2096 | **Silverplated Flatware**, Revised 4th Edition, Hagan | $14.95 |
| 1922 | Standard **Old Bottle** Price Guide, Sellari | $14.95 |
| 3892 | **Toy & Miniature Sewing Machines**, Thomas | $18.95 |
| 3828 | Value Guide to **Advertising Memorabilia**, Summers | $18.95 |
| 3977 | Value Guide to **Gas Station** Memorabilia | $24.95 |
| 3444 | **Wanted to Buy**, 5th Edition | $9.95 |